FROM MARX TO GRAMSCI

FROM MARX TO GRAMSCI

A Reader in Revolutionary Marxist Politics

Historical Overview and Selection by
PAUL LE BLANC

Haymarket Books
Chicago, Illinois

© 1996 and 2016 Paul Le Blanc

Previously published in 1996 by Humanity Books

This edition published in 2016 by
Haymarket Books
P.O. Box 180165
Chicago, IL 60618
773-583-7884
www.haymarketbooks.org
info@haymarketbooks.org

ISBN: 978-1-60846-623-8

Distributed to the trade in the US through Consortium Book Sales and
Distribution (www.cbsd.com) and internationally through Ingram
Publisher Services International (www.ingramcontent.com).

This book was published with the generous support of Lannan
Foundation and Wallace Action Fund.

Special discounts are available for bulk purchases by organizations and
institutions. Please call 773-583-7884 or email
info@haymarketbooks.org for more information.

Cover design by Rachel Cohen.

Entered into digital printing February 2019.

Printed in the United States.

Library of Congress Cataloging-in-Publication data is available.

To the memory of my teachers
Richard N. Hunt
and
Ernest Mandel
and to the memory of one of my dearest friends
Sarah Lovell

Contents

Preface to the 2016 Edition

Twenty years after the appearance of *From Marx to Gramsci*, it is gratifying that friends at Haymarket Books in the United States and Aakar Books in India are bringing it out in a new edition. This allows me to make modest corrections and add additional thoughts. While the corrections have been integrated into the text of this new edition, the book will remain basically as it was. The additional thoughts will be restricted to this brief introduction.

The Conception of This Book

The purpose of this book was, and remains to be, to provide a certain conceptualization of Marxism that connects it—as Marx intended—to revolutionary activism. This is important for students and scholars, in my opinion, simply to enable them to have an accurate understanding of what Marxism actually was and is about, regardless of whether or not one wants to apply it in political action. But also, as a decades-long political activist for whom Marxist theory has been important, I wanted to make easily available to other activists some basic explanations and texts that might be politically useful in their activism. Of course, these must be applied critically and creatively—more on that shortly.

Back in the 1930s, when Emile Burns offered militants in the Communist movement, and other interested readers, his fat *Handbook of Marxism* of more than one thousand pages, it seemed clear to him that he should offer Marx-Engels-Lenin-Stalin.[1] There have been others, fewer in number (but including some comrades I have admired), who would insist instead on Marx-Engels-Lenin-Trotsky. My own view, for reasons explained in this text, is that Stalin does not belong in the lineup. At the same time, it has seemed to me that the Marxist tradition is far richer than either of the four-person lineups.

I was not inclined to construct a polyglot anthology of various self-described "Marxists"—some of whom represent qualitatively different theoretical and political orientations. Good examples of this approach can be found in C. Wright Mills's *The Marxists* and David McLellan's *Marxism: Essential Writings.*[2] Both volumes have value, but as suggested above, this volume has a different purpose.

My organizing principle was to make use of the notion of "revolutionary Marxism." An old friend and mentor, Harry Magdoff, once challenged me when I used the term. He argued quite reasonably that Marxism is inherently revolutionary, making the adjective "revolutionary" redundant. But some who use Marx's concepts and perspectives in efforts to *understand the world,* and are certainly Marxists in that sense, have a different notion than Marx of how to change the world. My decision was to focus on several major figures whose proposed strategies of how to get from the "here" of capitalism to the proposed "there" of socialism are demonstrably grounded in the original revolutionary orientation of Karl Marx.

I then made a selection—not meant to be an exhaustive one—of the writings of Karl Marx and Frederick Engels, quite naturally, as well as Rosa Luxemburg, Vladimir Ilyich Lenin, Leon Trotsky, and Antonio Gramsci, and in the first 120 pages of the book sought to demonstrate that they all shared a common strategic orientation. There have been scholars and activists who argue that one or another of these had a significantly different approach than the others—but this book makes the case, with substantial documentation, that these six can best be understood as being close enough in methodological approach and practical political orientation to be grouped together.

I have indicated, at the same time, that each made distinctive contributions (grounded in different times, places, and circumstances) enriching revolutionary Marxism, but that the fundamentals of its strategic orientation consisted of a commonly shared approach. I then provided very short biographies of these figures and a sampling of some of their key texts focused on revolutionary strategy. Finally, I added extensive reading lists, on top of material presented in my reference notes, for those wishing to explore further. And that is the book you are now looking at.

New Thoughts

There are two modifications I would like to suggest here, and also an additional notion. Modifications first.

First of all, I believe I went too far in dividing my revolutionary Marxists from the presumably nonrevolutionary "Marxism of the Second International" of the period preceding the First World War. In fact, Engels, Luxemburg, Lenin and Trotsky were all associated with the Marxism of the Second International—they were part of what my friend Lars Lih has called "the best of Second International Marxism." Lars is among those providing a spirited defense (and, I have concluded, a valid defense) of the revolutionary qualities in the Marxist orientation of Karl Kautsky at least up until the year 1910. Two very large and very valuable collections of this "best of Second International Marxism," edited by Richard Day and Daniel Gaido—*Witnesses to Permanent Revolution* and *Discovering Imperialism*—are well worth examining. I believe it can be shown there were qualities in Lenin's Marxism that distinguish it from that of Kautsky, but the very substantial common ground that Lars Lih has insisted upon is given short shrift in this volume.[3]

Second, I have come to believe that there is greater complexity in the relationship between Maoism and revolutionary Marxism than I was inclined to acknowledge, especially given my recent experience of interacting with Indian revolutionaries associated with the Maoist tradition.

There is, of course, much more to be learned from the experience of the Chinese Revolution than I was able to cover in the few pages touching on it in my 1996 work. (See, for example, recent contributions by Pierre Rousset.) But there is more than just that. In his fine account of Maoism in the United States, *Revolution in the Air*, Max Elbaum has shown that many U.S. activists were drawn to the example of the Chinese Revolution and the writings of Mao Zedong (Mao Tse-tung)—and in many cases the writings of Joseph Stalin—precisely because they viewed these as manifestations of revolutionary Marxism.[4] They sought to interpret such things in a way that harmonized with the revolutionary qualities they were reaching for in their lives and which they found in the writings of Marx, Engels, and Lenin. The results are sometimes not reducible to something that can accurately be described simply as "Stalinism" or dismissed as simply wrong.

I continue to believe that the orientation represented by Mao is, in important ways, not consistent with the orientations of Marx and

Lenin. Problems associated with the Maoist approach have contributed to difficulties among revolutionaries connected with the Maoist tradition. Elbaum's discussion of theoretical and political limitations in U.S. Maoism and Tithi Bhattacharya's critique of Maoism in the global south (particularly India) provide valuable insights as to why this is so.[5]

Yet, consider the recent comments of Sirimane Nagaraj, once a top cadre in the Communist Party of India (Maoist), emerging from the underground as a leading figure in India's Revolutionary Communist Party (which has by no means rejected what Nagaraj terms "Marxism-Leninism-Maoism"):

> We are really the staunchest proponents of democracy. We are fighting to establish genuine democracy in society. Our view is that communism embodies the highest form of democracy. . . . What is being trumpeted here [in India] as democracy is not real democracy at all. Amdedkar [a prominent Dalit, or "untouchable," intellectual in the radical wing of the Indian independence movement] himself has said, way back in 1951, that a democracy that does not involve economic and social equality is not real democracy. We are coming into the democratic mainstream with the firm conviction that genuine democracy can be brought about through people's movements. . . . The masses have got some measure of democratic rights as a result of their struggles, over generations and centuries, putting forward democratic aspirations. . . . The rules are compelled to allow these democratic rights and facilities to the people. Yet they keep trying to restrict these, while people keep striving to save them and expand them. Our aim is to further expand what democratic opportunities and space people have by strengthening and bringing together these struggles and movements.[6]

The fact that this corresponds to revolutionary Marxism indicates that realities tend to be more complex than the exposition offered in *From Marx to Gramsci* might lead one to believe.

And this flows into the additional notion I want to speak to.

In the section of this book that concludes the first 120 pages—"Does Revolutionary Marxism Have a Future?"—I emphasize that the coherence of revolutionary Marxism does not mean revolutionary Marxist perspectives were triumphant. To a very large degree, the opposite is the case, which (intentionally) poses an obvious challenge. In addition, I argued that our world of the 1990s had changed in dramatic ways from what had existed in the time of Karl Marx or of Antonio Gramsci.

Ten years later, I emphasized yet further changes in *Marx, Lenin and the Revolutionary Experience*. And twenty years on, there are additional changes we can point to.[7]

To be true to the method of the creative and critical-minded revolutionaries we find in these pages—from Marx to Gramsci—we need to approach their revolutionary Marxism not in a rigid or dogmatic way, but as *a guide to action*. If we restrict ourselves to explaining the world in one or another way (while scolding those who somehow don't "measure up"), our work will of course be much easier. But if we try to use these perspectives in efforts to actually change the world, we will face many more challenges in struggling to determine how revolutionary Marxist perspectives can be applied effectively.

The Continuing Validity of Revolutionary Marxism

I believe the approach and insights provided by the revolutionaries presented in *From Marx to Gramsci* are (as stated in the conclusion of the initial survey in this volume) "irreplaceable for those wanting to come to grips with the past and the future." But those who would be revolutionary activists need to go beyond the six revolutionaries highlighted in this book, and need to do this in several ways.

One is to reach beyond them to the writings of their comrades that one cannot find in this book. Vibrant contributions were made by many dozens who were "part of the best" not only of the Second International, but also of the early Communist International, and the anti-Stalinist Left.

Another way we need to go beyond them is to be open—as they were—to learning from scholars and activists outside of their political tradition, integrating new insights into our understanding of a complex and volatile reality.

More than this, while respecting the seriousness and the integrity of their analytical and theoretical contributions, but also recognizing their elemental humanity, we must realize that they obviously had to be wrong about some things, and that there were necessarily limitations in even the best they had to offer. Approaching them, at one and the same time appreciatively but also critically enables us to strengthen the revolutionary Marxism that they represented.

And then, of course, one must go beyond their words as one attempts to use those words, to utilize their theories and conceptualizations, in new and ever-changing contexts that must, in at least some ways, be quite different from theirs.

To be most effective in such "going beyond" efforts, of course, one must have a grasp of the basic insights, experiences, and understandings represented by the revolutionary Marxism explored in this volume. To the extent that *From Marx to Gramsci* facilitates that, it will have served its purpose.

Notes

1. Emile Burns, *A Handbook of Marxism* (London: Victor Gollancz, 1935).
2. C. Wright Mills, *The Marxists* (New York: Dell, 1962); David McClellan, *Marxism, Essential Writings* (Oxford, UK: Oxford University Press, 1988).
3. See Lars Lih, *Lenin Rediscovered: What Is to Be Done? in Context* (Chicago: Haymarket Books, 2008) and "Kautsky When He Was a Marxist," http://www. historicalmaterialism.org/journal/online-articles/kautsky-as-marxist-data- base (accessed 21/7/2015). My current take on Kautsky can be found in Paul Le Blanc, "The Absence of Socialism in the United States: Contextualising Kautsky's 'American Worker,'" *Historical Materialism* 11, vol. 11, no. 4 (2003): 125–170, and in "Lenin's Revolutionary Marxism," *International Socialist Review* #97, Summer 2015, 155–171. Two collections of writings by "Second International Marxists" document the point: Richard B. Day and Daniel Gaido, eds., *Witnesses to Permanent Revolution: The Documentary Record* (Chicago: Haymarket Books, 2011) and Richard B. Day and Daniel Gaido, eds., *Discovering Imperialism: Social Democracy to World War I* (Chicago: Haymarket Books, 2012). The distinctiveness of Lenin's Marxism is well argued in three studies: Alan Shandro, *Lenin and the Logic of Hegemony: Political Practice and Theory in the Class Struggle* (Chicago: Haymarket Books, 2015), Tamás Krausz, *Reconstructing Lenin: An Intellectual Biography* (New York: Monthly Review Press, 2015), and Antonio Negri, *Factory of Strategy: Thirty-Three Lessons on Lenin* (New York: Columbia University Press, 2014).
4. Pierre Rousset, "People's Republic of China at 60: 1925–1949—Origins of the Chinese Revolution," *Links*, http://links.org.au/node/1268 (accessed 17/07/2015); Pierre Rousset, "People's Republic of China at 60: 1949–1969: Maoism and Popular Power," *Links*, http://links.org.au/node/1269 (accessed 17/07/2015); Max Elbaum, *Revolution in the Air: Sixties Radicals Turn to Lenin, Mao and Che* (London: Verso Books, 2002).
5. Tithi Bhattacharya, "Maoism in the Global South," *International Socialist Review* #97, January 2013, http://isreview.org/issue/87/maoism-global-south (accessed 17/07/2015).
6. "An Interview with Noor Zulfikar and Sirimane Nagarj," Daily Motion, 01/01/2015, http://www.dailymotion.com/video/x2dtrj4_an-interview-with- noor-zulfikar-and-sirimane-nagaraj_news (accessed 17/07/2015). Richard N. Hunt and August Nimtz, Jr.—coming from different perspectives—are among

those capably demonstrating what this Indian revolutionary insists upon, the radical democracy that is at the heart of Marx's communist goal and that permeates his strategic orientation. See Richard N. Hunt, *The Political Ideas of Marx and Engels, Volume I: Marxism and Totalitarian Democracy, 1818–1850* (Pittsburgh: University of Pittsburgh Press, 1975), and *The Political Ideas of Marx and Engels, Volume II: Classical Marxism, 1850–1895* (Pittsburgh: University of Pittsburgh Press, 1984); August Nimtz, *Marx and Engels: Their Contribution to the Democratic Breakthrough* (Albany: State University of New York Press, 2000), and *Marx, Tocqueville and Race in America: The "Absolute Democracy" or the "Defiled Republic"* (Lanham, MD: Lexington Books, 2003).

7.   Changing realities (and how Marxist perspectives can be applied to them) are discussed in Paul Le Blanc, *Marx, Lenin and the Revolutionary Experience: Studies of Communism and Radicalism in the Age of Globalization* (New York: Routledge, 2006) and Paul Le Blanc, *Unfinished Leninism: The Rise and Return of a Revolutionary Doctrine* (Chicago: Haymarket Books, 2014). Other volumes doing, in their own way, the same thing include Terry Eagleton, *Why Marx Was Right* (New Haven, CT: Yale University Press, 2012) and Colin Barker, Laurence Cox, John Krinsky, and Alf Gunvald Nilsen, eds., *Marxism and Social Movements* (Chicago: Haymarket Books, 2014).

Preface

Karl Marx and his closest comrades dedicated their lives to turning the world upside-down in order to get it rightside-up. The fact that they actually wanted to *do* this, rather than simply think and talk and write about it, is not clearly reflected in numerous Marxist studies produced by thousands of scholars and intellectuals during the last half of the 20th century. These studies generally focus on particular aspects of Marxism— as an approach to understanding philosophical, economic, sociological, historical, anthropological, cultural realities; as a way of thinking and as a body of analyses on a rich array of questions. Many of these studies are quite valuable and interesting, but few of them focus on Marxism as a guide to action, and even among these few there is a tendency to do this in an abstract or fragmentary way. The political impact of Marxism cannot be adequately understood, however, if we shrug off the fact that for Marx and his comrades it existed as a strategic perspective and a tactical orientation—deeply grounded, to be sure, in the humanities and social sciences, but culminating in practical political activity.

This disjuncture between theory and practice flows, in large measure, from an acceptance of Marx's general analyses and a rejection of his actual revolutionary-democratic strategic orientation within the organized workers' movement for many years. Marx's actual political orientation was abandoned due to the ascendancy of the reformist bureaucratism of Social Democracy in various forms and also due to the ascendancy of the brutal authoritarianism of Stalinism in its various incarnations. The present study outlines an authentic Marxist politics which grows naturally out of Marxist historical, social, and economic analyses. Nor is it the case that this "authentic Marxist politics" is simply the idiosyncratic contribution of one or another revolutionary sage (and certainly not the author). To be authentic, it would have to be more deeply rooted, more broadly held, more durable than that.

In fact, we can find a relatively consistent and coherent orientation, reflecting a considerable amount of practical experience of the labor and socialist movements, involving the analytical method and labors of an intellectual-political current which spans two centuries of struggle. It unites such theorists as Marx, Frederick Engels, Rosa Luxemburg, Vladimir Ilyich Lenin, Leon Trotsky, and Antonio Gramsci. Many scholars and polemicists have sought to prove that each of these revolutionaries was qualitatively different from—and in fundamental contradiction to—some or all of the others. And differences can certainly be found. Far more significant, I would argue, is the underlying continuity of theoretical orientation and practical political perspective which unites them. This was certainly the view of Luxemburg, Lenin, Trotsky, and Gramsci—none of whom sought to distinguish themselves from the revolutionary political orientation articulated by Marx and Engels. Perhaps one example will suffice. "'Trotskyism' does not exist as an original or independent theory," Trotsky complained in a 1937 interview for the U.S. press. "In the name of a fight against 'Trotskyism' the [Stalinist] bureaucracy combats and slanders the revolutionary essence of the teachings of Marx and Lenin." In his view, expressed clearly in a 1935 open letter, a revolutionary International should be established not upon specific theories of Trotsky, but on what he called "the *revolutionary Marxist foundation*."[1] Similar views were held by the others we have named.

It is hardly the case that no major or original contributions to revolutionary theory were made by these 20th-century followers of Marx. But it is very much the case that their contributions were seen by them—and by others—as an application of the political orientation of Marx and Engels to new (or newly perceived) realities, not as any kind of a break from that orientation. There are others—such as George Plekhanov or Karl Kautsky—who also claimed to be doing this. A serious examination of their political contributions, however, indicates significant divergences from the spirit and specifics of the *Communist Manifesto* and other political writings by Marx and Engels. This is why knowledgeable writers, former Marxists such as Sidney Hook and Bertram D. Wolfe—who never fully shook free from at least a residual appreciation for Marx but who did unambiguously reject the revolutionary orientation shared by Lenin, Trotsky, Luxemburg, and Gramsci—felt compelled to refer to Marx's "ambiguous legacy."[2]

Some may still object that the label "revolutionary Marxism" is redundant, since Marxism is *by definition* "revolutionary." But there are many who utilize decisive aspects of Marxist economic, social, and cultural analysis—who work in the broad analytical tradition of Marxism and who consider themselves Marxists—who nonetheless have diverse and sometimes contradictory notions about what one should do, or can do, to change the world. This can give rise to sterile debates about who is "really" a Marxist, and how one or another "self-proclaimed" Marxist is really nothing of the sort, etc. I am inclined to the view that anyone who accepts Marx's dialectical approach to reality, his method of historical materialism, his critique of capitalism, and his vision of a socialist future can be termed a Marxist. But there are some such people who do not embrace the particular revolutionary orientation which Marx first advanced and which was developed with considerable power and consistency by certain of his followers. This reality suggests the value of the two categories: Marxist (someone operating within a Marxist theoretical framework) but also *revolutionary Marxist* (a Marxist who embraces a particular approach to politics consistent with Marx's own, quite specific, revolutionary political orientation).

The first portion of this volume will offer a substantial essay which makes the case just sketched in this preface. After a general introduction to the nature of Marxism, we will focus on interrelated political ideas stretching from Marx to Gramsci, involving theories of capitalist development and the labor movement, and consequent theories of revolution and the transition to socialism. Some attention will be given to the contrasting outlooks and policies of different political currents claiming the mantle of Marxism, and also to some of the foremost critics of Marxism. Especially with the collapse of the USSR and the world Communist movement, there has been a triumphalism in the criticism of Marxism which has swept along many who once believed, or thought they believed, in Marxist ideas—but both the gist and specifics of such criticism can be found, often in more interesting form, in such earlier critics of the 1930s, '40s, and '50s as Sidney Hook, Bertram D. Wolfe, and James Burnham, as well as such mavericks as Daniel Bell, Robert Heilbroner, and C. Wright Mills, whose criticisms will be touched on here. It seems clear to me, however, that the intellectual coherence and moral authority of revolutionary Marxism are by no means obliterated by these criticisms, for reasons that will be suggested in what follows.

It is not enough for a serious scholar (let alone a revolutionary activist) to be content simply with commentaries on the great revolutionary theorists. The second portion of this volume will gather together some of the key political writings of the revolutionary Marxists. There have been previous collections of more diverse socialist writings, either linking revolutionary with Stalinist perspectives or representing a smorgasbord of different theoretical currents—utopians, anarchists, syndicalists, reformists, authoritarians, and more—mixed together with revolutionary Marxists.[3] But this is the first to draw together a representative selection of writings giving a clear sense of the revolutionary Marxist political orientation and at the same time demonstrating a continuity stretching from Marx and Engels to Luxemburg, Lenin, Trotsky, and Gramsci.

No single book can give a complete account of Marxism in all of its complexity, and many important questions will remain unexplored in what follows. We offer here an introduction to this body of revolutionary thought which highlights primary political concerns of those who created it, and the complex, *collective* nature of a political project involving a number of insightful, passionate thinkers and activists. A more complete understanding requires a more extensive reading of their works, and some study of the contexts in which the texts were written. The relevance of these works, of course, depends on their usefulness to those who want to overthrow all conditions in which men and women are degraded, enslaved, neglected, contemptible beings, and to those committed to creating a world in which the free development of each person is the condition for the free development of all.

I dedicate this book to the memory of three people. Richard N. Hunt taught history at the University of Pittsburgh, and his considerable knowledge, intellectual clarity, and personal integrity enriched those of us who were his students; his conscientious Marxist scholarship (despite social-democratic moderation!) reflected a deep commitment to a future in which there would be dignity, justice, and freedom for all. Ernest Mandel was an almost inexhaustible partisan for the cause of revolutionary socialism, and an often dazzling educator, whose boundless optimism and critical intelligence embraced all continents, all countries, all peoples. Sarah Lovell, from her teens to her 70s a thoughtful working-class activist and an outstanding representative of American Trotskyism, graced my life with her warmth and caring, and she inspired me with the courage of her final struggle. I miss these friends, but some of what they were has gone into this book.

Notes

1.   These quotations can be found, respectively, in "An interview for Americans," *Writings of Leon Trotsky, 1936–37*, second edition, ed. Naomi Allen and George Breitman (New York: Pathfinder Press, 1978), p. 96, and "Open Letter for the Fourth International," *Writings of Leon Trotsky, 1935–36*, second edition, ed. Naomi Allen and George Breitman (New York: Pathfinder Press, 1977), p. 25.

2.   Wolfe promises in the introduction to his *Marxism: One Hundred Years in the Life of a Doctrine* (New York: Dell, 1967) "to demonstrate . . . a multiple ambiguity in Marxism: ambiguity in the spirit of Marx himself, ambiguity in the heritage he left, and ambiguity in those who claimed to be his heirs" (p. xxiii). The same quality is stressed in the subtitle to Sidney Hook's study *Marx and the Marxists, An Ambiguous Legacy* (Princeton: D. Van Nostrand Co., 1955).

3.   In addition to Hook's volume cited above, see: Emile Burns, ed., *A Handbook of Marxism* (New York: Random House, 1935); C. Wright Mills, *The Marxists* (New York: Dell, 1962); Albert Fried and Ronald Sanders, *Socialist Thought, a Documentary History* (Garden City: Anchor Books, 1964); Irving Howe, *Essential Works of Socialism* (New York: Holt, Rinehart and Winston, 1970); and David McLellan, *Marxism: Essential Writings* (Oxford: Oxford University Press, 1988). Attempting a succinct survey of the main currents of Marxism, is David McLellan's *Marxism after Marx* (Boston: Houghton Mifflin Co., 1979)—which I find in some ways too tolerant, in other ways fragmentary or incomplete, but certainly more inclusive than George Lichtheim's "revisionist" classic *Marxism, an Historical and Critical Study* (New York: Praeger Publisher, 1961), and far less hostile to the subject than Leszek Kolakowski's three-volume philosophical polemic, *Main Currents of Marxism* (Oxford: Oxford University Press, 1978).

Acknowledgments

Every book is the fruit of what many people do. This one is dedicated to three, but there are others, too many to acknowledge by name here—family and friends, co-workers, students, activists, colleagues, and comrades—whose contributions have been important. Special thanks should be expressed to those at Humanities Press whose labors turned my manuscript into a book, under the guidance of production editor Terry Mares. I also give thanks to my brave companion, Carol McAllister, a creative scholar-activist who in the early stages of our friendship learned from me about the concept of uneven and combined development and then taught me how to understand it in theory and in life.

* * *

The heart of this book, of course, can be found in the writings of great revolutionaries that reflect the lives, struggles, triumphs and sacrifices of millions of working people and their families and partisans. These writings—which can be said to belong to the people for whom they were written and are mostly in the public domain—have come to us through the efforts of a number of translators, editors and publishers.

International Publishers in New York and Progress Publishers in Moscow have done the most to make available English translations (carried out through the years by many and sometimes unknown socialist and communist idealists) of works by Marx, Engels, Lenin, and Gramsci that can be found here (though in the case of Gramsci the Herculean translation efforts of Quintin Hoare and Geoffrey Nowell Smith have been decisive).

Rosa Luxemburg's translators—an anonymous associate of the New York Socialist Publication Society in 1918, Eden and Cedar Paul and

Patrick Lavin in the 1920s, someone who used the pen-name "Integer" in the 1930s, Rosemarie Waldrop in 1971—made it possible for this passionate revolutionary to share her insights with us in the writings reproduced here, which have been reprinted in various places but are most easily found in volumes published by Pathfinder Press and Monthly Review Press.

The works of Trotsky have had many translators—among the earliest were Morris Lewit, Max Eastman, and John G. Wright (Joseph Vanzler), some are unknown, and more recently dozens of others were drawn into the great collective project which George Breitman (aided by such people as Naomi Allen, Sarah Lovell, and George Saunders) coordinated under the auspices of Pathfinder Press.

It seems fitting that works seeking to advance human freedom through the struggle to achieve the collective ownership and control of society's resources should come to us through so rich a collective process.

PART ONE:

INTRODUCTION TO REVOLUTIONARY MARXIST POLITICS

1

The Revolutionary
Marxist Synthesis

Karl Marx (1818–1883) and Frederick Engels (1820–1895) together developed an approach to reality which they chose to call "scientific socialism" and which at the end of the 19th century came to be known as Marxism. Germans by birth, they had interests and knowledge (and, ultimately, influence) whose scope became global. Revolutionary activists intimately involved in the democratic and working-class movements of their time, they were also close observers, and in Engels's case a participant-observer, of the Industrial Revolution which was transforming civilization. More than activists and observers, they were highly educated scholars and intellectuals who were conversant in (and were to have a profound impact upon) almost all realms of human inquiry—ranging from philosophy and literature to the natural sciences, but especially the social sciences: what are now history, economics, sociology, anthropology, political science. They created a distinctive and expansive synthesis which blended classical German philosophy (Spinoza, Kant, Hegel, Feuerbach, and others), classical political economy predominant in England (Adam Smith, David Ricardo, and others), and French political thought (the thinkers of the Enlightenment, the ideologues of the French Revolution, the post-Revolution plebeian-radicals such as Babeuf, pioneering historians such as Michelet, Utopians such as Saint-Simon, Owen, and Fourier). Nor were the two men unaffected by the Romanticism which powerfully impacted on European thought in the early 19th century. Most profoundly shaping their distinctive synthesis, however, was the early working-class radicalism which arose in Britain, France, and Germany in the 1830s and '40s, in the wake of the Industrial Revolution.[1]

3

The synthesis which Marx and Engels developed was not simply meant to advance human knowledge in the abstract. Despite the relatively fortunate circumstances in which they were born, they saw human misery all around them. The lives and labor of the many were consumed in providing for the wealth and comfort of powerful minorities; the mental, cultural, and physical existence of mass laboring populations was degraded in the process. People suffered, and some died, under the innumerable assaults on their dignity and well-being, their potential for full human development stunted—all for the benefit of domineering and self-satisfied profiteers and rulers. Marx and Engels perceived this reality as being built into the social system of which they were part—not just the old order of aristocratic privilege, but also the rising order of bourgeois "progress." They were fired by what Marx called "the categorical imperative to overthrow all conditions in which man is a degraded, enslaved, neglected, contemptible being." The dual revolution wrought by the development of industrial capitalism and by the liberating upheavals in France had created, they believed, the material and conceptual basis for a future in which, as Engels put it, "Man, at last the master of his own form of social organization, becomes at the same time the lord over nature, master of himself—free." Convinced that the modern working class would "carry through this world-emancipating act," they believed that "it is the task of scientific socialism, the theoretical expression of the proletarian movement, to establish the historical conditions and, with these, the nature of this act, and thus to bring to the consciousness of the new oppressed class the conditions and nature of the act which it is its destiny to accomplish."[2]

The way that people perceive and analyze reality, the cluster of conceptions and definitions—or the theoretical framework—with which they make sense of their world, ultimately becomes a material force which can change the world. The Marxist paradigm, which was developed to do just that, has certainly influenced the course of modern history. The fact is, however, that this has evolved over the past century in a manner which is in no way simple or monochromatic. To get a sense of what is this complex thing called Marxism (there are, in fact, different "Marxisms," some of which have been in sharp and irreconcilable conflict with each other), it makes sense to survey the complex heritage from which it is derived.

Keystone of the Synthesis

In the early 1960s radical sociologist C. Wright Mills wrote *The Marxists*, an appreciative presentation of a multifaceted tradition of which Mills was prepared to be, at the same time, highly critical. "The cumulative effect of Mills's criticisms, largely culled without acknowledgement from criticisms made long before him, is so devastating that were it not for his tone of moral earnestness one would suspect that in calling himself 'a plain Marxist,' he was perpetrating an intellectual spoof." This was the shrewd judgment of the sophisticated ex-Marxist Sidney Hook, who added: "There is hardly a single notion of Marx which is not severely called into question by Mills—his theory of class, class interest, historical causation, state, political power, economic development, even the newly refurbished notion of alienation." One might argue that Mills, in drawing together and articulating the most plausible criticisms of Marx's thought, hoped to contribute to "clearing the decks," compelling Marxism to become stronger, more clear-minded, persuasive, vibrant. The fact remains, as Hook put it, that "Mills's criticisms could be used by schools devoted to the propagation of *anti*-Marxism."[3]

Mills insisted, however, on certain points which Hook was inclined to ignore. Marx, the sociologist wrote, "did not solve all of our problems; many of them he did not even know about." But "Karl Marx was *the* social and political thinker of the nineteenth century," and "to study his work today and then come back to our own concerns is to increase our chances of confronting them with useful ideas and solutions." He asserted that Marxism "is, after all, an explosive and liberating creed, and that the ends for which Marx hoped, and which are built into his thought, *are* liberating ends." One of its attractive qualities for Mills was precisely the fact that "Marxism is at once an intellectual and moral criticism" of society. As social science it provides "a more or less systematic inventory of the elements to which we must pay attention if we are to understand" social realities, but all of this acquires a dynamic quality because of Marx's explicit partisanship in favor of the struggles of the oppressed and his insistence on the need for revolutionary change. Even if Marx's intellectually disciplined yet passionate contribution "has to be reworked, extended, revised, even thoroughly remade, nonetheless it seems to many people an enormous truth." Mills concluded that while the specific doctrines and the general model developed by Marx had proved to be outdated and seriously flawed, "his method is a signal and lasting contribution to the best sociological ways of reflection and inquiry available."[4] Such an approach to Marxism, however, is somewhat problematical.

Another scholarly ex-Marxist, Bertram D. Wolfe, once rephrased Mills' point with a negative twist: "Marxism has been stripped down to a method that has yielded only invalid or unmeaningful results." Of course, Marxism has stubbornly refused to accept its frequently demonstrated invalidity and remains a force within the realm of intellectual discourse. Non-Marxist Robert Heilbroner has explained: "We turn to Marx . . . not because he is infallible, but because he is inescapable. Everyone who wishes to pursue the kind of investigation that Marx opened up, finds Marx there ahead of him, and must therefore agree with or confute, expand or discard, explain or explain away the ideas that are his legacy. . . . For those who want to explore the hidden dynamics of the life of society, Marx is the magisterial figure from whom we must all learn if we are to carry on the task of critical inquiry that he began." Thus Isaiah Berlin commented that "if to have turned into truisms what had previously been paradoxes is a mark of genius, Marx was richly endowed with it. His achievements . . . are necessarily ignored in proportion as their effects have become part of the permanent background of civilized thought."[5]

Yet we have seen that there is necessarily a sharper edge to Marx's contribution. "The essence of Marx and Engels' activity was that they theoretically anticipated and prepared the way for the age of proletarian revolution. If this is set aside, we end up with nothing but academic Marxism, that is, the most repulsive caricature." This intransigent declaration of Leon Trotsky might be seen as the other side of Bertram Wolfe's judgment: the failure of proletarian revolution means that Marxism is nothing—or worse than nothing. Both Wolfe (for the first half of his adult life) and Trotsky (for all of his adult life) saw Marxism as an awesome synthesis beginning from profound philosophical premises which were applied to the interpretation of history, out of which was developed an analysis of the historical forces that are unfolding in the existing social order, culminating in an orientation to the future, blending social-economic-political analysis with a call to practical action by masses of people and by each caring individual. In this way Marxism suggests a coherence and meaning in social existence which interlinks our personal lives with the society surrounding us and with all of history.[6]

Given the interrelationships stressed here, if the central pivot of this synthesis is removed, then especially for intensely committed individuals the synthesis as a whole loses coherence and meaning. And the central pivot of Marx's thought is proletarian revolution: the coming to political power of the working class, which will then transform the economy to create a society which is more free, more radically democratic, and better in innumerable ways than any society which has existed before.

Marx himself, in the early 1850s, asserted that "bourgeois historians had, long before me, described the historical development of this struggle of classes and bourgeois economists [had described] their economic anatomy." Marx believed that the distinctive elements in his synthesis involved "(1) to show that the existence of classes is simply bound up with *certain historical phases of the development of production*; (2) that the class struggle necessarily leads to the *dictatorship of the proletariat*; (3) that this dictatorship itself only constitutes the transition to the *abolition of all classes* and to a *classless society*." One of the most conscientious students of Marx's thought, Hal Draper, has demonstrated conclusively that by the term *dictatorship of the proletariat* Marx meant not some kind of elitist political domination in the name of the working class but rather the "rule of the proletariat" or the "conquest of political power by the proletariat." And in the passage we've quoted, "Marx was emphasizing that—though not the discoverer of classes and class struggle—he had shown why class struggle leads to *proletarian revolution*."[7]

An Outline of Marxism

Even if we restrict ourselves simply to the contributions of Karl Marx and Frederick Engels, Marxism constitutes what Rosa Luxemburg once called "a titanic whole," which has many more dimensions than the central commitment to proletarian revolution. As a body of thought and approach to reality it could be said to contain five fundamental components, which could be outlined in the following way:

ONE: Marxism involves a *philosophical approach to reality* that is

1. *dialectical* (reality is a complex, interacting, developing totality; it *evolves* through the contradictory interactions among and inherent within its component parts; things can only be understood in their contexts—i.e., their own course of development, and their interactions with other aspects of reality);

2. *materialist* (reality is based on the structure and dynamics of matter and energy; we may not yet understand all the laws of nature, but things that we cannot understand are not the result of "supernatural" or mystical causes; God is a creation of people, not the other way around; human beings and human societies can best be understood not on the basis of their expressed ideas but on the basis of how they live, their way of life);

3. *humanistic* (human beings are—for people—the most important part of reality; essential qualities of being human include: a striving toward self-determination [or freedom], creative labor, and community [or meaningful relations with others]; those things which stunt, mutilate, oppress or degrade people must be fought against; a society should be developed which allows for the free development of each person).

TWO: Marxism involves a *theory of history* which

1. sees human society as having evolved through stages: primitive "tribal" communism; slave civilizations; feudalism; capitalism (with some significant variations in non-European societies—for example, in some cases involving what Marx called "the Asiatic mode of production"); capitalism has not always existed and will not always exist;

2. integrates economics, political science, sociology, anthropology—emphasizing that the activities and relationships people enter into in order to get the things they need and want form a social structure and way of life (including power relationships among people) which must be grasped if we wish to make sense of their religious, intellectual and political practices, precepts and conflicts;

3. gives emphasis to technological development and economic productivity as helping to shape—often decisively—broader historical developments (for example: the creation of economic surpluses through agricultural innovations made possible the rise of slave civilizations; the creation of even greater productivity through the development of industrial technology under capitalism makes possible a future society of abundance for all);

4. stresses the centrality of class struggle in human history—which, from the time of the ancient slave civilizations, has involved ongoing tensions and conflicts ("now hidden, now open") between exploited,

laboring majoritiesand the privileged minorities who appropriate the economic surplus created by the majority's labor.

THREE: Marxism involves an *analysis of capitalism* in which (among other things)

1. capitalism can be defined as: an economy that is privately owned (by a minority), and basically controlled by the owners, used for the purpose of making profits for the owners; a form of generalized commodity production (that is, in which more and more aspects of life are drawn into a buying and selling—or market—economy);
2. it is grasped that under fully developed capitalism a majority of those in the labor force can only make their living by selling their labor-power (ability to labor) to the capitalists, and that the source of the capitalists' profits can be found in the actual labor that the employers are able to squeeze out of the workers;
3. it is understood that capitalism—in its necessary pursuit of profit—is incredibly dynamic, continually evolving (into highly concentrated and increasingly efficient economic enterprises) and expanding into ever more realms of social life as well as into ever more areas of the globe;
4. there is an identification of devastating internal contradictions within capitalism (such as the tendency toward overproduction; and a tendency of the rate of profit to fall, due to the utilization of more and more technology) leading to periodic economic depressions, and the contradiction between the social organization but private ownership of the economy generating a variety of other problems and dislocations;
5. related to this last point, innumerable social problems—including war, poverty, racism, sexism, erosion of democracy, ecological devastation, etc.—are traced to the economic dynamics and the structure of power inherent in capitalism itself.

FOUR: Marxism involves a *political program for the working class* which insists that the emancipation of the working class can only come from the workers themselves, while at the same time seeing this evolving majority-class as the key to the liberation of society from the problems generated by capitalism—but more specifically identifying the advance of the working class as coming from:

1. the organization of increasingly inclusive and socially conscious trade unions to defend the immediate interests of the workers;
2. overcoming competitive divisions that fragment the consciousness and power of the working class;
3. the formation of an independent political party of the working class which will seek "to win the battle of democracy";
4. the struggle for various social reforms being blended into a commitment to place political power exclusively in the hands of the working-class majority (that is, what is sometimes called "dictatorship of the proletariat," but *workers' state* or *workers' democracy* are clearer formulations);
5. an understanding that the capitalists may use violence to prevent the workers from taking power, and that the workers' movement must be prepared to see that such capitalist violence is not allowed to triumph;
6. the commitment of the triumphant working class to initiate the socialist reconstruction of society;
7. an understanding that the working class, combating the global capitalist system, must organize cooperatively across national boundaries and organize effective international organizations to advance their struggles; and that socialism too cannot triumph unless it is built on a global scale.

FIVE: Marxism involves a *vision of a socialist future* in which the economy is socially owned (by all), democratically controlled, utilized to meet the needs of all people, subject to democratic and humanistic planning based on the principle that "the free development of each will be the condition for the free development of all."[8]

Isaac Deutscher, in a thoughtful essay, once called Marxism "a way of thinking." V. I. Lenin stressed that it was "a guide to action."[9] Both were right. But here the trouble begins. Since the deaths of Marx and Engels in the late 19th century there has been a proliferation of ways of thinking and plans of action, some of them utterly incompatible with each other, which have appropriated the Marxist label. If we consider each of the five components of Marxism just listed, we can find at least several divergent interpretations regarding "what Marx really meant." In part, this flows from ambiguities which are inherent in "the titanic whole" of Marx's thought. Daniel Bell—the noted "end of ideology" sociologist whose fascination with Marxism has been lifelong—ably summarizes a number of the divergent interpretations that have been of particular interest to intellectuals such as himself:

Like all of us to this day, Marx was seeking to resolve a number of inherently irreconcilable dilemmas in the epistemology and sociology of the social sciences. Schematically, the contradictions are:

1. an activity theory of knowledge versus a copy theory;
2. voluntarism, according to which men make their own history, versus structural constraints or mechanistic determinism;
3. human nature seen as essence (*wesen*) versus human nature seen as re-created by history;
4. class role and persona of persons as against diverse individual motivations, and the mechanisms that mediate between the two concepts;
5. the "logic of history" versus moral condemnation of inhumanities;
6. scientific inquiry as either theoretical or historical, for it cannot be both simultaneously; thus one has either a logical explanation through a conceptual prism or an empirical explanation seeking to identify actual sequences;
7. a general theory of "society" and its determining mode (or even requisites) versus a historicist theory of specific, qualitatively different social formations.[10]

Bell asserts that "on almost all these issues, Marx was 'inconsistent,' and it is this inconsistency which allows so many individuals to construct their 'own' Marx." While many intellectuals who have an interest in Marxism focus precisely on such issues as these, this is not where we will find clues regarding the impact of Marxism on history and politics.

There are additional complexities, however, which go beyond simply academic "dilemmas in epistemology and sociology." The shape of Marxism was, for example, affected by the fact that within the early left-wing workers' movement throughout the world, the diffusion of the writings of Marx and Engels was uneven and limited. Only the *Communist Manifesto* and, to a lesser extent, the first volume of *Capital* plus Engels' popularization, *Anti-Dühring*, enjoyed a mass distribution, and many important works remained unavailable until the early decades of the 20th century. Ernest Mandel notes that "three successive generations of Marxists did not have access to an adequate overall view of the doctrine of Marx and Engels, often through only sheer lack of information and data." The first generations of socialists, beginning in the 1880s, were educated in Marxism largely through the popularizations offered by intellectuals and agitators whose own mastery of Marx's work was necessarily partial. The requirements of making even this "Marxism" accessible to masses of working people with varying educational levels introduced challenges that the popularizers grappled with in different ways, with more or less sophistication and vulgarization. The overall result tended to be, as Mandel puts it, "a rather summary version of Marxism, boiled down to a few central ideas: the class struggle; the socialist goal of that struggle through collective ownership of the means of production and exchange; the conquest of political power to achieve that goal; international solidarity of the workers." While this early form of popularized Marxism provided an integrated sense of history, economics, and politics considerably superior to the previous, narrower and more primitive orientations in the workers' movements of Europe, it failed to provide clear guidance in the face of new developments, for example, the far-reaching trends of the capitalist economy toward centralization and expansion (which meant the rise of imperialism, of the modern corporation, and of mass consumerism), the development of the scope of the modern state's activity (both within the nation—through economic regulation and social programs—and in the world arena), the profound impact of these things on culture and politics, and even the immense growth of the power and influence (and consequent integration into society and internal bureaucratization) of the labor movement itself.[11]

The Development and Proliferation of "Marxisms"

The most substantial organization influenced by Marxism before 1914 was the massive German Social Democratic Party (SPD), whose effective electoral work and trade union policies, well-organized local and regional structures, and vast educational, cultural, and social service apparatus made it a proletarian "state within a state." Because of its practical successes and the high quality of its Marxist intellectuals, the SPD came to be seen as a model by other parties in the Second (Socialist) International, a worldwide—though predominantly European—network of parties which represented twenty million people. Within the SPD and the Second International a revisionist current arose, led by Eduard Bernstein, asserting that ethical persuasion would be more important than class struggle in the transition from capitalism to socialism, which Bernstein and others saw as being brought about through the gradual accumulation of reforms. The revisionists argued that they were simply attempting to bring Marxism into line with contemporary realities and with the actual reformist practice of the Social Democratic movement. Against this challenge, revolutionaries such as Rosa Luxemburg insisted that if Marxism required any further development, it was simply in order to help the Social Democratic movement comprehend the necessity of more militant tactics to hasten the proletarian overthrow of an increasingly crisis-ridden, violent, and despotic capitalism. Taking a "center" position in this controversy stood the most authoritative theorist, Karl Kautsky, who sought to defend and develop Marxist "orthodoxy" against the "excesses" of SPD radicals and moderates. This became the majority position, in the SPD and throughout the Second International, as the highly bureaucratized leadership conservatively held on to the old-time radical rhetoric of Marx and Engels while, just as conservatively, drifting into an opportunistic accommodation with the *status quo*.[12]

When World War I erupted (1914–1918), a majority of the mass socialist parties of Europe felt compelled to abandon their revolutionary-internationalist rhetoric and accommodate themselves to the war efforts of their own capitalist governments. The fact that many hundreds of thousands of socialist workers "picked up the gun" in order to kill each other, and not their capitalist oppressors, seemed to throw into question Marx's high hopes for proletarian revolution.

In 1917 such a revolution took place, nonetheless, in Russia, under the leadership of Lenin and Trotsky. This momentous event and the new Soviet Republic established a rallying-point for those still committed to Marx's perspective of socialist revolution. Communist parties were formed throughout the world (including on continents where the Second International had limited or minimal presence: Asia, Africa, Latin America), and many of these new Communist parties established a mass following. A Third (Communist) International was established to guide the anticipated revolutionary upsurge of the 1920s. There was a creative renewal of Marxist thought, stimulated by the Russian Bolsheviks, the German followers of Luxemburg, and a new wave of vibrant activists and theorists in many other countries.

Yet new revolutionary triumphs of the 1920s failed to materialize. What's more, the young Communist parties soon became subservient to the new bureaucratic elite which consolidated its hold in the Soviet Union, after Lenin's death (1924), under the leadership of Joseph Stalin. The Stalinist version of Marxism was a rigid set of dogmas which were manipulatively utilized to justify all of the domestic and international policies of the new dictatorship. Stalin assumed a deity-like status unthinkable in the Bolsheviks' earlier "heroic" years. Under Stalinist leadership there was a "revolution from above" to collectivize agriculture and rapidly industrialize the country, with the use of extreme violence against all—peasants, workers, critical artists and intellectuals, political oppositionists, even dissident Communists—who got in the way. Throughout the 1930s and '40s, Stalin was especially interested in using the Communist parties in various countries, not to make socialist revolutions, but to make deals with liberal capitalists and help form capitalist governments that would be friendly to his own government.[13]

Meanwhile, the substantial remnants of the Second International continued on the trajectory of de-radicalization, reflected in an increasingly stilted "orthodoxy" and even bolder revisionism. The leaderships of the different Social-Democratic and Labor parties diluted Marxism with various gradualist notions which helped them make compromises with the capitalists of their respective countries, and they presented themselves as a credible alternative to Bolshevik violence and Stalinist totalitarianism. This allowed them to win certain reforms for the working class and to assume positions of prestige and authority; the socialist goal was postponed to the far-off future, or was eventually replaced with a more modest one: the capitalist welfare state.

The Great Depression which rocked the world capitalist economy in 1929 resulted in renewed working-class militancy but also in a welling-up of fascist reaction. With the rise of fascism throughout Europe in the 1930s there was a widespread belief among members of both the Second and Third Internationals that, as Communist spokesman George Dimitrov put it, "the toiling masses in a number of capitalist countries are faced with the necessity of making a *definite* choice, and of making it today, not between proletarian dictatorship and bourgeois democracy, but between bourgeois democracy and fascism."[14] The far-ranging and frankly class-collaborationist alliances which many self-designated Marxists helped to construct against fascism implicitly raised questions about the meaning of their own theories. The questions were rendered more profound by the fact that fascism was finally defeated not by proletarian revolution but by a devastating total war between major capitalist powers—with the USSR switching from anti-fascism to neutrality in 1939, and then in 1941 to membership in what would prove to be the winning alliance of World War II (1939–1945). While Communist and Socialist party members clung to old catch-words and ideals, the frankly reformist and often patriotic orientations that passed for Marxist politics in the Second and Third Internationals dulled many members to the dilemma posed by the failure of Marx's central category of proletarian revolution.

Rejecting the bland reformism of the Social Democrats and the sterile dogmas of the Stalinists, a number of European intellectuals developed different interpretations of Marxism which they hoped would restore and enhance its critical and revolutionary edge. Although many of them sharply disagreed with each other on a number of questions, they were eventually lumped together under the heading of "Western Marxism."

Some arose as dissidents, or at least maverick thinkers, within the Communist movement of the 1920s: Karl Korsch in Germany, Georg Lukács in Hungary, Antonio Gramsci in Italy. In the same period a group of independent left-wing scholars including Max Horkheimer, Theodor Adorno, and Herbert Marcuse established the Institute for Social Research in Frankfurt, Germany, and came to be known collectively as the Frankfurt School. Korsch, Lukács, Gramsci, and the Frankfurt School stressed the importance of the idealist philosopher Hegel in the formation of Marx's thought, and they were inclined to develop Hegelian interpretations of Marxism. Beginning in the late 1940s, in France, Jean-Paul Sartre and Maurice Merleau-Ponty attempted to blend existentialism (based on the ideas of Søren Kierkegaard, Karl Jaspers, and Martin Heidegger) with Hegelian-influenced Marxism.

On the other hand, in post-World War II Italy, Galvanno Della Volpe and Lucio Colletti developed a new interpretation of Marxism. First inside the Italian Communist Party, then outside of it, they rejected "Hegelianized Marxism" and urged that the ideas of other philosophers be used to revitalize the theories of Marx. Instead of Hegel, they preferred Rousseau and Kant. Joining Della Volpe and Colletti in their rejection of "Hegelianized Marxism" in the 1960s was the French Communist philosopher Louis Althusser, who claimed to have enriched Marxism with the structuralist theories associated with Ferdinand de Saussure, Roland Barthes, and Claude Levi-Strauss; many others were influenced by Althusser and made influential contributions of their own, such as the Greek Communist (later ex-Communist) Nicos Poulantzas.

As Perry Anderson has remarked, "to the exponents of the new Marxism that emerged in the West, the official Communist movement represented the sole real embodiment of the international working class with meaning for them—whether they joined it, allied with it or rejected it." There was no way to relate their creative thinking to the Stalinist dogmas and manipulative politics of that movement. A yawning gap appeared between theory and practice. "The result," notes Anderson,

> was a seclusion of theorists in universities, far from the life of the prole-
> tariat in their own countries, and a contraction of theory from economics
> and politics into philosophy. This specialization was accompanied by an
> increasing difficulty of language, whose technical barriers were a function
> of its distance from the masses. . . . The loss of any dynamic contact with
> working-class practice in turn displaced Marxist theory towards contem-
> porary non-Marxist and idealist systems of thought, with which it now
> typically developed in close if contradictory symbiosis.[15]

There arose in the late 1920s yet another alternative to Social Democracy and Stalinism which sought to keep alive the Bolshevik-Leninist heritage, cohering in the 1930s in the Fourth International led by Leon Trotsky. A small but often vital network of activists, primarily clustered in Europe, North America, Latin America, and Asia, it repre-sented a more coherent political orientation than that found within the overly intellectualized corridors of "Western Marxism." As Anderson has observed, "Trotsky's life from the death of Lenin onwards was devoted to a practical and theoretical struggle to free the international work-ers' movement from bureaucratic domination so that it could resume a successful overthrow of capitalism on a world scale. . . . One day, this other tradition—persecuted, reviled, isolated, divided—will have to be studied in all the diversity of its underground channels and streams. It may surprise future historians with its resources." In part through the efforts of Anderson and other colleagues of the British journal *New Left Review*, a synthesis of Trotskyist and Western Marxist (and other) cur-rents was achieved in the 1960s and 1970s. But the synthesis, to a very large extent, mirrored deficiencies that Anderson had seen in university-oriented and fashion-conscious Western Marxism—much to the annoy-ance of the relatively small clusters of Trotskyist activists.[16]

A far greater impact was exercised by what has been called Maoism, a complex phenomenon that became dominant in the Chinese Communist Party in the 1930s and which came to power in 1949. It has often been seen as a variant of Stalinism. As Mao Tse-tung himself put it in 1939: "Comrade Stalin is the leader of world revolution. . . . As you know, Marx is dead, and Engels and Lenin too are dead. If we did not have a Stalin, who would give the orders? This is indeed a fortunate circumstance." Yet analyst Pierre Rousset suggests that Maoism, "neither by its origins, doctrine or practice could . . . be reduced to Stalinism." Rather, Maoism was a form of "national communism," which was in part shaped by indigenous revolutionary traditions and a distinctive experience in the struggle for power within China itself. Of course, the Maoists, "despite their qualities . . . remained dependent on a context shaped by Stalinist supremacy over the international workers movement." Mao's lieutenant (and later his opponent and victim) Liu Shao-chi explained in 1945 that Mao's main contribution was "to transform Marxism from a European form to an Asian form." Mao had insisted: "There is no such thing as abstract Marxism, but only concrete Marxism. What we call concrete Marxism is Marxism that has taken on a national form, that is, Marxism applied to the concrete struggle in the concrete conditions prevailing in China, and not Marxism abstractly used." Among Maoism's distinctive perspectives were:

1. a stress on the peasantry (in place of the proletariat) as the decisive agent for revolutionary change;
2. the elevation of the Communist Party as the self-proclaimed proxy for the working class which would guide the peasant struggle;
3. a commitment to broad political and social alliances (including sections of the bourgeoisie) in "united fronts" against foreign invaders and indigenous reactionaries, alliances in which the other allies are to be subordinated to the leadership and control mechanisms of the Communist Party;
4. a populist insistence that intellectuals "become one with the people," subordinating their individualism to the needs of the masses (as defined by the leadership of the Communist Party);
5. a distinctive strategy of "people's war," establishing "liberated zones" in the countryside which ultimately surround and overwhelm the cities;

6. in the liberated zones controlled by the Communist party, utilizing participatory methods that involve the masses in policy-making, but in a manner that is ultimately controlled by the party leadership, and the utilization of mass mobilizations to carry out those policies;
7. an almost religious cult around the figure of Mao (here copying the example of Stalin).

In fact, despite important differences between Stalin and Mao, in important ways—such as the replacement of their own bureaucratic dictatorships for workers' democracy, the rejection of the perspective of organizing for a working-class revolution, the creation of their own personality cults, the intolerance of critical thought, the replacement of revolutionary internationalism by the belief in the possibility of creating socialism in one country—they were closer to each other than they were to the orientation of Karl Marx.[17]

The 1949 victory of the Chinese Revolution resulted in the Maoist model having a profound impact on the world Communist movement and on revolutionary-minded people attracted to Marxism. This was heightened when a split occurred between the leadership of the People's Republic of China and the leadership of the USSR (which was shifting from the more severe forms of Stalinism internally while seeking a greater accommodation to the capitalist world) in the 1960s. While Stalin had still been in power, forms of "national communism" had been brutally repressed (through pressure from the Communist Party of the Soviet Union and intervention by the Russian police apparatus) in the new Communist regimes of post-World War II Eastern Europe—with the exception of Josip Broz Tito's Communist Party and regime in Yugoslavia, which found it necessary to break openly with Stalin simply in order to survive as an independent entity. In Asia, on the other hand, such outside repression hadn't been possible; new Communist regimes in North Korea and North Vietnam didn't go so far as Mao, however, attempting instead to maintain their own distinctive character but also friendly relations with both the Soviet and the Chinese leaderships.

The disintegration of the Stalinist monolith was further advanced not only by the "de-Stalinization" campaign in the USSR but also by a process of "liberalization" and growing independence of Communist parties, particularly in Western Europe, whose orientation became increasingly similar to that of the reformist Social Democracy. Contributing to this growing heterogeneity was the development in Eastern Europe of "humanist-Marxist" currents (especially in Yugoslavia, Poland, Hungary—but even in the USSR) which brought into question much of the rigid orthodoxy that had passed for Marxism under Stalin.[18]

The post-World War II period saw the rise of anti-colonial and anti-imperialist sentiments, movements, and revolutions in Asia, Africa, and Latin America in which nationalist and modernizing elites often made use of socialist rhetoric and at least fragments of Marxist theory in order to develop ideological and programmatic orientations to advance mass struggles that would liberate their countries and bring them to power. This created confusing new "Marxist" variants which sometimes had little in common—in real, practical terms—with the actual approach of Marx and Engels.[19] In the course of the Cuban revolution, however, a new variant of Marxism emerged in Latin America with the encouragement of Fidel Castro and Che Guevara. As it evolved over time, it drew various elements from Marx, Engels, Lenin, Stalin, Trotsky, Mao, Gramsci, the Peruvian José Carlos Mariátegui, as well as such early revolutionary nationalists as José Martí and Augusto Cesar Sandino; eclectic and pragmatic, this variant of Marxism also characterized itself with a generous romanticism and revolutionary passion. The description by Donald Clark Hodges of "the new Marxism diffused by the Cuban Revolution" captures something of its flavor:

> The new Cuban Marxism was distinguished by its novel conviction that it is not always necessary to know the conditions of revolution in order to make one. . . . Together [Castro and Guevara] shifted the emphasis from Marxist theorizing to revolutionary practice, from the conditions of revolution that are independent of human volition to those dependent on our choices. . . . The established communist parties dedicate their energies to making Marxists as a prior condition of making revolution. Castro reversed the priorities by making revolution the best way of making Marxists. So did Che Guevara. In one of the many aphorisms that showed up in his conversations, "We walk by walking," he indicated that one learns to make a revolution by making one. . . . As Castro points out. . . Marxism is not a science or theory of revolution only: "Those who do not possess a truly revolutionary spirit cannot be called communists." As revolutionary action, Marxism includes a set of attitudes. "What defines a communist is his attitude toward the oligarchies, his attitude toward exploitation, his attitude toward imperialism; and on this

continent, his attitude toward the armed revolutionary movements". . . .
The independent character of Guevara's Marxism earned him the ani-
mosity of the communist parties throughout Latin America. . . . With
the same independence, Castro insisted that revolutionaries should learn
their Marxism not by rote but should acquire a critical understanding of
it. . . . Although Marxism is the theory, practice, and ideology of socialist
revolution, it should be interpreted critically in view of what is happening
in the world.[20]

Speaking of the orientation of Guevara's perspective in the "third
world," Michael Löwy wrote in 1970 that it means "rejection of rotten
compromises, opportunist maneuvers, 'peaceful coexistence'. . . . It means
the historical initiative of the revolutionary vanguard which launches
the guerilla struggle and mobilizes the masses. It means the concrete
international solidarity of brothers in arms in the common fight against
the imperialist yoke." Also, "while [Guevara] recognized that the fighting spirit of the workers of the imperialist countries had been weakened, he did not fall into the anti-European nihilism of [Franz] Fanon,"
Löwy added, "but on the contrary, prophesied in his 'Message to the
Tricontinental' that in Europe the 'contradictions will reach an explosive
stage during the next few years' (May 1968!) and that the class struggle
will eventually surge up in the very heart of the American imperialist
metropolis." This current had a profound impact not only among revolutionary insurgents in the "underdeveloped" countries of Asia, Africa,
and Latin America, but also among the "new left" and radicalizing youth
of Europe and North America. It contained within it contradictory elements—some of which shared many of the characteristics of the Mao
and Stalin perspective, some of which seemed more in harmony with the
original revolutionary project of Marx himself.[21]

In the cracks and crevices created by the proliferation of different
influential "Marxisms" after the World War II, additional distinctive currents developed. In Britain a number of creative scholars—E.
P. Thompson, Christopher Hill, E. J. Hobsbawm, Raymond Williams,
and others—came to the fore in the 1950s and '60s. In the United
States, grouped around the magazine *Monthly Review*, there were Paul
Sweezy, Leo Huberman, Paul Baran, Harry Magdoff, Harry Braverman.
Economists, sociologists, historians, anthropologists, literary critics, philosophers, and others in a number of countries began making independent contributions within a generalized but explicit Marxist orientation.

Recently, there have been new perspectives—analytical-Marxism, post-structuralist Marxism, post-modernist Marxism, post-Marxism, and more—which have brought their own complex vocabularies into the Marxist discourse.[22] No less important than theorists have been militant activists—from Central America, South America, Africa, Asia—who have been adding new dishes to the Banquet of Marxisms.

A Marxism Based on Working-Class Revolution

Or is it a Babel of Marxisms? The Tower of Babel was supposed to reach up into Heaven itself, but those who were building it found that each one of them was speaking a language incomprehensible to the others, resulting in chaos and collapse. Can the glittering and colorful swirls of theoretical divergence offer something of value to masses of people who yearn to move forward to a better life?

At this point we should step back from the multiplicity of interpretations in order to focus on the central issues that must concern us in this study. The question is not whether Marx's ideas generated an impressive array of influential and interesting perspectives. We can see that they did. Instead we must ask whether the central Marxist category of *proletarian revolution*—the working class rising up, smashing the bourgeois state, establishing its own political power, and maintaining that power in order to transform society along socialist lines—corresponds to some significant measure of historical reality. In the light of this question, many of the variants and interpretations of Marxism fade into the shadows.

Embedded in the question of proletarian revolution are additional questions which must be discussed in order to recover the revolutionary Marxist paradigm. If we are talking about Marxism in the 20th century, however, we must do more than consider how Marx and Engels dealt with these questions. We must also consider the views of those 20th-century adherents who remained true to the general structure and method of their thought and to their proletarian-revolutionary commitments, who had an opportunity actually to carry their approach into the 20th century. For this reason we will also make reference to theoretical contributions of Rosa Luxemburg, V. I. Lenin, Leon Trotsky, and Antonio Gramsci.[23]

Obviously we cannot assume that Marx and Engels would have agreed with all the views of these four people, just as the four didn't always agree with each other. Also, many commentators have argued that the Bolshevik tradition—with which Lenin, Trotsky, and Gramsci unambiguously identified—represents a profound divergence from the orientation of Marx himself. I am inclined, however, to accept the judgment of Eduard Bernstein: "The Bolsheviks are not unjustified in claiming Marx as their own. Do you know? Marx had a strong Bolshevik streak in him!" (The fact that Bolshevik Russia, in the face of brutal and unexpected realities, veered away from the Marxist goal of workers' democracy is an important—but separate—question which will be dealt with later in this study.) I am similarly inclined to accept this judgment of C. Wright Mills on Luxemburg: "She accepted Lenin's and Trotsky's revolution, but with early and important reservations. She was, first of all and continuously, a revolutionary . . . but she was also passionately for democracy and for freedom in all the decisive meanings of those terms." Mills (who had rejected as unrealistic the notion of proletarian revolution) critically notes that these two views—"For the Revolution" *and* "For Freedom"—are fused in her belief in the revolutionary nature of the working class. "She is in this respect a very close follower of Karl Marx. . . . What I have called, in my criticism of Marx, the labor metaphysic was for Rosa Luxemburg both a final fact and an ultimate faith." Along with Marx and Engels themselves, Luxemburg, Lenin, Trotsky, and Gramsci are revolutionary socialists, utilizing the materialist conception of history, who are committed to proletarian revolution and genuine working-class rule. Their extension of Marxist perspectives into the 20th century is permeated with this commitment.[24]

On the other hand, as a counter-balance, reference will also be made in these pages to individuals occupying different locations at the Marxist banquet table, and who developed different recipes out of 20th-century realities: Karl Kautsky, George Plekhanov, Joseph Stalin, and Mao Tse-tung. It is my belief that each of these figures represents lines of development which fundamentally compromise essential aspects of revolutionary Marxism. On the other hand, each of them represents influential and coherent alternatives to the theory and practice of the revolutionaries on whom we've chosen to focus; as such, they help us to better understand the meaning of that theory and practice.

In this study, it may be useful to discuss four aspects of Marxist theory: (1) the theory of capitalist development, (2) the theory of the labor movement, (3) the strategy of revolution, and (4) the conception of the transition to socialism. There is, of course, considerable overlap and interpenetration of these multifaceted aspects of Marxist theory. Also, there are a variety of interpretations of what Marx (and Engels, Luxemburg, Lenin, Trotsky, and Gramsci) "really meant," just as there are different stresses and nuances in the thinking of each of these revolutionaries—and also, from one time to another, significant shifts within the thought of each. There will be no serious attempt to deal with all of this here, for to do so would require a multivolume study. Instead, I will confine myself to what seem reasonable and coherent generalizations on each of the four selected theoretical questions, concluding with a summing up of key elements in the revolutionary Marxist paradigm.

Notes

1. See David Riazanov, *Karl Marx and Friedrich Engels, An Introduction to Their Lives and Work* (New York: Monthly Review Press, 1972), and Goran Thernborn, "The Working Class and the Birth of Marxism," *New Left Review*, May–June 1973. Two substantial and valuable discussions of the political thought of Marx and Engels are: Richard N. Hunt, *The Political Ideas of Marx and Engels*, 2 vols. (Pittsburgh: University of Pittsburgh Press, 1974, 1984), and the massive, multivolume work by Hal Draper, *Karl Marx's Theory of Revolution*, 5 vols. (New York: Monthly Review Press, 1977, 1978, 1986, 1990, and forthcoming). An indispensable resource is Tom Bottomore (with Laurence Harris, V. G. Kiernan, Ralph Miliband), ed., *A Dictionary of Marxist Thought*, second edition (London: Basil Blackwell, 1991). Useful essays which survey Marxist perspectives on culture, history, sociology, politics, economics, and philosophy can be found in David McLellan, ed., *Marx: The First Hundred Years* (Oxford: Fontana, 1985), and McLellan's own survey—*The Thought of Karl Marx, An Introduction* (New York: New York: Harper and Row, 1971)— also has merit. For a more revolutionary edge, see a collection of essays by Ernest Mandel, *Revolutionary Marxism and Social Reality in the 20th Century*, ed. Steve Bloom (Atlantic Highlands, N.J.: Humanities Press, 1994), dealing with figures and topics that are central to the present volume.
2. Karl Marx, "Toward the Critique of Hegel's Philosophy of Law: Introduction," *Writings of the Young Marx on Philosophy and Society*, ed. Loyd D. Easton and Kurt Guddat (Garden City: Anchor Books, 1967), pp. 257–258; Frederick Engels, "Socialism: Utopian and Scientific," in Marx and Engels, *Selected Works*, Vol. 3 (Moscow: Progress Publishers, 1973), p. 151; Frederick Engels, *Herr Dühring's Revolution in Science (Anti-Dühring)* (New York: International Publishers, 1966), p. 310.
3. Sidney Hook, "From 'Scientific Socialism' to Mythology," *Revolution, Reform and Social Justice, Studies in the Theory and Practice of Marxism* (New York: New York University Press, 1975), pp. 9–10.

4.   C. Wright Mills, *The Marxists* (New York: Dell Publishing Co., 1962), pp. 33–34, 35, 36, 102, 129, 472.

5.   Bertram D. Wolfe, *Marxism, One Hundred Years in the Life of a Doctrine* (New York: Dell Publishing Co., 1967), p. 357; Robert L. Heilbroner, *Marxism, For and Against* (New York: W. W. Norton, 1981), pp. 15, 18.

6.   Leon Trotsky, "Philosophical Tendencies of Bureaucratism," *The Challenge of the Left Opposition, 1928–29*, ed. Naomi Allen and George Saunders (New York: Pathfinder Press, 1981), p. 404; Heilbroner, *Marxism*, pp. 22–23.

7.   Hal Draper, *Karl Marx's Theory of Revolution, Volume III: The "Dictatorship of the Proletariat,"* (New York: Monthly Review Press, 1986), p. 248.

8.   Rosa Luxemburg, "Organizational Question of Social Democracy," *Rosa Luxemburg Speaks*, ed. Mary-Alice Waters (New York: Pathfinder Press, 1970), p. 111. The five-part outline offered here is suggested by: Bertram D. Wolfe, "The Basic Core of Marxism," *Workers Age*, June 29, 1940; Trotsky, "Philosophical Tendencies of Bureaucratism," pp. 396–398; V. I. Lenin, "Karl Marx," *Selected Works*, Vol. 1 (New York: International Publishers, 1967), esp. pp. 7–32.

9.   Isaac Deutscher, *Marxism in Our Time* (Berkeley: Ramparts Press, 1971), p. 17; V. I. Lenin, "Certain Features of the Historical Development of Marxism," *Collected Works*, Vol. 17 (Moscow: Progress Publishers, 1974), p. 43.

10.   Daniel Bell, "The Once and Future Marx," *The Winding Passage, Essays and Sociological Journeys 1960–1980* (New York: Basic Books, 1980), p. 107.

11.   Ibid.; Ernest Mandel, *The Place of Marxism In History* (Atlantic Highlands, N.J.: Humanities Press, 1994), pp. 72, 74.

12.   For an overview of the history of the socialist movement in Europe, see Wolfgang Abendroth, *A History of the European Working Class* (New York: Monthly Review Press, 1972). More detail can be found in the three-volume work by Julius Braunthal: *History of the International, 1864–1943*, 2 vols. (New York: Frederick A. Praeger, 1967), and *History of the International, 1943–1968* (Boulder, Co.: Westview Press, 1980). On the "revisionist" controversy in the SPD, see Peter Gay, *The Dilemma of Democratic Socialism: Eduard Bernstein's Challenge to Marx* (New York: Colliers, 1962).

13.   The Russian Revolution is the decisive event in the crystallization of the revolutionary Marxism on which we focus here. It is, now more than ever, a special target of intensified attacks by pro-capitalist scholars—such as Richard Pipes, *The Russian Revolution* (New York: Alfred A. Knopf, 1990), and Dmitri Volkoganov, *Lenin* (New York: Free Press, 1994), works by loyal functionaries in the Reagan-Bush administration and the Yeltsin regime, respectively—whose "stunning" and "magisterial" scholarship is breathlessly praised in the mass media, "conclusively proving" that the revolution inevitably led to the murderous totalitarianism associated with the Stalin dictatorship, a judgment unambiguously rejected by one of the most incisive and knowledgeable theorists of "totalitarianism" in Hannah Arendt, *The Origins of Totalitarianism*, second edition (New York: Meridian, 1958), pp. 318–323; also see Elisabeth

Young-Bruehl, *Hannah Arendt, For Love of the World* (New Haven: Yale University Press, 1982), pp. 410–411.

Honest and informative accounts remain easily available. A valuable reader especially designed for students is Ronald Suny and Arthur Adams, eds., *The Russian Revolution and the Bolshevik Victory* (Lexington, Mass.: D.C. Heath and Co., 1990). A fairly good popular history, presented in three well-written volumes, has been provided by W. Bruce Lincoln: *In War's Dark Shadow, The Russians before the Great War* (New York: Simon and Schuster, 1983); *Passage through Armageddon, The Russians in War and Revolution 1914–1918* (New York: Simon and Schuster, 1986), and *Red Victory, A History of the Russian Civil War* (New York: Simon and Schuster, 1989). There is also E. H. Carr's solid and standard history *The Bolshevik Revolution, 1917–1923*, 3 vols. (London: Macmillan Co., 1950).

For two evaluations of Stalin, one critical and one laudatory, see: Isaac Deutscher, *Stalin, A Political Biography*, second edition (Oxford: Oxford University Press, 1966), and Kenneth Neill Cameron, *Stalin, Man of Contradictions* (Toronto: NC Press Limited, 1987). An excellent anthology designed for students is Robert V. Daniels, ed., *The Stalin Revolution* (Lexington, Mass.: D.C. Heath and Co., 1990). Indispensable is Roy Medvedev, *Let History Judge, The Origins and Consequences of Stalinism* (New York: Columbia University Press, 1989). A valuable collection on the Stalinist legacy is Tariq Ali, ed., *The Stalinist Legacy, Its Impact on World Politics* (Harmondsworth: Penguin Books, 1984).

14.   Georgi Dimitroff, *The United Front, The Struggle against Fascism and War* (New York: International Publishers, 1938), p. 110. As the pro-Communist journalist Louis Fischer admiringly explained: "The Comintern realistically recognized in 1935 that the impending war could only be prevented if the Communists forsook active advocacy of revolution and extended their hand to all parties and persons who wanted to stop Fascist aggression" (*Men and Politics, An Autobiography* [New York: Duell, Sloan and Pearce, 1941], p. 308). Some Communist spokesmen later attempted to give this a "left spin," asserting that the primary function of a People's Front government, and the only sure way to crush fascism, involves taking "the necessary measures to break up the capitalist state machine, to disarm and repress reactionary capitalists, militarists, and landowners and to begin to move definitely toward Socialism," as U.S. Communist leader William Z. Foster put it when describing the People's Front conception in his booklet *In Defense of the Communist Party and the Indicted Leaders* (New York: New Century Publishers, 1949), p. 44. Foster called for a similar U.S. coalition to oppose "monopoly, fascism, and war" a coalition whose efforts, he claimed "would necessarily move toward Socialism" (pp. 88–92). Acknowledging that the allegedly revolutionary goal was not achieved, and that fascism was not smashed and world war not averted through the two foremost People's Front experiences of the 1930s (in France and Spain), Foster lamely placed all blame on the Communists' allies (pp. 44–45).

But his erstwhile comrade, Joseph Starobin, later noted in *American Communism in Crisis, 1943–1957* (Berkeley: University of California Press, 1975) that the conception was fundamentally flawed: "The basic forces with which Foster hoped to engineer an antimonopoly coalition were, by Communist definition, unreliable" due to "their belief that capitalism could be reformed" (p. 124). This "unreliability" is not surprising, given the fact that these forces largely consisted of small businessmen and liberal sectors of the capitalist class. And after all, the point of the People's Front, according to the Comintern leadership of 1935, is to create a coalition that will defend liberal capitalism (and at least minimal working-class rights under capitalism) from onslaughts of reactionary capitalism and fascism, a coalition which would be jeopardized by the sort of revolutionary and anticapitalist measures Foster prescribes (measures from which the Spanish and French Communist leaders, in fact, refrained). See Abendroth, *History of the European Working Class* (pp. 108–109), and more extensive discussions in Claudin and Mandel cited in note 19 below.

15. Perry Anderson, *Considerations on Western Marxism* (London: Verso, 1979), pp. 92–94.

16. Ibid., pp. 96, 98, 100. On the Trotskyist movement, see: Pierre Frank, *The Fourth International, The Long March of the Trotskyists* (London: Ink Links, 1977); Tom Barrett, ed., *Fifty Years of the Fourth International* (New York: Fourth Internationalist Tendency, 1990); Alex Callinicos, *Trotskyism* (Minneapolis: University of Minnesota Press, 1990); Robert J. Alexander, *International Trotskyism, 1929–1985: A Documented Analysis of the Movement* (Durham: Duke University Press, 1991); George Breitman, Paul Le Blanc, and Alan Wald, *Trotskyism in the United States, Historical Essays and Reconsiderations* (Atlantic Highlands, N.J.: Humanities Press, 1996).

17. Pierre Rousset, *The Chinese Revolution, Part I: The Second Chinese Revolution and the Shaping of the Maoist Outlook* (Amsterdam: International Institute for Research and Education, 1986), pp. 26, 27, 28, 30–31. Mao's views in his own words can be found in Stuart R. Schram, ed., *The Political Thought of Mao Tse-tung* (New York: Praeger Publishers, 1969), and Stuart Schram, ed., *Chairman Mao Talks to the People, Talks and Letters: 1956–1971* (New York: Pantheon Books, 1974). Maoism finds a critical defense in David Fernbach, *Mao Tse-tung, Marxist* (London: Anglo-Chinese Educational Institute, 1978), and Arif Dirlick, Paul Healy, Nick Knight, eds., Critical Perspectives on Mao Zedong's Thought (Atlantic Highlands, NJ: Humanities Press, 1997). A critical survey, with essential documentary material from Chinese dissidents, can be found in Gregor Benton and Alan Hunter, eds., *Wild Lilies, Prairie Fire: China's Road to Democracy, Yan'an to Tian'anmen 1942–1989* (Princeton: Princeton University Press, 1995). Additional critical points and sources can be found in the next chapter.

18. See: Fernando Claudin, *The Communist Movement, From Comintern to Cominform*, 2 vols. (New York: Monthly Review Press, 1975); Wolfgang Leonhard, *Three Faces of Marxism, The Political Concepts of Soviet Ideology*,

Maoism and Humanist Marxism (New York: Holt, Rinehart, Winston, 1975); and Ernest Mandel, *From Stalinism to Eurocommunism* (London: New Left Books, 1978).

19.   For incisive comments on "radical third-worldism" with a Marxist veneer, see Jean-Pierre Garnier and Roland Lew, "From the Wretched of the Earth to the Defense of the West: An Essay on Left Disenchantment in France," in *Socialist Register 1984*, ed. Ralph Miliband, John Saville, Marcel Liebman (London: Merlin Press, 1984). On Asian variants of Marxism, see: Colin Mackerras and Nick Knight, eds., *Marxism in Asia* (London: Croom Helm, 1985), and Hélène Carrère d'Encausse and Stuart Schram, eds., *Marxism and Asia* (London: Allen Lane, 1969). English-language works on Latin American Marxism include Sheldon Liss, *Marxist Thought in Latin America* (Berkeley: University of California Press, 1986), but especially Michael Löwy's superb anthology with commentary, *Marxism in Latin America From 1909 to the Present* (Atlantic Highlands, N.J.: Humanities Press, 1992).

20.   Donald C. Hodges, *Intellectual Foundations of the Nicaraguan Revolution* (Austin: University of Texas Press, 1986), pp. 174–175, 177, 178–179.

21.   Michael Löwy, *The Marxism of Che Guevara* (New York: Monthly Review Press, 1973), pp. 111, 114.

22.   See: Paul Buhle, *Marxism in the USA*, revised edition (London: Verso, 1991), esp. pp. 213–274; Bobbye S. Ortiz, ed., *History as It Happened: Selected Articles From "Monthly Review" 1949–1989* (New York: Monthly Review Press, 1990); Bertell Ollman and Edward Vernoff, eds., *The Left Academy, Marxist Scholarship on American Campuses* (New York: McGraw-Hill, 1982), Vols. 2 and 3 (New York: Praeger, 1984, 1986); and Antonio Callari, Stephen Cullenberg, and Carole Biewener, eds., *Marxism in the Postmodern Age, Confronting the New World Order* (New York: Guilford Press, 1995). The post-Marxist orientation is presented in Ernesto Laclau and Chantai Mouffe, *Hegemony and Socialist Strategy* (London: Verso, 1985), and Stanley Aronowitz, *The Politics of Identity: Class, Culture, Social Movements* (New York: Routledge, 1992); critiques are offered in Ellen Meiksins Wood and John Bellamy Foster, eds., *In Defense of History, Marxism and the Postmodern Agenda*—a special issue of *Monthly Review*, July–August 1995, and in Mas'ud Zavarzadeh, Teresa Ebert, Donald Morton, eds., *Post-Ality: Marxism and Postmodernism* (Washington, D.C.: Maisonneuve Press, 1995).

23.   It is useful to locate the ideas of these thinkers in their biographical and historical contexts. On Marx and Engels, see the dual biography by Riazanov, cited in note 1 above. On Luxemburg, see Paul Frölich, *Rosa Luxemburg: Her Life and Work* (New York: Monthly Review Press, 1972). On Lenin, three books taken together do the job: Leon Trotsky, *The Young Lenin* (New York: Doubleday and Co., 1972), N. K. Krupskaya, *Reminiscences of Lenin* (New York: International Publishers, 1970), and Moshe Lewin, *Lenin's Last Struggle* (New York: Vintage Books, 1970); Ronald Clark's competently researched and balanced study *Lenin, a Biography* (New York: Harper and Row, 1988) is also

quite serviceable. On Trotsky, see Isaac Deutscher's three-volume work, *The Prophet Armed, Trotsky 1879–1921* (London: Oxford University Press, 1954), *The Prophet Unarmed, Trotsky 1921–1929* (London: Oxford University Press, 1959), *The Prophet Outcast, Trotsky 1929–1940* (London: Oxford University Press, 1963). On Gramsci, see Giuseppe Fiori, *Antonio Gramsci, Life of a Revolutionary* (New York: Schocken Books, 1973).

24.   Mills, *The Marxists*, p. 149. Bernstein quoted in Sidney Hook, *Towards the Understanding of Karl Marx, A Revolutionary Interpretation* (New York: John Day Co., 1933), p. 43. Hook's pioneering study of 1933, written when he himself identified with revolutionary Marxism, remains one of the better works on the subject. Also worth reading is Hook's *From Hegel to Marx, Studies in the Intellectual Development of Karl Marx* (New York: John Day Co., 1936). Other valuable expositions which cover the philosophical ground—with some variations in interpretation—are: Henri Lefebvre, *Dialectical Materialism* (London: Jonathan Cape, 1968); Herbert Marcuse, *Reason and Revolution: Hegel and the Rise of Social Theory* (Atlantic Highlands, N.J.: Humanities Press 1992); and Bertell Ollman, *Alienation, Marx's Conception of Man in Capitalist Society*, Second Edition (Cambridge: Cambridge University Press, 1976). Georg Lukács' complex classic of 1923, *History and Class Consciousness, Studies in Marxist Dialectics* (Cambridge: MIT Press, 1971), is of special interest for those studying the intersection of Hegel and Marx.

2

Theory of Capitalist Development

The economy of a society involves the resources, tools, relationships, and activities through which its people "make a living," constituting "the way of life" of that society. This permeates and affects, often in complex ways, such things as its mores, cultural activity, politics, and the manner in which the society evolves, its history. Qualitatively more than previous forms of *class society* (where the labor of the majority of the people results in an economic surplus largely appropriated by economically and politically powerful minorities), capitalism involves a dynamic which militates against static and stable norms. In pre-capitalist societies the primary purpose of producing goods is the consumption of those goods; although some goods are produced for trade, the primary dynamic of the economy is not buying and selling but production for the purpose of consumption. Under capitalism, however, the purpose of production is profit. While elements of this capitalist dynamic can be found in previous forms of society, it is only from the 1400s onward that capitalism began its triumphal march of "progress," helping to set the stage for, and becoming the dominant form of economy through, the Industrial Revolution that was launched in the late 18th century. The capitalists—who purchase raw materials, tools and machinery, and the labor-power of free laborers in order to create goods to be sold in the marketplace—are naturally motivated to engage in activities that generate far-reaching transformations in society.

Accumulation and Expansion

"Accumulate, accumulate! That is Moses and the prophets!" wrote Marx of the central dynamic of capitalism. He quoted Adam Smith: "Industry

29

furnishes the material which saving accumulates," to which Marx added: "Therefore save, save, i.e. reconvert the greatest possible portion of surplus-value or surplus product into capital! Accumulate for the sake of accumulation, production for the sake of production: this was the formula in which classical economics expressed the historical mission of the bourgeoisie in the period of its domination."[1]

Marx adhered to the labor theory of value, according to which the value of a *commodity* (something produced for sale) is determined by the amount of socially necessary labor required to produce it; in a sense, labor equals value. The capitalist makes a living by purchasing commodities which are equivalent to a certain value, then combining those commodities in a certain way which creates new commodities that have a higher value, which yields him a profit at the marketplace. The secret is to be found in one of the commodities that he initially purchases—the labor-*power* of his workers. In the production process this labor-power is converted into *actual* labor which is absorbed into the newly produced commodity. This is largely unpaid labor, for the capitalist has only paid for the labor-power (i.e., wages which add up, more or less, to what it takes to sustain his employees), the cost of which is covered by the value produced for only part of the workday. The rest of the value produced in the workday is free to the capitalist, constituting what Marx called surplus-value.

Out of this surplus-value comes the capitalist's profits, but these are not simply consumed in the capitalist's quest for personal luxuries and pleasure (though a portion of them certainly are). A major portion of the surplus-value must be re-invested by the capitalist: into purchasing more raw materials, into maintaining machinery, into maintaining his labor force—*and into expanding his operations* (i.e., hiring additional workers, developing or acquiring new technology that will make "his" labor more productive, setting up new enterprises whether in the particular field he started out in or in others which may or may not be related to that field). Through this process, value is expanded. In the accumulation process, capital assumes different forms: capital (in the form of money) is invested into capital (in the form of industrial plants, technology, raw materials, labor power, and other such commodities) to produce capital (in the form of products to be sold at a higher value than the original capital). The laws of the market-place keep this wheel going round and round, drawing more and more elements and aspects of society and nature into its vortex. Capital is self-expanding value, accumulation. The competition between capitalists forces each to engage in this process—or be driven out of business and absorbed by more skillful and audacious competitors.

This dynamic involves a multiplicity of dynamics. One is a constant tension between the capitalist and his laborers (the class struggle), particularly at the point of production (i.e., the workplace), where the capitalist naturally and necessarily attempts to increase surplus-value through paying lower wages, extending the length of the workday, introducing more efficient standardized (though monotonous) work routines and speed-up, and utilizing labor-saving technology that will yield high productivity (that is, more product with less labor)—all of which represent one or another form of the degradation of labor, which the workers tend to resist. At the same time, more and more areas of life are drawn into the dynamic of the marketplace, more and more realms of labor are proletarianized; larger and more efficient concentrations of capital come to dominate the economy, and increasing numbers of people are unable to maintain themselves without selling their labor-power to the capitalists. Rapid industrialization, urbanization, increased national cohesion and consciousness, and what later social scientists would call "modernization" introduce massive dislocations and transformations. As Marx and Engels commented in the *Communist Manifesto*:

> The bourgeoisie cannot exist without constantly revolutionizing the instruments of production, and thereby the relations of production, and with them the whole relations of society. . . . Constant revolutionizing of production, uninterrupted disturbance of all social conditions, everlasting uncertainty and agitation distinguish the bourgeois epoch from all earlier ones. All fixed, fast-frozen relations, with their train of ancient and venerable prejudices and opinions, are swept away, all new-formed ones become antiquated before they can ossify. All that is solid melts into air, all that is holy is profaned, and man is at last compelled to face, with sober senses, his real conditions of life, and his relations with his kind.[2]

This "sobering" experience is propelled forward by other ramifications of the accumulation process. One of these is the periodic tendency for the capitalists to over-produce—to clog the market with more than can be purchased by consumers, resulting in a spiral of cutbacks in production, lay-offs, shrinking markets, factory closures, unemployment, etc.

Another ramification is the tendency for the rate of profit to fall in those industries where labor-saving technology has been introduced (since labor, not machinery, is the source of surplus-value from which profits are derived), a tendency which is mitigated by countervailing tendencies but which periodically can also generate a downward economic spiral. Far from constituting a collapse of capitalism as such, however, such depressions enable the stronger and more efficient capitalists to further transform the economy—and to secure greater domination.

The crises of the capitalist economy—whether resulting from over-production or the falling rate of profit—are often perceived as a sign of "the system" failing to work, even in its own terms, as capitalists are ruined, shopkeepers and farmers lose their enterprises, and workers are thrown out of work, with poverty and insecurity expanding dramatically. In an important sense this is true, but in another sense it is not. Periodic crises of capitalism, as Rosa Luxemburg put it, "are not 'derangements' in the usual sense of the word. They are 'derangements' without which capitalist economy could not develop at all." They "create the possibilities of the renewed advance of production" and are "the instruments of rekindling the fire of capitalist development. Their cessation—not temporary cessation, but their total disappearance in the world market—would not lead to the further development of the capitalist economy. It would destroy capitalism."[3] Economic crises are the means through which capitalism periodically becomes "modernized," more efficient, more technologically powerful, more centralized and integrated, while at the same time more expansive. While the effects can be devastating for particular sectors of the capitalist class and for the masses of people among the proletariat and other classes, these "derangements" are a beneficial aspect of the capitalist accumulation process—assuming, of course, that the mass discontent generated doesn't crystallize into an anti-capitalist revolution. They are beneficial for the predominant sectors of the capitalist class and for the system as such, and are a natural means through which the capitalist accumulation process periodically achieves a new equilibrium and moves forward.

Nor does the dynamic of accumulation restrict itself to one country. "The need of a constantly expanding market for its products chases the bourgeoisie over the whole surface of the globe. It must nestle every-where, settle everywhere, establish connections everywhere." So wrote Marx and Engels in the 1840s, although as Marx himself acknowledged in *Capital* twenty years later, capitalism "as yet exists only exceptionally on our earth!"[4] But he felt no compulsion to withdraw the futuristic prognosis of the *Communist Manifesto*:

> Modern industry has established the world market, for which the discovery of America paved the way. . . .
>
> The bourgeoisie has through its exploitation of the world market given a cosmopolitan character to production and consumption in every country. . . . All old-established national industries have been destroyed or are daily being destroyed. They are dislodged by new industries, whose introduction becomes a life and death question for all civilized nations, by industries that no longer work up indigenous raw material, but raw material drawn from the remotest zones; industries whose products are consumed, not only at home, but in every quarter of the globe. In place of the old wants, satisfied by the productions of the country, we find new wants, requiring for their satisfaction the products of distant lands and climes. . . .
>
> The bourgeoisie, by the rapid improvement of all instruments of production, by the immensely facilitated means of communication, draws all, even the most barbarian, nations into civilization. The cheap prices of its commodities are the heavy artillery with which it batters down all Chinese walls, with which it forces the barbarians' intensely obstinate hatred of foreigners to capitulate. It compels all nations, on pain of extinction, to adopt the bourgeois mode of production; it compels them to introduce what it calls civilization into their midst, i.e., to become bourgeois themselves. In one word, it creates a world after its own image.[5]

This could be interpreted in two very different ways. We can find both interpretations in the Marxist tradition—and both interpretations can be traced back to Marx himself.

Capitalism and "Progress"

Between the writing of the *Communist Manifesto* and *Capital*, Marx wrote *The Critique of Political Economy* (1859), whose preface asserted: "No social order ever perishes before all the productive forces for which there is room in it have developed; and new, higher relations of production never appear before the material conditions of their existence have matured in the womb of the old society itself." He added that "in broad outlines Asiatic, ancient, feudal, and modern bourgeois modes of production can be designated as progressive epochs in the modern formation of society," concluding that out of capitalism would emerge a socialist society so qualitatively superior to the previous modes of production that it would bring "the prehistory of human society to a close." Thanks particularly to the later contributions of anthropology, Marx and Engels came to the opinion that pre-class, communal societies had existed before the rise of "civilization" (and even persisted in some form on some parts of the globe), but this didn't necessarily alter the basic schema. As Engels elaborated it in *The Origin of the Family, Private Property and the State* (1884): "With slavery, which reached its fullest development in civilization, came the first great cleavage of society into an exploiting and an exploited class. This cleavage has continued during the whole period of civilization. Slavery was the first form of exploitation, peculiar to the world of antiquity; it was followed by serfdom in the Middle Ages, and by wage labor in modern times." The successive stages of civilization brought with them immense accomplishments, according to Engels, but these were achieved only "by playing on the most sordid instincts and passions of man, and by developing them at the expense of all his other faculties." He argued that "the increasing development of science and repeated periods of the fullest blooming of art" had occurred "only because without them the ample present-day achievements in the accumulation of wealth would have been impossible."[6] But at the same time, these accomplishments—which included the ability of modern economic technique to produce an immense surplus having the potential for providing for the well-being and full development of all people— provided the material basis which made possible a socialist future, to be ushered in by the uprising of the wage-laborers themselves. Or as Marx stated it in his 1853 article "The Future Results of the British Rule in India":

> The bourgeois period of history has to create the material basis of the new world—on the one hand the universal intercourse founded upon the mutual dependency of mankind, and the means of that intercourse; on the other hand the development of the productive powers of man and the transformation of material production into scientific domination of natural agencies. Bourgeois industry and commerce create these material conditions of a new world in the same way as geological revolutions have created the surface of the earth. When a great social revolution shall have mastered the results of the bourgeois epoch. . . . then only will human

progress cease to resemble that hideous pagan idol, who would not drink nectar but from the skulls of the slain.[7]

Regardless of its oppressive and degrading qualities, then, capitalist development was a necessary precondition for the rise of socialism; pre-capitalist societies must necessarily succumb to capitalist "progress" before their inhabitants could enjoy the liberation brought by the socialist future.

This perspective inspired the "father of Russian Marxism," George Plekhanov, to argue in the 1880s that "every factory founded in Petersburg . . . strengthens the 'flame of economic progress'" because the development of industrial capitalism "increases the possibility of a conscious movement of the working masses for their own economic emancipation." Karl Kautsky, writing in the early 1900s, agreed that "the bourgeoisie of Russia still has a revolutionary role to play," noting that "the Socialists active under Russian absolutism will have to take into consideration the most primitive conditions of their own country just as much as the most highly developed conditions of the other countries." Plekhanov's view was that "the old foundations of economic life are too narrow, heterogeneous and one-sided, and moreover too shaky, and new ones are as yet only being formed. The objective social conditions of production necessary for socialist organization have not yet matured." Even Lenin in 1905 (still considering himself a pupil of Plekhanov and Kautsky) stressed the "orthodox" Marxist view of "the bourgeois character of the Russian revolution" which, in overthrowing tsarist absolutism, "will, for the first time, really clear the ground for a wide and rapid European, and not Asiatic, development of capitalism."[8] Only after such development could a socialist revolution be possible.

Yet in the final decade of his life Marx himself had begun to develop his perspective along quite different lines—in contrast to aspects of his own previous writings. Even in the 1850s, in the massive notebooks he wrote in preparation for *Capital* which are known as the *Grundrisse* ("outline" or "floor plan"), Marx had clearly indicated that Western Europe was the only area to which was applicable the five-part schema: primitive communism—» slave society—» feudalism—» capitalism—» socialism. In Asia he detected something different arising after primitive communal society, a complex, and resilient (if somewhat vaguely understood) "Asiatic mode of production." In an 1877 letter to a Russian journal he explicitly warned against "transforming my historical sketch of the genesis of capitalism in Western Europe into a historico-philosophical theory of the general course fatally imposed on all peoples, whatever the historical circumstances in which they find themselves placed." Instead, he argued, it was necessary to carefully study specific forms of development in the world separately and then comparatively. "But success will never come with the master-key of a general historico-philosophical theory, whose supreme virtue consists in being supra-historical." What's more, by the 1860s the attitude of Marx and Engels regarding the "progressive" effects of Western capitalism on the "backward" countries had begun to shift. As Kinzo Mohri summarizes the evidence, Marx "became well aware that the destruction of the old society would not necessarily give rise to the material conditions for a new society." Instead he came to see "the forcible integration" of the old societies' into the world "market system" by Western capitalist powers as "depriving the precapitalist societies integrated into the world market system of the very preconditions for the balanced and systematic development of productive powers which would be indispensable for the construction of an independent national economy."[9]

What's more, as Teodor Shanin has commented, the final decade of Marx's life cannot be accurately characterized (as it has by many) as a period of "slow death" and "failing powers." Rather, it was a period in which he produced 30,000 pages of notes, reflecting an immense effort to deal seriously with "an increasing influx of 'stubborn data' which did not fully fit, and had to be digested. He was rethinking intensively, once more, his theoretical constructs, and moving into new fields." Marx's thought in this period was not in "decline or retreat but constant transformation, uneven as such processes are. His last decade was a conceptual leap, cut short by his death." In essence, Marx was developing a variant of what would later be called the concept of *uneven and combined development* associated with Trotsky. This can be found in the drafts of his 1881 letter to Vera Zasulich. While one can find important continuities between Marx's earlier thought and his thought in this final period, there is a dramatically new notion that socialist revolution is conceivable in countries where capitalism has *not* fully developed "all the productive forces for which there is room" and might even occur in "less developed" countries before occurring in "more advanced" ones.[10]

In his drafts for the letter to Zasulich, Marx argued that "the Western precedent would prove nothing at all about the 'historical inevitability' of this process" of capitalist development in non-Western countries. Nor did he believe that because primitive communal societies had been obliterated in the Western capitalist countries, all remaining forms of communal society in the world are doomed to extinction. "Primitive communities are not all cut according to the same pattern. On the contrary, they form a series of social groups which, differing in both type and age, mark successive phases of evolution." In Russia, despite the oppressive existence of tsarist absolutism and an exploitative landed nobility, communal forms persisted among the peasantry. "Russia is the only European country in which communal property has maintained itself on a vast, nationwide scale. But at the same time, Russia exists in a modern historical context: it is contemporaneous with a higher culture, and it is linked to a world market in which capitalist production is predominant." Marx believed that "to save the Russian commune, there must be a Russian Revolution," suggesting that "if the revolution takes place in time, if it concentrates all its forces to ensure the unfettered rise of the rural commune, the latter will soon develop as a regenerating element of Russian society and an element of superiority over the countries enslaved by the capitalist regime." He argued that "precisely because it is contemporaneous with capitalist production, the rural commune may appropriate all its positive achievements without undergoing its frightful vicissitudes." Against "the Russian admirers of the capitalist system" who denied that this would be possible, Marx challenged: "Did Russia have to undergo a long Western-style incubation of mechanical industry before it could make use of machinery, steamships, railways, etc.? Let them also explain how they managed to introduce, in the twinkling of an eye, that whole machinery of exchange (banks, credit companies, etc.) which was the work of centuries in the West." Against those who might protest that Marx is trading in progress for a romantic reversion to archaic forms, he could point out that many people among whom capitalism had "reached its highest peak in Europe and the United States of America seek only to break its chains by replacing capitalist with cooperative production, and capitalist property with a *higher form* of the archaic type of property, that is, communist property." Finally, in their 1882 preface to the *Communist Manifesto*, Marx and Engels integrated this conception into a rounded revolutionary-internationalist formulation: "If the Russian revolution becomes the signal for proletarian revolution in the West, so that the two complement each other, then Russia's peasant communal land-ownership may serve as the point of departure for a communist development."[11]

The Highest Stage of Capitalism

Yet this entire approach was not incorporated into the Marxist "orthodoxy" which Kautsky and Plekhanov had come to represent. The 30,000 pages of notes which Marx wrote in his last decade remained mostly unpublished for many years, as did the *Grundrisse*. The letter to Zasulich and all the drafts were not made public until 1924 by the great Marxist archivist and historian David Riazanov. As for the 1882 preface to the *Manifesto*, shortly before his death in 1895 Engels himself seemed to close the book on it, commenting that "there has been no revolution in Russia," and that "all the foundations of the capitalist mode of production were laid in Russia in a short time. But then the axe was also taken to the roots of the Russian village community. There is no point in complaining about this now."[12] This contributed to "mainstream" Marxists being able to ignore Marx's own challenge against a more or less unilinear historical scheme in which the grim necessities of capitalist development inexorably paved the way for a brighter socialist future.

Nonetheless, there almost naturally arose within the revolutionary wing of the Marxist movement interpretations and theoretical developments which went in the direction of elaborating, completing, or complementing the unknown or unfinished elements in Marx's thought. Consider the way Rosa Luxemburg described capitalism's expansion across the face of the globe:

> Capitalist desire for imperialist expansion, as the expression of its highest maturity in the last period of its life, has the economic tendency to change the whole world into capitalistically producing nations, to sweep away all superannuated, precapitalistic methods of production and society, to subjugate all the riches of the earth and all means of production to capital, to turn the laboring masses of the peoples of all zones into wage slaves. In Africa and in Asia, from the most northern regions to the southernmost point of South America and in the South Seas, the remnants of old communistic social groups, of feudal society, of patriarchal systems, and of ancient handicraft production are destroyed and stamped out by capitalism. Whole peoples are destroyed, ancient civilizations are

levelled to the ground, and in their place profiteering in its most modern forms is being established.[13]

This reflected the views of revolutionary Marxists in general in the early decades of the 20th century. The "progressive" impact of capitalist civilization upon the "backward" peoples was seen as a fraud. Luxemburg explained:

> To capitalist economists and politicians, railroads, matches, sewerage systems and warehouses are progress and culture. Of themselves such works, grafted upon primitive conditions, are neither culture nor progress, for they are too dearly paid for with the sudden economic and cultural ruin of the peoples who must drink down the bitter cup of misery and horror of two social orders, of traditional agricultural landlordism, of supermodern, superrefined capitalist exploitation, at one and the same time.[14]

With Luxemburg and others on the Marxist left who shared her revulsion, however, there was a serious-minded effort to develop a theoretical analysis of this phenomenon which had assumed qualitatively new dimensions after Marx's death. The first substantial effort along these lines was the Austro-Marxist Rudolf Hilferding's *Finance Capital* (1910), followed by Luxemburg's own *The Accumulation of Capital* (1913), the Bolshevik theorist Nikolai Bukharin's *Imperialism and the World Economy* (1915), and Lenin's *Imperialism, the Highest Stage of Capitalism* (1916). "Despite their divergent methods and different conclusions," says a recent history of socialist economic thought, "all four of them share a common central problem: the relationship between the continuing accumulation and centralization of capital in the metropolis [i.e., advanced capitalist centers] on the one hand, and the imperialist expansion of capital on the other."[15] Here we will touch briefly, however, only on the views of Luxemburg and Lenin.

According to Luxemburg, the logic of the capitalist system involves on the one hand *the drive to produce increasing quantities of goods* and on the other hand *the drive to keep down the wages* (and thus the living standards and, for that matter, the purchasing power) of the working class, in order to increase capitalist profits. This leads to a contradiction: society's ability to consume ultimately lags behind its ability to produce. Capitalism's drive to subordinate all areas of life to the mechanisms of the market, and the natural tendency for capital to become concentrated, results in the overwhelming majority of the population being

proletarianized. To the extent "that there are no other classes but capitalists and workers. . . . there is no way that the capitalists as a class can get
rid of the surplus goods in order to change the surplus value into money,
and thus accumulate capital." Unchecked, this will lead to a downward
economic spiral and finally economic collapse. The need to accumulate
pushes capitalists beyond their national borders to portions of the globe
"where capitalist production has only scattered roots" and "where capital
not only finds the possibility of realizing surplus value in hard cash for
further capitalization, but also receives various commodities to extend
production, and finally wins new proletarianized labor forces by disinte-
grating the non-capitalist forms of production." Yet this only postpones
the final reckoning, at the same time bringing about "a chain of economic catastrophes: world crises, wars, revolution." In fact, "the absolute
and undivided rule of capital aggravates class struggle throughout the
world and the international economic and political anarchy to such an
extent that, long before the last consequences of economic development,
it must lead to the rebellion of the international proletariat against the
existence of the rule of capital."[16]

Other Marxists argued, against Luxemburg's model, that capitalism
has greater flexibility than she attributed to it, and also that Marx himself provided tools for a richer and more satisfactory analysis of modern
capitalism's contradictions. "Unlike Marx," Paul Sweezy has commented,
"Rosa Luxemburg, in rejecting 'the limitlessness of capital accumulation,'
set up a concept of mechanical breakdown." Her conception of imperialism tended to coincide with what John Weeks has criticized as "narrow
reference to the economic and political relationship between advanced
capitalist countries and backward countries," in which "the word imperialism has become synonymous with the oppression and 'exploitation'
of weak, impoverished countries by powerful ones."[17] A broader conception, however, was articulated by V. I. Lenin.

According to Lenin, Marx's analysis held that under capitalist development "free competition gives way to the concentration of production,
which, in turn, at a certain stage of development, leads to monopoly."
Offering a specific periodization, Lenin argued that capitalism has consequently "been transformed into imperialism" since the opening of
the 20th century. In this period, "although commodity production still
'reigns' and continues to be regarded as the basis of economic life, it has
in reality been undermined and the bulk of the profits go to the 'geniuses'

of financial manipulation." He perceived that "the 20th century marks the turning-point from the old capitalism to the new, from the domination of capital in general to the domination of finance capital." He defined *finance capital* as "the concentration of production; the monopolies arising therefrom; the merging or coalescence of the banks with industry." He identified this period as one in which "a monopoly . . . inevitably penetrates into *every* sphere of public life, regardless of the form of government and all other 'details,'" with a tendency by the state to identify the needs of the massive firms with the national interest. It is also a period in which "the ownership of capital is separated from the application of capital to production,. . . and that the rentier who lives entirely on income obtained from money capital, is separated from the entrepreneur and all who are directly concerned in the management of capital." Financial-managerial interests assume heightened importance. Under the old capitalism, the export of goods was typical, while under the new capitalism the more important dynamic is the export of capital. The logic of the accumulation process leads to the fact that "surplus capital will be utilized not for the purpose of raising the standard of living of the masses in a given country, for this would mean a decline of profits for the capitalists, but for the purpose of increasing profits by exporting capital abroad to the backward counties. In these backward countries profits are usually high, for capital is scarce, the price of land is relatively low, wages are low, raw materials are cheap." Thus, rather than the bleakly inexorable push which Luxemburg saw as driving capital abroad, Lenin perceived a magnetically inexorable pull. Nonetheless, the new capitalism continued to increase and intensify "the anarchy inherent in capitalist production *as a whole*," certainly for workers affected by capital flight to far-off lands. For Lenin, however, imperialism involved not simply the quest for profits in formally colonized areas (such as the case of the British Empire), but also the drive to invest in independent countries, sometimes "semi-colonies" for all practical purposes, but sometimes enjoying even greater autonomy than that—creating "diverse forms of dependent countries which, politically, are formally independent, but in fact, are enmeshed in the net of financial and diplomatic dependence." While this might "to a certain extent. . . arrest development in the capital-exporting countries, it can only do so by expanding and deepening the further development of capitalism throughout the world." In contrast to Luxemburg, Lenin stressed that expanding capital sought entry into *"not only* agrarian territories, but even most highly industrialized regions. . . . because (1) the fact that the world is already partitioned obliges those contemplating a *redivision* to reach out for *every kind* of territory, and (2) an essential feature of imperialism is the rivalry between several great powers in the striving for hegemony."[18] Lenin wrote:

> The epoch of the latest stage of capitalism shows us that certain relations between capitalist associations grow up, *based* on the economic division of the world; while parallel to and in connection with it, certain relations grow up between political alliances, between states, on the basis of the territorial division of the world, of the struggle for colonies, of the "struggle for spheres of influence."[19]

The end result of all this, for Lenin no less than for Luxemburg, was what she had called the chain of catastrophes: world crises, wars, revolutions—and the ultimate intensification of struggles by oppressed working people throughout the world. Lenin cautioned, however, that the process was complex because divisions could be created between workers—not simply along national lines but even within countries: "Imperialism has the tendency to create privileged sections also among the workers, and to detach them from the broad masses of the proletariat."[20]

Even among influential 20th-century economic, social, and political analysts who have rejected Marxism (in the United States such a politically diverse lot as John Kenneth Galbraith, James Burnham, Daniel Bell, Walt Whitman Rostow), we can find views similar to those just summarized: the immense expansion in scale of the capitalist firm, encompassing varied fields of enterprise; the key importance of the managerial strata to the new form of capitalist economy; the interpenetration of the state and the expanded capitalist entities; the international scope and interdependence of national capitalist economies; the capacity of the new capitalism to win over sections of the working class. There are significant differences, of course, in that Luxemburg and Lenin stress what they view as destructive contradictions, the negative effects on the independence of "less developed" countries, the exploitation and oppression of the laboring populations of both imperialist and imperialist-dominated countries. And both of them saw an indissoluble link between inter-imperialist rivalries and the new phenomenon of devastating world wars.

Against the views shared by Luxemburg and Lenin that imperialism had become inseparable from the nature and existence of capitalism, Karl Kautsky advanced a profoundly different analysis which insisted that "imperialism is a particular kind of capitalist policy, just like Manchesterism [i.e., free trade], which it replaces." It simply involved "the struggle of every big capitalist state to expand its own colonial empire in conflict with other kingdoms of this kind," and it represented "only one among various means of expanding capitalism." Not only is it not "necessary for the continuation of the capitalist mode of production," but it is "becoming a barrier" to capitalist development. According to Kautsky "the capitalist economy . . . is extremely threatened by the conflicts between its states. Every far-sighted capitalist today must call to his comrades: Capitalists of the world unite!" A system of cooperation between advanced capitalist countries, which Kautsky saw as a possible future development that he termed ultra-imperialism, would constitute "dissolving imperialism by a holy alliance of the imperialists." This would not, he admitted, eliminate the subjugation of agrarian countries for their raw materials by the advanced capitalist countries— only the overthrow of capitalism by the working class or independence struggles by the colonized peoples could bring this to an end. George Lichtheim has characterized Kautsky's conception of ultra-imperialism as "a planetary economy controlled by a unified elite of scientifically trained managers who have left the national state behind and merged their separate identities in the formation of a global cartel linking all the industrially advanced centers of the world." But Kautsky—who saw ultra-imperialism as something "which of course we must fight against just as energetically as we fought against imperialism"—was optimistic. "Socialism, that is general well-being within modern civilization," he argued, "would only be possible through a powerful development of the productive forces which capitalism brings into existence, and with the aid of the enormous riches which it concentrates into the hands of the capitalist class." Noting that "the various states of the world are at very different stages of economic and political development," he asserted (in line with the unilinear schema which was part of his own brand of Marxist orthodoxy) that "the more a state is capitalistic on the one hand and democratic on the other, the nearer it is to socialism."[21]

Uneven and Combined Development

The first Marxist of the 20th century to offer a clearly formulated challenge to this unilinear view was Leon Trotsky. Whereas many had little difficulty in perceiving the *unevenness* of development among the societies of the world, Trotsky added an essential new element to understanding "the very different stages of economic and political development" among nations that Kautsky spoke of. In *The History of the Russian Revolution* (1932) he wrote:

> The laws of history have nothing in common with pedantic schematism. Unevenness, the most general law of the historic process, reveals itself most sharply and complexly in the destiny of the backward countries. Under the whip of external necessity their backward culture is compelled to make leaps. From the universal law of unevenness thus derives another law which, for the lack of a better name, we may call the law of *combined development*—by which we mean a drawing together of the different stages of the journey, a combining of separate steps, an amalgam of archaic with more contemporary forms. Without this law, to be taken of course in its whole material content, it is impossible to understand the history of Russia and indeed of any country of the second, third or tenth cultural class.[22]

Particularly in the 1960s and '70s, this perspective became an issue in debates over dependency theory in Latin America. George Novack commented: "The principal issue of historical theory in the so-called 'dependency debate' is: what caused the relative backwardness of Latin America with all the fateful consequences of its underdevelopment? Collaterally, why have the Latin American bourgeoisies had so feeble and stunted a development, and played so limited a progressive role, compared with their North American and Western European counterparts?" Novack insisted that "the law of uneven and combined development can help clarify these problems," which of course have been raised in Asia and Africa as well. Its application to 20th century realities was summed up, during the debate, by Timothy Harding: "Capitalism as it spread everywhere across the world swallowed up earlier systems without totally destroying them and employed them in modified ways for the capitalist purpose of commodity production for profit." This approach differed profoundly from Kautsky's and Plekhanov's orderly "pattern of historical development," as Trotsky put it, "according to which every bourgeois society sooner or later secures a democratic regime, after which the proletariat, under conditions of democracy, is gradually organized and educated for socialism." This older perspective "considered democracy and socialism, for all peoples and countries, as two stages in the development of society which are not only distinct but also separated by great distances of time from each other."[23] Given the dynamics which Trotsky perceived, however, the old schema was profoundly unrealistic.

Trotsky, along with all other Marxists of his time, believed that certain "democratic tasks" remained to be accomplished in the "underdeveloped" countries. Michael Löwy has systematized the general notions of what these tasks were held to be:

(1) *The agrarian democratic revolution*: the bold and definitive abolition of all residues of slavery, feudalism and "Asiatic despotism"; the liquidation of all pre-capitalist forms of exploitation (*corvée*, forced labor, etc.); and the expropriation of the great landowners and the distribution of the land to the peasantry.

(2) *National liberation*: the unification of the nation and its emancipation from imperialist domination; the creation of a unified national market and its protection from cheaper foreign goods; the control of certain strategic national resources; etc.

(3) *Democracy*. . . . not only the establishment of democratic freedoms, a democratic republic and the end of military rule, but also the creation of the social and cultural conditions for popular participation in political life by the reduction of the working day to eight hours and through universal education.[24]

Variations of these democratic tasks had been among the goals of the great revolutions of the 17th, 18th, and 19th centuries, which were termed "bourgeois-democratic revolutions" because they had helped clear the way for the full development of capitalism. Due to the dynamics of uneven and combined development and the emergence of modern imperialism, however, in the "less developed" countries there had arisen what Harding has characterized as "weak bourgeoisies incapable of making their own democratic national revolutions." Internally weak, the national bourgeoisie in countries dominated by imperialism became intimately linked to foreign capital. This implied an inability to lead the struggle for national autonomy—a mass movement raised to seize imperialist property might devour the property of local capital as well. This also suggests an inability to carry through agrarian reform, inasmuch as the mobilization of the peasantry to eliminate semi-feudal privileges might also threaten the bourgeoisie, which was tied very closely to the landlords. Nor would the bourgeoisie be able to offer consistent leadership in establishing a genuinely democratic state, because this could also enable the insurgent masses to carry through policies that might jeopardize the situation of the relatively weak capitalist layer. "Confronted with such a threat to its privileges," Löwy has noted, "the indigenous bourgeoisie would tend to opt for a more moderate and conciliatory policy towards foreign capitalism and domestic reaction." Even capitalist economic development in which the domestic bourgeoisie was interested would often be distorted and stunted by these dynamics. While Trotsky never denied that the national bourgeoisie, in collaboration with foreign interests, would be capable of achieving a certain degree of industrialization or of advancing *any* aspects of the democratic tasks, he insisted on "the limited, half-hearted and frequently *ephemeral* character of such 'progress,'" as Löwy has put it, concluding that "a complete and genuine solution to the national and democratic tasks in the countries of peripheral capitalism would be impossible under the leadership of the national bourgeoisie."[25]

This analytical approach formed the basis for Trotsky's theory of permanent revolution. He saw that the majority sectors of the population—the newly proletarianized labor force, the impoverished peasantry, aspiring and democratic-minded elements among the petty-bourgeoisie (artisanal, petty-commercial and professional layers)—did have a vital interest in the achievement of the democratic tasks. Among these forces, the urban and largely industrial working class had sufficient cohesion, leverage, and (through educational and organizing efforts of the socialist movement) consciousness and will to provide consistent leadership in the democratic struggles. "So far as its direct and indirect tasks are concerned," he wrote in the wake of the 1905 uprising, "the Russian revolution is a 'bourgeois' revolution because it sets out to liberate bourgeois society from the chains and fetters of absolutism and feudal ownership. But the principal driving force of the Russian revolution is the proletariat, and that is why, so far as its method is concerned, it is a proletarian revolution." This working-class hegemony in the struggle had a logic, Trotsky insisted, which "leads directly . . . to the dictatorship of the proletariat and puts socialist tasks on the order of the day." He argued that the working class "is being impelled towards power by the entire course of the revolution," that "once the proletariat has taken power in its hands it will not give it up without a desperate resistance," and that "the proletariat, on taking power, must, by the very logic of its position, inevitably be urged forward to the introduction of state management of the economy." Trotsky agreed with the classical Marxist view that socialism could not be realized in an impoverished and economically underdeveloped country, particularly given "the character of the world economy, of the world development of productive forces and the world scale of the class struggle. . . . In an isolated proletarian dictatorship, the internal and external contradictions grow inevitably along with the successes achieved. If it remains isolated, the proletarian state must finally fall to these contradictions. The way out for it lies only in the victory of the proletariat of the advanced countries." He was convinced that "the revolution in the East will infect the Western proletariat with a revolutionary idealism and rouse a desire to speak to their enemies 'in Russian.'" Thus he believed that "a national revolution is not a self-contained whole; it is only a link in the international chain. The international revolution constitutes a permanent process, despite temporary declines and ebbs."[26]

It should be noted that similar conceptions were developed independently by Lenin in the period 1914–1917, and this orientation underlay the Bolshevik Revolution of 1917 and guided the Communist International from its inception in 1919 until approximately 1925. Attacked as "Trotskyism," it became a point of fierce controversy in the world Communist movement beginning in 1924. Ultimately it was rejected by the triumphant current led by Joseph Stalin, in favor of the conviction that socialism could be built in a single country (the USSR). The Stalinist orientation to struggles in the "less developed" countries reverted to something resembling the older Kautsky-Plekhanov outlook. In regard to China in 1927, for example, Stalin and his co-thinkers argued that "China is a semi-colonial country oppressed by imperialism," which meant that the revolution in China was "a bourgeois revolution of an anti-imperialist type," resulting in the consequence that "the Chinese bourgeoisie may, under certain conditions and for a certain period, support the Chinese Revolution" even if it involved the prominent participation of the Chinese Communist Party. In the 1930s the leaders of that party held, as Mao put it, that "the Trotskyists conclude that the nature of the Chinese Revolution at present is not bourgeois but proletarian.

Without any hesitation we are opposed to this viewpoint." As late as 1945 Mao—following Stalin—insisted that the Chinese Revolution would "allow capitalism to develop broadly in China," because "to replace the oppression of foreign imperialism and native feudalism with the development of capitalism is not only an advance, but also an unavoidable process; it benefits the bourgeoisie as well as the proletariat." Those following this line of thought were naturally inclined to exclude from their methodology Marx's later insights into social development. In his essay on dialectical and historical materialism, Stalin stressed the unilinear schema that "five *main* types of relations of production are known to history: primitive communal, slave, feudal, capitalist and socialist," going on to highlight Marx's 1859 statement that "no social order ever disappears before all the productive forces for which there is room in it have been developed." Yet reality is more complex than formal statements. Despite an official adherence to "Marxist-Leninist" conceptions, and despite an apparently genuine embrace of the Stalinist orientation, the Chinese Communist Party pragmatically sought to maintain itself and to move forward to take power—basing itself on the innovative strategy of peasant war. But with a different political methodology and a different strategic orientation, Mao and his followers achieved a goal somewhat different from that of bringing the working class to power as advocated by the revolutionary Marxists who have been our focus.[27]

The critique of capitalist development in underdeveloped countries, and the alternative to it which was developed by Trotsky, clearly is in harmony with the perspectives developed by others who preceded him, as well as by certain of his contemporaries. Thus, Marian Sawer's interesting comment on Trotsky applies as well to Marx, Engels, Luxemburg, and Lenin:

> Trotsky's analysis of how non-Western types of historical development give rise to non-Western forms of the industrialization process has been amply confirmed by events. His ideas on how the integrative force of the world economy would eventually bring about, though by different paths, a universal type of socialism based on the Western European conception of it, have not been confirmed in the same way.[28]

This question can be generalized: Even if the revolutionary Marxist analysis of capitalist development is accepted, it is not clear (at least to many observers) that the working class will come to power and create

socialist democracies in non-Western countries—or even in Western
countries! This leads to matters which are the focus of the remainder of
this study.

Notes

1. Karl Marx, *Capital, A Critique of Political Economy*, Vol. 1 (New York: Vintage
   Books, 1976), p. 742. Among the outstanding expositions of Marx's analysis
   are Paul M. Sweezy's 1942 classic—from which I respectfully adopt the present chapter title—*The Theory of Capitalist Development* (New York: Monthly
   Review Press, 1968), and Ernest Mandel's *Marxist Economic Theory*, 2 vols.
   (New York: Monthly Review Press, 1968). A succinct and lucid comparison of
   the Marxist theory of capitalist development with those of Max Weber, Joseph
   Schumpeter, and Friedrich A. Hayek can be found in Tom Bottomore, *Theories
   of Modern Capitalism* (London: George Allen and Unwin, 1985).
2. "Manifesto of the Communist Party," in Marx and Engels, *Selected Works*, Vol.
   1 (Moscow: Progress Publishers, 1973), p. 111.
3. "Reform or Revolution," in *Rosa Luxemburg Speaks*, ed. Mary-Alice Waters
   (New York: Pathfinder Press, 1970), pp. 61, 62.
4. "Manifesto of the Communist Party," in Marx and Engels, *Selected Works*, Vol.
   1, p. 112; Marx, *Capital*, p. 653.
5. "Manifesto of the Communist Party," in Marx and Engels, *Selected Works*, Vol.
   1, pp. 110, 112.
6. Karl Marx, "Preface to *A Contribution to the Critique of Political Economy*," in
   ibid., p. 504; Frederick Engels, *The Origin of the Family, Private Property and
   the State*, in Marx and Engels, *Selected Works*, Vol. 3, pp. 331–333.
7. "The Future Results of British Rule in India," in Karl Marx and Frederick
   Engels, *On Colonialism* (New York: International Publishers, 1972), p. 87.
8. George Plekhanov, "Socialism and the Political Struggle," *Selected Philosophical
   Works*, Vol. 1 (Moscow: Progress Publishers, 1977), pp. 60, 61–62, 97–98; Karl
   Kautsky, "To What Extent Is the *Communist Manifesto* Obsolete?" reprinted in
   Bulletin in Defense of Marxism, March 1988.
9. Teodor Shanin, ed., *Late Marx and the Russian Road, Marx and "the Peripheries
   of Capitalism"* (New York: Monthly Review Press, 1983), p. 136; Kinzo Mohri,
   "Marx and 'Underdevelopment,'" *Monthly Review*, April 1979, pp. 40–41. Also
   see Horace B. Davis, *Nationalism and Socialism: Marxist and Labor Theories of
   Nationalism to 1917* (New York: Monthly Review Press, 1967), esp. Chapter
   3; Eric J. Hobsbawm, "Introduction" to Karl Marx, *Pre-Capitalist Economic
   Formations* (New York: International Publishers, 1967); and Anne M. Bailey
   and Josep R. Llobera, eds., *The Asiatic Mode of Production, Science and Politics*
   (London: Routledge and Kegan Paul, 1981).
      There have developed some sharply divergent perspectives—within a more
   or less Marxist framework—of how and when transitions from pre-capitalist

to capitalist societies occurred. Justice cannot be done to the richness of the literature, but a few of the salient works can be mentioned. An early, sophisticated, and still valuable work of Marxist popularization on the rise of capitalism is Leo Huberman, *Man's Worldly Goods, The Story of the Wealth of Nations* (New York: Harper and Brothers, 1936; still in print through Monthly Review Press). An early controversy on the transition to capitalism is documented in Rodney Hilton, ed., *The Transition from Feudalism to Capitalism* (London: Verso, 1978). A related but later controversy is presented in T. H. Aston and C. H. E. Philipin, eds., *The Brenner Debate* (Cambridge: Cambridge University Press, 1985).

Perry Anderson's ambitious synthesis is offered in *Passages from Antiquity to Feudalism* (London: Verso, 1978) and *Lineages of the Absolutist State* (London: Verso, 1979). In a similar vein are Rodney Hilton, *Class Conflict and the Crisis of Feudalism, Essays in Medieval Social History* (London: Verso, 1990), and Colin Mooers, *The Making of Bourgeois Europe, Absolutism, Revolution and the Rise of Capitalism in England, France and Germany* (London: Verso, 1991). Compatible with these is Eric J. Hobsbawm's four-volume history of the modern world—*The Age of Revolution, 1789–1848* (New York: Mentor Books, 1962), *The Age of Capital, 1848–1875* (New York: Mentor Books, 1979), *The Age of Empire, 1875–1914* (New York: Vintage Books, 1989), and *The Age of Extremes, 1914–1990* (New York: Pantheon Books, 1995).

Somewhat different approaches, providing critical insights, are pursued by Immanuel Wallerstein, *The Capitalist World Economy* (Cambridge: Cambridge University Press, 1979), Peter Worsley, *The Three Worlds, Culture and Development* (Chicago: University of Chicago Press, 1984), and Eric Wolf, *Europe and the People Without History* (Berkeley: University of California Press, 1982).

10.   Shanin, ed., *Late Marx*, pp. 32, 33; especially useful for balance, however, is the essay by Derek Sayer and Philip Corrigan in the same volume, pp. 77–94.

11.   Karl Marx, Drafts of a reply to Vera Zasulich (February 16 to March 8, 1881), in Shanin, ed., *Late Marx*, pp. 101, 102, 106, 116–17, 118, 139.

12.   David Ryazanov (Riazanov), "The Discovery of the Drafts (1924)," Shanin ed., *Late Marx*, pp. 127–133; Frederick Engels, "On Social Relations in Russia," Marx and Engels, *Selected Works*, Vol. 2, pp. 407, 408. It is by no means clear that Engels was correct in writing off the Russian peasant communes. In his study of Russian society at the end of the 19th century, *Russia as a "Developing Society"* (New Haven: Yale University Press, 1986), Teodor Shanin writes: "In the period we are interested in, the commune was a major factor of peasant life in Russia. It proceeded to play that role until the early 1930s to the unending surprise of many peasants-watchers. It was the persistence of the commune and the way it could drop out of sight only to resurface later on, that puzzled most of the non-peasants looking at it" (p. 80). Also see Moshe Lewin, *Russian Peasants and Soviet Power, A Study of Collectivization* (New York: W. W. Norton, 1975), pp. 26–27, 85–93.

13. "The Junius Pamphlet: The Crisis in the German Social Democracy," *Rosa Luxemburg Speaks*, p. 325.
14. Ibid.
15. Gerd Hardach, Dieter Karras, and Ben Fine, *A Short History of Socialist Economic Thought* (New York: St. Martin's Press, 1979), p. 38. Also see Charles A. Barone, *Marxist Thought on Imperialism, Survey and Critique* (Armonk, N.Y.: M.E. Sharpe, 1985), pp. 18–56, and Anthony Brewer, *Marxist Theories of Imperialism, A Critical Survey* (London: Routledge and Kegan Paul, 1980), pp. 27–130.
16. Hardach, et al., *Short History*, pp. 42–45; Rosa Luxemburg, "The Accumulation of Capital—An Anti-Critique," in Luxemburg and Nikolai Bukharin, *Imperialism and the Accumulation of Capital*, ed. Ken Tarbuck (New York: Monthly Review Press, 1972), pp. 58, 59, 60.
17. Sweezy, *The Theory of Capitalist Development*, p. 207; John Weeks, "Imperialism and the World Market," in Tom Bottomore et al., eds., *A Dictionary of Marxist Thought*, second edition (London: Basil Blackwell, 1991), p. 253. Also see Harry Magdoff, *Imperialism: From the Colonial Age to the Present* (New York: Monthly Review Press, 1978).
18. Lenin, "Imperialism: The Highest State of Capitalism," *Selected Works*, Vol. 1 (New York: International Publishers, 1967), pp. 688, 690, 694, 695, 710, 711, 720, 721, 723, 724, 725, 726, 742–743, 747.
19. Ibid., p. 734.
20. Ibid., p. 760.
21. Karl Kautsky, "Accumulation and Imperialism," *Selected Political Writings*, ed. Patrick Goode (London: Macmillan Press, 1983), pp. 86, 87, 88; George Lichtheim, *Imperialism* (New York: Praeger Publishers, 1971), p. 12; Karl Kautsky, *The Dictatorship of the Proletariat* (Ann Arbor: University of Michigan Press, 1964), pp. 92, 96.
22. Leon Trotsky, *The History of the Russian Revolution*, three volumes in one, Vol. 1 (New York: Simon and Schuster, 1936), pp. 5–6.
23. George Novack, "The Law of Uneven and Combined Development and Latin America," *Latin American Perspectives*, Spring 1976, p. 101; Timothy Harding, "Dependency, Nationalism and the State in Latin America," *Latin American Perspectives*, Fall 1976, p. 4; Leon Trotsky, *Permanent Revolution*, p. 131.
24. Michael Löwy, *The Politics of Combined and Uneven Development* (London: Verso, 1980), p. 89. One could argue that all of this has relevance beyond the so-called "backward" countries. While not making explicit reference to Trotsky's theory, Arno J. Mayer has produced rich and provocative studies on modern European history—*The Persistence of the Old Regime: Europe to the Great War* (New York: Pantheon Books, 1981) and *Why Did the Heavens Not Darken?: The "Final Solution" in History* (New York: Pantheon Books, 1988)—which suggest the broader applicability of the concept of uneven and combined development.

25. Harding, p. 4; Löwy, *The Politics of Combined and Uneven Development*, pp. 90, 91.

26. Leon Trotsky, *1905* (New York: Vintage Books, 1972), p. 49; Trotsky, *Permanent Revolution and Results and Prospects* (New York: Pathfinder Press, 1978), pp. 66–67, 115, 131, 133.

27. Joseph Stalin, *The Essential Stalin, Major Theoretical Writings, 1905–52*, ed. Bruce Franklin (Garden City: Anchor Books, 1972), pp. 196, 322, 332; Nym Wales [Helen Foster Snow], *Inside Red China* (New York: Doubleday, Doran and Co., 1939), p. 223; Conrad Brandt, Benjamin Schwartz, and John K. Fairbank, eds., *A Documentary History of Chinese Communism* (New York: Atheneum, 1967), p. 304. Some historical perspective for making sense of all this is offered in John King Fairbank, *The United States and China* (Cambridge: Harvard University Press, 1972). More on divergent perspectives for the Chinese Revolution can be found in Les Evans and Russell Block, eds., *Leon Trotsky on China* (New York: Monad Press, 1976), which includes important writings by Chen Tu-hsiu and Peng Shu-tse (founders and central leaders of the Chinese Communist Party until 1927)—who understood the disastrous consequences of Stalin's line and sought to develop a revolutionary Marxist orientation appropriate to Chinese realities; their role is discussed in Benjamin I. Schwartz, *Chinese Communism and the Rise of Mao* (New York: Harper and Row, 1958), and additional insights are available in Wang Fan-hsi, *Memoirs of a Chinese Revolutionary* (New York: Columbia University Press, 1991). Key studies on the Chinese Revolution include: Edgar Snow, *Red Star Over China* (New York: Grove Press, 1968); Agnes Smedley, *Battle Hymn of China* (New York: Alfred A. Knopf, 1943); Jack Belden, *China Shakes the World* (New York: Monthly Review Press, 1970); James Pinkney Harrison, *The Long March to Power* (New York: Praeger Publishers, 1972); Gregor Benton, *China's Urban Revolutionaries: Explorations in the History of Chinese Trotskyism, 1921–1952* (Atlantic Highlands, N.J.: Humanities Press, 1995).

28. Marian Sawer, *Marxism and the Question of the Asiatic Mode of Production* (The Hague, Netherlands: Martinus Nijhoff, 1977), p. 187.

3

Theory of the Labor Movement

According to Marx and Engels, the two dominant classes in capitalist society are the bourgeoisie and the proletariat. As Engels explained in 1888: "By bourgeoisie is meant the class of modern capitalists, owners of the means of social production and employers of wage-labor. By proletariat, the class of modern wage-laborers who, having no means of production of their own, are reduced to selling their labor-power in order to live." In proportion as capitalist economy develops, the general population tends to undergo a process of proletarianization; intermediate classes are increasingly eliminated, and the ranks of (and occupational categories within) the working class are expanded. "These laborers, who must sell themselves piecemeal, are a commodity, like every other article of commerce, and are consequently exposed to all the vicissitudes of competition, to all the fluctuations of the market." While outside of the workplace they are subjected to profound insecurity, inside the workplace they are subjected to authoritarian pressures designed to convert their labor-power into ever higher degrees of actual labor, in order to increase the amount of surplus-value for the employer: "They are daily and hourly enslaved by the machine, by the overlooker, and, above all, by the individual bourgeois manufacturer himself. The more openly this despotism proclaims gain to be its end and aim, the more petty, the more hateful and the more embittering it is." There is a natural tendency for the capitalist to keep wages low, to keep the workday long, to increase the pace of work—and a natural tendency for the worker to resist all of this. What's more, even when increased productivity allows for the rise of wages and the improvement of workers' material conditions, at the same time it gives the employer more power over the employees, "the working class increases and enlarges the power that is hostile to it, the wealth that does not belong to it and that rules over it, the more favorable will be the conditions under which it is allowed to labor anew at increasing bourgeois wealth, at enlarging the power of capital, content with forging for itself the golden chains by which the bourgeoisie drags it in its train."[1]

The Historic Line of March

This constitutes an irreconcilable antagonism between workers and capitalists, an ongoing struggle between the classes, "an uninterrupted, now hidden, now open fight" in which the genuine gains for one class can only be secured at the expense of the other. This must ultimately end "either in a revolutionary reconstitution of society at large, or in the common ruin of the contending classes." Marx and Engels believed the "more or less veiled civil war, raging within existing society," would finally break out "into open revolution, where the violent overthrow of the bourgeoisie lays the foundation for the sway of the proletariat." To the extent that capitalism grows stronger—dominating and centralizing the economy and the state—it at the same time prepares the way for the triumph of the proletarian revolution. "The proletarian movement is the self-conscious, independent movement of the immense majority, in the interests of the immense majority. The proletariat, the lowest stratum of our present society, cannot stir, cannot raise itself up, without the whole superincumbent strata of official society being sprung into the air." Working people could then "take their conditions of existence . . . under their own control."[2] The new proletarian state, establishing majority rule for the first time in history, would establish social ownership and control of society's economic resources. The technology and the social organization of the economy developed under capitalism would, in the new communist society, be utilized to meet human needs; class divisions and antagonisms would give way to a society of abundance and freedom in which each individual would be enabled to develop to the highest of his or her abilities.

This could only be brought about, however, as the culmination of an extended process through which the workers would "make themselves fit to take power."[3]

Marx and Engels described the "stages of development" of the workers struggle as beginning with "the contest. . . carried on by individual laborers, then by the workpeople of a factory, then by the operatives of one trade, in one locality, against the individual bourgeois who directly exploits them." At first, they noted, workers directed their attacks not against capitalist relations of production, but instead against the instruments of production—new technology which they associated with the increased oppression they experienced at the workplace. Discussing early labor disputes in Russia, Lenin commented that "even the primitive revolts expressed the awakening consciousness to a certain extent." But, Marx and Engels noted, "at this stage the laborers still form an incoherent mass scattered over the whole country, and broken up by their mutual competition." With the development of industry, however, the working class increases in numbers and becomes concentrated in industrial centers. The competition between rival capitalists, the periodic commercial crises, and the further development of technology "make the wages of the workers ever more fluctuating" and "makes their livelihood more and more precarious." In the face of this situation, "collisions" develop between workers and capitalists, and "the workers thereupon begin to form combinations (Trades' Unions) against the bourgeois; they club together in order to keep up the rate of wages; they found permanent associations in order to make provision beforehand for these occasional revolts." As Lenin noted in regard to Russian trade union developments in the 1890s, "the strikes . . . revealed far greater flashes of consciousness; definite demands were advanced, the strike was carefully timed, known cases and instances in other places were discussed, etc." These "systematic strikes represented the class struggle in embryo, but only in embryo." In order to be effective, the workers of different localities must link up with each other, wrote Marx and Engels, in order to "centralize the numerous local struggles, all of the same character, into one national struggle between the classes." But since "every class struggle is a political struggle," the class-wide organization of the workers will eventually lead to the formation of a workers party which will lead the fight for defense of the proletariat's immediate interests and eventually for its coming to power.[4]

Trade Unionism

Marx and Engels viewed trade unions as essential components of the developing class struggle. As early as 1844, Engels' study of the British working class described strikes as "first skirmishes" which "sometimes result in weighty struggles," asserting: "They are the school of war of the workingmen in which they prepare themselves for the great struggle that cannot be avoided. . . . And as schools of war they are unexcelled. In them is developed the peculiar courage of the English." In the mid-1860s Marx offered an economic analysis which gave even greater stress to their importance. Marx's analysis held that the value of commodities is determined by the amount of socially necessary labor which it takes to produce them; thus, the value of the labor-power which the workers sell to the capitalist for wages is determined by the amount of socially necessary labor it takes to feed, clothe, house, and otherwise maintain the workers. "By comparing the standard wages or values of labor in different countries," he noted, "and by comparing them in different historical epochs of the same country, you will find that the *value of* labor itself is not a fixed but a variable magnitude." He remarked that wages generally fluctuate between the mere physical minimum necessary to keep the worker alive and the usually somewhat higher "traditional standard of life. . . springing from the social conditions in which people are placed and reared up." The standard of living (and therefore "the value of labor") is established at a particular level, as are the hours of labor and the working conditions, only "by the continuous struggle between capital and labor." Trade unions, which keep workers from competing with each other and instead combine their individual energies into a cohesive force, to fight for their common interests, becomes a factor as "the matter resolves itself into a question of the respective powers of the combatants." Whatever gains the workers win, Marx asserted, are threatened by the capitalists' investment in technological improvements to increase the productivity of labor (and diminish the leverage of the organized workers). "The very development of modern industry must progressively turn the scale in favor of the capitalist against the working man, and . . . consequently the general tendency of capitalistic production is not to raise, but to sink the average standard of wages, or to push the *value of labor* more or less to its *minimum limit*." Yet trade union activity continues to be essential because if the workers abandoned "their resistance to the encroachments of capital, they would be degraded to one level mass of broken wretches past salvation."[5]

Effective defense of the workers' interests, however, requires that trade unions do more than concentrate on the wages, hours, and working conditions of their members. Marx felt that, as of the late 1860s, they were "too exclusively bent upon the local and immediate struggles with capital" and had "not yet fully understood their power of acting against the system of wages slavery itself." He outlined what he believed must be their future trajectory:

> Apart from their original purposes, they must now learn to act deliberately as organizing centers of the working class in the broad interest of its *complete emancipation*. They must aid every social and political movement tending in that direction. Considering themselves and acting as the champions and representatives of the whole working class, they cannot fail to enlist the non-society men [i.e., non-union members] into their ranks. They must look carefully after the interests of the worst paid trades, such as the agricultural laborers, rendered powerless by exceptional circumstances. They must convince the world at large that their efforts, far from being narrow and selfish, aim at the emancipation of the downtrodden millions.[6]

In the *Communist Manifesto* Marx and Engels described "the ever-expanding union of the workers," which places "the workers of different localities in contact with one another. It was just this contact that was needed to centralize the numerous local struggles, all of the same character, into one national struggle between classes. But every class struggle is a political struggle." In part this is because, as Marx put it later, "the lords of land and the lords of capital will always use their political privileges for the defense of their economical monopolies." Marx explained: "The attempt to obtain forcibly from individual capitalists a shortening of the working hours in some individual factory or some individual trade by means of a strike, etc., is a purely economic movement. On the other hand, a movement forcibly to obtain an eight-hour *law*, etc., is a political movement." He added that "in this way a *political* movement grows everywhere out of the individual economic movement of the workers, i.e., a movement of the *class* to gain its ends in a general form, a form which possesses compelling force in a general social sense."[7]

Class-Conscious Politics

Later Marxists such as Lenin expanded upon this: "When the workers of a single factory or of a single branch of industry engage in struggle against their employer or employers, is this class struggle? No, this is only a weak embryo of it. The struggle of the workers becomes a class struggle only when all the foremost representatives of the entire working class of the whole country are conscious of themselves as a single working class and launch a struggle that is directed not against individual employers, but against the *entire class* of capitalists and against the government that supports that class." Only when individual conflicts in one or another factory were animated by this consciousness could they be seen as fully a part of the class struggle. In the same manner, Lenin denied that proletarian class-consciousness is simply whatever happens to be the consciousness of one or another group of workers. "The workers' class-consciousness," he explained, "means the workers' understanding that the only way to improve their conditions and to achieve their emancipation is to conduct a struggle against the capitalist and factory-owner class created by the big factories. Further, the workers' class-consciousness means their understanding that the interests of all the workers of any particular country are identical, that they constitute one class, separate from all the other classes in society. Finally, the class-consciousness of the workers means the workers' understanding that to achieve their aims they have to work to influence the affairs of the state, just as the landlord and the capitalists did, and are continuing to do now."[8] Lenin provided some of the boldest characterizations of the breadth of this kind of class-consciousness:

> Working-class consciousness cannot be genuine political consciousness unless the workers are trained to respond to *all* cases of tyranny, oppression, violence and abuse, no matter *what class* is affected—unless they are trained, moreover, to respond from a Social-Democratic [i.e., socialist] point of view and no other. The consciousness of the working masses cannot be genuine class-consciousness, unless the workers learn, from concrete and above all from topical political facts and events to observe *every* other social class in *all* the manifestations of its intellectual, ethical and political life; unless they learn to apply in practice the materialist analysis and the materialist estimate of *all* aspects of the life and activity of *all* classes, strata, and groups of the population. Those who concentrate the attention, observation, and consciousness of the working class exclusively, or even mainly, upon itself alone are not Social-Democrats; for the self-knowledge of the working class is indissolubly bound up, not solely with the clear theoretical understanding—or rather, not so much with the theoretical, as with the practical understanding—of the relationships between *all* the various classes of modern society, acquired through the experience of political life.[9]

What's more, as Marx put it, "the emancipation of labor is neither a local nor a national, but a social problem, embracing all countries in which modern society exists, and depending for its solution on the concurrence, practical and theoretical, of the most advanced countries." He and Engels had commented in the *Manifesto* that the expansion of "the bourgeoisie over the whole surface of the globe" was increasingly subordinating national differences "to uniformity in the mode of production and in the conditions of life corresponding thereto," so that "in the national struggles of the proletarians of the different countries" it was essential to "point out and bring to the front the common interests of the entire proletariat, independently of all nationality." In his *Inaugural Address of the International Workingmen's Association* (1864), Marx warned: "Past experience has shown how disregard of that bond of brotherhood which ought to exist between the workmen of different countries, and incite them to stand firmly by each other in all their struggle for emancipation, will be chastised by their common discomfiture of their incoherent efforts." He thundered against the bourgeois governments' "foreign policy in pursuit of criminal designs, playing upon national prejudices, and squandering in piratical wars the people's blood and treasure." He called instead for an independent foreign policy of labor "to vindicate the simple laws of morals and justice, which ought to govern the relations of private individuals, as the rules paramount of the intercourse of nations," insisting: "The fight for such a foreign policy forms part of the general struggle for the emancipation of the working classes."[10]

Later Marxists continued to stress these points. "Capitalist domination is international," Lenin stressed. "That is why the workers' struggle in all countries for their emancipation is only successful if the workers fight jointly against international capital."[11] In discussing the *Communist Manifesto*, Trotsky wrote:

> The international development of capitalism has predetermined the international character of the proletarian revolution. "United action of the leading civilized countries, at least, is one of the first conditions for the emancipation of the proletariat." The subsequent development of capitalism has so closely knit all sections of our planet, both "civilized" and "uncivilized," that the problem of the socialist revolution has completely and decisively assumed a world character.[12]

Many considering themselves to be Marxists have viewed the practical application of this—at least in wartime—as "a ticklish question," as Karl Kautsky put it during World War I, to be approached "with great caution," because it is difficult for even a party animated by proletarian internationalism to take "action against the war without harming one's own country." He explained: "As long as the time does not seem ripe for the conclusion of peace, the practical question is no longer: war or peace. It is: war or the defeat of one's own country.... The only question remaining after the outbreak of war is: victory or defeat?" Against this, Rosa Luxemburg insisted: "We stand today, as Friedrich Engels prophesied more than a generation ago, before the awful proposition: either the triumph of imperialism and the destruction of all culture, and, as in ancient Rome, depopulation, desolation, degeneration, a vast cemetery; or, the victory of socialism, that is, the conscious struggle of the international proletariat against imperialism, against its methods, against war."[13] Along with Trotsky and Lenin, she believed that "even" in wartime (especially in wartime) working-class internationalism dictates the need for labor's independent foreign policy, which is ultimately linked to—and hopefully would culminate in—socialist revolution.

Problems of the Workers' Party

An essential aspect of the Marxist theory of the labor movement is the conception of the working-class party. "Against the collective power of the propertied classes," Marx and Engels believed, "the working class cannot act as a class except by constituting itself into a political party distinct from, and opposed to, all old parties formed by the propertied classes." They believed that the "organization of the proletarians into a class, and consequently into a political party" was essential because although the numerical strength of the workers could "raise the proletariat to the position of ruling class, to win the battle of democracy," their "numbers weigh only in the balance, if united by combination and led by knowledge." A *trade union*, of course, is certainly a combination of workers, yet, as Antonio Gramsci argued, it is unrealistic to think that "the trade union possesses in itself the ability to overcome capitalism," because its function is in large measure that of "a commercial society, of a type purely capitalistic, which tends to realize in the interest of the proletariat the maximum price for labor-power and to realize a monopoly of this commodity in the national and international arena." Trotsky explained similarly that "trade unions do not offer and, in line with their task, composition and manner of recruiting membership, cannot offer a finished revolutionary program; in consequence, they cannot replace the *party*."[14]

Among Marxist theorists of the party concept, Lenin was among those who gave the most careful attention to the role of the organization in "combining" the different strata of the working class.

"The history of the working-class movement in all countries," he observed, "shows that the better-situated strata of the working class respond to the ideas of socialism more rapidly and more easily. From among these come, in the main, the advanced workers that every working-class movement brings to the fore, those who can win the confidence of the laboring masses, who devote themselves entirely to the education and organization of the proletariat, who accept socialism consciously, and who even elaborate independent socialist theories." (This layer would ultimately merge with non-proletarian revolutionaries such as Lenin himself, who—contrary to many interpretations—did not favor as a principle the tutelage of "middle class" intellectuals over the workers.) Below this "working-class intelligentsia" is a "broad stratum of average workers" who also have a degree of political awareness and sympathy for socialism but are primarily "absorbed by *local* practical work and interested mainly in the events of the working class movement." Below this stratum is "the mass that constitutes the lower strata of the proletariat. It is quite possible that a socialist newspaper will be completely or well-nigh incomprehensible to them."[15] The function of the revolutionary party is to facilitate the interconnection of these different strata of the working class in a way that raises the general level of working-class consciousness and the general level of the class struggle. It must utilize a variety of means—legal when possible, illegal when necessary—including educational and cultural work, electoral activity, trade union and other forms of organizing, mass demonstrations, mass actions, etc. for the purpose of advancing the interests of the working class, which as we've seen are defined quite broadly. The party must be prepared to participate in struggles for all democratic rights and for economic and social reforms that benefit workers and the oppressed, forming alliances with elements of other social classes, but always safeguarding the politically independent standpoint of the proletariat and striving to establish working-class hegemony in the progressive struggles.

Although there tended to be formal agreement among Marxists on these generalities, problems developed in the socialist movement which generated controversies and new lines of thought. In Germany, for example, Rosa Luxemburg observed a conservative tendency among Social Democratic trade union leaders to be "constantly absorbed in the economic guerrilla war whose plausible task it is to make the workers place the highest value on the smallest economic achievement." They therefore tended to lose "the power of seeing the larger connections and of taking a survey of the whole position." This "specialization of professional activity as trade union leaders," which developed especially on the basis of "disconnected economic struggles in a peaceful period," inevitably resulted in a tendency toward "bureaucratism and a certain narrowness of outlook." This led to an inclination to see the trade union organization as "an end in itself, a precious thing, to which the interests of the struggle should be subordinated." Thus came the temptation to shrink from an extension or deepening of the class struggle and "the overvaluation of the trade union method of struggle itself, its prospects and its successes." This "quite understandable *but irrational* illusion" could result in the movement simply being "swept aside by the rush of events."[16]

It is not always the case, however, that they are bypassed by events. "In periods of acute class struggle, the leading bodies of the trade unions aim to become masters of the mass movement in order to render it harmless." As it turned out, the conservative trade union wing of the German Social Democracy became predominant after 1905, despite the party's continued formal adherence to Marxist "orthodoxy." Karl Kautsky gave it all a theoretical gloss with his critique of "the strategy of overthrow" in which "either we deeply disappoint the masses or with one mighty leap we take the Junkers [aristocratic upper classes] by the throat, either to overthrow them or be overthrown by them." To this he counterposed the more prudent "strategy of attrition," which he believed would allow the Social Democrats "to keep our powder dry for the next great battle." He described the preferred strategy in these terms: "In the attrition strategy, the commander-in-chief initially avoids any decisive battle; he aims to keep the opposing army on the move by maneuvers, without giving it the opportunity of raising the morale of its troops by gaining victories; he strives to gradually wear them out by continual exhaustion and threats and to continually reduce their resistance and paralyze them." This tried-and-true orientation of the Social Democracy made sense, he argued, "not just because the given political rights offered a basis for this, but also because the Marxist theory of class struggle gave it the assurance that, whether or not it can electrify the masses with success or new sensations, it can always count on the class-conscious proletariat, as long as it energetically represents its class interests." This corresponded to Kautsky's own optimistic-fatalist interpretation of Marxism, which held that objective forces would inevitably bring about capitalism's collapse and the triumph of socialism, that revolutions "come with inevitable necessity, when the conditions which render them necessary exist." His sanguine conclusion: "The Socialist party is a revolutionary party, but not a revolution-making party. We know that our goal can be attained only through a revolution. We also know that it is just as little in our power to create this revolution as it is in the power of our opponents to prevent it. It is no part of our work to instigate a revolution or to prepare for it." Kautsky envisioned the possibility of the revolution coming about "if the proletariat in a democratic state grows until it is numerous and strong enough to conquer political power by making use of the liberties which exist."[17] This perspective—combined with the increasingly conservative influence of the trade union leaders—led to the strengthening of the kind of party apparatus described by Richard N. Hunt:

> Created during a long period of social stability and economic expansion, it was hired to run election campaigns, handle finances, disseminate the press, and do everything possible to attract new members and voters. It was not expected to mount the barricades or overturn existing society, but only to work within it for the attainment of a socialist majority. Oriented toward winning over half-convinced and marginal voters, the functionaries wanted a moderate, easy-to-sell program appealing to the widest possible audience. They resented criticism of this tactic and opposed any thought of changing it, even when the social stability and economic prosperity upon which it rested ceased to exist.[18]

Despite the Marxist rationale of theoreticians such as Kautsky, the German party and trade union bureaucracies, in the name of discipline and orthodoxy, increasingly restricted, slandered, and penalized left-wing elements which counterposed a revolutionary Marxist orientation to this gradualist practice. (Ultimately, in 1919 and after, when the reformist section of the SPD held state power, it utilized fiercely repressive measures which resulted in the murder of Luxemburg and many others in the militant wing of the labor and socialist movements.) In coming to terms with this phenomenon—particularly after the German Social Democratic decision to support the capitalist war-effort in 1914—Luxemburg, Trotsky, and Lenin added new elements to the Marxist theory of the labor movement.

Luxemburg commented that as early as the 1890s "it was characteristic of party conditions at the time that the socialist parliamentarians should have the decisive word alike in theory and practice. . . . frittering away the energies of the labor movement. . . . What passed officially for Marxism became a cloak for all possible kinds of opportunism, for persistent shirking of the revolutionary class struggle, for every conceivable half measure. Thus the German social democracy, and the labor movement, the trade union movement as well, were condemned to pine away within the framework of capitalist society." Even in 1905, Trotsky later confessed, he'd had the premonition "that the gigantic machine of the German Social Democracy might, at a critical moment for the bourgeois society, prove to be the mainstay of the conservative order. At the time, however, I did not foresee to what extent this theoretical presumption would be confirmed by the facts." In discussing the case of Kautsky, Trotsky argued that "the age of revolution is Marxism's school of advanced study. . . . Kautsky did not have this irreplaceable living experience of revolution. He accepted Marxism as a ready-made system and popularized it like a schoolmaster of scientific socialism. The heyday of his activity came in the middle of the deep trough between the crushing of the Paris Commune and the first Russian revolution." In 1915, discussing Kautsky's generation, he commented that it lacked "the apostolic zeal of the generation that was connected with the First International," adding: "Hindered in its first steps by the power of victorious imperialism, forced to adapt itself to the traps and snares of the anti-Socialist laws, this generation grew up in the spirit of moderation and constitutional distrust of revolution. They are now men of fifty to sixty years old, and they are the very ones who are now at the head of the unions and the political organizations. Reformism is their political psychology, if not also their doctrine." In later years he deepened his analysis. "There is one common feature in the development," Trotsky wrote in 1940, "or more correctly the degeneration, of modern trade union organizations throughout the world: it is their drawing closely to and growing together with the state power," a tendency transcending ideological predilections of unions leaders because it "derives from social conditions common for all unions" in the epoch of monopoly capitalism. In that epoch "they have to confront a centralized capitalist adversary, intimately bound up with state power," resulting in "the need of the trade unions—insofar as they remain in reformist positions, i.e., on positions of adapting to private property—to adapt themselves to the capitalist state and to contend for its cooperation." Hoping to draw the state to "their side" in the confrontation with capital, "the labor bureaucrats do their level best in words and deeds to demonstrate to the 'democratic' state how reliable and indispensable they are in peacetime and especially in time of war." Thus trade unionism (which had been a key in the Social Democracy's de-radicalization) became an either/or proposition for revolutionaries, evolving in one way or another depending on whether or not revolutionaries were able to win a majority of union members to their own program and leadership:

> The trade unions in the present epoch cannot simply be the organs of democracy as they were in the epoch of free capitalism and they cannot any longer remain politically neutral, that is, limit themselves to serving the daily needs of the working class. . . . The trade unions of our time can either serve as secondary instruments of imperialist capitalism for the subordination and disciplining of workers and for obstructing the revolution, or, on the contrary, the trade unions can become the instruments of the revolutionary movement of the proletariat.[19]

Unlike their contemporary, the sociologist Robert Michels, whose critical study of the German Social Democracy referred to "an iron law of oligarchy" inherent in all organization (making genuine democracy, and therefore socialism, impossible), these theorists perceived this phenomenon as arising from specific historical conditions which, therefore, could be transcended. Lenin was among the first to take the analysis further by seeking a material basis for opportunism in the labor movement; he argued that "the better-situated strata of the working class" (precisely those most inclined to respond to the ideas of socialism) can be disoriented by narrow economistic ideological perspectives. The reformist wing of the movement, according to Lenin, is "working hand-in-hand with the imperialist bourgeoisie *precisely* towards creating an imperialist Europe on the backs of Asia and Africa," adding that "objectively *opportunists* are a section of the petty bourgeoisie and of a certain strata of the working class who have been bribed out of imperialist super-profits," although "the trusts, the financial oligarchy, high prices, etc., *while permitting* the bribery of a handful of people in the upper layers, are increasingly oppressing, crushing, ruining and torturing the *mass* of the proletariat and the semi-proletariat." The reformist leaders "are in reality betraying and selling the interests of the masses," and are only "defending the temporary privileges of a minority of the workers" while acting as "the vehicles of bourgeois ideas and influences."[20] He later warned (in 1920):

> The industrial workers cannot fulfill their world-historical mission of emancipating mankind from the yoke of capital and from wars if these workers concern themselves exclusively with their narrow craft, narrow trade interests, and smugly confine themselves to care and concern for improving their own, sometimes tolerable, petty bourgeois conditions. This is exactly what happens in many advanced countries to the "labor aristocracy" which serves as the base of the alleged Socialist parties of the Second International.[21]

New Bureaucratic Obstacles

In the first two decades of the 20th century, then, important elements received particular stress in the evolving Marxist theory of the labor movement. Socialist revolution is not inevitable. Such a revolution can only be made by the working class, but important sectors of that class can be disoriented and misled. Different currents arise in the labor movement, offering counterposed (reformist vs. revolutionary) orientations. The fate of the working class and of humanity is dependent in large measure on whether revolutionaries guided by scientific socialism are able to win leadership in the workers' movement. If a program resulting in an advance to socialism is not triumphant, the alternative—as Luxemburg put it—may be "a reversion to barbarism."[22]

As the 20th century "progressed" into its third and fourth decades, the rise of fascism and Stalinism added new meaning to this somber forecast. And further developments in the Marxist theory of the labor movement necessarily resulted, in large measure through the contributions of Trotsky and Antonio Gramsci. An examination of these questions will also enable us to highlight Marxist views on the nature of the revolutionary party and its relationship to the working class as a whole, and also on dynamics of the revolutionary process.

In regard to analyses of the phenomenon which came to be known as Stalinism, we will have cause to touch on them later in this study. But important insights, relevant to our discussion here, were offered openly by Trotsky in his oppositional writings and elliptically by Gramsci in his prison notebooks. In large measure, their critiques have much in common with earlier revolutionary critiques of the bureaucratic conservatism which arose in the old Social Democracy. And yet there are important differences, flowing from the fact that Stalinism had its roots not in a segment of the labor movement maintaining itself within the framework of capitalist society, but rather in the governing apparatus of Soviet Russia, where a proletarian revolution had overturned capitalism. As Trotsky explained: "On the foundation of the dictatorship of the proletariat—in a backward country, surrounded by capitalism—for the first time a powerful bureaucratic apparatus has been created from the upper layers of the workers, that is raised above the masses, that lays down the law to them, that has at its disposal colossal resources, that is bound together by an inner mutual responsibility, and that intrudes into the policies of a workers' government its own interests, methods, and regulations."[23]

These methods and regulations were, in fact, extended throughout the Third International in the 1920s and '30s. "A *revolutionist*," Stalin had asserted, "is one who unreservedly, unconditionally, frankly and honestly . . . will defend the USSR, for the USSR is the first proletarian revolutionary state in the world that builds socialism. *An internationalist* is one who is unreservedly, unwaveringly, unconditionally ready to defend the USSR, for the USSR is the base of the world revolutionary movement and it is impossible to defend, to advance that revolutionary movement apart from and against the USSR." This was translated into unquestioningly following the leadership of the Russian Communist Party. As a leading spokesman for the Third International, O. W. Kuusinen, put it, "the Communist International possesses in the Russian leadership, in the person of its chairman and of the Russian delegation as well as of the Central Committee of the RCP, an accumulated stock of far-reaching revolutionary experience, of Marxian leadership and of proven ability, which are requisite to the historical tasks of the Communist International." Another Stalinist ideologist, V. Sorin, explained: "The Party is governed by leaders. If the Party is the vanguard of the working class then the leaders are the advanced post of the vanguard. . . . The special feature of the Communist Party is its strictest discipline, i.e., the unconditional and exact observance of all directives coming from their Party organizations. . . . The Party must be sure that each of its members will do what the Party tells him even if he disagrees with it. . . . Discipline, firm and unrelenting, is necessary not only during the period of underground work and struggle against Tsarism, not only during civil war, but even during peaceful times. . . . The stricter the discipline, the stronger the Party, the more dangerous is it to the capitalists." As Stalin exulted after the final crushing of all major opposition to him in the Communist Party of the Soviet Union: "When 99 percent of our Party vote for the Party and against the opposition, that is real, genuine proletarian unity as there has not been in our Party before."[24]

In his reflections from within a fascist prison in this period, Gramsci wrote that "the prevalence of bureaucratic centralism in the State indicates that the leading group is saturated, that it is turning into a narrow clique which tends to perpetuate its selfish privileges by controlling or even by stifling the birth of oppositional forces—even if these forces are homogeneous with the fundamental dominant interests," i.e., with the interests of the working class. Commenting that "every type of society and State has had its own problem of functionaries," he noted that "a new type of functionary is increasingly being produced—what could be described as 'career' functionaries, technically trained for bureaucratic work." He posed the question: "Has this process been a necessary one, or, as the 'pure' liberals claim, a degeneration in respect of the ideal of *self-government*?" In contrast to Stalin's celebration of unity, he argued that "in the end there is no unity but a stagnant swamp, on the surface calm and 'mute,'" and that "the party in this . . . case is a simple, unthinking executor. It is then technically a policing organism, and its name of 'political party' is simply a metaphor of a mythological character."[25]

This paralleled Trotsky's observation: "Industrialization and collectivization are being put through by the one-sided and uncontrolled laying down of the law to the laboring masses by the bureaucracy. . . . The bureaucracy cannot exercise its pressure upon workers and peasants except by depriving them of all possibility of participating in decisions upon questions that touch their own labor and their entire future."[26] This had relevance for the entire world Communist movement:

The ruling and uncontrolled position of the Soviet bureaucracy is conducive to a psychology which in many ways is directly contradictory to the psychology of a proletarian revolutionist. Its own aims and combinations in domestic as well as international politics are placed by the bureaucracy above the tasks of the revolutionary education of the masses and have no connection with the tasks of the international revolution. In the course of a number of years the Stalinist faction demonstrated that the interests and the psychology of the prosperous engineer, administrator, Chinese bourgeois intellectual, and British trade-union functionary were much closer and more comprehensible to it than the psychology and the needs of the unskilled laborer, the peasant poor, the Chinese national masses in revolt, the British strikers, etc.[27]

Indeed, Stalin (even as he slandered, persecuted, and ultimately imprisoned or slaughtered those inside the USSR who were resistant to his "revolution from above") looked forward to a "period of 'co-existence' with the capitalist states in which we are entering into rich and wide commercial relations with the capitalist world on a more or less wide scale," arguing that "the co-existence of two opposite systems is possible" and that Soviet foreign policy was committed to "preserving peace and strengthening trade relations with all countries." He repeated this time and again: "We stand for peace and the strengthening of business relations with all countries. That is our position; and we shall adhere to this position as long as these countries maintain like relations with the Soviet Union, and as long as they make no attempt to trespass on the interests of our country." Asked by a U.S. journalist if "the Soviet Union has to any degree abandoned its plans and intentions for bringing about a world revolution," Stalin insisted: "We never had any such plans. . . . This is the product of a misunderstanding." The journalist asked: "A tragic one?" Stalin replied: "No, a comical one. Or, perhaps, tragi-comic."[28]

Of course, the fact that other countries did not always "maintain like relations with the Soviet Union" and sometimes engaged in policies interpreted as trespassing on the interests of the USSR could generate less genial attitudes and rhetoric from the Stalin leadership. Nonetheless, this basic orientation had a profound impact on the world Communist movement. In 1938 Trotsky, seeing Stalinist policies as equally detrimental to the workers' cause as the reformism of Social Democracy, wrote:

In a society based upon exploitation, the highest moral is that of the social revolution. All methods are good which raise the class consciousness of the workers, their trust in their own forces, their readiness for self-sacrifice in the struggle. The impermissible methods are those which implant fear and submissiveness in the oppressed before their oppressors, which crush the spirit of protest and indignation or substitute for the will of the masses—the will of the leaders; for conviction—compulsion; for an analysis of reality—demagogy and frame-up. That is why Social Democracy, prostituting Marxism, and Stalinism—the antithesis of Bolshevism—are both mortal enemies of the proletarian revolution and its morals.[29]

The Revolutionary Vanguard

In contradistinction to the bureaucratic, distorted "internationalism" of the Stalinized Third International, Trotsky favored maintaining a revolutionary-internationalist orientation in which, as Marx and Engels had put it, "the proletariat of each country must, of course, first of all settle matters with its own bourgeoisie." To do this, a party was necessary "in order to construct an intellectual-moral bloc which can make politically possible the intellectual progress of the mass and not only of small intellectual groups," as Gramsci put it; it must reject "the intention that there must always be rulers and ruled," instead striving "to create the conditions in which this division is no longer necessary." Although the party must absorb "traditional intellectuals" who have been won to Marxism, it must facilitate the development of "organic intellectuals" who are (and remain) part of the working class—in a sense "all members of a political party should be regarded as intellectuals"—and the revolutionary organization must "work incessantly to raise the intellectual level of ever-growing strata of the populace, to give a personality to the amorphous mass element." It must be "linked organically to a national-popular mass," seeking to "stimulate the formation of homogeneous, compact social blocs, which will give birth to their own intellectuals, their own commanders, their own vanguard—who will in turn react upon those blocs in order to develop them." Although the revolutionary party "is the decisive element in every situation" involving revolution, there is a danger of "neglecting, or worse still despising, so-called 'spontaneous' moments" of mass action among the workers and the oppressed. In fact, "unity between 'spontaneity' and 'conscious leadership' or 'discipline' is precisely the real political action of the subaltern classes, in so far as this is mass politics and not merely an adventure by groups claiming to represent the masses." The essential organic quality necessary for such revolutionary politics cannot be found in the bureaucratic centralism characteristic of Stalinism. Gramsci insisted that it "can only be found in democratic centralism, which is so to speak a 'centralism' in movement— i.e. a continual adaptation of the organization to the real movement, a matching of thrusts from below with orders from above, a continuous insertion of elements thrown up from the depths of the rank and file into the solid framework of the leadership apparatus which ensures continuity and the regular accumulation of experience."[30]

Gramsci's perspective on the function of the party and the meaning of democratic centralism was consistent with that of Luxemburg, Lenin, and Trotsky. Luxemburg saw the party as "the most enlightened, most class-conscious vanguard of the proletariat," interacting with "every spontaneous people's movement" to "hasten the development of things and endeavor to accelerate events," and she called for a "social-democratic centralism" which would be "the 'self-centralism' of the advanced sectors of the proletariat." Lenin also believed that "the Party, as the vanguard of the working class, must not be confused . . . with the entire class," but believed that a "varied, rich, fruitful" interrelationship with the working class as a whole must be facilitated by "the full application of the democratic principle in the Party organization," and that "the principles of democratic centralism" involved "guarantees for the rights of all minorities and for all loyal opposition. . . . the autonomy of every [local] Party organization. . . . recognizing that all Party functionaries must be elected, accountable to the Party and subject to recall." In his opinion "the workers' Social-Democratic organizations must be united, but in these united organizations there must be wide and free discussion of Party questions, free comradely criticism and assessments of events in Party life." The interplay of vanguard with masses—he emphasized in the wake of the 1905 revolution—was a key to making possible the revolutionary upsurge: "The working class is instinctively, spontaneously Social-Democratic, and more than ten years of work put in by the Social-Democracy has done a great deal to transform this spontaneity into consciousness." Trotsky wrote: "The proletariat can take power only through its vanguard. In itself the necessity for state power arises from an insufficient cultural level of the masses and their heterogeneity. In the revolutionary vanguard, organized in a party, is crystallized the aspiration of the masses to obtain their freedom." He also argued that "revolutionary education requires a regime of internal democracy. Revolutionary discipline has nothing to do with blind obedience," for "the will to struggle has on every occasion to be independently renewed and tempered." He asserted: "We must not forget that even if we are *centralists*, we are *democratic* centralists who employ centralism only for the revolutionary cause and not in the name if the 'prestige' of the officials." This approach generated "a combination of the highest revolutionary audacity and political realism," facilitating "the only relation between vanguard and class that can assure victory."[31]

If Revolution Fails

Yet the triumphant rise of fascism in Italy and Germany in the 1920s and '30s demonstrated once again—in the wake of the political collapse following World War I and the chaos engendered by the worldwide economic depression—that the victory of socialism was by no means inevitable. Gramsci described fascism as a form of political reaction and repression exceeding all others, in part because it was a mass movement which "has opened its gates to all applicants" and "with its promise of impunity enabled a formless multitude to cover over the savage outpouring of hatreds and desires with a varnish of vague and nebulous political ideals." Made up initially of military personnel, lower echelon officers, and veterans, "it thinks it can cure unemployment by pistol-shots; it thinks it can assuage the tears of the women of the people with bursts of machine-gun fire." Aimed largely against left-wing peasant organizations, trade unions, and the socialist movement, it "won the support of the capitalists and the authorities," especially "agrarian capitalist interests," but also white-collar workers, small shopkeepers, and small manufacturers. Gramsci noted the importance to this movement of "a broad stratum of intermediate classes [that] stretches between the proletariat and capitalism: classes which seek to carry on, and to a certain extent succeed in carrying on, policies of their own, with ideologies which often influence broad strata of the proletariat, but which particularly affect the peasant masses." Trotsky noted a similar phenomenon in Germany in the early 1930s, commenting that "when revolutionary hope embraces the whole proletarian mass, it inevitably pulls behind it on the road of revolution considerable and growing sections of the petty bourgeoisie," but in Germany "counterrevolutionary despair embraced the petty-bourgeois mass with which force that it drew behind it many sections of the proletariat."[32]

The fascists took decisive action against symbols of subversion and disorder, with a bold populist rhetoric and brutal audacity that proved exhilarating to those swept up in its activities, which included "attacks on trade union leaders, violent opposition to strikes, terrorism against the masses; opposition to all forms of [left-wing] organization, help for the regular police in repressive activity and arrests, help for blacklegs [scabs or strikebreakers] in agitation involving strikes and lockouts . . . individual assassination attempts . . . the introduction into the class struggle of military methods of assault and surprise attack." Gramsci made the important observation—almost in passing—that such fascist violence took place not during but *after* a radical upsurge of the workers: "It waited to move until working-class organization had entered a period of passivity and then fell upon it, striking it as such, not for what it 'did' but for what it 'was'—in other words, as the source of links capable of giving the masses a form and physiognomy." He saw the dynamic of this violence as "an unchaining of elemental forces which cannot be restrained under the bourgeois system of economic and political government," suggesting that "fascism, as a general phenomenon, as a scourge which transcends the will and disciplinary means of its [bourgeois] exponents—with its violence, with its monstrous and arbitrary actions, with its destruction at once systematic and irrational—can be extirpated only by . . . a state whose power is in the hands of the proletariat."[33] This last optimistic flourish, however, seemed inconsistent with Gramsci's 1924 description of the fascist onslaught:

> It set out to destroy even that minimum to which the democratic system was reduced in Italy—i.e. the concrete possibility to create an organizational link at the base between workers, and to extend this link gradually until it embraced the great masses in movement. . . . The strength and capacity for struggle of the workers for the most part derive from the existence of these links, even if they are not in themselves apparent. What is involved is the possibility of meeting, of discussing; of giving these meetings and discussions some regularity; of choosing leaders through them; of laying the basis for an elementary organic formation, a league, a cooperative or a party section. What is involved is the possibility of giving these organic formations a continuous functionality; of making them into the basic framework for an organized movement. . . . After

three years of this kind of action, the working class has lost all form and all organicity; it has been reduced to a disconnected, fragmented, scattered mass.[34]

What occurred, rather than proletarian revolution, was an accommodation of the fascist movement with the bourgeoisie and the state apparatus, resulting in the consolidation of a powerful fascist regime which placed Gramsci himself in prison for the decade before his death in 1937. It remained for Leon Trotsky to offer an explanation of how fascism could triumph over the massive left-wing labor movements which had existed in Italy and Germany, which he traced to "a spent or missed revolutionary situation, at the conclusion of a revolutionary crisis" in each country.[35] He summarized his analysis in 1940—as the triumph of fascism was culminating in World War II—in the following manner:

> Both theoretical analysis and the rich historical experience of the last quarter of a century have demonstrated with equal force that fascism is each time the final link of a specific political cycle composed of the following: the gravest crisis of capitalist society; the growth of the radicalization of the working class; the growth of sympathy toward the working class and a yearning for change on the part of the rural and urban petty bourgeoisie; the extreme confusion of the big bourgeoisie; its cowardly and treacherous maneuvers aimed at avoiding the revolutionary climax; the exhaustion of the proletariat; growing confusion and indifference; the aggravation of the social crisis; the despair of the petty bourgeoisie, its yearning for change; the collective neurosis of the petty bourgeoisie, its readiness for violent measures; the growth of hostility towards the proletariat which has deceived its expectations. These are the premises for a swift formation of a fascist party and its victory.[36]

Both in Italy and in Germany the massive Socialist and Communist workers' movements suffered, on the one hand, from the indecisiveness of reformism and, on the other hand, from sectarianism and inexperience. Thus there was "the lack of a revolutionary party that would be regarded by the popular masses as the acknowledged revolutionary leader," and although socioeconomic crises had generated an immense upsurge of working-class militancy, "the proletarian vanguard revealed its inability to put itself at the head of the nation and change the fate of all its classes, the petty bourgeoisie included." In Germany in particular, he believed, the influence of Stalinism in the Communist Party had resulted in "mistakes, defeats, fictions, and the direct deception of the masses" which undermined the confidence of its own supporters. "Without an internal confidence in itself, the party will not conquer the class. Not to conquer the proletariat means not to break the petty-bourgeois masses away from fascism. One is inextricably bound up with the other."[37] The inability to move forward to socialist revolution made inevitable the downward slide into barbarism.

As we can see, the Marxist theory of the labor movement as it developed in the 19th century was predominantly concerned with why and how the working class would usher in a transition from capitalism to socialism, while in the 20th century it increasingly was compelled to deal with obstacles to that transition. Nonetheless, the revolutionaries we have been examining remained convinced that, *given* a correct strategic orientation for the workers' movement, such a transition was possible. It is to this strategy for revolution that we will now turn our attention.

Notes

1.   Marx and Engels, "Manifesto of the Communist Party," and Marx, "Wage-Labor and Capital," in *Selected Works*, Vol. 1 (Moscow: Progress Publishers, 1973), pp. 108, 114, 115, 167–168.

Among the most persistent critiques of Marxism is that developed by the former Marxist Selig Perlman in *A Theory of the Labor Movement* (New York: Macmillan Co., 1928), from which the present chapter title is taken. A more extensive examination can be found in Simeon Larson and Bruce Nissen, eds., *Theories of the Labor Movement* (Detroit: Wayne State University Press, 1987). Perlman insists that "organic" working-class consciousness finds its culmination in trade unionism within capitalism, not in a working-class revolution leading to socialism (the latter notion being imported from "outside" the working class by romantic intellectuals). A serious problem with the Perlman theory is the narrowness with which he views the working class as such, and his narrow equation of "labor movement" with "trade union." For a broader conception, see: E. P. Thompson, *The Making of the English Working Class* (New York: Vintage Books, 1968); E. J. Hobsbawm, *Labouring Men, Studies in the History of Labour* (Garden City: Anchor Books, 1967); Eric Hobsbawm, *Workers: Worlds of Labor* (New York: Pantheon Books, 1984); Herbert Gutman, *Work, Culture and Society in Industrializing America* (New York: Vintage Books, 1977); Herbert Gutman, *Power and Culture, Essays on the American Working Class* (New York: Pantheon Books, 1987); Ira Katznelson and Aristide Zolberg, eds., *Working-Class Formation: Nineteenth-Century Patterns in Western Europe and the United States* (Princeton: Princeton University Press, 1986).

2.   "Manifesto of the Communist Party," Marx and Engels, *Selected Works*, Vol. 1, pp. 109, 118–119; Marx and Engels, "The German Ideology," in *Writings of the Young Marx on Philosophy and Society*, ed. Loyd D. Easton and Kurt H. Guddat (Garden City: Anchor Books, 1967), p. 460.

3.   Franz Mehring, *Karl Marx, The Story of His Life* (Ann Arbor: University of Michigan Press, 1962), p. 206.

4.   "Manifesto of the Communist Party" in Marx and Engels, *Selected Works*, Vol. 1, pp. 115–117; "What Is to Be Done?" in Lenin, *Selected Works*, Vol. 1 (New York: International Publishers, 1967), pp. 121–122.

5.   A. Lozovsky, *Marx and the Trade Unions* (New York: International Publishers, 1935), p. 122; "Wages, Price and Profit," in Marx and Engels, *Selected Works*, Vol. 2, pp. 71–76.

6.   "Trades Unions: Their Past, Present and Future," in Marx and Engels, *Selected Works*, Vol. 2, p. 83.

7.   "Manifesto of the Communist Party," in Marx and Engels, *Selected Works*, Vol. 1, p. 116; "Inaugural Address of the International Workingmen's Association," in Marx and Engels, *Selected Works*, Vol. 2, p. 17; Lozovsky, *Marx and the Trade Unions*, p. 20.

8.   "Our Immediate Task," in Lenin, *Collected Works*, Vol. 4 (Moscow: Progress Publishers, 1972), p. 216; "Draft and Explanation for a Program of the Social-Democratic Party," in Lenin, *Collected Works*, Vol. 2 (Moscow: Progress Publishers, 1963), pp. 112–113.

9.   "What Is to Be Done?" in Lenin, *Selected Works*, Vol. 1, pp. 154–155.

10.   "Inaugural Address" and "General Rules for the International Workingmen's Association," in Marx and Engels, *Selected Works*, Vol. 2, pp. 17, 18, 19; "Manifesto of the Communist Party," in Marx and Engels, *Selected Works*, Vol. 1, pp. 112, 120, 125.

11.   "Draft and Explanation for a Program of the Social-Democratic Party," Lenin, *Collected Works*, Vol. 2, p. 108.

12.   "Ninety Years of the Communist Manifesto," *Writings of Leon Trotsky, 1937–38*, second edition, ed. Naomi Allen and George Breitman (New York: Pathfinder Press, 1976), p. 21.

13.   "The Social Democracy in War Time," in Karl Kautsky, *Selected Political Writings*, ed. Patrick Goode (London: Macmillan Press, 1983), p. 93; "The Junius Pamphlet: The Crisis in the German Social Democracy," in *Rosa Luxemburg Speaks*, ed. Mary-Alice Waters (New York: Pathfinder Press, 1970), p. 269.

14.   Monty Johnstone, "Marx and Engels and the Concept of the Party," *Socialist Register 1967* (London: Merlin, 1967), p. 121; "Manifesto of the Communist Party," in Marx and Engels, *Selected Works*, Vol. 1, pp. 117, 126; "Inaugural Address of the International Workingmen's Association," in Marx and Engels, *Selected Works*, Vol. 2, p. 17; Frank R. Annunziato, "Gramsci's Theory of Trade Unionism," *Rethinking Marxism*, Summer 1988, p. 156; Leon Trotsky, *On the Trade Unions* (New York: Pathfinder Press, 1969), p. 60. More on this can be

found in Ralph Miliband, *Marxism and Politics* (Oxford: Oxford University Press, 1977), pp. 118–153, and John Molyneux, *Marxism and the Party* (London: Pluto Press, 1978), esp. pp. 11–35. Also see Paul Le Blanc, *Lenin and the Revolutionary Party* (Atlantic Highlands, N.J.: Humanities Press, 1990).

15. "A Retrograde Trend in Russian Social-Democracy," in Lenin, *Collected Works*, Vol. 4, pp. 280–282.

16. "The Mass Strike, the Political Party, and the Trade Unions," in *Rosa Luxemburg Speaks*, pp. 207, 214, 215, 218.

17. Trotsky, *On the Trade Unions*, p. 60; "The Mass Strike," in Kautsky, *Selected Political Writings*, pp. 54, 60–61, 62, 73; Karl Kautsky, *The Road to Power* (Chicago: Samuel A. Bloch, 1909), pp. 6, 50; Karl Kautsky, *The Dictatorship of the Proletariat* (Ann Arbor: University of Michigan, 1964), p. 9.

18. Richard N. Hunt, *German Social Democracy, 1918–1933* (Chicago: Quadrangle Books, 1970), p. 59. Also see: Vernon L. Lidtke, *The Outlawed Party: Social Democracy in Germany, 1878–1890* (Princeton: Princeton University Press, 1966); Vernon L. Lidtke, *The Alternative Culture, Socialist Labor in Imperial Germany* (Oxford: Oxford University Press, 1985); Carl Schorske, *German Social Democracy, 1905–1917* (Cambridge: Harvard University Press, 1955); W. L. Guttsman, *The German Social Democratic Party, 1875–1933* (London: Allen and Unwin, 1981). An outstanding account of a decisive "moment" in the development of the German workers' movement can be found in William A. Pelz, *The Spartakusbund and the German Working Class Movement 1914–1919* (Lewiston, N.Y.: Edwin Mellen Press, 1987). An informative and very fine memoir by one whose life took a revolutionary turn in the wake of that "moment" is Oskar Hippe's *And Red Was the Colour of Our Flag, Memories of Sixty Years in the Workers' Movement* (London: Index Books, 1991).

19. "Speech to the Founding Convention of the German Communist Party," in *Rosa Luxemburg Speaks*, pp. 410, 411; Leon Trotsky, *My Life* (New York: Pathfinder Press, 1970), p. 204; Leon Trotsky, "Karl Kautsky," in *Portraits, Political and Personal*, ed. George Breitman and George Saunders (New York: Pathfinder Press, 1977), pp. 30–31; Leon Trotsky, *The War and the International* (Columbo, Sri Lanka: Young Socialist Pamphlets, 1971), p. 60; Trotsky, *On the Trade Unions*, pp. 68–69, 71. Also see Gramsci's elaboration of this last point, and his discussion of how winning; trade union leadership is an educational and democratic process, in Frank Annunziato, "Gramsci's Theory of Trade Unionism," *Rethinking Marxism*, Summer 1988, pp. 156, 161.

20. Lenin, *Selected Works* (1930s ed.), Vol. XI, pp. 752, 759, 762–763. Also see Robert Michels's 1915 classic, *Political Parties, A Sociological Study of the Oligarchical Tendencies of Modern Democracy* (New York: Dover Publications, 1959), which argues that powerful oligarchical tendencies in ostensibly the most democratic of organizations—the German Social Democratic Party—threw into doubt the capacity of the working class (or any other force) to bring about genuine "rule by the people." This finds elaboration in Max Nomad, *Aspects of Revolt* (New York: Noonday Press, 1961). Early attempts at a Marxist critique of the

"iron law of oligarchy" conception can be found in Nikolai Bukharin, *Historical Materialism, A System of Sociology* (Ann Arbor: University of Michigan Press, 1969), pp. 309–311, and Sidney Hook, *Towards the Understanding of Karl Marx, A Revolutionary Interpretation* (New York: John Day Co., 1933), pp. 311–313. More recent—and more satisfactory—responses can be found in Hal Draper, "Is Oligarchy Inevitable?" in *Socialism from Below*, ed. E. Haberkern (Atlantic Highlands, N.J.: Humanities Press, 1992), pp. 183–197, and Ernest Mandel, *Power and Money, A Marxist Theory of Bureaucracy* (London: Verso, 1992), esp. pp. 93–96.

21.   Quoted in E. J. Hobsbawm, "Lenin and the 'Aristocracy of Labor,'" *Monthly Review*, April 1970, pp. 50–51.

22.   "The Junius Pamphlet: The Crisis in the German Social Democracy," *Rosa Luxemburg Speaks*, p. 269. Also see Michael Löwy, "Rosa Luxemburg's Conception of 'Socialism or Barbarism,'" *On Changing the World: Essays in Political Philosophy, From Karl Marx to Walter Benjamin* (Atlantic Highlands, N.J.: Humanities Press, 1993).

23.   Leon Trotsky, "What Next? Vital Questions for the German Proletariat," *The Struggle against Fascism in Germany*, ed. George Breitman and Merry Maisel (New York: Pathfinder Press, 1971), p. 213.

24.   Stalin quoted in Louis Fischer, *Russia's Road from Peace to War, Soviet Foreign Relations, 1917–1941* (New York: Harper and Row, 1969), p. 177; O. W. Kuusinen, "Under the Leadership of Russia," *The Communist International*, No. 1, 1924, p. 134; V. Sorin, *Lenin's Teachings about the Party* (Bell Gardens, Calif.: October League, 1973), pp. 7, 30, 32, 37; Joseph Stalin, *Political Report of the Central Committee to the Fifteenth Congress of the C.P.S.U. (B)* (Moscow: Foreign Languages Publishing House, 1950), p. 132.

25.   Antonio Gramsci, "The Modern Prince," *Selections from the Prison Notebooks*, ed. Quintin Hoare and Geoffrey Nowell Smith (New York: International Publishers, 1973), pp. 185–186, 186–187, 187, 155. There are, however, ambivalences and ambiguities in Gramsci—discussed, for example, in: Perry Anderson, "Antinomies of Antonio Gramsci," *New Left Review*, No. 100, November 1976-January 1977; Frank Rosengarten, "The Gramsci-Trotsky Question (1922–1932)," *Social Text*, Winter 1984–85; Livio Maitan, "The Revolutionary Marxism of Antonio Gramsci," *International Marxist Review*, Summer 1987. A valuable exposition is offered by Dante Germino, *Antonio Gramsci, Architect of a New Politics* (Baton Rouge: Louisiana State University Press, 1990).

26.   Trotsky, "What Next? Vital Questions for the German Proletariat," *The Struggle Against Fascism in Germany*, pp. 219, 220.

27.   Ibid., pp. 214–215.

28.   Stalin's reports to the 14th Party Congress (December 18, 1925), 15th Party Congress (December 3, 1927), the 17th Party Congress (January 26, 1934), and the 18th Party Congress (March 10, 1939) in Myron Rush, ed., *The International Situation and Soviet Foreign Policy, Key Reports by Soviet Leaders*

from the Revolution to the Present (Columbus, Oh.: Charles Merrill Publishing Co., 1970), pp. 47, 61, 84, 95; Joseph Stalin, *The Stalin-Howard Interview* (New York: International Publishers, 1936), p. 7.

29. Leon Trotsky, *The Transitional Program for Socialist Revolution*, third edition, ed. George Breitman and Fred Stanton (New York: Pathfinder Press, 1977), p. 148.

30. "Manifesto of the Communist Party," in Marx and Engels, *Selected Works*, Vol. 1, p. 118; Gramsci, *Selections From the Prison Notebooks*, pp. 16, 144, 185, 188–189, 198, 199, 204–5, 332–333, 340.

31. Luxemburg, "The Mass Strike, the Political Party and the Trade Unions," and "Organizational Questions of Social Democracy," in *Rosa Luxemburg Speaks*, pp. 119, 200; Lenin, "One Step Forward, Two Steps Back," in *Selected Works*, Vol. 1, p. 306; Lenin, "The Reorganization of the Party," and "An Appeal to the Party by Delegates to the Unity Congress Who Belonged to the Faction of 'Bolsheviks,'" *Collected Works*, Vol. 10 (Moscow: Progress Publishers, 1972), pp. 32, 33, 314; "Stalinism and Bolshevism," *Writings of Leon Trotsky, 1936–37*, second edition, ed. Naomi Allen and George Breitman (New York: Pathfinder Press, 1978), pp. 426, 430; "Questions for Communists," *Writings of Leon Trotsky, 1932*, ed. George Breitman and Sarah Lovell (New York: Pathfinder Press, 1973), p. 326; Leon Trotsky, *History of the Russian Revolution*, three vols, in one (New York: Simon and Schuster, 1936), Vol. 3, p. 165; "The Crisis of the German Left Opposition," *Writings of Leon Trotsky, 1930–31*, ed. George Breitman and Sarah Lovell (New York: Pathfinder Press, 1973), p. 155. Contrary to many interpretations, I would argue that Luxemburg and Lenin had largely similar views on "the organization question," a position that is documented in Paul Le Blanc, "Luxemburg and Lenin on Revolutionary Organization," *International Marxist Review*, Summer 1987.

32. Antonio Gramsci, "On Fascism 1921" and "Democracy and Fascism," in David Beetham, ed., *Marxists in the Face of Fascism* (Manchester: Manchester University Press, 1983), pp. 83, 84, 85, 87, 125; Trotsky, "The Turn in the Communist International and the Situation in Germany," *The Struggle Against Fascism in Germany*, p. 59.

33. Gramsci, "On Fascism 1921" and "The International Situation and the Struggle against Fascism," in Beetham, *Marxists in the Face of Fascism*, pp. 83, 84, 85, 121.

34. Ibid., pp. 121–122.

35. Trotsky, "The Turn in the Communist International and the Situation in Germany," p. 59.

36. Trotsky, "Bonapartism, Fascism and War," in *The Struggle against Fascism in Germany*, p. 447.

37. Trotsky, "The Turn in the Communist International and the Situation in Germany," pp. 59, 63.

4

The Strategy of Revolution

We can see from our previous discussion that the revolutionary Marxist current did not assume a socialist majority would automatically come into being or that capitalism would inevitably be overthrown. Socialism will not be achieved, Rosa Luxemburg explained, "either as a result of the victorious violence of a minority or through the numerical superiority of a majority," but rather "as a result of economic necessity— and the comprehension of that necessity—leading to the suppression of capitalism by the working masses." She saw the economic necessity as manifesting itself "above all in the anarchy of capitalist production," the devastating effects of the capitalist accumulation process on the lives of millions of human beings; but these millions must come to *comprehend* this reality and must organize to take the action of *suppressing* capitalism.[1] The function of revolutionary socialist strategy is to advance this process—increasing the understanding and knowledge of workers and other oppressed groups, organizing them into a powerful force capable of taking action, mobilizing them to actually overturn capitalism.

Marx and Engels had insisted that the workers cannot come to power and achieve the realization of their class interests without passing through a process of development. Luxemburg explained that this process of development "consisted of trade union work, of agitation for social reforms and the democratization of existing political institutions," all of which should be "considered to be the means of guiding and educating the proletariat in preparation for the task of taking over power." It was important, within this context, that those guided by scientific-socialist knowledge "fight for the attainment of the immediate aims, for the enforcement of the momentary interests of the working class; but in the movement of the present, they also represent and take care of the future of the movement," as Marx and Engels put it. The organization

81

and socialist education of working-class activists were interrelated
necessities, for the numerical strength of the proletariat would "weigh
only in the balance, if united by combination and led by knowledge."[2]
This commitment to building a mass socialist workers movement guided
not only the German Social Democracy that Luxemburg described but
also the Bolshevik organization that Lenin led in tsarist Russia. As one
of his foremost lieutenants Gregory Zinoviev explained:

> Comrade Lenin's main idea was that we had to remain with the work-
> ing class and be a mass party and not coop ourselves up exclusively in
> the underground and turn into a narrow circle. If the workers are in the
> trade unions then we must be there too; if we can send just one man into
> the Tsar's Duma [parliament] then we shall: let him tell the workers the
> truth and we can publish his speeches as leaflets. If something can be
> done for the workers in the workers' clubs then we shall be there. We
> have to use every legal opportunity, so as not to divorce ourselves from
> the masses. . . .[3]

The importance of this economic, electoral, and cultural activity
involving mass layers of the working class, too often not understood by
small groups of isolated would-be revolutionaries, is that it describes the
realities of the socialist movement in the early decades of the 20th century and also that—for Marx and Engels, Luxemburg, Lenin, Trotsky,
Gramsci, and others—it is a necessary precondition for realizing the
Marxist strategy of revolution.

Working-Class Hegemony and Unity

The struggle for reforms, however, must involve a commitment to
working-class political independence, a dynamic toward working-class
hegemony in the struggle, and an interweaving of reform struggles with
the struggle for working-class revolution.

Marx and Engels insisted that in such struggles the workers "must
do the utmost for their final victory by clarifying their minds as to what
their class interests are, by taking up their position as an independent
party as soon as possible and by not allowing themselves to be seduced
for a single moment by the hypocritical phrases of the democratic petty
bourgeois into refraining from the independent organization of the party
of the proletariat." This included independence in the electoral arena:
"Even where there is no prospect whatsoever of their being elected, the

workers must put up their own candidates in order to preserve their independence, to count their forces and to bring before the public their revolutionary attitude and party standpoint. In this connection they must not allow themselves to be seduced by such arguments of the democrats as, for example, that by doing so they are splitting the democratic party and making it possible for the reactionaries to win. The ultimate intention of all such phrases is to dupe the proletariat."[4]

The hegemony (or predominance) of the working class in struggles for social and political reforms is necessary because, as Marx and Engels put it, it is "the workers who, in the main, will have to win the victory by their courage, determination and self-sacrifice." Lenin argued similarly that "in the fight against the autocracy, the working class must single itself out, for it is the *only* thoroughly consistent and unreserved enemy of the autocracy, *only* between the working class and autocracy is no compromise possible, *only* in the working class can democracy find a champion who makes no reservations, is not irresolute and does not look back." Critically surveying the dynamics and inconsistencies of the other discontented social strata, he concluded: "The proletariat alone can be the *vanguard fighter* for political liberty and for democratic institutions." He stressed that to the extent that the working class assumed that hegemonic role in such struggles, all other elements in the democratic struggle would be pushed toward "an irrevocable rupture with the whole of the political and social structure of present society."[5]

Embedded in this conception of proletarian hegemony was a notion which was later given the label of *united front*. As Marx and Engels expressed it: "The relation of the revolutionary workers' party to the petty-bourgeois democrats is this: it marches together with them against the faction which it aims at overthrowing, [but] it opposes them in everything whereby they seek to consolidate their position in their own interests." Gregory Zinoviev described a similar dynamic in the Bolsheviks' anti-tsarist struggle in Russia: "All the first phase of the history of our party is nothing other than at first a semiconscious and then a fully-conscious struggle of proletarian revolutionaries against bourgeois revolutionaries. In so far as it was a case of a struggle against Tsarism we had, I repeat, a united front. But as soon as the struggle to win the masses and the soul of the working class was unleashed, our paths diverged." Or as Lenin put it, "no practical alliances with other groups of revolutionaries can, or should, lead to compromises or concessions on matters of theory, program or banner." The meaning of the united front for Lenin is further clarified if we examine his response to an appeal for unified revolutionary action in 1905. This has particular relevance to the problem of divisions in the labor movement and between socialists, for the appeal was for an agreement on practical action among "all the socialist parties of Russia."[6]

Lenin hailed the proposal as "possible, useful and essential," noting that it allowed for "the preservation of complete independence by each separate party on points of principle and organization" in the context of "a fighting unity of these parties." He argued: "We must be very careful, in making these endeavors, not to spoil things by vainly trying to lump together heterogeneous elements. We shall inevitably have to . . . march separately, but we can . . . strike together more than once and particularly now." He went further and called for the inclusion of non-socialist groups in the united front, warning that "we must not confound or allow anyone to ever confound the immediate democratic aims with our ultimate aims of socialist revolution." Yet he stressed that unity in action among the different "parties, trends, and shades" should not be permitted to obscure the differences between them, insisting on the necessity of an ongoing process of political clarification. As he put it:

> In the interests of the revolution our ideal should by no means be that all parties, all trends and shades of opinion fuse in a revolutionary chaos. On the contrary, the growth and spread of the revolutionary movement, its constantly deeper penetration among the various classes and strata of the people, will inevitably give rise (all to the good) to constantly newer trends and shades. Only full clarity and definiteness in their attitude towards the revolutionary proletariat can guarantee maximum success for the revolutionary movement. Only full clarity in mutual relations can guarantee the success of an agreement to achieve a common immediate aim.[7]

Several points should be made about this united front perspective. As we can see, there was a conviction that the proletariat would need to ally itself with different social strata. For Lenin, the most important alliance was between the working class and the masses of the peasantry (which in Russia between 1905 and 1917 tended to provide a base for the Socialist-Revolutionary Party—hence the advisability of a united front with that organization when possible). Lenin agreed with the perspective which

Marx had articulated regarding "the possibility of backing the proletarian revolution by some second edition of the Peasant War."[8] More than a possibility, he viewed the worker-peasant alliance as a vital necessity for largely agrarian countries such as Russia, going far beyond the exigencies of the united front tactic.

Also, Lenin recognized that working-class activists were often themselves divided (in Russia between Bolshevik and Menshevik wings of the Russian Social Democratic Labor Party, as well as between the RSDLP and the Socialist Revolutionaries and anarchist groups—hence the advisability of a united front between those organizations when possible). This perspective was further developed after 1919, when the international workers movement was divided between the revolutionary Third International and the reformist Second International. The reformist leaders, he commented, "need a united front, for they hope to weaken us by inducing us to make excessive concessions for the purpose of convincing the workers that the reformist tactics are correct and that revolutionary tactics are wrong. We need a united front because we hope to convince the workers of the opposite." Speaking for the Communist International in this period, Leon Trotsky elaborated on "our readiness, within certain limits and on specific issues, to correlate in practice our actions with those of reformist organizations, to the extent to which the latter still express today the will of important sections of the embattled proletariat." But built into this orientation was a commitment to the process of political clarification which would win workers and militant activists to the revolutionary workers' party: "Any sort of organizational agreement which restricts our freedom of criticism and agitation is absolutely unacceptable to us. We participate in a united front as an independent detachment. It is precisely in the course of the struggle that broad masses must learn from experience that we fight better than the others, that we see more clearly than the others, that we are more audacious and resolute."[9]

Revolutionary Approach to Struggles

This brings us to the question of the difference between reformist and revolutionary perspectives, and to the manner in which reform struggles are seen as interweaving with the struggle for socialist revolution. Rosa Luxemburg argued that "reform and revolution are not different methods of historic development that can be picked out at pleasure from the counter of history, just as one chooses hot or cold sausages." Reformists, who counterpose struggles for reform to the conquest of political power and social revolution, "do not really choose a more tranquil, calmer and slower road to the *same* goal, but a *different* goal," one which involves "not the realization of *socialism*, but the reform of *capitalism*; not the suppression of the system of wage labor, but the diminution of exploitation, that is, the suppression of the abuses of capitalism instead of the suppression of capitalism itself." Revolutionaries approach reform struggles differently, seeking—in Lenin's words—"to ensure that these demands for partial concessions are raised to the status of a systematic, implacable struggle of a revolutionary working-class party."[10]

One aspect of this approach to reform struggles involved the manner in which they were conducted. Lenin rejected the notion of appealing to liberal political leaders for the purpose of persuading them to present the workers' demands to the government. He argued that "precisely because they are bourgeois democrats, the liberal democrats will never be able to understand 'our' demands and to advocate them sincerely, consistently and resolutely." He added that "if we are strong enough to exercise serious influence on bourgeois democrats in general, . . . we are also strong enough to present our demands to the government independently." This should be done in a manner through which the workers' movement could "widen and strengthen its organization among the masses tenfold, to take advantage of every vacillation of the government," particularly through "calling meetings, scattering leaflets, organizing demonstrations wherever it has sufficient forces to do so." He called upon revolutionary socialists to organize "*mass* demonstrations (because demonstrations that are not mass demonstrations have no significance whatever)," indicating an orientation in which "the workers will rise still more fearlessly, in still greater numbers, . . . to conquer by force for *themselves* that which Messieurs the liberal bourgeoisie promise to give them as charity." Marx and Engels had similarly favored mass action to "counteract, as much as possible, . . . the bourgeois endeavors to allay the storm," organizing "actions . . . so aimed as to prevent the direct revolutionary excitement from being suppressed," but rather to "keep it alive as long as possible."[11]

Rosa Luxemburg further developed this mass action orientation—taking it well beyond the perspective of simply militant demonstrations—in her discussion of what she called the *mass strike*. The workings and contradictions of capitalism, she believed, can sometimes result in a "violent sudden jerk which disturbs the momentary equilibrium of everyday social life," aggravating "deep-seated, long-suppressed resentment" among workers and other social layers, resulting in an explosive and spontaneous reaction on a mass scale—in the form of strikes spreading through an industry and sometimes involving many, most, or all occupations and workplaces. "The mass strike is not artificially 'made,' not 'decided' at random, not 'propagated,' but it is a historically made phenomenon which, at a given moment, results from social conditions with historical inevitability." Mass strikes go far beyond economic issues and are the means by which workers seek to "grasp at new political rights or attempt to defend existing ones."[12] Once such strikes begin, there can occur tremendous solidarity, discipline, and effective organization. But they have an elemental quality which defies any notion of revolutionary blueprints being drawn up in advance. Consider Luxemburg's description of 1905 events in Russia:

> The mass strike ... is such a changeable phenomenon that it reflects all phases of the political and economic struggle, all stages and factors of the revolution. Its adaptability, its efficiency, the factors of its origins are constantly changing. It suddenly opens new and wide perspectives of the revolution when it appears to have already arrived in a narrow pass and where it is impossible for anyone to reckon upon it with any degree of certainty. It flows now like a broad billow over the whole kingdom, and now divides into a gigantic network of narrow streams; now it bubbles forth from under the ground like a fresh spring and now is completely lost under the earth. Political and economic strikes, mass strikes and partial strikes, demonstrative strikes and fighting strikes, general strikes of individual branches of industry and general strikes in individual towns, peaceful wage struggles and street massacres, barricade fighting—all these run through each other, run side by side, cross one another, flow in and over one another—it is a ceaselessly moving, changing sea of phenomena. And the law of motion of these phenomena is clear: it does not lie in the mass strike itself nor in its technical details, but in the political and social proportions of the forces of revolution.[13]

Luxemburg by no means believed that such upsurges would necessarily result in socialist revolution. But neither did she believe that they would wreck labor organizations. Rather, they became "the starting point of a feverish work of organization." While labor and socialist bureaucrats might "fear that the organizations will fall in pieces in a revolutionary whirlwind like rare porcelain," the opposite is the case: "From the whirlwind and the storm, out of the fire and glow of the mass strike and the street fighting rise again, like Venus from the foam, fresh, young, powerful, buoyant trade unions." Some segments of the working class cannot be unionized through "the form of quiet, systematic, partial trade union struggles." On the other hand, "a powerful and reckless fighting action of the proletariat, born of a revolutionary situation, must surely react upon the deeper-lying layers, and ultimately draw all those into a general economic struggle who, in normal times, stand aside from the daily trade union fight."[14]

At the same time, Luxemburg believed that this phenomenon, under certain circumstances, would lead far beyond trade union victories and the winning of reforms. "The mass strike," she wrote, "is the first natural, impulsive form of every great revolutionary struggle of the proletariat and the more highly developed the antagonism is between capital and labor, the more effective and decisive must mass strikes become." This "process of the proletarian mass struggle" could culminate in "the fight at the barricades, the open conflict with the armed power of the state," resulting in "the last historical necessary goal [which] can only be the *dictatorship of the proletariat.*"[15] Given the spontaneous quality of the mass strike, however, how could it fit into the conscious strategy of the revolutionary party? Luxemburg offered this answer:

> The social democrats are the most enlightened, most class-conscious vanguard of the proletariat. They cannot and dare not wait, in a fatalistic fashion, with folded arms for the advent of the "revolutionary situation," to wait for that which in every spontaneous people's movement, falls from the clouds. On the contrary, they must now, as always, hasten the development of things and endeavor to accelerate events. They cannot do this, however, by suddenly issuing the "slogan" for a mass strike at random at any odd moment, but first and foremost, by making clear to the widest layers of the proletariat the *inevitable advent* of this revolutionary period, the inner *social factors* making for it and the *political consequences* of it. If the widest proletarian layer should be won for a political mass action of the social democrats, and if, vice versa, the social democrats should seize and maintain the real leadership of a mass movement—should they become, in a *political* sense, the rulers of the whole movement, then they must, with the utmost clearness, consistency and resoluteness, inform the . . . proletariat of their tactics and aims in the period of coming struggle.[16]

Transitional Program

The kind of demands and slogans put forward by a revolutionary organization, and the manner in which these are fought for, can help serve this function. In the pre-1914 Social Democracy, a distinction was commonly made between the minimum program (reforms to be achieved under capitalism) and the maximum program (the ultimate goal of socialism). Increasingly, revolutionary Marxists advanced what Trotsky later called a *transitional program*, intertwining three types of demands: (1) immediate demands concerned with the defense of decent living standards, living conditions, and working conditions; (2) democratic demands concerned with freedom of expression, control of one's own person, legal and political equality, popular sovereignty, the right of self-determination, etc.; and (3) transitional demands, which seem reasonable to masses of people but cannot be implemented without immediately and seriously undermining the capitalist system. Such demands would be formulated and combined in such a way as to help generate and guide mass struggles—independent of bourgeois leadership and outside the framework of "politics as usual"—helping to build up the numbers, the self-confidence, and the revolutionary consciousness of the participants. "It is necessary to help the masses in the process of daily struggle to find the bridge between present demands and the socialist program of the revolution,"Trotsky wrote. "This bridge should include a system of *transitional demands*, stemming from today's conditions and from today's consciousness of wide layers of the working class and unalterably leading to one final conclusion: the conquest of power by the proletariat." Such demands—seeming fair and desirable and necessary to growing sectors of the working class prepared to struggle for them—would, as it became clear that they were unrealizable under the specific capitalist conditions, lead formerly "non-revolutionary" workers into the struggle for socialist revolution. As Marx and Engels had put it in 1850, the workers' movement must "drive the proposals of the democrats to their logical extreme . . . and transform these proposals into direct attacks on private property."[17] And in the midst of World War I, Lenin articulated such a transitional approach in regard to democratic demands:

> The proletariat cannot be victorious except through democracy, i.e., by giving full effect to democracy and by linking up with each step of its

struggle democratic demands formulated in their most resolute terms. It is absurd to *contrapose* the socialist revolution and the revolutionary struggle against capitalism to a *single* of problem of democracy. . . . We must *combine* the revolutionary struggle against capitalism with a revolutionary program and tactics on *all* democratic demands: a republic, a militia, the popular election of officials, equal rights for women, self-determination of nations, etc. While capitalism exists, these demands—all of them—can only be accomplished as an exception, and even then in an incomplete and distorted form. Basing ourselves on democracy as already achieved, and exposing its incompleteness under capitalism, we demand the overthrow of capitalism and the expropriation of the bourgeoisie, as a necessary basis both for the abolition of the poverty of the masses and for the *complete* and *all-round* institution of *all* democratic reforms. Some of these reforms will be started before the overthrow of the bourgeoisie, others *in the course* of that overthrow, and still others after it. The social revolution is not a single battle, but a period covering a series of battles over all sorts of problems of economic and democratic reform, which are consummated only by the expropriation of the bourgeoisie. It is for the sake of this final aim that we must formulate *every one* of our democratic demands in a consistently revolutionary way. It is quite conceivable that the workers of a particular country will overthrow the bourgeoisie *before* even a single fundamental democratic reform has been fully implemented. But it is, however, quite inconceivable that the proletariat, as a historical class, will be able to defeat the bourgeoisie, unless it is prepared for that by being educated in the spirit of the most consistent and resolutely revolutionary democracy.[18]

Vanguard, Majority and Revolutionary Situation

The strategic approach which we have been examining is in sharp contrast to that which had become predominant in the pre-1914 Social Democracy. In the most powerful of its organizations, the German Social Democratic Party, the dilemma of how to obtain an electoral majority had "weighed like a nightmare," as Luxemburg put it, on the organization. "As bred-in-the-bone disciples of parliamentary cretinism," she wrote, "these German social democrats have sought to apply to revolutions the homemade wisdom of the parliamentary nursery: in order to carry anything, you must first have a majority. The same, they say, applies to revolution: first let's become a 'majority.' The true dialectic of revolutions, however, stands this wisdom of parliamentary moles on its head: not through a majority to revolutionary tactics, but through revolutionary tactics to a majority—that is the way the road runs."[19]

The revolutionary Marxists were not in favor of a minority *putsch*. Luxemburg's formulation is not that a majority is won after the revolution is made, but rather that only revolutionary tactics can win majority support for making a revolution. This was Lenin's view as well. Explaining the Bolshevik revolution, he noted that "we were victorious in Russia not only because the undisputed majority of the working class was on our side. . . . but also because half the army, immediately after our seizure of power, and nine-tenths of the peasants, in the course of some weeks, came over to our side." In the months before the Bolsheviks won a majority in the soviets (workers' councils), Lenin was against a revolutionary seizure of power by the Bolshevik minority. "So long as we remain in the minority," he wrote, "we carry on the work of criticism and of explaining errors, advocating all along the necessity of transferring the entire state power to the Soviets of Workers' Deputies, so that the masses may learn from experience how to rid themselves of their errors."[20] Only with majority support—gained through persuasive education and agitation, combined with militant tactics in a revolutionary situation—could the socialist revolution be carried out.

Another important component of the revolutionary Marxist strategic perspective is the concept of a national crisis and a revolutionary situation. This involves a rejection of the idea that a majority can be won and a revolution made simply through the efforts of the revolutionary party. As Lenin put it in *Left-Wing Communism, An Infantile Disorder* (1920), "revolution is impossible without a nation-wide crisis (affecting both the exploited and the exploiters)," a crisis which will weaken the confidence of the ruling class, strengthen the resolve of the vanguard sectors of the proletariat, politicize the hitherto apathetic masses of workers and the oppressed, weaken the government, and make possible a revolutionary overturn.[21] In *The Collapse of the Second International* (1915) Lenin offered this sketch of the revolutionary situation:

(1) it is impossible for the ruling classes to maintain their power unchanged; there is a crisis "higher up," taking one form or another; there is a crisis in the policy of the ruling class; as a result, there appears a crack through which the dissatisfaction and the revolt of the oppressed classes burst forth. If a revolution is to take place, it is usually insufficient that "one does not wish way below," but it is necessary that "one is incapable above" to continue in the old way; (2) the wants and sufferings of the oppressed classes become more acute than usual; (3) in consequence of

the above causes, there is a considerable increase in the activity of the masses who in "peace time" allow themselves to be robbed without protest, but in stormy times are drawn both by the circumstances of the crisis and *by the "higher-ups" themselves* into independent historic action.[22]

According to Lenin, "without these objective changes, which are independent not only of the will of separate groups and parties but even of separate classes, a revolution, as a rule, is impossible." Yet when all of these objective conditions exist, the revolutionary situation will not always result in revolution. "Why? Because a revolution emerges not out of every revolutionary situation, but out of such situations where, to the above-mentioned objective changes, subjective ones are added, namely, the ability of the revolutionary *classes* to carry out revolutionary mass actions *strong* enough to break (or to undermine) the old government, it being the rule that never, not even in a period of crises, does a government 'fall' of itself without being 'helped to fall.'"[23]

In the absence of a revolutionary situation, it is the function of the revolutionary party to prepare for it. Through practical work, organizing and mobilizing workers and the oppressed around immediate economic and democratic struggles which are audaciously, militantly conceived and carried out, while at the same time carrying out revolutionary socialist educational work among those drawn into or affected by the struggles, the party seeks to create revolutionary socialist hegemony within the working class and working-class hegemony within the broader struggles and the population as a whole. The experience, consciousness, and organizations created through this process provide the subjective factor which can combine, at moments of national crisis, with revolutionary objective factors, leading to socialist revolution—mass mobilizations which overturn the capitalist state and replace it with new organizations and institutions of working-class power.

Hegemony and Revolutionary Movement-Building

In the early congresses of the Communist International the struggle for hegemony between the bourgeoisie and the proletariat was given some attention. "The proletariat becomes a revolutionary class only in so far as it does not restrict itself to the framework of a narrow corporatism and acts in every manifestation and domain of social life as the guide of the whole working and exploited population." On the other hand, "the bourgeoisie always seeks to separate politics from economics, because it understands very well that if it succeeds in keeping the working class within a corporative framework, no serious danger can threaten its hegemony." Trotsky stressed that it was easier for Russian revolutionaries to overcome bourgeois hegemony "in the cultural and political backwardness of a country that had just cast off Tsarist barbarism," unlike "in countries that are older in the capitalist sense, and with a higher culture."[24] Antonio Gramsci made a similar point in 1926:

> In the advanced capitalist countries, the ruling class possesses political and organizational reserves which it did not possesses, for instance, in Russia. This means that even the most serious economic crises do not have immediate repercussions in the political sphere. Politics always lags behind economics, far behind. The state apparatus is far more resistant than is often possible to believe; and it succeeds, at moments of crisis, in organizing greater forces loyal to the regime than the depth of the crisis might lead one to suppose. This is especially true of the more important capitalist states.[25]

More than most Marxists, Gramsci gave special attention to the development of this concept of hegemony, which involved a class believing in and persuading broad social layers of the legitimacy of its leadership and the validity of its world-view (ideology), through a variety of cultural and political mechanisms. He warned that the undermining of capitalist hegemony by great social crises would not automatically generate positive change:

> That aspect of the modern crisis which is bemoaned as a "wave of materialism" is related to what is called the "crisis of authority." If the ruling class has lost its consensus, i.e. is no longer "leading" but only "dominant," exercising coercive force alone, this means precisely that the great masses have become detached from their traditional ideologies, and no longer believe what they used to believe previously, etc. The crisis consists precisely in the fact that the old way is dying and the new cannot be born; in this interregnum a great variety of morbid symptoms appear.[26]

Only if the working-class movement was able to develop itself as a viable alternative in the eyes of substantial social layers could both bourgeois hegemony and the "interregnum of morbid symptoms" be overcome, but this must involve opening "the struggle for an autonomous and superior culture" which would enable the working class to become "really autonomous and hegemonic, thus bringing into being a new form of State" and generating "the concrete birth of a need to construct a new intellectual and moral order, that is, a new type of society."[27] There must be protracted struggles and multi-faceted movement-building around immediate, democratic, and transitional demands, involving a variety of united fronts and alliances, undergirded with broad and multi-level socialist education. Through these methods the revolutionary party could establish strong positions on the social, cultural, and political field that would enable it to triumph over the powerful positions of the bourgeoisie when revolutionary situations developed.

Some scholars have argued that Gramsci's thought was so unique that it represented a qualitative shift away from the traditional revolutionary Marxist framework. It seems more accurate, however, to understand it as an important elaboration and development of certain aspects of the framework.[28] Gramsci himself saw it in these terms. Similar points can be made regarding the other theorist we've examined who survived into the fourth decade of our century, Leon Trotsky—particularly in regard to his theory of permanent revolution, which highlights essential elements in the Marxist revolutionary strategy.

Permanent Revolution

We've already touched on Trotsky's theory. Here it will suffice to indicate its three fundamental components and indicate where they fit into the questions we've been examining: the internal dynamics of the revolutionary struggle (examined earlier in this chapter), the internal dynamics of post-revolutionary development, and the international character of the revolutionary process.

1. *The internal dynamics of the revolutionary struggle.* The struggle for democracy and for the immediate needs of workers and the oppressed, if waged *consistently*, inevitably spills over into the struggle for socialism. The realization of democracy and human needs cannot be fully or adequately achieved within a capitalist framework. Nor can bourgeois democracy be a stable half-way mark at which revolutionary forces pause. The pro-capitalist liberals will be much more willing to make compromises with reactionaries and imperialists than to rely on alliances with a powerful and militant labor movement. If the struggle does not go forward through an alliance of the hegemonic proletariat with other oppressed social layers—in agrarian countries particularly with the peasantry—it will be compromised, undermined, perhaps even crushed

in a barbaric onslaught by the panic-stricken forces of capitalist reaction. If the struggle fully triumphs under working-class leadership, this means political power is in the hands of the working class.

2. *The internal dynamics of post-revolutionary development.* When the working class takes political power, the question of a transition to socialism is posed. The socialist revolution is not a cataclysmic event which with a single blow establishes the new society. It is a process involving long-term, or permanent, dynamism and change. "For an indefinitely long time and in constant internal struggle," wrote Trotsky, "all social relations undergo transformation. Society keeps changing its skin. . . . Revolutions in economy, technique, science, the family, morals and everyday life develop in complex reciprocal action and do not allow society to achieve equilibrium."[29] (This touches on questions examined more fully in the next chapter.)

3. *The international character of the revolutionary process.* The reality of the world economy and the profound interdependence of various countries and continents necessitates an internationally based strategy for revolutionaries of each country and guarantees that they will be affected by each other's setbacks and victories. Trotsky insisted that "not a single communist party can establish its program by proceeding solely or mainly from conditions and tendencies of developments in its own country," but instead "can base itself only upon an international program corresponding to the character of the present epoch, the epoch of the highest development and collapse of capitalism."[30] This means that socialism cannot be achieved in a single country, and that in particular the success of the socialist reconstruction of society in less industrially developed countries is dependent on the triumph of socialist revolution in other (especially more industrially developed) countries. But it means more. As Trotsky put it in 1929:

> Socialist construction is conceivable only on the foundation of the class struggle, on a national and international scale. This struggle, under the conditions of an overwhelming predominance of capitalist relationships on the world arena, must inevitably lead to explosions, that is, internally to civil wars and externally to revolutionary wars. Therein lies the permanent character of the socialist revolution as such, regardless of whether it is a backward country that is involved, which only yesterday accomplished its democratic revolution, or an old capitalist country which already has behind it a long epoch of democracy and parliamentarism.[31]

Thus "a national revolution is not a self-contained whole; it is only a link in the international chain. The international revolution constitutes a permanent process, despite temporary declines and ebbs."[32]

A striking, yet hardly surprising, feature of the revolutionary Marxist strategic orientation is the implications it has for what comes *after* the proletarian revolution—the transitional period from capitalism to socialism. This final component of the Marxist paradigm will be examined in the next chapter.

Notes

1.   "Reform or Revolution," *Rosa Luxemburg Speaks*, ed. Mary-Alice Waters (New York: Pathfinder Press, 1970), p. 66.

2.   Ibid., p. 57; Marx and Engels, "Manifesto of the Communist Party," *Selected Works*, Vol. 1 (Moscow: Progress Publishers, 1973), p. 136; Marx, "Inaugural Address of the International Workingmen's Association," *Selected Works*, Vol. 2 (Moscow: Progress Publishers, 1973), p. 17.

3.   Gregory Zinoviev, *History of the Bolshevik Party, A Popular Outline* (London: New Park, 1973), pp. 153–154.

4.   "The Civil War in France," Marx and Engels, *Selected Works*, Vol. 1, pp. 182, 185.

5.   Marx and Engels, "Address of the Central Committee to the Communist League (March 1850)," *The Revolutions of 1848: Political Writings of Karl Marx, Vol. I*, ed. David Fernbach (Harmondsworth: Penguin, 1973), p. 330; Lenin, "The Tasks of the Russian Social Democrats," *Collected Works*, Vol. 2 (Moscow: Progress Publishers, 1963), pp. 335, 336.

6.   Marx and Engels, "Address of the Central Committee to the Communist League (March 1850)," *Selected Works*, Vol. 1, pp. 177–178; Zinoviev, *History of the Bolshevik Party*, p. 25; Lenin, "The Tasks of the Russian Social Democrats," *Collected Works*, Vol. 2, p. 331.

7.   Lenin, "A Militant Agreement for the Uprising," *Collected Works*, Vol. 8 (Moscow: Progress Publishers, 1963), pp. 163–164, 165.

8.   "Marx to Engels, April 16, 1856," *Selected Works*, Vol. 1, p. 529.

9.   Lenin, "We Have Paid Too Much," *Collected Works*, Vol. 33 (Moscow: Progress Publishers, 1973), p. 334; Trotsky, "On the United Front," *The First Five Years of the Communist International*, Vol. 2 (New York: Pathfinder Press, 1972), pp. 93–96.

10.   Luxemburg, "Reform or Revolution," *Rosa Luxemburg Speaks*, pp. 77, 78; Lenin, *Selected Works*, Vol. 1, p. 94.

11.   Lenin, *Selected Works* (1930s ed.), Vol. II, pp. 477, 489, 490; Marx and Engels, "Address of the Central Committee to the Communist League," *Selected Works*, Vol. 1, p. 180.

12. "The Mass Strike, the Political Party and the Trade Unions," *Rosa Luxemburg Speaks*, pp. 160–161, 192, 193.

13. Ibid., pp. 181–182.

14. Ibid., pp. 176, 192, 194.

15. Ibid., pp. 202, 206.

16. Ibid., p. 200.

17. Trotsky, *The Transitional Program for Socialist Revolution*, second edition (New York: Pathfinder Press, 1974), p. 75; Marx and Engels, "Address of the Central Committee to the Communist League (March 1850)," *The Revolutions of 1848*, ed. Fernbach, p. 329.

18. Lenin, "The Revolutionary Proletariat and the Right of Nations to Self-Determination," *Collected Works*, Vol. 21 (Moscow: Progress Publishers, 1974), pp. 408–409.

19. "The Russian Revolution," *Rosa Luxemburg Speaks*, p. 374.

20. Lenin, "Speech in Defense of the Tactics of the Third International," *Selected Works*, Vol. 3, p. 630; Lenin, "The Tasks of the Proletariat in the Present Revolution," *Selected Works*, Vol. 2, pp. 14–15.

21. Lenin, *"Left-Wing" Communism—An Infantile Disorder*, in *Selected Works*, Vol. 3, p. 392. This element of Lenin's thought is put forward with special clarity in Daniel Bensaid, *Revolutionary Strategy Today* (Amsterdam: Institute for Research and Education, 1987), pp. 8–10.

22. Lenin, "The Collapse of the Second International," *The Imperialist War* (New York: International Publishers, 1930), p. 279.

23. Ibid., pp. 279–280.

24. Comintern analysis quoted in Perry Anderson, "The Antinomies of Antonio Gramsci," *New Left Review*, November 1976-January 1977, p. 18; Trotsky, "Report on the New Soviet Economic Policy and the Perspectives of the World Revolution," *The First Five Years of the Communist International*, Vol. 2, pp. 220–221.

25. Gramsci, "The International Situation and the Struggle against Fascism," David Beetham, ed., *Marxists in the Face of Fascism* (Manchester: Manchester University Press, 1983), p. 125.

26. Gramsci, "State and Civil Society," *Selections from the Prison Notebooks*, ed. Quintin Hoare and Geoffrey Nowell Smith (New York: International Publishers, 1973), pp. 275–276.

27. Gramsci, "Problems of Marxism," *Selections from the Prison Notebooks*, p. 388.

28. An "epistemological break" of Gramsci from Lenin is argued, for example, in Carl Boggs, *Gramsci's Marxism* (London: Pluto Press, 1976). My own interpretation follows Perry Anderson, "The Antinomies of Antonio Gramsci," New Left Review, No. 100 (November 1976-January 1977); John Molyneux, *Marxism and the Party* (London: Pluto Press, 1978); and Livio Maitan, "The Legacy of Antonio Gramsci," *International Marxist Review*, Summer 1987. Also relevant is a fine study by Dante Germino, *Antonio Gramsci, Architect of a New Politics* (Baton Rouge: Louisiana University Press, 1990).

Important aspects of creating the "new moral order" to which Gramsci referred intersect with other works, of considerable interest, having to do with the interpenetration of class with race, gender, sexuality, and culture. Relevant explorations include: Leon Trotsky, *Problems of Everyday Life and Other Writings on Culture and Science* (New York: Pathfinder Press, 1973); Alexandra Kollontai, *Selected Writings*, ed. Alix Holt (New York: W. W. Norton, 1980); Wilhelm Reich, *Sex-Pol Essays, 1929–1934*, ed. Lee Baxandall (New York: Random House, 1972); Raymond Williams, *Resources of Hope: Culture, Democracy, Socialism*, ed. Robin Gable (London: Verso, 1989); Sheila Rowbotham, *Women, Resistance and Revolution* (New York: Vintage Press, 1972); Jamie Gough and Mike Macnair, *Gay Liberation in the Eighties* (London: Pluto Press, 1985); Roger N. Lancaster, *Life Is Hard: Machismo, Danger, and the Intimacy of Power in Nicaragua* (Berkeley: University of California Press, 1992); Scott McLemee and Paul Le Blanc, eds., *C. L. R. James and Revolutionary Marxism, Selected Writings 1939–1949* (Atlantic Highlands, N.J.: Humanities Press, 1994); Anna Grimshaw, ed., *The C. L. R. James Reader* (London: Basil Blackwell, 1992); Sonia Kruks, Rayna Rapp, Marilyn Young, eds., *Promissory Notes, Women in the Transition to Socialism* (New York: Monthly Review Press, 1989); W. E. B. DuBois, *An ABC of Color* (New York: International Publishers, 1969); Neville Alexander, *Education and the Struggle for National Liberation in South Africa* (Trenton, N.J.: Africa World Press, 1992); Carol McAllister, *Matriliny, Islam and Capitalism: Combined and Development in the Lives of Negeri Sembilan Women* (Ann Arbor: University Microfilms International, 1987); Penny Duggan and Heather Dashner, eds., *Women's Lives in the New Global Economy* (Amsterdam: International Institute for Research and Education, 1994); Maynard Solomon, ed., *Marxism and Art: Essays Classic and Contemporary* (New York: Vintage Books, 1972); Frederic Jameson, *Postmodernism or, The Cultural Logic of Late Capitalism* (Durham: Duke University Press, 1991); Jeremy Brecher, John Brown Childs, Jill Cutler, eds., *Global Visions: Beyond the New World Order* (Boston: South End Press, 1993).

29.   Trotsky, *Permanent Revolution* (New York: Pathfinder Press, 1978), p. 132.

30.   Leon Trotsky, *The Third International after Lenin* (New York: Pathfinder Press, 1970), pp. 3–4.

31.   Trotsky, *Permanent Revolution*, pp. 278–279.

32.   Ibid., p. 133. Some interpretations of Trotsky's theory of permanent revolution assert (incorrectly, in my opinion) that it was meant to be applied only to industrially "backward" countries. Although it was formulated first with "backward Russia" in mind and has special relevance for such countries in Asia, Africa, and Latin America, the dynamics it identifies are not irrelevant to more "advanced" societies. Also, a distinction should be made between utilizing the theory as 1) a generally applicable analytical tool that can help guide revolutionaries, 2) an agitational formula for socialist revolution deemed to be practical in every situation, and 3) a policy orientation for revolutionary governments to rapidly nationalize the economy of whatever country in which they happen to exercise power. While many self-styled Trotskyists can be identified with these last two points, only the first can be accurately attributed to Trotsky himself.

5

The Conception of the Transition to Socialism

"The test of Marxism," Robert Heilbroner has asserted, "emerges in its relation to socialism, not to capitalism."[1] There is something to be said for this paradoxical notion. One can acknowledge the power and validity of Marxist descriptions, analyses, and insights regarding capitalist development, the history of the labor movement, and the dynamics of revolution—yet to the extent that the possibility of working-class rule and the realizability of socialism are thrown into question, Marxism itself is thrown into question. These are precisely the tests which Marxism has yet to "pass." Of course, Marxist interpretations on all the rest can be—and have been—fiercely challenged; but capable and often illuminating Marxist responses to the challenges can be—and have been—developed. Marxist perspectives have consequently been a powerful influence within—and to some extent have been integrated into—the social sciences, the humanities, and even the natural sciences. Only when it comes to what happens after the overturn of capitalism have Marxists found themselves on weaker ground: on the one hand, there is pure (if educated) speculation on what might be possible; on the other hand, there are the examples of so-called "actually existing socialism" (which many would label "failed experiments"), where such words as "proletarian democracy" have been dogmatic slogans rather than vibrant descriptions. Here we will briefly examine revolutionary Marxist expectations regarding the transition to socialism. Then we will examine counterposed explanations—claiming some connection with Marxist perspectives—as to why historical experience did not conform to these expectations.

Not surprisingly, Marxist conceptions of the transition to socialism have been organically interconnected to Marxist theory of capitalist

99

development and the labor movement, and to the Marxist strategy for revolution. As we examine this question of transition, we will have cause to refer to points made earlier in this study. This can provide us with a useful review of essential aspects of the Marxist paradigm, at the same time highlighting its coherence.

Transition as Process

Marx and Engels viewed socialism not as an abstract ethical ideal but as a product of historical processes. Since the dissolution of primitive communal societies at the dawn of civilization, the history of humanity has been a history of class struggles, forming "a series of evolutions in which, nowadays, a stage has been reached where the exploited and oppressed class—the proletariat—cannot attain its emancipation from the sway of the exploiting and ruling class—the bourgeoisie—without, at the same time, and once and for all, emancipating society at large from all exploitation, oppression, class distinctions and class struggles." They predicted and supported "the formation of the proletariat into a class, [the] overthrow of the bourgeois supremacy, [the] conquest of political power by the proletariat," which they believed would mean "to raise the proletariat to the position of ruling class, to win the battle of democracy."[2]

With the establishment of working-class political power (which has sometimes been labeled the *dictatorship of the proletariat*, sometimes a *proletarian state* or *workers' state*, sometimes a *workers' democracy*), the workers would "wrest, by degrees, all capital from the bourgeoisie. . . . centralize all instruments of production in the hands of the State, i.e., of the proletariat organized as the ruling class; and . . . increase the total productive forces as rapidly as possible." This new socialist (or communist) order would run all "branches of production on behalf of society as a whole, i.e. according to a social plan and with the participation of all members of society." According to Marx and Engels, "in Communist society, accumulated labor is but a means to widen, to enrich, to promote the existence of the laborer. . . . In place of the old bourgeois society, with its classes and class antagonisms, we shall have an association, in which the free development of each is the condition for the free development of all."[3]

Prior to the development of industrial capitalism, Marx and Engels believed, the material basis for such a social order did not exist. The productive capacities which had developed under capitalism created, for the first time in human history, a sufficient economic surplus to allow humanity to move from the realm of necessity to the realm of freedom. As Marx explained it, "this development of productive forces . . . is an absolutely necessary practical premise [of communism] because without it *want* is merely made general, and with *destitution* the struggle for necessities and all the old filthy business would necessarily be reproduced."[4]

The two men also saw socialist revolution as an international process. Because "modern industry has established the world-market," the struggle between workers and capitalists—although "first a national struggle"—is actually a national struggle only "in form, though not in substance." In fact, "in national struggles of the proletarians of the different countries, they [i.e., Communists] point out and bring to the front the common interests of the entire proletariat, independently of all nationality." As Marx stressed in 1864, "the emancipation of labor is neither a local nor a national, but a social problem, embracing all countries in which modern society exists, and depending for its solution on the concurrence, practical and theoretical, of the most advanced countries." Several years later, Marx noted that the weakness of the international workers' movement had contributed to the 1871 defeat of the revolutionary workers of Paris: "The revolution needs solidarity, and we have a great example of it in the Paris Commune, which fell because a great revolutionary movement corresponding to that supreme rising of the Paris proletariat did not arise in all centers, in Berlin, Madrid and elsewhere."[5] Marx and Engels' internationalist perspective can also be seen in their view that a revolution in a backward country such as Russia could help generate upheavals in more advanced capitalist countries which, in turn, could help the more backward countries advance along non-capitalist lines.

In countries with a substantial agrarian population, Marx and Engels believed that relations between the working class and the peasantry constituted a profoundly important question for the transition process. Marx argued that "the peasants find their natural ally and leader in the *urban proletariat*, whose task is to overthrow the bourgeois order." But such an alliance cannot be realized automatically, and Marx warned that the peasant "either . . . hinders each workers' revolution, makes a wreck of it, as he has formerly done in France, or the proletariat (for the peasant proprietor does not belong to the proletariat, and even where his condition is proletarian, he believes himself not to be) must as government take measures through which the peasant finds his condition immediately improved, so as to win him for the revolution." He stressed that if the working class "is to have any chance of victory, it must be able to do immediately as much for the peasants as the French bourgeoisie . . . did in its revolution for the French peasants of that time." Sensitive to the peasantry's individualistic attachment to the soil, Marx believed in the necessity of a revolutionary workers' state to institute "measures which will at least provide the possibility of easing the transition from private ownership of the land to collective ownership, so that the peasant arrives at this of his own accord, from economic reasons. It must not hit the peasant over the head."[6]

The socialist revolution, as may be surmised from all of this, would not be a simple *act*, but rather an immense and complex *process*. A communist society would not come into being full-blown, directly based on totally new foundations, but would "in every respect, economically, morally and intellectually, still [be] stamped with the birthmarks of the old society from whose womb it emerges." Marx stressed more than once that "defects are inevitable in the first phase of communist society as it is when it has just emerged after prolonged birthpangs from capitalist society. Right can never be higher than the economic structure of society and its cultural development conditioned thereby." Marx and Engels rejected utopian blueprints that would be schematically imposed on society by socialistic reformers, but the basic thrust of the democratic collectivist process they envisioned was quite clear. "You cannot decree the development of the masses," Engels explained. "This is conditioned by the development of the conditions in which these masses live and hence evolve gradually." The first step, "the political liberation of the proletariat by a democratic state of society" would lead immediately to measures "guaranteeing the proletariat the means for its existence," for example: by progressive taxation (hitting the wealthy) and restricting the right of capitalists to give away things like factories, coal mines, and railroads through their wills (instead these things would be taken over by the democratic state); creating jobs for all through public works projects and national industries; offering a full, well-rounded public education to all children; and the gradual socialization of the entire economy. This would profoundly transform human relationships, culture, and psychology. "Just as the peasant and the worker in manufacture in the last [18th] century were forced to change the whole of their habits and customs, and even had to become totally different human beings when they were swept into the current of large-scale industry," Engels commented, "so also, communal production by the whole of society and the resulting new development of production will need entirely different men, and, indeed, will produce them." But this transformation would emerge from a democratic transformation of the society's way of life:

> The general association of all members of society for the purpose of common and planned utilization of the productive forces, the expansion of production so that it suffices to provide for the needs of all, the cessation of that condition whereby the satisfaction of the needs of one is effected only at the cost of the needs of others, the complete destruction of classes and their antagonisms, the all-round development of the talents of all the members of society by means of industrial education, the variations of activities, the participation of all in the enjoyments produced by all, the unification of town and countryside—such are the main results of the abolition of private ownership.[7]

The State

A crucial aspect of this transitional period is the role of the state.

Marx and Engels viewed the state as a product of class society, designed to maintain "order" in the face of tensions and antagonisms that are generated by class oppression—in short, "an engine of class despotism." Under developed capitalism, in Marx's words, "the State power, apparently soaring high above society, was at the same time itself the greatest scandal of that society and the very hotbed of all its corruptions. . . . Imperialism is, at the same time, the most prostitute and the ultimate form of the State power which nascent middle-class [i.e., bourgeois] society had commenced to elaborate as a means of its own emancipation from feudalism, and which full-grown bourgeois society had finally transformed into a means for the enslavement of labor by capital."[8]

We have seen that the state was central, however, to the socialist program, a point that Marx and Engels repeated frequently: "The proletariat seizes political power and turns the means of production into state property." Yet "the working class cannot simply lay hold of the ready-made state machinery, and wield it for its own purposes." The solution, as stated by Marx in 1875, was this: "Between capitalist and communist society lies the period of the revolutionary transformation of the one into the other. Corresponding to this is also a political transition period in which the state can be nothing but the *revolutionary dictatorship of the proletariat.*" In the same year, Engels explained that this proletarian state "is only a transitional institution which is used in the struggle, in the revolution, to hold down one's adversaries by force." He added that "so long as the proletariat still *uses* the state, it does not use it in the interests of freedom but in order to hold down its adversaries, and as soon as it becomes possible to speak of freedom the state as such ceases to exist."[9]

Marx and Engels viewed this as a *class dictatorship*, which for the proletariat could only be realized through democratic forms (despite its repressive function toward those seeking to overturn working-class rule). "Do you want to know what this dictatorship looks like?" asked Engels in 1891. "Look at the Paris Commune. That was the Dictatorship of the Proletariat." Twenty years earlier, Marx had described it as follows: "The Commune was formed of municipal councillors, chosen by universal suffrage in the various wards of the town, responsible and revocable at short terms. The majority of its members were naturally working men, or acknowledged representatives of the working class. The Commune was to be a working, not a parliamentary, body, executive and legislative at the same time." Significantly, the Commune was governed not by a single political party but by representatives of several different parties.[10]

Marx and Engels believed that "with the introduction of the socialist order of society, the state will disappear." Seeing the essential characteristic of the state as its repressive apparatus, they believed that even the Paris Commune "was no longer a state in the proper sense of the word," because the working-class majority in society was assuming power and responsibility which had been divorced from it previously and which had been concentrated instead in the state apparatus that functioned in the interests of bourgeois society. According to Engels, in *Socialism: Utopian and Scientific* (1880): "As soon as there is no longer any social class to be held in subjection; as soon as class rule, and the individual struggle for existence based upon our present anarchy in production, with collisions and excesses arising from these, are removed, nothing more remains to be repressed, and a special repressive force, the state, is no longer necessary. . . . State interference in social relations becomes, in one domain after another, superfluous, and then dies out of itself."[11]

This represents the "higher phase of communist society" to which Marx refers in his *Critique of the Gotha Program* (1875), "after the productive forces have also increased with the all-round development of the

individual, and all the springs of cooperative wealth flow more abun-
dantly . . . and society [can] inscribe on its banners: From each according to his ability, to each according to his needs!"[12]

Workers' Power and Mixed Economy

In developing his theory of permanent revolution, Trotsky gave special
attention to the dynamics of the early phase of the transition process.
Under the impact of the revolutionary upsurge of 1905, and partially
through re-studying the experience of history's first proletarian dictatorship, the Paris Commune of 1871, Trotsky made the obvious (but
important) point that the dictatorship of the proletariat is not premised
on the establishment of a collectivized, planned economy under workers'
control. He believed the reverse to be true: "The Paris Commune of 1871
was not, of course, a socialist commune: its regime was not even a developed regime of socialist revolution. The commune was only a prologue.
It established the dictatorship of the proletariat, the necessary premise
of the socialist revolution."[13] Trotsky believed that national-democratic
struggles in "backward" capitalist countries would result—if carried out
in a consistent, uncompromising manner under proletarian hegemony—
in the establishment of working-class rule and would move in a socialist
direction. But he did not believe that this would necessarily mean rapid
nationalizations of the various sectors of the economy. His formulation
of the question is worth quoting at length:

> The Parisian workers, says Marx, did not demand miracles from the
> Commune. Now too, we must not expect the dictatorship of the proletar-
> iat to produce miracles instantly. State power is not all-powerful. It would
> be absurd to think that all the proletariat has to do is acquire power and
> it can replace capitalism by socialism by means of a few decrees. The
> economic structure is not a product of the activity of the state. The pro-
> letariat can only apply state power, with all its energy, so as to ease and
> shorten the path of economic evolution in the direction of collectivism.
>
> The proletariat will begin with those reforms which enter into the so-
> called minimum program—and directly from them, by the very logic of
> its position, will be forced to go over to collectivist measures.
>
> To introduce the eight-hour day and a heavily-progressive income tax
> will be a comparatively simple business, although here, too, the center of
> gravity lies not in the publication of the "act" but in the organization of its
> execution. But the main difficulty (and here we go over to collectivism!)

will consist in the organization of production by the state in those factories and plants which will be closed by their owners in answer to the publication of these acts. . . .

Expropriation with compensation offers political advantages but financial difficulties; expropriation without compensation offers financial advantages but political difficulties. But greater than either the financial or political difficulties will be the economic and organizational difficulties.

We repeat: a government of the proletariat does not mean a government of miracles.

The socialization of production will begin with those branches which present the least difficulties. In the first period the socialized sector of production will have the appearance of oases connected with private economic enterprises by the laws of commodity exchange.[14]

In other words, the dictatorship would pursue policies resulting in a kind of "mixed economy." Part of the reason for this was the impossibility of achieving socialism in a single country: "The Russian proletariat . . . will be able to carry its great cause to its conclusion only under one condition—that it knows how to break out of the national framework of our great revolution and make it the prologue to the world victory of labor."[15]

It is worth noting that the "mixed economy under workers' rule" scenario did not originate with Trotsky. We've already noted that in the *Communist Manifesto* Marx and Engels envisioned the proletarian state wresting "by degrees" economic power from the capitalists. "Of course," they wrote, "in the beginning this cannot be effected except by means of despotic inroads on the rights of property and on the conditions of bourgeois production; by means of measures, therefore, which appear economically insufficient and untenable, but which, in the course of the movement outstrip themselves, necessitate further inroads upon the old social order, and are unavoidable as a means of entirely revolutionizing the mode of production."[16]

Proletarian Democracy

While the pace of economic transformation can be more or less rapid or gradual, the essential element in the transition to socialism is *the coming to power of the workers*. This is also the essential link between the revolutionary strategy of Marxism and the Marxist conception of the transition to socialism. "The most indubitable feature of a revolution is the direct interference of the masses in historic events," wrote Trotsky. "In ordinary times that state, be it monarchical or democratic, elevates itself above the nation, and history is made by specialists in that line of business—kings, ministers, bureaucrats, parliamentarians, journalists. But at those crucial moments when the old order becomes no longer endurable to the masses, they break over the barriers excluding them from the political arena, sweep aside their traditional representatives, and create by their interference the initial groundwork for a new regime." He concluded that "the history of a revolution is for us first of all a history of the forcible entrance of the masses into the realm of rulership over their own destiny."[17] Rosa Luxemburg stressed the same point, underscoring the necessity of proletarian democracy:

> Bourgeois class rule has no need of the political training and education of the entire mass of the people, at least not beyond certain narrow limits. But for the proletarian dictatorship that is the life element, the very air without which it is not able to exist. . . . Only experience is capable of correcting and opening new ways. Only unobstructed, effervescing life falls into a thousand new forms and improvisations, brings to light creative force, itself corrects all mistaken attempts. . . . The whole mass of the people must take part. . . . Socialism in life demands a complete spiritual transformation in the masses degraded by centuries of class rule. Social instincts in place of egotistical ones, mass initiative in place of inertia, idealism which conquers all suffering, etc. . . . The only way to a rebirth is the school of public life itself, the most unlimited, the broadest democracy and public opinion.[18]

Lenin offered a similar conception, describing socialism as "a rapid, genuine, truly mass forward movement, embracing first the *majority* and then the whole population, in all spheres of public and private life." From this dynamic vision of socialism, he explained the nature of the state and how it would evolve with the coming working-class revolution. "Democracy is a form of the state," Lenin explained, "one of its varieties. Consequently, it, like every state, represents on the one hand, the organized, systematic use of force against persons; but, on the other hand, it signifies the formal recognition of equality of citizens, the equal right of all to determine the structure of, and to administer, the state." Such democracy could be utilized by the revolutionary movement to organize and mobilize for workers' power, ultimately overturning the capitalist state, to substitute for bourgeois democracy "a *more* democratic state machine, but a state machine nonetheless, in the shape of the armed workers who proceed to form a militia, involving the entire population." With the mass diffusion of political power, quantity is transformed into quality: "*Such* a degree of democracy implies overstepping the boundaries of bourgeois society and beginning its socialist reorganization. If really *all* take part in the administration of the state, capitalism cannot retain its hold." Like other Marxists, of course, Lenin assumed this would occur on the high level of economic productivity and potential abundance made possible by capitalism. But the "subjective" factor and the initiative and creativity within the working class were no less important. Lenin saw the "vital creativity of the masses" as the "fundamental factor in the new society," arguing: "Let the workers take on the creation of workers' control in their works and factories, let them supply the countryside with manufactured goods in exchange for bread. . . . Socialism is not created by orders from on high. Its spirit is alien to state-bureaucratic automatism. Socialism is vital and creative, it is the creation of the popular masses themselves." As self-government became the norm, "the *necessity* of observing the simple, fundamental rules of the community will very soon become a *habit*," and "the more complete the democracy, the nearer the moment when it becomes unnecessary." The internalization of human solidarity, social consciousness, and democratic values on a mass scale, and the diffusion of knowledge and organizational expertise throughout society—these represented for Lenin the meaning of socialism and the means through which it would develop to ever higher levels of civilization.[19]

Antonio Gramsci similarly viewed working-class self-rule in expansive terms, making the same point—that under such circumstances the state essentially dissolves into the population as whole: "The people's consent does not end at the moment of voting, quite the contrary. The consent is presumed to be permanently active; so much so that those who give it may be considered as 'functionaries' of the State, and elections as a means of voluntary enrollment of State functionaries of a certain type—a means which in a certain sense may be related to the idea of *self-government*. . . . Since elections are held on the basis not of vague, generic programs, but of programs of immediate, concrete work, anyone who gives his consent commits himself to do something more . . . towards their realization."[20]

Explaining Bureaucratic Dictatorship

And yet, in Gramsci's fertile and sometimes contradictory *Prison Notebooks*, in his attempt to deal with the realities of Stalinism (as it was beginning to manifest itself in the late 1920s and early '30s) without turning away from the Communist mainstream, he wrote: "The war of position [between world capitalism and world communism] demands enormous sacrifices by indefinite masses of people. So an unprecedented concentration of hegemony is necessary, and hence a more 'interventionist' government, which will take the offensive more openly against the oppositionists and organize permanently the 'impossibility' of internal disintegration—with controls of every kind, political, administrative, etc., reinforcement of the hegemonic 'positions' of the dominant group, etc."[21] This seems applicable to the rise of authoritarianism both in the capitalist and post-capitalist societies and could be seen as a justification for Stalinism (although, as we've suggested earlier, Gramsci's critical-minded position on such questions was hardly one of clear-cut endorsement for authoritarian policies).

It is worth turning to Joseph Stalin's 1927 discussion of the future society which he claimed to be building in the USSR:

> Briefly, the anatomy of Communist society may be described as follows: It is a society in which (a) there will be no private ownership of the instruments and means of production, but social, collective ownership; (b) there will be no classes or state power, but there will be working people in industry and agriculture who manage economic affairs as a free association of working people; (c) the national economy, organized according to plan, will be based on the highest level of technique, both in industry and agriculture; (d) there will be no antithesis between town and country, between industry and agriculture; (e) products will be distributed according to the principle of the old French Communists: "from each according to his ability, to each according to his needs"; (f) science and art will enjoy conditions sufficiently favorable for them to attain full flowering; (g) the individual, freed from concern about his daily bread and from the necessity of adapting himself to the "powers that be," will become really free.[22]

Noting that this statement "is still strongly reminiscent of Marx and Engels," Wolfgang Leonhard has demonstrated that by 1952, in Stalin's later description of the characteristics of communist society, little remained of this list—"neither the free association of the workers

nor the absence of state power, neither the liberation of the human personality nor the free development of science and art to full flower. . . .
According to Stalin's new definition, even the Communist society of
the future would be marked by differences between 'leading personnel'
and rank-and-file workers." In language consistent with his trajectory as
the supreme representative of a bureaucratic order, Stalin offered what
he called *the basic law of socialism*: "the securing of the maximum satisfaction of the constantly rising material and cultural requirements of
the whole society through the continuous expansion and perfection of
socialist production on the basis of higher techniques."[23]

An interesting defense of Stalinism (though not necessarily of its
more repressive and murderous "excesses") was put forward by Donald
C. Hodges in the early 1980s, critical of Lenin, Luxemburg, and Trotsky
because in their description of post-capitalist society "they retreat from
scientific to utopian socialism on the basis of a literal interpretation of
Marx's and Engels's writings," whereas "Stalin was the first to adapt
Marxism to the new world ushered in by the Bolshevik Revolution of
October 1917." Although critical of Stalin for attempting to lay claim
to Marxist orthodoxy by distorting Marxist texts and introducing self-
serving elements into his description of the new social order, Hodges
nonetheless approves of the fact that "Stalin replaced the traditional
Marxist forecasts of a postcapitalist order with a description of the new
social reality, whereas his critics on the left stuck to the original forecasts
and to a socialist ideal that has little substance in fact." Hodges goes on
to develop a more lucid defense of Stalinist practice. Lacking administrative ability to maintain by themselves the state apparatus and to
coordinate the functioning and development of the economy, politically
reliable Communists must make concessions to non-communists whose
adminstrative abilities are needed in the process of socialist development. "Owing to the party's lack of professional cadres, we may conclude,
either socialism becomes bureaucratized or there will be no socialism."[24]

According to Hodges, the organization and initiative of the working
class has proved to be decisive "at critical moments . . . as in Russia during the first decade after October 1917 and in China during the early
stages of its revolution." But it is utopian to expect the working class to
maintain its own democratic rule during the period of socialist transformation. Even though the workers are displaced from actual power by
a bureaucratic elite, however, they still recognize that "bureaucratized

socialism" (the only kind of socialism that is possible) is a progressive stage of society which functions in their interests:

> Once ordinary workers squarely face the obstacles to establishing and then maintaining a dictatorship of their own, once they recognize that the conditions of a classless society are still a long way off, then they no longer have reason to criticize communist parties for "betraying the revolution." Claims of treason will have been put to rest along with the ultraleft sects nourishing them. [Here one assumes that Hodges does *not* mean "laying them to rest" in the manner that Stalin utilized during the period of the purges.] Because a bureaucratic-type political and social revolution is a necessary stage to a communist or classless society . . . the proletariat has an interest in supporting it. Despite the auxiliary role of workers under socialism, they have thus far benefited from a socialist transformation.[25]

Hodges makes a distinction between socialism (which is necessarily bureaucratic) and communism, which he defines in terms similar to those which we've quoted from Marx, Engels, Luxemburg, Lenin, Trotsky, and Gramsci. He argues:

> A strategy for establishing communism may become viable once the socialist system becomes consolidated, but it is hardly practical before that time—at least not in the developed socialist countries. In his own day, Marx supported the efforts to extend the capitalist system throughout Europe as a prior condition of the struggle for socialism. Today, and for the same reason, Marxists support the new socialist or bureaucratic order as a prior condition of the struggle for communism.[26]

Hodges' analysis is not unique. A sympathizer of the Stalin regime in the 1930s, *New York Times* correspondent Walter Duranty, also argued that Stalin's revisions of the revolutionary Marxist orientation "were most fitted to the Russian character and folkways in that they established Asiatic absolutism and put the interests of Russian Socialism before those of international Socialism." Duranty was one of many observers who predicted that this would provide the basis for the eventual development of a higher form of society. More recently, some theorists have utilized the concept of the Asiatic Mode of Production to make a similar argument. This concept offers the model of a knowledgeable state bureaucracy whose more or less authoritarian domination over society in ancient China and other parts of Asia was accepted by the populace because it effectively coordinated the organization and maintenance of socially useful or necessary public works (such as irrigation systems). Important elements of this model are said to have existed in pre-revolutionary Russia and China, later to be taken over by Stalin and Mao and integrated into a "tutelary socialism" that brings about modernization and industrialization. "According to Marx," Marian Sawer has explained, "the role of Western capital in *breaking down* the old structure of Asiatic society and providing the conditions for development in its own image was an essential element of the universal progress towards socialism. The notion that (contrary to Marx's beliefs) industrialization and capitalism may be logically and historically separable has given rise to an interesting change of terminology in Marxist writing." One terminological change involves a definition of socialism as a collectivized, planned economy in which a strong, centralized state carries out policies of modernization and industrial development *without* genuine (democratic) working-class rule. As Sawer puts it, "the 'Asiatic' form of industrialization cannot give rise to popular socialism (i.e., the Marxist conception of socialism) as contrasted with tutelary socialism until the class of functionaries is abolished and the state becomes identified with the people as a whole," which can only happen after an extended process of development under bureaucratic rule.[27]

As we can see, this line of reasoning stands in stark contrast to the traditional perspectives of revolutionary Marxism. More, it distorts Marx's own views—particularly as developed in the final decade of his life. We have noted that he believed industrialization and socialism could come to countries like Russia without a period of capitalist development, provided that the international revolutionary struggle brought more developed industrial countries into the process of creating a socialist world. It is questionable whether he would have recognized the bureaucratized or tutelary "socialism" described here as socialism at all, so alien is it from his own analysis of what socialism represents. There is yet another fact of some significance: the apparent quality of hard-headed reasoning in this sophisticated-Stalinist line of argument evaporates as it becomes apparent that this "actually-existing socialism" lacked sufficient durability (and popular support) to remain in existence for more than a few decades in the USSR and Eastern Europe. In China, the Communist Party dictatorship has overseen the increasingly exploitative integration of the Chinese economy into the global capitalist economy.

A Marxist Critique of Bureaucratic Dictatorship

Rosa Luxemburg was the first to identify developments which would undermine the Russian Revolution and give an authoritarian connotation to Communism. But one must understand the context. In 1917 a workers' revolution established Soviet power—democratic councils in which Bolsheviks were predominant. From 1918 to 1921, the infant Soviet Republic was engulfed by foreign invasion and internal counterrevolution, economic blockade and collapse, and a brutalizing civil war. Victor Serge, who lived through this period as a Bolshevik militant, recalled twenty years later:

> In the midst of the proletarian revolution, the civil war brings about little by little the disappearance of democratic liberties. It would be necessary to sketch here a picture of those terrible years, to show the revolution hemmed in by its foes, undermined at home by Vendees [peasant rebellions], by conspiracies, by sabotage, by famine, by the disorganization of transports, by epidemics, by schisms, to show the conflict between the battling vanguard of the working class and its backward elements, the least conscious and most selfish, those least inclined to make sacrifices demanded by the general interest. The misfortune of the dissident parties or groups in those times is that their opposition runs the risk of rallying these discouraged rearguards who are ready unconsciously to second a counter-revolution.[28]

"If the Bolshevik dictatorship fell," Serge believed, "it was only a short step to chaos, and through chaos to a peasant rising, the massacre of the Communists, the return of the *emigres*, and in the end, through sheer force of events, another dictatorship, this one anti-proletarian." This outlook generated the dictatorial policies that stood in stark contradiction to the radical-democratic and libertarian perspectives which had been essential components of revolutionary Marxism.[29]

It was this that Rosa Luxemburg explained with luminous clarity in 1918. "Socialism in life demands a complete spiritual transformation in the masses degraded by centuries of class rule," she wrote, and "the only way to a rebirth is the school of public life itself, the most unlimited, the broadest democracy and public opinion." The demoralizing repression imposed by Russia's revolutionary regime made this impossible. "But with the repression of political life in the land as a whole, life in the soviets [the councils on which the regime was based] must also become more and more crippled," she noted. "Without general elections, without unrestricted freedom of press and assembly, without a free struggle of opinion, life dies out in every public institution, becomes a mere semblance of life, in which only the bureaucracy remains as the active element."[30]

Repression during the civil war period was seen as a temporary expedient, to be set aside when Soviet Russia's dangerous isolation had been overcome by the spread of socialist revolutions to other countries. When the civil war ended and the economy revived in the 1920s, the repression eased considerably—only to be murderously reimposed by the early 1930s under Stalin's leadership. A deeper analysis was required to explain all this.

The attempt to analyze the authoritarian degeneration of the Russian Revolution in a manner consistent with revolutionary Marxism was pioneered by Trotsky. The primary reason for this degeneration, he argued, was "the number of defeats of the proletariat in Europe and Asia," ensuring the Soviet Republic's isolation in a hostile capitalist world. "The 'vast masses' which, according to Lenin, decide the outcome of the struggle, became tired of internal privations and of waiting too long for the world revolution. The mood of the masses declined. The bureaucracy won the upper hand. It cowed the revolutionary vanguard, trampled upon Marxism, prostituted the Bolshevik Party. Stalinism conquered." He explained that "the Bolshevik revolution, with all its repressions, meant an upheaval of social relations in the interest of the masses, whereas the Stalinist thermidorian upheaval accompanies the transformation of Soviet society in the interest of a privileged minority." Trotsky concluded that "certainly Stalinism 'grew out' of Bolshevism, not logically, however, but dialectically; not as a revolutionary affirmation but as a Thermidorian negation. It is by no means the same."[31] (Thermidor was late July, after the changing of the names of the months during the French Revolution; in Thermidor 1794 conservative elements in the revolutionary camp overturned the radical regime of Robespierre to establish their own dictatorship.) We can see that Trotsky viewed the rise of bureaucratic rule not as a necessary or universal stage in the development of post-capitalist society but as an historically specific phenomenon which is neither desirable nor inevitable.

"Had the level of technology in Russia been as high as in Germany or the United States," Trotsky asserted, "the socialist economy would from the start have produced everything needed to satisfy the everyday needs of the people. Under those circumstances, the Soviet bureaucracy would not have been able to play an important role, since a high level of technology would also mean a high cultural level, and the workers would never have permitted the bureaucracy to order them about." Instead, Russia was compelled to carry out its economic development after the revolution on the basis of immense poverty. "The basis of bureaucratic rule is the poverty of society in objects of consumption, with the result-ing struggle of each against all. When there is enough goods in a store, the purchasers can come whenever they want. When there is little goods, the purchasers are compelled to stand in line. When the lines are very long, it is necessary to appoint a policeman to keep order. Such is the starting point of the power of the Soviet bureaucracy. It 'knows' who is to get something and who has to wait."[32] And of course, the bureau-crat-policeman knew that *he* should be the first to "get something," and enough of "something" to maintain his own morale—in the interests of the revolution, to be sure. Thus a privileged bureaucratic layer developed a material interest and an ideology to maintain power relationships that were antithetical to the socialist goal. Trotsky summed up his analysis as follows:

> The Soviet Union is a contradictory society halfway between capital-ism and socialism, in which: (a) the productive forces are still far from adequate to give the state property a socialist character; (b) the tendency toward primitive accumulation created by want breaks out through innu-merable pores of the planned economy; (c) norms of distribution pre-serving a bourgeois character lie at the basis of a new differentiation of society; (d) the economic growth, while slowly bettering the situation of the toilers, promotes a swift formation of privileged strata; (e) exploit-ing the social antagonisms, a bureaucracy has converted itself into an uncontrolled caste alien to socialism; (f) the social revolution, betrayed by the ruling party, still exists in [collectivized] property relations and in the consciousness of the toiling masses; (g) on the road to capitalism the counterrevolution would have to break the resistance of the workers; (h) on the road to socialism the workers would have to overthrow the bureaucracy. In the last analysis, the question will be decided by a struggle of living social forces, both on the national and the world arena.[33]

The collapse of the Soviet Union five and a half decades later gives at least some vindication for Trotsky's analysis—although for many it has also raised questions about the possibility of the working class realizing a transition to socialism, and therefore about the entire revolutionary Marxist perspective. Some would respond to this that such questions were actually posed when the working class of the USSR found itself effectively disenfranchised by the bureaucracy many years before. Additional questions are posed: If the "economic democracy" of socialism is not achievable, is it possible that democracy itself is simply a utopian notion? And if the revolutionary Marxist critique of capitalism is basically correct, is it really the case that there can be no democratic and rational alternative to it?

Notes

1. Robert L. Heilbroner, *Marxism: For and Against* (New York: W. W. Norton, 1980), p. 173.
2. Frederick Engels, "Preface to the English Edition of 1888," *The Revolutions of 1848*, ed. David Fernbach (Harmondsworth: Penguin Books, 1973), p. 65; "Manifesto of the Communist Party" in Karl Marx and Frederick Engels, *Selected Works*, Vol. 1 (Moscow: Progress Publishers, 1973), pp. 120, 126.
3. "Manifesto of the Communist Party," *Selected Works*, Vol. 1, pp. 88, 120, 121, 126, 127.
4. Ibid., pp. 37, 88.
5. Ibid., pp. 110, 118, 120; Karl Marx, "The Hague Conference," *Selected Works*, Vol. 2, pp. 293–294.
6. Karl Marx to Frederick Engels (April 16, 1856), and Karl Marx, "The Eighteenth Brumaire of Louis Bonaparte," *Selected Works*, Vol. 1, pp. 482, 529; Karl Marx, "Conspectus of Bakunin's *Statism and Anarchy*," in *The First International and After*, ed. David Fernbach (Harmondsworth: Penguin Books, 1973), p. 334.
7. Karl Marx, "Critique of the Gotha Program," *Selected Works*, Vol. 3, pp. 17, 19; Engels, "Draft of the Communist Confession of Faith" and "Principles of Communism," in Dirk Struik, ed., *Birth of the Communist Manifesto* (New York: International Publishers, 1971), pp. 167, 168, 180–182, 184, 185.
8. Karl Marx, "The Civil War in France," *Selected Works*, Vol. 2, pp. 217, 218, 219. The same insight can be found in Marx's 1843 comment: "While politics ideally is superior to financial power, in actual fact it has become its serf." (This point is made in "On the Jewish Question," in *Writings of the Young Marx on Philosophy and Society*, ed. Loyd D. Easton and Kurt H. Guddat [Garden City, N.Y.: Anchor Books, 1967], p. 245.)
9. Frederick Engels, "Socialism: Utopian and Scientific" and *The Origin of the Family, Private Property and the State*, Karl Marx, "Critique of the Gotha

Program," Engels to August Bebel (March 18–28, 1875), *Selected Works*, Vol. 3, pp. 26, 34–35, 146, 217.

10. Marx, "The Civil War in France" in Marx and Engels, *Selected Works*, Vol. 2, pp. 189, 220. Also see Monty Johnstone, "The Paris Commune and Marx's Conception of the Dictatorship of the Proletariat," in John Hicks and Robert Tucker, eds., *Revolution and Reaction, The Paris Commune of 1871* (Amherst: University of Massachusetts Press, 1971).

11. Frederick Engels to August Bebel (March 18–28, 1875), and Frederick Engels, "Socialism: Utopian and Scientific," *Selected Works*, Vol. 3, pp. 34, 147.

12. Marx, "Critique of the Gotha Program," *Selected Works*, Vol. 3, p. 19.

13. Leon Trotsky, *On the Paris Commune* (New York: Pathfinder Press, 1970), p. 13.

14. Ibid., pp. 13, 25, 26.

15. Ibid., p. 26.

16. "Manifesto of the Communist Party," *Selected Works*, Vol. 1, p. 126.

17. Leon Trotsky, *History of the Russian Revolution*, three volumes in one (New York: Simon and Schuster, 1936), p. xvii.

18. Rosa Luxemburg, "The Russian Revolution," *Rosa Luxemburg Speaks*, ed. Mary-Alice Waters (New York: Pathfinder Press, 1970), pp. 389–391.

19. Lenin, "The State and Revolution," *Selected Works*, Vol. 2 (New York: International Publishers, 1967), pp. 343–345; S. A. Smith, *Red Petrograd: Revolution in the Factories, 1917–1918* (Cambridge: Cambridge University Press, 1986), p. 156. All of this has been criticized, even by many who are sympathetic to Marxism, as one of the most utopian (unrealistic, unrealizable) strands in the revolutionary Marxist perspective. For an intriguing defense, however, see Richard N. Hunt, *The Political Ideas of Marx and Engels, Volume 2: Classical Marxism, 1850–1895* (Pittsburgh: University of Pittsburgh Press, 1984), pp. 212–265, although Hunt (incorrectly, in my opinion) separates the Bolsheviks from this libertarian strand.

20. Antonio Gramsci, "Once Again on the Organic Capacities of the Working Class," *Selections From Political Writings, 1921–1926* (New York: International Publishers, 1978), pp. 418–420.

21. Antonio Gramsci, *Selections from the Prison Notebooks*, ed. Quintin Hoare and Geoffrey Nowell Smith (New York: International Publishers, 1973), pp. 238–239; also see Livio Maitan's insightful discussion in "The Legacy of Antonio Gramsci," *International Marxist Review*, Vol. 2, No. 3, Summer 1987, pp. 7–39.

22. Quoted in Wolfgang Leonhard, *Three Faces of Marxism: The Political Concepts of Soviet Ideology, Maoism, and Humanist Marxism* (New York: G. P. Putnam's Sons, 1974), p. 113.

23. Ibid., pp. 113, 114; Stalin, "Economic Problems of Socialism in the U.S.S.R.," *The Essential Stalin*, ed. Bruce Franklin (Garden City, N.Y.: Anchor Books, 1972), p. 476.

24. Donald C. Hodges, *The Bureaucratization of Socialism* (Amherst: University of Massachusetts Press, 1983), pp. xi, xii, 183.

25. Ibid., p. 183.

26.   Ibid. Marx and Engels and the early Marxists saw "socialism" and "communism" as synonyms. In *Critique of the Gotha Program* Marx had made a distinction between a lower stage of communism (with a workers' state) and a higher stage of communism where the state had withered away. In *State and Revolution* Lenin labeled the first stage socialism and the second communism. Based on this, Hodges adds his own innovation.

27.   Walter Duranty, *I Write as I Please* (New York: Halcyon House, 1935), p. 274; Marian Sawer, *Marxism and the Question of the Asiatic Mode of Production* (The Hague, Netherlands: Martinus Nijhoff, 1977), pp. 220, 221–222. Additional variations on this mode of analysis are discussed in Tracy B. Strong and Helene Keyssar, *Right in Her Soul, The Life of Anna Louise Strong* (New York: Random House, 1983), and David Caute, *The Fellow Travellers, A Postscript to the Enlightenment* (New York: Macmillan Co., 1973).

28.   Victor Serge, *Russia Twenty Years After* (New York: Hillman-Curl, 1937), p. 142.

29.   Victor Serge, *Memoirs of a Revolutionary* (London: Writers and Readers, 1984), p. 129.

30.   Rosa Luxemburg, "The Russian Revolution," p. 391.

31.   "Stalinism and Bolshevism," in *Writings of Leon Trotsky, 1936–37*, second edition, ed. Naomi Allen and George Breitman (New York: Pathfinder Press, 1978), pp. 420, 422.

32.   "The Meaning of the Struggle against 'Trotskyism,'" *Writings of Leon Trotsky, 1938–39*, ed. Naomi Allen and George Breitman (New York: Pathfinder Press, 1974), pp. 42–43; Leon Trotsky, *The Revolution Betrayed, What Is the Soviet Union and Where Is It Going?* (Garden City, N.Y.: Doubleday, Doran and Co., 1937), p. 112.

33.   Trotsky, *The Revolution Betrayed*, p. 255.

6

Does Revolutionary Marxism Have a Future?

In our review of Marxist thought, we have seen that there are substantial divergences and qualitative differences among those identifying with the Marxist tradition. Even among those whom we've identified as "revolutionary Marxist," there are significant differences, and each of the five thinkers has also offered distinctive contributions—although it has been argued here that these can be harmonized with each other, adding up to a powerfully coherent whole. Regardless of how one feels about the orientations and activities of these five revolutionaries, all of them have offered significant ideas which can contribute to an understanding of contemporary realities. While not attempting to do justice to all aspects of the revolutionary Marxist synthesis, we can list some of the central ideas, indicating a cogent theoretical paradigm. After doing this, we should ponder some of the challenges posed for this paradigm by the realities of the 20th century.

Summing Up Revolutionary Marxism

1. Capitalism is an historically evolved (and evolving) socioeconomic system which has created the material basis for generalized abundance and freedom but which contains contradictions (between exploiting and exploited classes, between the social organization and the private ownership of the economy, etc.) which block the possibility of realizing this potential. These contradictions generate tensions and conflicts and will lead to capitalism's downfall, but the social organization and technological development generated by capitalism have provided a basis on which a better society can be built.

119

2. Democracy is possible and desirable. Democratic struggles coin-
   cided with and were intertwined in the struggle of the rising capitalist order for freedom from traditionalist restraints and aristocratic
   privilege. But under capitalism—with its gross material inequalities,
   concentrations of economic power (particularly decision-making
   power) in a few hands, and authoritarianism in the workplace—
   democracy cannot be fully realized. It continues to be worth fighting
   for, but its actualization requires overturning capitalism and implies
   the creation of socialism, of which democracy is an essential component. The struggle for authentic democracy thus overflows into the
   struggle against capitalism itself. Ultimately, under advanced socialist civilization, democracy will become a habit and will not require a
   state apparatus for its realization.

3. Capitalism and strong bourgeois nation-states arose out of pre-
   capitalist forms of society, but a similar evolution of strong capitalist national economies in today's "underdeveloped" countries is
   prevented by the present stage of the world capitalist economy. The
   more developed capitalist regions subordinate the development of
   the newer capitalist nations (often former colonies or semi-colonies)
   to the needs of the existing world market, perpetuating "backward"
   and "underdeveloped" features in the socioeconomic life of the dominated countries and fusing these with modern features of capitalism
   to create hybrid forms, preventing the less developed countries from
   copying the trajectories (and from enjoying the consequent benefits)
   of the more advanced capitalist countries.

4. The working class, evolving into a majority class, has the power
   and the objective interest to create a movement to fight against the
   injustice, exploitation, and oppression generated by capitalism, and
   also to struggle for socialism. This is a natural tendency but is not
   automatically triumphant. Various obstacles—divisions in the working class, competition among workers and between different sectors
   of the working class, the power of capitalist authority-relations and
   ideology, etc.—counteract the development of radical working-class
   consciousness. On the other hand, the realities of capitalist development and its contradictions contribute to the development of such
   consciousness. The organizational and political development of the
   working class along revolutionary socialist lines is possible and is

also necessary for the overturn of capitalism, the establishment of working-class democracy, and the socialist reconstruction of society.

5.   A revolutionary vanguard, guided by scientific socialist theory, is needed to develop an effective program capable of mobilizing workers and the oppressed in the fight against capitalist injustice and in the struggle for socialism. The development of such a vanguard—composed of those with the greatest commitment to devoting attention and energy to the struggle—takes place naturally, but is neither a simple nor unproblematical process. Without it, however, the struggle of the working class will not move forward to socialist revolution.

6.   The fact that post-capitalist societies created through popular revolutions have resulted in bureaucratic dictatorships instead of socialist democracies can be explained not by the impossibility of socialism or democracy but by specific historical circumstances which were not inevitable and which can be overcome. Socialism can only be realized on a world scale, and particularly requires that advanced industrial countries be involved in bringing it into being.

7.   Advanced capitalist countries have a vital stake in the forms of development which the other countries of the world undergo, because these countries are an important arena within which the capitalist accumulation process is realized. It is particularly important for such countries as the United States (from the capitalist vantage-point) to prevent revolutions and other upheavals which might in any way deny capitalist corporations raw materials, markets, and investment opportunities. Backed up by political (including military) power from the advanced capitalist countries, this inevitably introduces distortions in the political, cultural, and economic life of the underdeveloped countries, which are often detrimental to their populations—and in some ways detrimental to the populations (especially the working class) of the advanced capitalist countries as well, such as the drift of industry to "cheap labor" regions, increased military spending (adversely affecting resources available for maintaining popular living standards), wars, and so forth.

8.   To the extent that advanced capitalism is able to perpetuate itself, it will generate tendencies which undermine and do violence to democracy, community, culture, the quality of life, and life itself. Increasingly, humanity faces a choice between socialism or barbarism.

The revolutionary Marxist paradigm has an impressive coherence, but coherence is not necessarily enough. Before concluding, we should discuss the failure of revolutionary Marxism in the late 20th century. For it is absolutely unquestionable that it has failed to achieve the goals advanced by the theorists on whom we have focused our attention.

Workers' States and the Fall of Communism

Many make the case that the collapse of the Communist regimes in the Soviet Union and Eastern Europe in the late 1980s and early '90s, and the utter failure of their Marxist-Leninist ideologies to prevent or even coherently explain what happened, conclusively demonstrates the obsolescence of the revolutionary Marxist perspective. There is an effective response to this: that the official ideology of Marxism-Leninism—far from embracing the critical method and revolutionary perspectives of Marx and Lenin—was simply a set of rigid dogmas and political rationalizations to justify the dictatorship of a corrupt, self-interested, often vicious bureaucratic layer which had as much to do with the socialism of Marx as the Spanish Inquisition had to do with the Christianity of Jesus. Genuine Marxism (as we have seen in this study) provides tools for analyzing and understanding the Stalinist degeneration, and the ultimate disintegration, of the Soviet workers' state—and it also provided tools for resisting such developments, and for posing the positive alternative of a radical democracy: a genuine workers' democracy, a healthy workers state, the Marxist vision of the full-blooded and vital political rule by the working class.[1]

There are several problems with this. One is that the power of a correct theory generally has much less impact on popular consciousness than the power of a mighty collapse. Related to this, the revolutionary Marxism discussed here was embraced throughout the 20th century by immensely fewer people than the many millions who perceived the now-discredited Communist ideology as authentic Marxism. Also, many people's perceptions of these complex realities are profoundly influenced by a massively wealthy colossus, the multifaceted news and opinion apparatus, which is hostile to any substantial challenge to capitalism. This pro-capitalist news-and-opinion apparatus generally slants the news and limits the range of opinions to be presented to the public in a manner consistent with this inherent bias.[2] But in addition to problems of perception, there are problems of substance that must be acknowledged.

To what extent is a "workers state" as envisioned by the revolutionary Marxists—Marx and Engels, Luxemburg, Lenin, Trotsky, Gramsci—a genuine possibility? This problematic may be illuminated if we refer to points made by some of the keenest minds ever drawn to and subsequently repelled from a revolutionary understanding of Marxism— Sidney Hook, Bertram D. Wolfe, James Burnham—whose ideas are being repeated today (usually without acknowledgment) by many latter-day "post-Marxists" whose own disillusionment is of recent vintage. The nub of the critique can be found in Sidney Hook's comment: "In the end it must be admitted that Rosa Luxemburg's faith in the workers outstripped the evidence."[3] In a tone of bitter wisdom, Bertram D. Wolfe elaborated:

> And what if History fails to force the working class to accept the goal that Marx's science has assigned to it? What if enslavement and degradation, or corruption, or willfulness, or caprice, should be such as to unfit it for, or cause it to reject, the mission of redeeming all mankind? What if the proletariat stubbornly continues to choose other goals or other methods than this "science" prescribes?[4]

As if in response, Hook explains that, from a Marxist perspective, "the working class cannot succeed in its historical task without a leadership to enlighten and guide it. This leadership is supplied by those socialists who have taken to heart Marx's theories. . . . As the number of his followers increased, Marx actively encouraged them to organize or transform existing working-class groups into Marxist parties."[5] These would provide the leadership necessary for the working class to take political power. To which Wolfe responds: "Once such a government, by whatever means, comes to power, can it permit its decisions and its actions, based as they are on science, to be challenged, or outvoted, or reversed by ignorant numbers from whatever class or classes?"[6]

To illustrate this problem, James Burnham offers a case-study on the fate of "workers' control of industry" in revolutionary Russia. Noting that this had "been a slogan of the Leninist wing of Marxism," he explained: "According to the formal ideology of socialism, private ownership (control) in industry is to be eliminated—that is, as socialism understands it, control is to be vested in the masses as a whole. The crucial revolutionary act, therefore, would presumably be the actual taking over of control in industry by the workers themselves."[7] This notion animated the factory committees which in 1917 became an important base for the worker-Bolsheviks helping to lead their class forward to the revolutionary seizure of power. But once the Bolsheviks had come to power, this all became increasingly problematical. Burnham puts it this way:

> In the first place, the separate factories and other instruments of production were not run very well under workers' control exercised at the source; and there were even greater difficulties in the co-ordination of the efforts of various factories. It is needless to speculate on exactly why this was so. Elected committees of the workers themselves, the members of which are subject to momentary recall and who have, besides, no technical training for, or background in, the managerial tasks, do not seem to make a good job of running modern factories or mines or railroads. It is even harder for them to collaborate effectively in directing entire branches of industry or industry as a whole. Perhaps new democratic mechanisms and sufficient time to gain experience would overcome the troubles. As things actually work out, time is not granted, and the mechanisms are not available.[8]

By 1918 a battle had opened up within the Bolshevik Party and within the new Soviet republic on this question. Very quickly the majority of Bolsheviks were won to the idea that experienced specialists and authoritative managers—not democratic committees of the workers—must run the factories. At least some workers, Burnham writes, felt that "the freedom and end of privilege, which they had thought the revolution was to bring about, were giving way to a new form of class rule," and there was widespread resistance. "Lenin and Trotsky, both, in the early years of the revolution, wrote pamphlets and speeches arguing the case of the specialists, the technicians, the managers. Lenin, in his forceful way, used to declare that the manager had to be a *dictator* in the factory." The irony was obvious and ominous: "'Workers' democracy' in the state, Lenin said in effect, was to be founded upon a managerial dictatorship in the factory."[9]

Regardless of what quibbles one might have with the accuracy of Burnham's account and the adequacy of his particular interpretation, the underlying issue is posed clearly. Even a revolutionary-minded working class may sometimes not be able to clearly understand—as a whole, or in its majority—how to harmonize its radical-democratic aspirations with the practical needs of maintaining a national economy and of surviving in a complex and hostile world. To what extent can a revolutionary working-class government afford to "let the people decide" when what is at stake are fundamental questions of survival, for reasons that can be understood only by the minority of the working class that has a certain level of economic understanding and political experience—but not enough votes to carry the day? On the other hand, it is precisely such reasoning which can be utilized to justify the erosion of workers' democracy for the benefit of arrogant (and perhaps self-interested) elites. At the very least, we have identified a profound tension in the revolutionary Marxist conception of the *workers' state.*

The question is, how can such a tension be resolved? Hook, Wolfe, and Burnham found one of the simplest ways: the rejection of Marxism. But similar questions can be raised about the possibility of democracy as such (indeed, Burnham concluded by openly rejecting the possibility of "rule by the people"), and it is not clear that any resolution to such dilemmas are possible outside of the revolutionary Marxist framework. To reject the Marxist goals of rule by the working-class majority and social justice for all, to embrace some notion of permanent inequality and elite rule, does not seem to yield a better form of politics or society than that for which Lenin and Trotsky struggled. If one is committed to the belief that our political life must consist of rule by the people and that we must have a society in which the free development of each is the condition for the free development of all, then it is necessary to seek other means than those of the ex-Marxists for resolving the contradiction.

"At first the Bolshevik leaders did not try to belittle or embellish the predicament or deceive their followers," Isaac Deutscher tells us about the regime of Lenin as it contended with unbearable difficulties. "They attempted to uphold their courage and hope with words of truth." Yet as realities deteriorated, resort was increasingly made to "the soothing lie," which gradually became a cover for the crystallization of a bureaucratic dictatorship whose totalitarian potential Lenin perceived with alarm as he lay dying. And ultimately those who remained true to the ideals of revolutionary Marxism, Deutscher notes, "rose to expose and denounce the lie and to invoke against it the revolution's broken promise."[10] For those who wish to be true to revolutionary Marxist perspectives, it could be argued, a first principle is to be honest about what one knows and sees and thinks.

But one must go much further than this. A revolutionary Marxist would insist that neither faith in impersonal historic forces, nor scholarly research in libraries, nor simply speaking one's mind can resolve such contradictions as identified here. This can only come through a process of deepening understanding, practical experiment, and conscious political struggle. It is possible and necessary to learn from past mistakes as well as previous achievements, to educate the cadres and also the mass membership of the revolutionary movement in these lessons, and to move forward to learn new lessons—and at least in part to overcome old dilemmas—in continuing efforts to achieve working-class rule and a transition to socialism.[11]

This process presupposes the existence of a mass revolutionary socialist movement throughout the world. And throughout the 20th century there have been international movements claiming a Marxist orientation and a socialist goal. The problem is that the revolutionary Marxism described here has generally been a minority voice—and often an ineffectual presence—within these movements. This brings us to yet another aspect of revolutionary Marxism's failure. Such a failure is heavy with implications, and its causes are complex. While we cannot do justice to it here, it makes sense to offer the beginning of a discussion.

Revolutionary Marxism and the Socialist Movement

First of all, we should ponder the words of Rosa Luxemburg, written from a prison cell during World War I, when she stressed that socialism is not inevitable, that it "can only be won by a long chain of powerful struggles, in which the proletariat, under the leadership of the socialist movement, will learn to take hold of the rudder of society to become instead of the powerless victim of history, its conscious guide." The failure of such struggles, she warned, would be a "reversion to barbarism," which in the imperialist age would involve "depopulation, desolation, degeneration, a vast cemetery. . . ."[12] Luxemburg noted that the mass imperialist slaughter of World War I was, consequently, not only a hideous reality of the present but also disastrous for the future:

> It is the mass destruction of the European proletariat. . . . Millions of human lives were destroyed in the Vosges, in the Ardennes, in Belgium, in Poland, in the Carpathians and on the Save; millions have been hopelessly crippled. But nine-tenths of these millions come from the ranks of the working class of the cities and the farms. It is our strength, our hope that was mowed down there, day after day, before the scythe of death. They were the best, the most intelligent, the most thoroughly schooled

forces of international socialism, the bearers of the holiest traditions, of the highest heroism, the modern labor movement, the vanguard of the whole world proletariat, the workers of England, France, Belgium, Germany and Russia who are being gagged and butchered en masse. . . .

For the advance and victory of socialism we need a strong, educated, ready proletariat, masses whose strength lies in knowledge as well as in numbers. And these very masses are being decimated all over the world. The flower of our youthful strength, hundreds of thousands whose social- ist education in England, in France, in Belgium, in Germany and in Russia was the product of decades of education and propaganda, other hundreds of thousands who were ready to receive the lessons of socialism have fallen, and are rotting upon the battlefields. The fruit of the sacrifices and the toil of generations is destroyed in a few short weeks, the choic- est troops of the international proletariat are torn out by the life roots . . . . Another such war, and the hope of socialism will be buried under the ruins of imperialistic barbarism. . . . [13]

The degree of slaughter generated by the Second World War certainly exceeded that of the First, and many more hundreds of thousands of irreplaceable working-class activists—educated, trained, and seasoned in the socialist and revolutionary movements—were also destroyed. One may question whether this actually "buried the hope of socialism," as Luxemburg had put it, but one cannot deny its profound and devastating impact on the future of the revolutionary socialist movement.

In the terrible years after this First World War leading up to the Second World War (years filled with civil wars, numerous "small" wars, fascist and Nazi violence on a massive scale—rivaled by Stalinism's vio- lence against others on the Left and sometimes against its own cad- res), many hundreds of thousands of irreplaceable revolutionary leaders and activists were destroyed. In the midst of such interwar persecutions, Trotsky expressed the hope that his revolutionary followers might be able to constitute themselves as a political force in the midst of struggle, but he added that effective revolutionary parties "may also be formed considerably later, in a number of years, in the midst of the ruins and the accumulation of debris following upon the victory of fascism and war." Observing that "not a single revolutionary grouping in world history has yet experienced such terrible pressure" as those currently sharing his own orientation in 1936, he stressed that the pressure of fascism was combined with the pressure of Stalinism as well as pressures of the "democratic" imperialist countries. Trotsky concluded: "In the event of the outbreak of war, the united forces of imperialism and Stalinism will inflict upon the revolutionary internationalists immeasurably more furious persecutions than those which the generals of the Hohenzollerns [the German monarchy] together with the Social Democratic butchers inflicted in their time upon Luxemburg, Liebknecht, and their supporters."[14]

A year later, he provided a sketch of the coming global conflagration: "Since a new war of nations will start where the old one left off, the extermination of human lives and the expenditure of war materials will, from the very beginning, be several times greater than at the beginning of the last war, and will at the same time have a tendency to further rapid increase. The tempos will be more feverish, the destructive forces more grandiose, the distress of the population more unbearable. . . . Not a single country will escape the heavy consequences of the war. In pains and convulsions the whole world will change its face." Although over-optimistically projecting the overthrow of the Stalin regime by a democratic working-class political revolution, he also made some quite accurate predictions at this time: the fascist nations would be defeated; France would emerge from the war as a second-rate power; a weakened Britain would lose its empire; and the "domination over our planet will fall to the lot of the United States." Trotsky foresaw this as a "domination over decadence and destruction, over hunger, epidemics, and savagery," adding that "a protracted decay of humanity as a result of the new war is not excluded." But he also believed that "the further progress of war, with its train of destitution, savagery and despair, will of necessity not only regenerate but also develop to the extreme all the frictions, antagonisms, and centrifugal tendencies, which sooner or later will find their expression in insurrections and revolutions."[15]

So it was that while the global holocaust of 1939–1945 destroyed and devastated many people, and while it destroyed many irreplaceable revolutionaries (irreplaceable because of the decades-long process of education and experience that had shaped them), it also helped to create many new revolutionaries. But the new revolutionaries were quite simply that—*new*. Less educated and less experienced in Marxist politics, they tended to flock rather uncritically (contrary to Trotsky's hopes) to the organizations which seemed to them to represent the vision of a better future—the existing mass organizations of the working class, associated one way or another with the goal of socialism, but under the leadership either of reformist Social Democrats or of Stalinists. These were the organizations with which they were most familiar, to which they had more ready access, and which themselves had very substantial resources. Groups with Marxist orientations that had not been so utterly compromised were considerably smaller than the mass Stalinist and Social-Democratic parties, and consequently much less able to appeal to masses of leftward moving militants. The problem was that the programs and leaderships of these mass parties were not capable of bringing about socialism. Instead, the Social-Democratic and Labor parties which were swept into office in the postwar upsurge were determined (as they had been in similar situations in the 1930s) to avoid any transition to an actual socialist democracy, instead initiating a more modest program of "welfare state" social reforms—leaving the economy under the control of the corporate executives and the dynamics of capitalism. The Communist parties divided between 1) those which refrained from a struggle for power—and channeled popular revolutionary energy into non-revolutionary channels—in accordance with the "spheres of influence" agreements made between the USSR, the United States, and Britain in the Teheran and Yalta conferences, and 2) those which established—under such phrases as "people's democracy" and "socialist republics"—bureaucratic dictatorships destined, sooner or later, to become despised by their own working classes.

Essential to the revolutionary Marxist response, regarding the failure of its perspectives to guide the organized workers' movements, would be the point that a renewal of these movements must come with the influx of new working-class members who are prepared—by their own experience—to move beyond bureaucratic modes of functioning and non-revolutionary orientations. But this points out yet another failure of revolutionary Marxism.

Revolutionary Marxism and the Working Class

The tendency toward widespread bureaucratization of the workers' movement, and the effects of this bureaucratization, are questions which—as we have seen—had been a focal-point for revolutionary Marxists. But we must go beyond this to examine deeper causes for changes in the workers' movement in the advanced capitalist countries. After all, it was precisely in such countries that Marx had expected the class struggle would first bring the workers to power. How can the failure of revolutionary Marxism to sustain a mass base in such countries be explained?

The working class, from a strictly Marxist standpoint, consists of those of us who have no means of making our living except through the sale of labor-power, as opposed to making a living through the ownership of businesses. Included in this working class, then, are blue-collar and white-collar (industrial and service) employees of various skill and income levels, plus family members who are dependent on the wages and salaries of these workers, plus unemployed workers and their families (whom Marx called "the reserve army of labor"). As defined here, the working class constitutes the majority of people in an advanced capitalist society such as the United States. But a majority of such workers do not automatically or necessarily have a sense of themselves as being part of something called the working class. (In fact, being neither very rich nor very poor, most working people in the United States since the 1950s have tended to define themselves as middle class, with active encouragement from the mass media as well as mainstream politicians and academics.) They don't necessarily believe that they can best improve their conditions by joining with other workers in the struggle against the big businessmen, the capitalists, who own and run our economy. They don't automatically or necessarily see themselves as having common interests with working-class people of other countries (or even of working-class people of their own country who have different racial or ethnic backgrounds, different occupations and income levels, different sexual identities and orientations, and so on). These beliefs—(1) that there is something called the working class to which we belong, (2) that our interests are necessarily counterposed to the interests of the capitalists against whom we must struggle, (3) that we should identify with and have solidarity with *all* members of our class, and (4) that the working class should struggle for political power in order to bring about the socialist transformation of society—these beliefs have traditionally been seen as constituting the *class consciousness* of the proletariat.

This brings us to the reflections, from the mid-1960s, of a disillusioned former adherent of Marx and Lenin, the late Bertram D. Wolfe, who cites the inspiring words of "The International," the revolutionary anthem of the workers' movement: "We have been naught, We shall be all." He then quotes Henrik Brugmans: "Those who, being naught were to become all, become something—and then the whole scheme loses its tidy outlines." The fact that Wolfe apparently sees workers as being exclusively male should not distract us from the general point he was trying to make:

> For the workingman has never accepted the "mission" which Marx assigned to him, nor consented to becoming ever more miserable, impoverished, proletarianized, or pauperized. It is precisely in fighting this supposed inexorable law of his increasing impoverishment and degradation that he has displayed tireless courage, skill, solidarity, stubbornness, incapacity to know when he has been defeated, ability to enlist sympathy of much of the rest of society. The workingmen have had no stomach for becoming naught in order to prepare themselves for becoming all. It is against this reduction to naught that their real "class" struggle has been steadily directed. They have striven for political rights, for social status, for rights as workingmen, and for rights as citizens and men.[16]

Emphasizing the achievement and the impact of universal suffrage, Wolfe noted that "along with considerable political influence, labor has won a surprising measure of social security and economic improvement," involving "state regulation of economic life, the legal limitation of the working day, minimum wage, regulation of sanitary, safety, and other working conditions, legalization of the right to organize [unions], to assemble, to petition (or demand), institutionalizing of collective bargaining, and the whole astonishing sweep of social security legislation." Claiming that "in democratic countries the labor vote and the farm vote have become far more important than the banker or broker or businessman vote," Wolfe argued that the *laissez-faire* capitalism against which Marx thundered had given way to a managerial-run corporate economy interconnecting with a dramatically growing democratic government (including a mushrooming sector of government employees)—which meant that "the very boundaries between the private and the public sectors of a mixed economy tend to blur."[17]

Before dealing with the theoretically interesting aspect of Wolfe's comments, it is necessary and instructive to give attention to what—especially in hindsight—is a profound deficiency in his characterization of the political and economic system that he was describing in the 1960s. As noted earlier in this study, 20th-century Marxists were hardly fixated on an outdated conception of *laissez-faire* capitalism, but characterized modern capitalism as involving corporations led by substantial managerial strata, which were increasingly interlocked with each other and with the state. While it was fashionable in the 1950s and '60s to argue that this—combined with various welfare-state reforms—constituted some sort of post-capitalist "mixed economy," the illusory nature of this analysis had become clear by the 1980s and '90s. More than this, the limited nature of what was labeled democracy in the advanced industrial capitalist countries—the fact that there was by no means actual *rule by the people*, that real power was in the hands of multinational corporations interlocked with governmental bureaucracies and self-seeking political machines, that minimal opportunity existed for meaningful popular participation in the political process, and that voter alienation affected a majority of the electorate—had become clear to serious observers.[18]

But all of this hardly obliterates Wolfe's basic point: Rather than seeking to realize an alleged "revolutionary potential," the bulk of the workers quite naturally sought to improve their situation very much within the framework of the existing capitalist system. The struggles of the sectors of the working class organized into trade unions (never much more than one-third of the U.S. labor force) were focused on raising living standards and securing dignity on the job, combined with pressing for legislation that would extend such living standards and dignity off the job as well. Through militant actions in the 1930s and '40s, and thanks to an unprecedented period of economic expansion and prosperity after World War II, this—and not socialist revolution—was achieved in advanced industrial capitalist countries in North America and Western Europe. Nor can it be argued that there was no link between the unambiguously non-revolutionary goals espoused by the reformist leaders of the labor movement and the consciousness of masses of workers in the 1950s and '60s. Consider the 1952 comments of U.S. Trotskyist leader James P. Cannon, describing the evolution of the once left-wing United Auto Workers union, and the Congress of Industrial Organizations, led by the exsocialist Walter Reuther:

> Now what have we got today? We have eleven years of unchanged prosperity. For us that is an episode, comrades. Why do we say it is an episode? Because we took the advice of Comrade [Murry] Weiss and we studied Comrade Marx, and we think in historic terms and we know that it is not only an episode but that it is going to change and must change as a result of the contradictions of the capitalist system itself. But how does it impress the ordinary worker? All he knows is that for eleven years

he has been working more or less steadily and enjoying better wages than he knew before. Do you mean to say that has not had a conservatizing effect on his psychology? I don't think you read it correctly if you say it hasn't. . . . The privileged section of the unions, formerly the backbone of the left wing, is today the main social base of the conservative Reuther bureaucracy. They are convinced far less by Reuther's clever demagogy than by the fact that he really articulates their own conservative moods and patterns of thought.[19]

Two salient points emerge from this.

First of all, the "episode" Cannon refers to—post-World War II prosperity and the wage-and-benefits concessions that were extended to much of the working class, blended with the welfare-state social policies inaugurated by Franklin D. Roosevelt's New Deal in the 1930s but more or less maintained by Democrats and Republicans alike down through the 1970s—has quite unambiguously come to an end. Marx had, on the basis of considerable research and observation, argued that the capitalist economy runs in cycles of boom and bust, rising production and prosperity leading to overproduction and economic depression, acceleration and stagnation in the capital accumulation process. For reasons that can certainly be explained (and have been explained) within a Marxist economic framework, the U.S. economy has since the 1970s increasingly been experiencing a downturn. This contributed to an incredibly strong resurgence of conservative ideology among the upper classes, who felt a greater intolerance than ever toward the strong trade unions, government economic regulations, generous health-education-welfare and social security programs, and taxes on the corporate rich extolled in the 1965 comments of Bertram D. Wolfe. "The political right took control of most governments in the Group of Seven nations—the United States, Japan, Canada, Britain, France, Germany, and Italy," notes the maverick conservative Kevin Phillips, whose summary can hardly be improved upon:

It is true that inequality and polarization had begun intensifying in the 1970s, years in which Democratic, Liberal and Labour regimes governed in the United States, Canada and Britain, so that Ronald Reagan and Margaret Thatcher were not the initial or sole perpetrators. . . . Nevertheless, the key, which too many observers ignore . . . is that economics, politics and ideology run in broadly similar patterns, and that during the 1980s the broad pattern of government and politics in the prosperous Western nations was conservative. The result was to intensify favoritism to the upper brackets. . . . The new conservatism, which shaped the political economies of the major industrial nations, began as a move to limit big government, but by the late 1980s had revealed a less popular aspect: a developing inattentiveness to public-sector functions, economic fairness and jobs. . . .

Glorification of the unfettered marketplace soon came to include a permissiveness toward securities markets, real estate speculation and corporate reorganizations that helped bring about a level of speculative tremors and financial jitters unseen since the 1930s. . . . Meanwhile, the postwar middle-class [i.e., middle-income blue-collar/white-collar *working-class*] "social contract" broke down. . . . By 1990 corporate chief executives, whose 1980 compensation had been 30 to 40 times higher than that of their average worker, were being paid sums 130 to 140 times greater. In this climate, top executives lost compunctions about terminating blue-collar and middle class jobs in order to make their companies "competitive." They moved production to Taiwan and Mexico, liquidated company pension plans and reduced other employee benefits. Upper-middle-class professionals and vendors of private services were also able to charge rapidly escalating prices for health care, legal costs, banking services, college tuition, entertainment tickets, cable television charges and the like. . . . Financial booms that produce new fortunes [as in the Reagan-Bush period] inevitably bring record levels of debt, leverage and speculation. . . . Then the boom disappears in an implosion of assets—crumbling savings and loan institutions, banks and commercial real estate—and pain spreads to the real economy, where ordinary families live and work. Popular bitterness grows.[20]

The second point to be drawn from Cannon's remarks has to do with the way that the consciousness of the working class develops. As Bertram Wolfe insisted, there is no automatic inclination on the part of the actual "members" of the working class to embrace any kind of revolutionary mission. This was most succinctly expressed many years before by Rosa Luxemburg when she discussed "opportunism in the labor movement" (understanding opportunism to mean not outright graft and corruption, but rather a pragmatic approach to gaining reforms without any active concern for revolutionary or socialist principles):

Marxist theory offers us a reliable instrument enabling us to recognize and combat typical manifestations of opportunism. But the socialist movement [in Germany and other countries of the early 1900s] is a mass movement. Its perils are not the product of the insidious machinations of individuals and groups. They arise out of unavoidable social conditions. We cannot secure ourselves in advance against all possibilities of opportunist deviation. Such dangers can be overcome only by the movement itself—certainly with the aid of Marxist theory, but only after the dangers in question have taken tangible form in practice. *Looked at from this angle, opportunism appears to be a product and an inevitable phase of the historic development of the labor movement* [emphasis added].[21]

Under qualitatively different circumstances than those existing from 1945 to 1980, many workers in the advanced industrial countries of the late 20th century have experienced troubling and frustrating and often painful realities that were less common in that earlier "golden age," and in the face of diminishing opportunities (and therefore shrinking possibilities for "opportunist" success), a process of rethinking and recomposition has been taking place within the consciousness of those who make up the working class. There is certainly considerable unevenness in this consciousness—which we will discuss later in this chapter—but there also appears to be a greater possibility than seemed likely in the golden age that significant sectors of the working class will, as in the past, be drawn to something like the revolutionary Marxist orientation outlined in this book. The failure of revolutionary Marxism to sustain a substantial base in the working class—a failure which can best be explained in a Marxist framework—can be seen as necessarily permanent only by closing one's eyes to incredibly dynamic world realities. But this dynamism raises additional questions.

Revolutionary Marxism and Technological Progress
The comments of Bertram D. Wolfe can again be used to illuminate tough questions:

The industrial revolution that Marx studied in *Das Kapital* (the change from man, animal, wind and waterpower to steampower, and from cottage handicraft and small tool artisanship to large factories and machinofacture) was but the first of a series of industrial revolutions. It was to be followed by a second: from the age of steam to the age of electricity. And by a third, fourth, fifth and nth: conveyor belt, combustion engine, synthetic chemistry, mechanized agriculture, electronics, automation, atomic fission, atomic fusion . . . and the end of the development of the productive forces under this [capitalist] "system," whose only fixed point is that it has change built into it, is not in sight.[22]

This poses the questions of (a) whether capitalism is an inherently progressive system with an unlimited capacity for solving problems and meeting human needs through a continually developing technology, and (b) whether the conceptions and political perspectives of revolutionary Marxism—shaped in a qualitatively different material world—have become outmoded by the amazing new world created by modern technology. The way we have posed the questions, of course, is in harmony with the anti-Marxist thrust of Wolfe's argument. There is nothing wrong with doing this, but in order to squeeze more meaning out of the argument it is necessary to pose additional questions which raise doubts about his whole line of thought. For example (c), is it the case that the competitive and private profit-oriented dynamics inherent in the capitalist system negatively affect the way that technology is developed and the purposes to which it is put to use—enhancing the wealth and power of capitalist minorities in a manner that is destructive to the natural environment and to the needs of society as a whole, at the same time undermining the power and dignity of the working-class majority?

Historian Paul Kennedy, an honest scholar who seems liberal but hardly Marxist, has recently surveyed the global spread and impact of the never-ending Industrial Revolution by commenting that "new factories, assembly plants, road systems, airports, and housing complexes not only reduce the amount of natural land but contribute to the demand for more energy (especially electricity) and more automobiles and trucks, infrastructure, foodstuffs, paper and packaging, cement, steel ores, and so on. All of this increases the ecological damage: more polluted rivers and dead lakes, smog-covered cities, industrial waste, soil erosion, and devastated forests litter the earth." More than this, "human economic activities are creating a dangerous 'greenhouse effect' of global warming, with consequences for the earth's entire ecosystem and for the way of life of rich and poor societies alike." Kennedy judges that "piecemeal international agreements" are unlikely to safeguard "the future of the earth's thin film of life."[23]

New advances in our never-ending Industrial Revolution, Kennedy shows us, may also further tilt wealth and power from the poor nations to the rich ones: "As with global finance, biotechnology, and multinationals, we are once again looking at a technology-driven revolution that could keep poorer countries at the bottom of the heap, or weaken them further." More than this, amazing technological developments in manufacturing, communications, transportation, and the like enable multinational corporations to exercise greater flexibility at the expense of the world's labor forces—"multinational corporations in certain industries, already switching production from one country to another according to differentiated labor costs, will gain further advantage of assessing whether developing-world wages are greater or less than the [industrial] robot's 'costs' in the automated factory back home." More than this, "any government which offends international finance's demand for unrestricted gain—by increasing personal taxes, for example, or by raising fees in financial transactions—will find its capital has fled and its currency weakened. . . . If, say, a French Socialist government is conscientiously attempting to provide better schools, health care, housing, and public utilities for its citizenry, by what means can it raise the necessary funds without alarming international investors who may not be at all interested in the well-being of those citizens but merely in their own profits?" Kennedy reminds us of the point that Wolfe seems to have forgotten: "The rational market, by its very nature, is not concerned with social justice and fairness." And he makes an additional point that dovetails with Kevin Phillips's observation: "Skilled blue-collar employees—the core of the traditional high-percapita-income U.S. workforce, and the backbone of the Democratic Party—have lost jobs in the millions as American firms wilted under international competition and relocated industrial production to other countries with lower labor costs."[24]

What remains of Bertram Wolfe's argument is a point that still raises questions about *the viability of the revolutionary Marxist strategic orientation in the face of technological "advances,"* although from a gloomier angle than he might have accepted. One question: Is there time to bring about socialism before the environment of the planet is ruined? But also there are other unanswered questions. For example, the development of technology has greatly enhanced the power of capital and eroded the traditional industrial proletariat, greatly weakening the power of the working class as a whole—although ongoing industrial development, largely thanks to the multinational corporations' "globalization" strategy, has created more extensive proletarianized layers of the international labor force than ever before. Still, it is not clear in what ways the balance

of power can be tipped back in the favor of the working-class majority. Some left-wing analysts—in the spirit of the *Communist Manifesto*'s
call for workers of all countries to unite—have emphasized the need to
organize workers on an international scale in order to limit the ability of
international capitalism to erode working-class living standards of the
various regions, and to prevent the corporations from undermining the
various national labor movements by pitting workers of different countries against each other. But achieving the international organization of
the working class is easier said than done, and it brings us to another of
revolutionary Marxism's failures.

Revolutionary Marxism and Uneven Development

A key aspect of the failure of revolutionary Marxism was identified by
Marx himself in 1872. Reflecting on the defeat of history's first working-class government, he commented that "the Paris Commune . . . fell
because a great revolutionary movement corresponding to that supreme
rising of the Paris proletariat did not arise in all centers, in Berlin,
Madrid, and elsewhere."[25]

This has happened more than once. But if socialism can only triumph
on a world scale, and if no workers' revolution in a single country can
escape degeneration or collapse (or both) without workers' revolutions
spreading to other countries, and if the ability of the working class simply to turn back the assaults of today's global capitalism is dependent
on the effective international organization of the working class, then
such limitations on the practical realization of working-class solidarity throws the entire strategic perspective of revolutionary Marxism in
doubt. The lack of practical solidarity is rooted, to a large extent, in the
uneven development of the working class. The experiences of workers
in the United States, for example, are profoundly different from those
of workers in Brazil, and the experience of workers in Russia are different from those in Korea, South Africa, and Sweden. All of these workers share certain things in common, but there are significant differences
which result in variation in the forms and levels of class consciousness,
class organization, and class struggle in each country.

In fact, *within* each country there is also unevenness in the experience, consciousness, and struggle of various sectors of the working class.
This unevenness can be traced along occupational lines and geographical
lines, and especially along the lines of race, ethnicity, and gender, as well

as age, sexual orientation, and so on. In the United States during the 1960s and early '70s—when there was relative economic prosperity, a conservatized labor movement, and a blurred notion of class (most people seeing themselves as middle class)—masses of people were moved into political and social struggles not by notions of class, but by important issues of civil liberties and civil rights, war, the environment, race, gender, and so on, having to do with seemingly "non-class" issues and identities. More recently, many "post-modernist" and post-Marxist radical theorists have argued that such non-class "identities" (and questions of culture rather than economics) should be our focal-point, that these "identities"—which define the actuality of each human individual in our society as much as does class, and which often more decisively shape the consciousness of the individual (and the perceptions of others)—are generated by cultural factors that are relatively autonomous from economics.

Those continuing to embrace the revolutionary socialist orientation as developed by Marx, on the other hand, believe that the fundamental class relationships arising from the structure of the economy—the basis for human subsistence—do not obliterate but instead *permeate and connect* all other forms of identity and oppression which exist in capitalist society. The interpenetration of the various dimensions of human identity and relationships must be grasped in order to achieve a more complete understanding of social dynamics: an understanding of the distinct dynamics of sexual oppression, of gender oppression, of racial oppression are essential for grasping the social totality, but this must be combined with an understanding of class oppression if we want to illuminate the realities of race, sexuality, gender, and class. "The class dimension *is* privileged, if only circumstantially and politically (not analytically)," notes Marxist ethnographer Roger Lancaster, "and by this index: class exploitation necessarily produces an exploiting minority, and an exploited majority. The same cannot be said of other dimensions of oppression. Whether one is seeking to reform or to overthrow *any* system of exploitation, the dynamics of class and class resistance remain, in Marx's sense, strategic and paramount."[26] The fact remains, however, that there is an "unevenness" in the consciousness—and in the circumstances—of the various sectors of the working class which facilitates the fragmentation of the working class and the defeat of each of the fragments.

Earlier in this study we noted the revolutionary explosiveness of uneven *and combined* development within the cultural life and political economies of various countries. To the extent that there is uneven *but not combined* development within the working class inside a country and among the working classes of various countries, the viability of the revolutionary Marxist strategic orientation will be open to question. Only if a "combining" process takes place—through education, organization, and struggle—can this orientation be realized. This is by no means a new insight. The very same 1872 speech by Marx—about the International Workingmen's Association, the First International—from which we quoted at the beginning of this section focuses precisely on this: "Citizens, let us think of the fundamental principle of the International, solidarity! It is by establishing this vivifying principle on a strong basis, among all the working people of all countries, that we shall achieve the great goal we have set ourselves."[27]

While there has been a pattern of educational and organizational efforts to overcome the effects of this uneven development of the working class, however, there has also very clearly been a pattern of breakdown and disappointment. In the 1990s the international organizations of the working class seem weaker than ever. If anything, present trends within capitalism itself seem to be creating bases on which bridges can be built to overcome the uneven development of the various working classes: the globalization of capitalist production and distribution operations, the advances of communication and transportation technologies, and the commercial creation of common elements of a mass culture on a global scale. On the other hand, while powerful elements of revolutionary working-class consciousness may be latent among the workers of all countries, there are also (and always have been) powerful countervailing tendencies working to erode or prevent the crystallization of such consciousness. It is unlikely that we will ever see the automatic or "inevitable" or spontaneous resurgence of the working-class consciousness which is so central to the revolutionary Marxist perspective. History has shown that a considerable amount of conscious effort and painstaking work are required to evoke the latent class-consciousness of the working class to make it possible for the workers of all countries (or even within a particular country) to unite.

FROM MARX TO GRAMSCI   141

Conclusion

To utilize revolutionary Marxist tools to explain why revolutionary Marxism failed to triumph in the 20th century does not magically whisk away the fact that its project is in a shambles. The fact remains that capitalism continues to exist without having eliminated class oppression and consequent class struggles, and it continues to generate innumerable problems which raise some doubts about the future possibility of democracy, civilization, and human existence.

It is not possible to establish here whether the revolutionary Marxist orientation can be translated into a relevant plan of action, or can be transcended by something more adequate. But as one of the most comprehensive and intellectually powerful prescriptions for social change ever developed, the perspective elaborated in various ways by Marx and Engels, Luxemburg, Lenin, Trotsky, and Gramsci adds up to an approach to reality and a body of thought which is irreplaceable for those wishing to come to grips with the past and the future.

Notes

1.   One example of the conservative "fall of communism" genre is Kenneth Murphy's extended anti-socialist polemic *Retreat from the Finland Station, Moral Odysseys in the Breakdown of Communism* (New York: The Free Press, 1992), which was touted as a tour de force updating the less ideologically tidy, and more honest, 1950 anti-Communist classic *The God That Failed*, edited by Richard Crossman (New York: Harper and Row, 1950) and "completing" Edmund Wilson's 1940 classic study of Marxism, *To the Finland Station, A Study in the Writing and Acting of History* (New York: Farrar, Strauss and Giroux, 1972). The author—who is no Edmund Wilson—explains that "violent, destructive, greedy, fallible as we are, men demand a vision of harmony and order," namely, the "debased people" and "debased faith" of socialism, but that "socialism demands the construction of a tyranny far more oppressive than the one it was designed to replace"—though at long last the collapse of Communist Party regimes has spelled the death of "the totalitarian pretence, the claims of Marx and Lenin and their myriad followers in this century," and so on (pp. x, 133, 380). A left-wing variant of the "fall of communism" genre— seeking to retrieve socialist hopes while rejecting the alleged revolutionary folly of Bolshevism—is offered by many of the essays in Robin Blackburn, ed., *After the Fall, The Failure of Communism and the Future of Socialism* (London: Verso, 1991), which almost appears to react to the rottenness of Stalinism as if it were a revelation. Illuminating analyses of the bankruptcy of the Stalinized

variant of "Communism," which demonstrate the value of the revolutionary Marxist orientation (and the gulf dividing that orientation from Stalinism), were provided at least as early as the 1930s and are being added to down to the present; see: C. L. R. James, *World Revolution 1917–1936, The Rise and Fall of the Communist International* (Atlantic Highlands, N.J.: Humanities Press, 1993; originally published 1937); Victor Serge, *Russia Twenty Years After* (Atlantic Highlands, N.J.: Humanities Press, 1996; originally published 1937); Marilyn Vogt-Downey, ed., *The USSR 1987–1991: Marxist Perspectives* (Atlantic Highlands, N.J.: Humanities Press, 1993); and Thomas Barrett, ed., *China, Marxism and Democracy: Selections from "October Review"* (Atlantic Highlands, N.J.: Humanities Press, 1996).

2.   One of the earliest exposés is Upton Sinclair's classic, *The Brass Check, A Study in American Journalism* (Long Beach, Calif.: Published by Author, 1928; first ed. 1920). More recent studies include: Robert Cirino, *Don't Blame the People: How the News Media Use Bias, Distortion and Censorship to Manipulate Public Opinion* (New York: Vintage Books, 1972); Erik Barnouw, *The Sponsor, Notes on a Modern Potentate* (Oxford: Oxford University Press, 1978); Herbert J. Gans, *Deciding What's News: A Study of CBS Evening News, NBC Evening News, "Newsweek," and "Time"* (New York: Vintage Books, 1980); Ben H. Bagdikian, *The Media Monopoly* (Boston: Beacon Press, 1982); Edward S. Herman and Noam Chomsky, *Manufacturing Consent, The Political Economy of the Mass Media* (New York: Pantheon Books, 1988); Mark Hertsgaard, *On Bended Knee: The Press and the Reagan Presidency* (New York: Schocken Books, 1989); Eric Alterman, *Sound and Fury: The Washington Punditocracy and the Collapse of American Politics* (New York: HarperCollins, 1992).

3.   Sidney Hook, *Marx and the Marxists, An Ambiguous Legacy* (Princeton: D. Van Nostrand Co., 1955), p. 107.

4.   Bertram D. Wolfe, *Marxism: One Hundred Years in the Life of a Doctrine* (New York: Dell Publishing Co., 1967), p. 207.

5.   Hook, *Marx and the Marxists*, pp. 31, 32.

6.   Wolfe, *Marxism*, p. 207. A similar approach is elaborated by neo-conservative Thomas Sowell, who asserts: "The supreme irony of Marxism was that a fundamentally humane and egalitarian creed was so dominated by a bookish perspective that it became blind to facts and deaf to humanity and freedom" (Thomas Sowell, *Marxism, Philosophy and Economics* [New York: William Morrow, 1985], p. 221).

7.   James Burnham, *The Managerial Revolution* (New York: John Day Co., 1941), p. 212. Later works dealing, from different standpoints, with these questions are Carmen Sirianni, *Workers Control and Socialist Democracy, The Soviet Experience* (London; Verso, 1982), and—more satisfactory—S. A. Smith, *Red Petrograd, Revolution in the Factories 1917–18* (Cambridge: Cambridge University Press, 1985).

8.   Burnham, *Managerial Revolution*, pp. 212–213.

9. Ibid., p. 214. Among the worthwhile accounts of the Russian Revolution that are relevant to this discussion are those found in: Victor Serge, *Year One of the Russian Revolution* (Chicago: Holt, Rinehart and Winston, 1972); William Henry Chamberlin, *The Russian Revolution*, 2 vols. (New York: Grossett and Dunlap, 1965); Robert Service, *The Russian Revolution 1900–1927* (London: Macmillan, 1986); Daniel H. Kaiser, ed., *The Workers' Revolution in Russia 1917, the View from Below* (Cambridge: Cambridge University Press, 1987); Ronald Suny and Arthur Adams, eds., *The Russian Revolution and the Bolshevik Victory* (Lexington, Mass.: D.C. Heath and Co., 1990); Lewis H. Siegelbaum, *Soviet State and Society Between Revolutions, 1918–1929* (Cambridge: Cambridge University Press, 1992); John Rees, "In Defense of October," *International Socialism*, August 1991.

10. Isaac Deutscher, *The Prophet Unarmed, Trotsky: 1921–1929* (London: Oxford University Press, 1959), pp. 2, 3.

11. Among the works relevant to this question are: Richard R. Fagen, Carmen Diana Deere, and Jose Luis Coraggio, eds., *Transition and Development: Problems of Third World Socialism* (New York: Monthly Review Press, 1986); Paul Le Blanc, *Workers and Revolution: A Comparative Study of Bolshevik Russia and Sandinist Nicaragua* (Ann Arbor: University Microfilms International, 1989); Harry E. Vanden and Gary Prevost, *Democracy and Socialism in Sandinista Nicaragua* (Boulder, Colo.: Lynne Rienner Publishers, 1993); John Brentlinger, *The Best of What We Are: Reflections on the Nicaraguan Revolution* (Amherst: University of Massachusetts Press, 1995). Received too late for consideration in this study, but of obvious relevance, is a massive work by István Mészáros, *Beyond Capital, Towards a Theory of Transition* (New York: Monthly Review Press, 1995).

12. "The Junius Pamphlet: The Crisis in German Social Democracy," *Rosa Luxemburg Speaks*, ed. Mary-Alice Waters (New York: Pathfinder Press, 1970), p. 269.

13. Ibid., pp. 326–327.

14. "The Way Out," *Writings of Leon Trotsky 1934–35*, second edition, ed. George Breitman and Bev Scott (New York: Pathfinder Press, 1974), p. 81.

15. "On the Threshold of a New World War," *Writings of Leon Trotsky, 1936–37*, ed. Naomi Allen and George Breitman (New York: Pathfinder Press, 1978), pp. 391–392, 396.

16. Wolfe, *Marxism*, pp. 317, 333.

17. Ibid., pp. 331, 332.

18. Some of these points are made in such conservative works as Garry Wills, *Confessions of a Conservative* (Middlesex, England: Penguin Books, 1980), and James Burnham, *The Machiavellians, Defenders of Freedom* (New York: John Day Co., 1943); others by the non-leftist political philosopher Hannah Arendt in *On Revolution* (London: Penguin Books, 1990), pp. 215–281, and *Crises of the Republic* (New York: Harcourt Brace Jovanovich, 1972), as well as other political theorists as Peter Bachrach in *The Theory of Democratic Elitism, A Critique*

(Boston: Little, Brown and Co., 1967), and Carole Pateman in *Participation and Democratic Theory* (Cambridge: Cambridge University Press, 1970); also see M. I. Finley, *Democracy Ancient and Modern*, revised edition (New Brunswick, N.J.: Rutgers University Press, 1985). Persuasive anarchist and Marxist analyses are presented, respectively, in Paul Goodman, "Getting into Power," *Seeds of Liberation*, ed. Paul Goodman (New York: George Braziller, 1964), pp. 433–444, and Paul Baran and Paul Sweezy, *Monopoly Capital, An Essay on the American Economic and Social Order* (New York: Monthly Review Press, 1968). Substantial factual analyses—from different perspectives—can be found in: Walter Dean Burnham, *The Crisis in American Politics* (Oxford: Oxford University Press, 1977); Tom Bottomore and Robert J. Brym, eds., *The Capitalist Class, An International Study* (New York: New York University Press, 1989); G. William Domhoff, *Who Rules America Now? A View for the '80s* (New York: Simon and Schuster, 1983); Michael Parenti, *Democracy for the Few* (New York: St. Martin's, 1977); Edgar Wilson, *A Very British Miracle: The Failure of Thatcherism* (London: Pluto Press, 1992); Kevin Phillips, *The Politics of Rich and Poor: Wealth and the American Electorate in the Reagan Aftermath* (New York: Harper Collins, 1991); Michael D. Yates, *Longer Hours, Fewer Jobs: Employment and Unemployment in the United States* (New York: Monthly Review Press, 1994).

19.   James P. Cannon, *Speeches to the Party* (New York: Pathfinder Press, 1973), pp. 47, 58. For additional information on the U.S. working class that Cannon was discussing, see: Andrew Levison, *The Working Class Majority* (New York: Coward, McCann and Geohegan, 1974); Harry Braverman, *Labor and Monopoly Capital, The Degradation of Labor in the Twentieth Century* (New York: Monthly Review Press, 1974); John C. Leggett, *Class, Race, and Labor: Working-Class Consciousness in Detroit* (London: Oxford University Press, 1971); James R. Green, *The World of the Worker, Labor in Twentieth-Century America* (New York: Hill and Wang, 1980); James Green, ed., *Workers' Struggles, Past and Present: A "Radical America" Reader* (Philadelphia: Temple University Press, 1984); Michael Goldfield, *The Decline of Organized Labor in the United States* (Chicago: University of Chicago Press, 1987); Kim Moody, *An Injury to All, The Decline of American Unionism* (London: Verso, 1988); Janet Zandy, ed., *Liberating Memory, Our Work and Our Working-Class Consciousness* (New Brunswick, N.J.: Rutgers University Press, 1994).

20.   Kevin Phillips, *Boiling Point: Democrats, Republicans and the Decline of Middle-Class Prosperity* (New York: HarperCollins, 1993), pp. xxii, xxiii–xxiv, 36; also see Joyce Kolko, *Restructuring the World Economy* (New York: Pantheon Press, 1988); Bennett Harrison and Barry Bluestone, *The Great U-Turn, Corporate Restructuring and the Polarizing of America* (New York: Basic Books, 1988); Paul Sweezy and Harry Magdoff, *The Irreversible Crisis* (New York: Monthly Review Press, 1988); Ernest Mandel, *Long Waves of Capitalist Development, A Marxist Interpretation*, Revised Edition (London: Verso, 1995).

21. "Organizational Question of Russian Social Democracy," *Rosa Luxemburg Speaks*, p. 129.
22. Wolfe, *Marxism*, pp. 330–331.
23. Paul Kennedy, *Preparing for the Twenty-First Century* (New York: Random House, 1993), pp. 97, 105, 121.
24. Phillips., pp. 56, 59, 91, 93–94.
25. "The Hague Congress," in Karl Marx and Frederick Engels, *Selected Works*, Vol. 2 (Moscow: Progress Publishers, 1973), p. 294.
26. Roger N. Lancaster, *Life Is Hard: Machismo, Danger, and the Intimacy of Power in Nicaragua* (Berkeley: University of California Press, 1992), p. 282. Works giving attention to stratification, divisions, and special oppression within the working class, which nonetheless highlight the centrality of class, include: William Form, *Divided We Stand: Working-Class Stratification in America* (Urbana: University of Illinois Press, 1985); Martin Oppenheimer, *White Collar Politics* (New York: Monthly Review Press, 1985); Melvin M. Leiman, *The Political Economy of Racism, A History* (London: Pluto Press, 1993); Teresa Amott, *Caught in the Crisis: Women and the U.S. Economy Today* (New York: Monthly Review Press, 1993); Trevor Blackwell and Jeremy Seabrook, *A World Still to Win: The Reconstruction of the Post-War Working Class* (London: Faber and Faber, 1985); Harry Braverman, "The Making of the U.S. Working Class," *Monthly Review*, November 1994; John Hinshaw and Paul Le Blanc, eds., *U.S. Labor in the Twentieth Century, Studies in Working-Class Fragmentation and Insurgency* (Atlantic Highlands, N.J.: Humanities Press, 1997 forthcoming).
27. Marx, "The Hague Congress," p. 293.

PART TWO:

READINGS, FROM MARX TO GRAMSCI

Marx and Engels*

Karl Marx (1818–1883) and Frederick Engels (1820–1895) were born in what would soon become Germany, sons respectively of a well-to-do lawyer and a prosperous textile manufacturer. As youths and university students, both were profoundly influenced by the ideas of the Enlightenment and Romanticism, as well as the radical-democratic political thought generated by the French Revolution and the immense changes that were being generated by the Industrial Revolution. As they sought to understand the world around them, they drew from German philosophical currents (especially those developing radical interpretations of G. W. F. Hegel, such as Ludwig Feuerbach), French political and historical works, and the studies in political economy advanced in Britain by Adam Smith and David Ricardo. Utopian socialists such as Charles Fourier, Claude Henri Saint-Simon, and Robert Owen were also an important influence. The two young men were most profoundly affected by the rise of an organized working-class movement—the Chartists, who struggled to extend the right to vote to the working class in England, early efforts at trade unionism in various countries, numerous reform activities, radical and socialist study groups, and so forth.

In the late 1840s they joined the predominantly working-class Communist League (with members in a number of European countries), for which they agreed to write a manifesto to explain the group's general outlook and political orientation. This was the *Communist Manifesto* (READING #1), which appeared just as a revolutionary upheaval swept through Europe. Diverse currents of revolutionary nationalism, liberal constitutionalism, radical democracy, and working-class social reform animated this mass upsurge, which seemed on the verge of sweeping away a variety of monarchist, semi-feudal, reactionary obstacles to "progress."

Instead, the revolutionary wave broke apart as liberal capitalist forces turned against the radicalizing working class. In their 1850 "Address of the Central Committee to the Communist League," in Engels's *Revolution and Counter-Revolution in Germany*, and in Marx's *The Eighteenth Brumaire of Louis Bonaparte*, the two comrades sought to draw the lessons of this experience, in which they were very active participants. The Communist League collapsed under the weight of the defeated revolutions; Marx and Engels—who had formed an intimate political-intellectual partnership lasting for the rest of their lives—concluded that, since industrial capitalism was obviously going through a period of powerful expansion, many more years would pass before a working-class movement could arise that would be capable of bringing about socialism. Marx turned his attention to economic studies of capitalism—a project to which Engels lent considerable intellectual and (with his profits from running a capitalist enterprise) financial support. The result was a massive feat of scholarship, yielding *A Critique of Political Economy* (1859), culminating in 1867 with the first volume of Marx's masterwork, *Capital*, which Engels was able to summarize in a review for the English-speaking public (READING #2).

The early 1860s saw a resurgence of working-class organizations and radical currents throughout Europe and North America, many of which joined in the International Workingmen's Association (IWA, later known as the First International) in 1864. Marx became a central figure and guiding spirit within the IWA, translating the perspectives of the *Communist Manifesto* into a form relevant to non-revolutionary times (READING #3). In 1871, however, an unexpected revolutionary upsurge in France created the world's first working-class government, the short-lived Paris Commune. Marx defended the Commune and sought to draw the lessons taught by its life and death in *The Civil War in France*, advancing key ideas on the state and revolution which would be elaborated especially by Lenin in future years. The defeat of the Commune and the sharp increase of government repression throughout Europe—combined with controversies within the IWA dividing trade union moderates, revolutionary socialists, and anarchists—resulted in the IWA being moved to the United States; after Marx's militant explanation of the need for revolutionary internationalism at its 1872 congress (READING #4), it passed out of existence as a force in Europe.

In the last decade of his life, Marx was forced to cope with the precipitous decline of his wife's health and his own. Nonetheless, he labored to complete the final two volumes of *Capital*, at the same time initiating important new research on Asia and Russia, as well as in anthropology, plus assisting Engels with the popularization contained in the 1877–78 polemic *Herr Eugen Dühring's Revolution in Science (Anti-Dühring)*, portions of which provided the basis for Engels's important short book *Socialism: Utopian and Scientific* (1880). Throughout these years Marx also maintained an extensive and intensive correspondence with working-class and revolutionary activists and organizations throughout Europe and North America. At certain points he made significant interventions in debates and discussions—for example, in his "Critique of the Gotha Program" (1875) of the newly united German Social-Democratic Party, and in his 1881 response to Vera Zasulich on issues facing Russian revolutionaries.

After Marx's death, Engels sought to continue his work—bringing out the second and third volumes of *Capital* (1885, 1894) and producing *The Origin of the Family, Private Property and the State* (1888), among other works which helped to explain and popularize the approach, analyses, and political orientation which Marx and he had developed. Through a voluminous correspondence and personal contacts he also helped to strengthen the growing labor and socialist movements in a variety of countries, which in 1889 established the Socialist International (the Second International). The general orientation of this new International was essentially Marxist; although as its member parties gained ground in Europe there was a growing tendency toward moderating or diluting the revolutionary politics essential to the orientation of both Marx and Engels. Despite tensions with some of his comrades over this, Engels was optimistic that the ongoing impact of capitalist oppression and experience of class struggle would win working-class majorities throughout the world to the revolutionary socialist orientation he had shared with Marx.

READING #1: *Communist Manifesto* (excerpts)—1848
READING #2: "Marx's *Capital*"—1868
READING #3: "Inaugural Address of the International Workingmen's Association"—1864
READING #4: "The Hague Congress of the IWA"—1872

---

* A NOTE ON A CONFUSING TERM: Marx and Engels sometimes utilize the term "middle class," which can be confusing. Originally this referred to capitalists who once occupied a social position between the upper class of landed aristocrats

and the less fortunate lower classes. When Marx and Engels occasionally used the term "middle class," they meant capitalists.

Later some attached the term "middle class" to the intermediate strata of small shopkeepers, self-employed artisans, and independent craftsmen sandwiched between the new capitalist upper class and the proletarian lower class; sometimes peasants, farmers, "professionals" and white-collar employees are also placed in the "middle class" grab bag. The occasional and loose mention by Marx and Engels of the "lower middle class" refers to the intermediate petty-bourgeois strata.

More recently in the United States the term "middle class" has been used to identify those who sell their labor-power for wages or salaries to make a living and are neither very rich nor very poor—which includes most of the U.S. working class. Marx and Engels unambiguously placed these social layers in the proletariat and did not refer to them as "middle class" (a term they reserved for those who made a living through the ownership of businesses).

Regardless of what Marx and Engels thought, however, studies show that as early as 1940 between 79 and 88 percent of the U.S. population *regarded* themselves as middle class (as cited in Stanislaw Ossowski, *Class Structure in the Social Consciousness* (London: Routledge and Kegan Paul, 1979), p. 103—and most of these working people would understandably be put off by criticisms of the "middle class." On the other hand, according to Federal Reserve figures of 1989, 20 percent of U.S. households own 80 percent of the country's wealth, with the top 1 percent of the households owning 40 percent of the wealth (*New York Times*, April 17, 1995).

The following readings suggest that the sympathies of Marx and Engels would have been with the 80 percent of Americans who have only 20 percent of wealth—whom the two revolutionaries would have described not as middle class but, in the words of the *Communist Manifesto*, as proletarianized sectors of the population capable of becoming a "self-conscious, independent movement of the immense majority, in the interests of the immense majority."

READING #1

Marx and Engels
Manifesto of the Communist Party
(excerpts)

A spectre is haunting Europe—the spectre of communism. All the powers of old Europe have entered into a holy alliance to exorcise this spectre: pope and czar, Metternich and Guizot, French Radicals and German police spies.

Where is the party in opposition that has not been decried as communistic by its opponents in power? Where the opposition that has not hurled back the branding reproach of communism, against the more advanced opposition parties, as well as against its reactionary adversaries?

Two things result from this fact.

I. Communism is already acknowledged by all European powers to be itself a power.

II. It is high time that communists should openly, in the face of the whole world, publish their views, their aims, their tendencies, and meet this nursery tale of the spectre of communism with a Manifesto of the party itself.

To this end, communists of various nationalities have assembled in London, and sketched the following Manifesto, to be published in the English, French, German, Italian, Flemish, and Danish languages.

1. Bourgeois and Proletarians*

The history of all hitherto existing society** is the history of class struggles.

Freeman and slave, patrician and plebeian, lord and serf, guildmaster*** and journeyman, in a word, oppressor and oppressed, stood in constant opposition to one another, carried on an uninterrupted, now hidden, now open fight, a fight that each time ended either in a revolutionary

---

* By bourgeoisie is meant the class of modern capitalists, owners of the means of social production and employers of wage-labor. By proletariat, the class of modern wage-laborers who, having no means of production of their own, are reduced to selling their labor-power in order to live. [Note by Engels to the English edition of 1888.]

** That is, all written history. In 1847, the prehistory of society, the social organization existing previous to recorded history, was all but unknown. Since then, Haxthausen discovered common ownership of land in Russia, Maurer proved it to be the social foundation from which all Teutonic races started in history, and by and by village communities were found to be, or to have been, the primitive form of society everywhere from India to Ireland. The inner organization of this primitive communistic society was laid bare, in its typical form, by Morgan's crowning discovery of the true nature of the gens and its relation to the tribe. With the dissolution of these primeval communities, society begins to be differentiated into separate and finally antagonistic classes. I have attempted to retrace this process of dissolution in "The Origin of the Family, Private Property and the State." [Note by Engels to the English edition of 1888.]

***Guildmaster, that is, a full member of a guild, a master within, not a head of a guild. [Note by Engels to the English edition of 1888.]

reconstitution of society at large or in the common ruin of the contending classes.

In the earlier epochs of history, we find almost everywhere a complicated arrangement of society into various orders, a manifold gradation of social rank. In ancient Rome we have patricians, knights , plebeians, slaves; in the Middle Ages, feudal lords, vassals, guildmasters, journeymen, apprentices, serfs; in almost all of these classes, again, subordinate gradations.

The modern bourgeois society that has sprouted from the ruins of feudal society has not done away with class antagonisms. It has but established new classes, new conditions of oppression, new forms of struggle in place of the old ones.

Our epoch, the epoch of the bourgeoisie, possesses, however, this distinctive feature: it has simplified the class antagonisms. Society as a whole is more and more splitting up into two great hostile camps, into two great classes directly facing each other: bourgeoisie and proletariat.

From the serfs of the Middle Ages sprang the chartered burghers of the earliest towns. From these burgesses the first elements of the bourgeoisie were developed.

The discovery of America, the rounding of the Cape, opened up fresh ground for the rising bourgeoisie. The East Indian and Chinese markets, the colonization of America, trade with the colonies, the increase in the means of exchange and in commodities generally, gave to commerce, to navigation, to industry, an impulse never before known, and thereby, to the revolutionary element in the tottering feudal society, a rapid development.

The feudal system of industry, under which industrial production was monopolized by closed guilds, now no longer sufficed for the growing wants of the new markets. The manufacturing system took its place. The guildmasters were pushed on one side by the manufacturing middle class; division of labor between the different corporate guilds vanished in the face of division of labor in each single workshop.

Meantime the markets kept ever growing, the demand ever rising. Even manufacture no longer sufficed. Thereupon, steam and machinery revolutionized industrial production. The place of manufacture was taken by the giant, modern industry, the place of the industrial middle class, by industrial millionaires, the leaders of whole industrial armies, the modern bourgeois.

Modern industry has established the world market, for which the discovery of America paved the way. This market has given an immense development to commerce, to navigation, to communication by land. This development has, in its turn, reacted on the extension of industry; and in proportion as industry, commerce, navigation, railways extended, in the same proportion the bourgeoisie developed, increased its capital, and pushed into the background every class handed down from the Middle Ages.

We see, therefore, how the modern bourgeoisie is itself the product of a long course of development, of a series of revolutions in the modes of production and of exchange.

Each step in the development of the bourgeoisie was accompanied by a corresponding political advance of that class. An oppressed class under the sway of the feudal nobility, an armed and self-governing association in the medieval commune;* here independent urban republic (as in Italy and Germany), there taxable "third estate" of the monarchy (as in France), afterwards, in the period of manufacture proper, serving either the semifeudal or the absolute monarchy as a counterpoise against the nobility, and, in fact, cornerstone of the great monarchies in general, the bourgeoisie has at last, since the establishment of modern industry and of the world market, conquered for itself, in the modern representative state, exclusive political sway. The executive of the modern state is but a committee for managing the common affairs of the whole bourgeoisie.

The bourgeoisie, historically, has played a most revolutionary part.

The bourgeoisie, wherever it has gotten the upper hand, has put an end to all feudal, patriarchal, idyllic relations. It has pitilessly torn asunder the motley feudal ties that bound man to his "natural superiors," and has left remaining no other nexus between man and man than naked self-interest, than callous "cash payment." It has drowned the most heavenly ecstasies of religious fervor, of chivalrous enthusiasm, of philistine

---

* "Commune" was the name taken, in France, by the nascent towns even before they had conquered from their feudal lords and masters local self-government and political rights as the "Third Estate." Generally speaking, for the economic development of the bourgeoisie, England is here taken as the typical country; for its political development, France. [*Note by Engels to the English edition of 1888.*]

This was the name given their urban communities by the townsmen of Italy and France, after they had purchased or wrested their initial rights of self-government from their feudal lords. [*Note by Engels to the German edition of 1890.*]

sentimentalism, in the icy water of egotistical calculation. It has resolved personal worth into exchange value, and in place of the numberless indefeasible chartered freedoms, has set up that single, unconscionable freedom—free trade. In one word, for exploitation, veiled by religious and political illusions, it has substituted naked, shameless, direct, brutal exploitation.

The bourgeoisie has stripped of its halo every occupation hitherto honored and looked up to with reverent awe. It has converted the physician, the lawyer, the priest, the poet, the man of science, into its paid wage-laborers.

The bourgeoisie has torn away from the family its sentimental veil and has reduced the family relation to a mere money relation.

The bourgeoisie has disclosed how it came to pass that the brutal display of vigor in the Middle Ages, which Reactionists so much admire, found its fitting complement in the most slothful indolence. It has been the first to show what man's activity can bring about. It has accomplished wonders far surpassing Egyptian pyramids, Roman aqueducts, and Gothic cathedrals; it has conducted expeditions that put in the shade all former exoduses of nations and crusades.

The bourgeoisie cannot exist without constantly revolutionizing the instruments of production, and thereby the relations of production, and with them the whole relations of society. Conservation of the old modes of production in unaltered form was, on the contrary, the first condition of existence for all earlier industrial classes. Constant revolutionizing of production, uninterrupted disturbance of all social conditions, everlasting uncertainty and agitation distinguish the bourgeois epoch from all earlier ones. All fixed, fast-frozen relations, with their train of ancient and venerable prejudices and opinions, are swept away, all new-formed ones become antiquated before they can ossify. All that is solid melts into air, all that is holy is profaned, and man is at last compelled to face, with sober senses, his real conditions of life and his relations with his kind.

The need of a constantly expanding market for its products chases the bourgeoisie over the whole surface of the globe. It must nestle everywhere, settle everywhere, establish conditions everywhere.

The bourgeoisie has, through its exploitation of the world market, given a cosmopolitan character to production and consumption in every country. To the great chagrin of Reactionists, it has drawn from under the feet of industry the national ground on which it stood. All old-established national industries have been destroyed or are daily being destroyed. They are dislodged by new industries, whose introduction becomes a life-and-death question for all civilized nations, by industries that no longer work up indigenous raw material, but raw material drawn from the remotest zones; industries whose products are consumed not only at home, but in every quarter of the globe. In place of the old wants, satisfied by the productions of the country, we find new wants, requiring for their satisfaction the products of distant lands and climes. In place of the old local and national seclusion and self-sufficiency, we have inter-course in every direction, universal interdependence of nations. And as in material, so also in intellectual production. The intellectual creations of individual nations become common property. National one-sidedness and narrow-mindedness become more and more impossible, and from the numerous national and local literatures, there arises a world literature.

The bourgeoisie, by the rapid improvement of all instruments of pro-duction, by the immensely facilitated means of communication, draws all, even the most barbarian, nations into civilization. The cheap prices of its commodities are the heavy artillery with which it batters down all Chinese walls, with which it forces the barbarians' intensely obsti-nate hatred of foreigners to capitulate. It compels all nations, on pain of extinction, to adopt the bourgeois mode of production; it compels them to introduce what it calls civilization into their midst, i.e., to become bourgeois themselves. In one word, it creates a world after its own image.

The bourgeoisie has subjected the country to the rule of the towns. It has created enormous cities, has greatly increased the urban population as compared with the rural, and has thus rescued a considerable part of the population from the idiocy of rural life. Just as it has made the coun-try dependent on the towns, so it has made barbarian and semibarbarian countries dependent on the civilized ones, nations of peasants on nations of bourgeois, the East on the West.

The bourgeoisie keeps more and more doing away with the scattered state of the population, of the means of production, and of property. It has agglomerated population, centralized means of production, and has concentrated property in a few hands. The necessary consequence of this was political centralization. Independent or but loosely connected prov-inces, with separate interests, laws, governments, and systems of taxa-tion, became lumped together into one nation, with one government, one code of laws, one national class interest, one frontier, and one customs tariff.

The bourgeoisie, during its rule of scarce one hundred years, has created more massive and more colossal productive forces than have all preceding generations together. Subjection of nature's forces to man, machinery, application of chemistry to industry and agriculture, steam navigation, railways, electric telegraphs, clearing of whole continents for cultivation, canalization of rivers, whole populations conjured out of the ground—what earlier century had even a presentiment that such productive forces slumbered in the lap of social labor?

We see then: the means of production and of exchange, on whose foundation the bourgeoisie built itself up, were generated in feudal society. At a certain stage in the development of these means of production and of exchange, the conditions under which feudal society produced and exchanged, the feudal organization of agriculture and manufacturing industry, in one word, the feudal relations of property, became no longer compatible with the already developed productive forces; they became so many fetters. They had to be burst asunder; they were burst asunder.

Into their place stepped free competition, accompanied by a social and political constitution adapted to it and by the economic and political sway of the bourgeois class.

A similar movement is going on before our own eyes. Modern bourgeois society with its relations of production, of exchange, and of property, a society that has conjured up such gigantic means of production and of exchange, is like the sorcerer who is no longer able to control the powers of the nether world whom he has called up by his spells. For many a decade past, the history of industry and commerce is but the history of the revolt of modern productive forces against modern conditions of production, against the property relations that are the conditions for the existence of the bourgeoisie and of its rule. It is enough to mention the commercial crises that by their periodic return put on trial, each time more threateningly, the existence of the entire bourgeois society. In these crises a great part not only of the existing products, but also of the previously created productive forces are periodically destroyed. In these crises there breaks out an epidemic that, in all earlier epochs, would have seemed an absurdity—the epidemic of overproduction. Society suddenly finds itself put back into a state of momentary barbarism; it appears as if a famine, a universal war of devastation, had cut off the supply of every means of subsistence; industry and commerce seem to be destroyed; and why? Because there is too much civilization, too much means of subsistence, too much industry, too much commerce. The productive forces at the disposal of society no longer tend to further the development of the conditions of bourgeois property; on the contrary, they have become too powerful for these conditions, by which they are fettered, and so soon as they overcome these fetters, they bring disorder into the whole of bourgeois society, endanger the existence of bourgeois property. The conditions of bourgeois society are too narrow to comprise the wealth created by them. And how does the bourgeoisie get over these crises? On the one hand by enforced destruction of a mass of productive forces; on the other, by the conquest of new markets and by the more thorough exploitation of the old ones. That is to say, by paving the way for more extensive and more destructive crises and by diminishing the means whereby crises are prevented.

The weapons with which the bourgeoisie felled feudalism to the ground are now turned against the bourgeoisie itself.

But not only has the bourgeoisie forged the weapons that bring death to itself; it has also called into existence the men who are to wield those weapons—the modern working class—the proletarians.

In proportion as the bourgeoisie, i.e., capital, is developed, in the same proportion is the proletariat, the modern working class, developed—a class of laborers, who live only so long as they find work and who find work only so long as their labor increases capital. These laborers, who must sell themselves piecemeal, are a commodity, like every other article of commerce, and are consequently exposed to all the vicissitudes of competition, to all the fluctuations of the market.

Owing to the extensive use of machinery and to division of labor, the work of the proletarians has lost all individual character and, consequently, all charm for the workman. He becomes an appendage of the machine, and it is only the most simple, most monotonous, and most easily acquired knack that is required of him. Hence, the cost of production of a workman is restricted, almost entirely, to the means of subsistence that he requires for his maintenance and for the propagation of his race. But the price of a commodity, and therefore also of labor, is equal to its cost of production. In proportion, therefore, as the repulsiveness of the work increases, the wage decreases. Nay more, in proportion as the use of machinery and division of labor increases, in the same proportion the burden of toil also increases, whether by prolongation of the working hours, by increase of the work exacted in a given time, or by increased speed of the machinery, etc.

Modern industry has converted the little workshop of the patriarchal master into the great factory of the industrial capitalist. Masses of laborers, crowded into the factory, are organized like soldiers. As privates of the industrial army they are placed under the command of a perfect hierarchy of officers and sergeants. Not only are they slaves of the bourgeois class and of the bourgeois state; they are daily and hourly enslaved by the machine, by the overlooker, and, above all, by the individual bourgeois manufacturer himself. The more openly this despotism proclaims gain to be its end and aim, the more petty, the more hateful, and the more embittering it is.

The less the skill and exertion of strength implied in manual labor, in other words, the more modern industry becomes developed, the more is the labor of men superseded by that of women. Differences of age and sex have no longer any distinctive social validity for the working class. All are instruments of labor, more or less expensive to use, according to their age and sex.

No sooner is the exploitation of the laborer by the manufacturer, so far, at an end, and he receives his wages in cash, than he is set upon by the other portions of the bourgeoisie, the landlord, the shopkeeper, the pawnbroker, etc.

The lower strata of the middle class—the small trades people, shopkeepers, and retired tradesmen generally, the handicraftsmen and peasants—all these sink gradually into the proletariat, partly because their diminutive capital does not suffice for the scale on which modern industry is carried on and is swamped in the competition with the large capitalists, partly because their specialized skill is rendered worthless by new methods of production. Thus the proletariat is recruited from all classes of the population.

The proletariat goes through various stages of development. With its birth begins its struggle with the bourgeoisie. At first the contest is carried on by individual laborers, then by the work people of a factory, then by the operatives of one trade, in one locality, against the individual bourgeois who directly exploits them. They direct their attacks not against the bourgeois conditions of production, but against the instruments of production themselves; they destroy imported wares that compete with their labor, they smash to pieces machinery, they set factories ablaze, they seek to restore by force the vanished status of the workman of the Middle Ages.

At this stage the laborers still form an incoherent mass scattered over the whole country and broken up by their mutual competition. If anywhere they unite to form more compact bodies, this is not yet the consequence of their own active union but of the union of the bourgeoisie, which class, in order to attain its own political ends, is compelled to set the whole proletariat in motion and is moreover yet, for a time, able to do so. At this age, therefore, the proletarians do not fight their enemies, but the enemies of their enemies, the remnants of absolute monarchy, the landowners, the nonindustrial bourgeois, the petty bourgeoisie. Thus the whole historical movement is concentrated in the hands of the bourgeoisie; every victory so obtained is a victory for the bourgeoisie.

But with the development of industry the proletariat not only increases in number; it becomes concentrated in greater masses, its strength grows, and it feels that strength more. The various interests and conditions of life within the ranks of the proletariat are more and more equalized, in proportion as machinery obliterates all distinctions of labor and nearly everywhere reduces wages to the same low level. The growing competition among the bourgeois, and the resulting commercial crises, make the wages of the workers ever more fluctuating. The unceasing improvement of machinery, ever more rapidly developing, makes their livelihood more and more precarious; the collisions between individual workmen and individual bourgeois take more and more the character of collisions between two classes. Thereupon the workers begin to form combinations (trades' unions) against the bourgeois; they club together in order to keep up the rate of wages; they found permanent associations in order to make provision beforehand for these occasional revolts. Here and there the contest breaks out into riots.

Now and then the workers are victorious, but only for a time. The real fruit of their battles lies, not in the immediate result, but in the ever-expanding union of the workers. This union is helped on by the improved means of communication that are created by modern industry and that place the workers of different localities in contact with one another. It was just this contact that was needed to centralize the numerous local struggles, all of the same character, into one national struggle between classes. But every class struggle is a political struggle. And that union, to attain which the burghers of the Middle Ages, with their miserable highways, required centuries, the modern proletarians, thanks to railways, achieve in a few years.

This organization of the proletarians into a class, and consequently into a political party, is continually being upset again by the competition between the workers themselves. But it ever rises up again, stronger, firmer, mightier. It compels legislative recognition of particular interests of the workers, by taking advantage of the divisions among the bourgeoisie itself. Thus the ten-hours bill in England was carried.

Altogether collisions between the classes of the old society further, in many ways, the course of development of the proletariat. The bourgeoisie finds itself involved in a constant battle. At first with the aristocracy; later on, with those portions of the bourgeoisie itself whose interests have become antagonistic to the progress of industry; at all times, with the bourgeoisie of foreign countries. In all these battles it sees itself compelled to appeal to the proletariat, to ask for its help, and thus to drag it into the political arena. The bourgeoisie itself, therefore, supplies the proletariat with its own elements of political and general education; in other words, it furnishes the proletariat with weapons for fighting the bourgeoisie.

Further, as we have already seen, entire sections of the ruling classes are, by the advance of industry, precipitated into the proletariat or are at least threatened in their conditions of existence. These also supply the proletariat with fresh elements of enlightenment and progress.

Finally, in times when the class struggle nears the decisive hour, the process of dissolution going on within the ruling class, in fact within the whole range of old society, assumes such a violent, glaring character, that a small section of the ruling class cuts itself adrift, and joins the revolutionary class, the class that holds the future in its hands. Just as, therefore, at an earlier period a section of the nobility went over to the bourgeoisie, so now a portion of the bourgeoisie goes over to the proletariat, and in particular, a portion of the bourgeois ideologists who have raised themselves to the level of comprehending theoretically the historical movement as a whole.

Of all the classes that stand face to face with the bourgeoisie today, the proletariat alone is a really revolutionary class. The other classes decay and finally disappear in the face of modern industry; the proletariat is its special and essential product.

The lower middle class, the small manufacturer, the shopkeeper, the artisan, the peasant, all these fight against the bourgeoisie to save from extinction their existence as fractions of the middle class. They are therefore not revolutionary, but conservative. Nay more, they are reactionary, for they try to roll back the wheel of history. If by chance they are revolutionary, they are so only in view of their impending transfer into the proletariat, they thus defend not their present, but their future interests, they desert their own standpoint to place themselves at that of the proletariat.

The "dangerous class," the social scum, that passively rotting mass thrown off by the lowest layers of old society, may, here and there, be swept into the movement by a proletarian revolution; its conditions of life, however, prepare it far more for the part of a bribed tool of reactionary intrigue.

In the conditions of the proletariat, those of old society at large are already virtually swamped. The proletarian is without property; his relation to his wife and children has no longer anything in common with the bourgeois family relations; modern industrial labor, modern subjection to capital, the same in England as in France, in America as in Germany, has stripped him of every trace of national character. Law, morality, religion are to him so many bourgeois prejudices, behind which lurk in ambush just as many bourgeois interests.

All the preceding classes that got the upper hand sought to fortify their already acquired status by subjecting society at large to their conditions of appropriation. The proletarians cannot become masters of the productive forces of society except by abolishing their own previous mode of appropriation and thereby also every other previous mode of appropriation. They have nothing of their own to secure and to fortify; their mission is to destroy all previous securities for, and insurances of, individual property.

All previous historical movements were movements of minorities, or in the interests of minorities. The proletarian movement is the self-conscious, independent movement of the immense majority, in the interests of the immense majority. The proletariat, the lowest stratum of our present society, cannot stir, cannot raise itself up, without the whole superincumbent strata of official society being sprung into the air.

Though not in substance, yet in form, the struggle of the proletariat with the bourgeoisie is at first a national struggle. The proletariat of each country must, of course, first of all settle matters with its own bourgeoisie.

In depicting the most general phases of the development of the proletariat, we traced the more or less veiled civil war, raging within existing society, up to the point where that war breaks out into open revolution and where the violent overthrow of the bourgeoisie lays the foundation for the sway of the proletariat.

Hitherto, every form of society has been based, as we have already seen, on the antagonism of oppressing and oppressed classes. But in order to oppress a class, certain conditions must be assured to it under which it can, at least, continue its slavish existence. The serf, in the period of serfdom, raised himself to membership in the commune, just as the petty bourgeois, under the yoke of feudal absolutism, managed to develop into a bourgeois. The modern laborer, on the contrary, instead of rising with the progress of industry, sinks deeper and deeper below the conditions of existence of his own class. He becomes a pauper, and pauperism develops more rapidly than population and wealth. And here it becomes evident that the bourgeoisie is unfit any longer to be the ruling class in society and to impose its conditions of existence upon society as an overriding law. It is unfit to rule because it is incompetent to assure an existence to its slave within his slavery, because it cannot help letting him sink into such a state that it has to feed him, instead of being fed by him. Society can no longer live under this bourgeoisie; in other words, its existence is no longer compatible with society.

The essential condition for the existence, and for the sway of the bourgeois class, is the formation and augmentation of capital; the condition for capital is wage-labor. Wage-labor rests exclusively on competition between the laborers. The advance of industry, whose involuntary promoter is the bourgeoisie, replaces the isolation of the laborers, due to competition, by their revolutionary combination, due to association. The development of modern industry, therefore, cuts from under its feet the very foundation on which the bourgeoisie produces and appropriates products. What the bourgeoisie, therefore, produces, above all, is its own gravediggers. Its fall and the victory of the proletariat are equally inevitable.

11. Proletarians and Communists

In what relation do the communists stand to the proletarians as a whole?

The communists do not form a separate party opposed to other working-class parties.

They have no interests separate and apart from those of the proletariat as a whole.

They do not set up any sectarian principles of their own, by which to shape and mold the proletarian movement.

The communists are distinguished from the other working-class parties by this only: (1) In the national struggles of the proletarians of the different countries, they point out and bring to the front the common interests of the entire proletariat, independently of all nationality. (2) In the various stages of development which the struggle of the working class against the bourgeoisie has to pass through, they always and everywhere represent the interests of the movement as a whole.

The communists, therefore, are on the one hand, practically, the most advanced and resolute section of the working-class parties of every country, that section which pushes forward all others; on the other hand, theoretically, they have over the great mass of the proletariat the advantage of clearly understanding the line of march, the conditions, and the ultimate general results of the proletarian movement.

The immediate aim of the communists is the same as that of all the other proletarian parties: formation of the proletariat into a class, overthrow of the bourgeois supremacy, conquest of political power by the proletariat.

The theoretical conclusions of the communists are in no way based on ideas or principles that have been invented, or discovered, by this or that would-be universal reformer.

They merely express, in general terms, actual relations springing from an existing class struggle, from a historical movement going on under our very eyes. The abolition of existing property relations is not at all a distinctive feature of communism.

All property relations in the past have continually been subject to historical change consequent upon the change in historical conditions.

The French revolution, for example, abolished feudal property in favor of bourgeois property.

The distinguishing feature of communism is not the abolition of property generally, but the abolition of bourgeois property. But modern bourgeois private property is the final and most complete expression of the system of producing and appropriating products, that is based on class antagonisms, on the exploitation of the many by the few.

In this sense, the theory of the communists may be summed up in the single sentence: Abolition of private property.

We communists have been reproached with the desire of abolishing the right of personally acquiring property as the fruit of a man's own labor, which property is alleged to be the groundwork of all personal freedom, activity, and independence.

Hard-won, self-acquired, self-earned property! Do you mean the property of the petty artisan and of the small peasant, a form of property that preceded the bourgeois form? There is no need to abolish that; the development of industry has to a great extent already destroyed it and is still destroying it daily.

Or do you mean modern bourgeois private property?

But does wage-labor create any property for the laborer? Not a bit. It creates capital, i.e., that kind of property which exploits wage-labor and which cannot increase except upon condition of begetting a new supply of wage-labor for fresh exploitation. Property, in its present form, is based on the antagonism of capital and wage-labor. Let us examine both sides of this antagonism.

To be a capitalist is to have not only a purely personal, but a social *status* in production. Capital is a collective product, and only by the united action of many members, nay, in the last resort, only by the united action of all members of society, can it be set in motion.

Capital is, therefore, not a personal, it is a social power.

When, therefore, capital is converted into common property, into the property of all members of society, personal property is not thereby transformed into social property. It is only the social character of the property that is changed. It loses its class character.

Let us now take wage-labor.

The average price of wage-labor is the minimum wage, i.e., that quantum of the means of subsistence which is absolutely requisite to keep the laborer in bare existence as a laborer. What, therefore, the wage-laborer appropriates by means of his labor merely suffices to prolong and reproduce a bare existence. We by no means intend to abolish this personal appropriation of the products of labor, an appropriation that is made for the maintenance and reproduction of human life and that leaves no surplus wherewith to command the labor of others. All that we want to do away with is the miserable character of this appropriation, under which the laborer lives merely to increase capital and is allowed to live only in so far as the interest of the ruling class requires it.

In bourgeois society, living labor is but a means to increase accumulated labor. In communist society, accumulated labor is but a means to widen, to enrich, to promote the existence of the laborer.

In bourgeois society, therefore, the past dominates the present; in communist society, the present dominates the past. In bourgeois society capital is independent and has individuality, while the living person is dependent and has no individuality.

And the abolition of this state of things is called by the bourgeois, abolition of individuality and freedom! And rightly so. The abolition of bourgeois individuality, bourgeois independence, and bourgeois freedom is undoubtedly aimed at.

By freedom is meant, under the present bourgeois conditions of production, free trade, free selling and buying.

But if selling and buying disappears, free selling and buying disappears also. This talk about free selling and buying, and all the other "brave words" of our bourgeoisie about freedom in general, have a meaning, if any, only in contrast with restricted selling and buying, with the fettered traders of the Middle Ages, but have no meaning when opposed to the communistic abolition of buying and selling, of the bourgeois conditions of production, and of the bourgeoisie itself.

You are horrified at our intending to do away with private property. But in your existing society, private property is already done away with for nine-tenths of the population; its existence for the few is solely due to its nonexistence in the hands of those nine-tenths. You reproach us, therefore, with intending to do away with a form of property, the necessary condition for whose existence is the nonexistence of any property for the immense majority of society.

In one word, you reproach us with intending to do away with your property. Precisely so; that is just what we intend.

From the moment when labor can no longer be converted into capital, money, or rent, into a social power capable of being monopolized, i.e., from the moment when individual property can no longer be transformed into bourgeois property, into capital, from that moment, you say, individuality vanishes.

You must, therefore, confess that by "individual" you mean no other person than the bourgeois, than the middle-class owner of property. This person must, indeed, be swept out of the way and made impossible.

Communism deprives no man of the power to appropriate the products of society; all that it does is to deprive him of the power to subjugate the labor of others by means of such appropriation.

It has been objected that upon the abolition of private property all work will cease, and universal laziness will overtake us.

According to this, bourgeois society ought long ago to have gone to the dogs through sheer idleness; for those of its members who work, acquire nothing, and those who acquire anything, do not work. The whole of this objection is but another expression of the tautology: that there can no longer be any wage-labor when there is no longer any capital.

All objections urged against the communistic mode of producing and appropriating material products have, in the same way, been urged against the communistic modes of producing and appropriating intellectual products. Just as, to the bourgeois, the disappearance of class property is the disappearance of production itself, so the disappearance of class culture is to him identical with the disappearance of all culture.

That culture, the loss of which he laments, is, for the enormous majority, a mere training to act as a machine.

But don't wrangle with us so long as you apply, to our intended abolition of bourgeois property, the standard of your bourgeois notions of freedom, culture, law, etc. Your very ideas are but the outgrowth of the conditions of your bourgeois production and bourgeois property, just as your jurisprudence is but the will of your class made into a law for all, a will whose essential character and direction are determined by the economic conditions of existence of your class.

The selfish misconception that induces you to transform into eternal laws of nature and of reason, the social forms springing from your present mode of production and form of property—historical relations that rise and disappear in the progress of production—this misconception you share with every ruling class that has preceded you. What you see clearly in the case of ancient property, what you admit in the case of feudal property, you are of course forbidden to admit in the case of your own bourgeois form of property.

Abolition of the family! Even the most radical flare up at this infamous proposal of the communists.

On what foundation is the present family, the bourgeois family, based? On capital, on private gain. In its completely developed form this family exists only among the bourgeoisie. But this state of things finds its complement in the practical absence of the family among the proletarians and in public prostitution.

The bourgeois family will vanish as a matter of course when its complement vanishes, and both will vanish with the vanishing of capital.

Do you charge us with wanting to stop the exploitation of children by their parents? To this crime we plead guilty.

But, you will say, we destroy the most hallowed of relations when we replace home education by social.

And your education! Is not that also social and determined by the social conditions under which you educate, by the intervention, direct or indirect, of society, by means of schools, etc.? The communists have not invented the intervention of society in education; they do but seek to alter the character of that intervention and to rescue education from the influence of the ruling class.

The bourgeois claptrap about the family and education, about the hallowed co-relation of parent and child, becomes all the more disgusting, the more, by the action of modern industry, all family ties among the proletarians are torn asunder, and their children transformed into simple articles of commerce and instruments of labor.

But you communists would introduce community of women, screams the whole bourgeoisie in chorus.

The bourgeois sees in his wife a mere instrument of production. He hears that the instruments of production are to be exploited in common and, naturally, can come to no other conclusion than that the lot of being common to all will likewise fall to the women.[*]

---

[*] EDITOR'S NOTE. Many readers have found these passages confusing. A lucid passage from an earlier draft by Engels clarifies the point: "*What influence will the communist order of society have upon the family?* It will make the relations between the sexes a purely private affair, which concerns only the persons involved, and calls for no interference by society. It is able to do this because it abolishes private property and educates children communally, destroying thereby the two foundation stones of hitherto existing marriage—the dependence of the wife upon her husband and of the children upon the parents conditioned by private property. This is an answer to the outcry raised by moralizing philistines against the communistic community of wives. Community of wives is a relationship belonging entirely to bourgeois society and existing today in perfect form in prostitution.

He has not even a suspicion that the real point aimed at is to do away with the status of women as mere instruments of production.

For the rest, nothing is more ridiculous than the virtuous indignation of our bourgeois at the community of women which, they pretend, is to be openly and officially established by the communists. The communists have no need to introduce community of women; it has existed almost from time immemorial.

Our bourgeois, not content with having the wives and daughters of their proletarians at their disposal, not to speak of common prostitutes, take the greatest pleasure in seducing each other's wives.

Bourgeois marriage is in reality a system of wives in common and thus, of the most, what the communists might possibly be reproached with is that they desire to introduce, in substitution for a hypocritically concealed, an openly legalized community of women. For the rest, it is self-evident that the abolition of the present system of production must bring with it the abolition of the community of women springing from that system, i.e., of prostitution both public and private.

The communists are further reproached with desiring to abolish countries and nationality.

The working men have no country. We cannot take from them what they have not got. Since the proletariat must first of all acquire political supremacy, must rise to be the leading class of the nation, must constitute itself *the* nation, it is, so far, itself national, though not in the bourgeois sense of the word.

National differences and antagonisms between peoples are daily more and more vanishing, owing to the development of the bourgeoisie, to freedom of commerce, to the world market, to uniformity in the mode of production and in the conditions of life corresponding thereto.

The supremacy of the proletariat will cause them to vanish still faster. United action, of the leading civilized countries at least, is one of the first conditions for the emancipation of the proletariat.

In proportion as the exploitation of one individual by another is put an end to, the exploitation of one nation by another will also be put an end to. In proportion as the antagonism between classes within the

Prostitution, however, is rooted in private property and falls with it. Hence, the communistic organization rather than establishing the community of women, puts an end to it." (Engels, "Principles of Communism," Marx and Engels *Selected Works*, Vol. 1, p. 94.)

nation vanishes, the hostility of one nation to another will come to an end.

The charges against communism made from a religious, a philosophical, and, generally, from an ideological standpoint are not deserving of serious examination.

Does it require deep intuition to comprehend that man's ideas, views, and conceptions, in one word, man's consciousness, changes with every change in the conditions of his material existence, in his social relations, and in his social life?

What else does the history of ideas prove, than that intellectual production changes its character in proportion as material production is changed? The ruling ideas of each age have ever been the ideas of its ruling class.

When people speak of ideas that revolutionize society, they do but express the fact that within the old society, the elements of a new one have been created, and that the dissolution of the old ideas keeps even pace with the dissolution of the old conditions of existence.

When the ancient world was in its last throes, the ancient religions were overcome by Christianity. When Christian ideas succumbed in the eighteenth century to rationalist ideas, feudal society fought its death battle with the then-revolutionary bourgeoisie. The ideas of religious liberty and freedom of conscience merely gave expression to the sway of free competition within the domain of knowledge.

"Undoubtedly," it will be said, "religious, moral, philosophical, and juridical ideas have been modified in the course of historical development. But religion, morality, philosophy, political science, and law constantly survived this change."

"There are, besides, eternal truths, such as Freedom, Justice, etc., that are common to all states of society. But communism abolishes eternal truths, it abolishes all religion and all morality, instead of constituting them on a new basis; it therefore acts in contradiction to all past historical experience."

What does this accusation reduce itself to? The history of all past society has consisted in the development of class antagonisms, antagonisms that assumed different forms at different epochs.

But whatever form they may have taken, one fact is common to all past ages, namely, the exploitation of one part of society by the other. No wonder, then, that the social consciousness of past ages, despite all the multiplicity and variety it displays, moves within certain common forms, or general ideas, which cannot completely vanish except with the total disappearance of class antagonisms.

The communist revolution is the most radical rupture with traditional property relations; no wonder that its development involves the most radical rupture with traditional ideas.

But let us have done with the bourgeois objections to communism.

We have seen above that the first step in the revolution by the working class is to raise the proletariat to the position of ruling class, to win the battle of democracy.

The proletariat will use its political supremacy to wrest, by degrees, all capital from the bourgeoisie, to centralize all instruments of production in the hands of the state, i.e., of the proletariat organized as the ruling class, and to increase the total of productive forces as rapidly as possible.

Of course, in the beginning, this cannot be effected except by means of despotic inroads on the rights of property and on the conditions of bourgeois production; by means of measures, therefore, which appear economically insufficient and untenable, but which, in the course of the movement, outstrip themselves, necessitate further inroads upon the old social order, and are unavoidable as a means of entirely revolutionizing the mode of production.

These measures will of course be different in different countries.

Nevertheless in the most advanced countries, the following will be pretty generally applicable.

1. Abolition of property in land and application of all rents of land to public purposes.
2. A heavy progressive or graduated income tax.
3. Abolition of all right of inheritance.
4. Confiscation of the property of all emigrants and rebels.
5. Centralization of credit in the hands of the state, by means of a national bank with state capital and an exclusive monopoly.
6. Centralization of the means of communication and transport in the hands of the state.
7. Extension of factories and instruments of production owned by the state; the bringing into cultivation of wastelands, and the improvement of the soil generally in accordance with a common plan.

8. Equal liability of all to labor. Establishment of industrial armies, especially for agriculture.
9. Combination of agriculture with manufacturing industries; gradual abolition of the distinction between town and country by a more equable distribution of the population over the country.
10. Free education for all children in public schools. Abolition of children's factory labor in its present form. Combination of education with industrial production, etc., etc.

When, in the course of development, class distinctions have disappeared, and all production has been concentrated in the hands of a vast association of the whole nation, the public power will lose its political character. Political power, property so called, is merely the organized power of one class for oppressing another. If the proletariat during its contest with the bourgeoisie is compelled, by the force of circumstances, to organize itself as a class, if, by means of a revolution, it makes itself the ruling class, and, as such, sweeps away by force the old conditions of production, then it will, along with these conditions, have swept away the conditions for the existence of class antagonisms and of classes generally and will thereby have abolished its own supremacy as a class.

In place of the old bourgeois society, with its classes and class antagonisms, we shall have an association, in which the free development of each is the condition for the free development of all.

IV. Position of the Communists in Relation to the Various Existing Opposition Parties

Section II has made clear the relations of the communists to the existing working-class parties, such as the Chartists in England and the Agrarian Reformers in America.

The communists fight for the attainment of the immediate aims, for the enforcement of the momentary interests of the working class; but in the movement of the present, they also represent and take care of the future of that movement. In France the communists ally themselves with the Social Democrats,* against the conservative and radical

---

*   The party when represented in Parliament by Ledru-Rollin, in literature by Louis Blanc, in the daily press by the *Réforme.* The name of Social Democracy signified, with these its inventors, a section of the democratic or republican party more or less tinged with socialism. [*Note by Engels to the English edition of 1888.*]

bourgeoisie, reserving, however, the right to take up a critical position in regard to phrases and illusions traditionally handed down from the great revolution.

In Switzerland they support the Radicals, without losing sight of the fact that this party consists of antagonistic elements, partly of democratic socialists, in the French sense, partly of radical bourgeois.

In Poland they support the party that insists on an agrarian revolution as the prime condition for national emancipation, that party which fomented the insurrection of Cracow in 1846.

In Germany they fight with the bourgeoisie whenever it acts in a revolutionary way, against the absolute monarchy, the feudal squirearchy, and the petty bourgeoisie.

But they never cease, for a single instant, to instill into the working class the clearest possible recognition of the hostile antagonism between bourgeoisie and proletariat, in order that the German workers may straightway use, as so many weapons against the bourgeoisie, the social and political conditions that the bourgeoisie must necessarily introduce along with its supremacy, and in order that, after the fall of the reactionary classes in Germany, the fight against the bourgeoisie itself may immediately begin.

The communists turn their attention chiefly to Germany, because that country is on the eve of a bourgeois revolution that is bound to be carried out under more advanced conditions of European civilization, and with a much more developed proletariat, than that of England was in the seventeenth and of France in the eighteenth century, and because the bourgeois revolution in Germany will be but the prelude to an immediately following proletarian revolution.

In short, the Communists everywhere support every revolutionary movement against the existing social and political order of things.

In all these movements they bring to the front, as the leading question in each, the property question, no matter what its degree of development at the time.

Finally, they labor everywhere for the union and agreement of the democratic parties of all countries.

The party in France which at that time called itself Socialist-Democratic was represented in political life by Ledru-Rollin and in literature by Louis Blanc; thus it differed immeasurably from present-day German Social Democracy. [*Note by Engels to the German edition of 1890.*]

The communists disdain to conceal their views and aims. They openly declare that their ends can be attained only by the forcible overthrow of all existing social conditions. Let the ruling classes tremble at a communistic revolution. The proletarians have nothing to lose but their chains. They have a world to win.

WORKING MEN OF ALL COUNTRIES, UNITE!

READING #2

Engels
"Marx's *Capital*"

1

As long as there have been capitalists and workers on earth, no book has appeared which is of as much importance for the workers as the one before us. The relation between capital and labor, the hinge on which our entire present system of society turns, is here treated scientifically for the first time and with a thoroughness and acuity possible only for a German. Valuable as the writings of an Owen, Saint-Simon, Fourier are and will remain, it was reserved for a German first to climb to the height from which the whole field of modern social relations can be seen clearly and in full view just as the lower mountain scenery is seen by an observer standing on the topmost peak.

Political economy up to now has taught us that labor is the source of all wealth and the measure of all values, so that two objects whose production has cost the same labor-time possess the same value and must also be exchanged for each other, since on the average only equal values are exchangeable for one another. At the same time, however, it teaches that there exists a kind of stored-up labor which it calls capital; that this capital, owing to the auxiliary sources contained in it, raises the productivity of living labor a hundred and a thousandfold, and in return claims a certain compensation which is termed profit or gain. As we all know, this occurs in reality in such a way that the profits of stored-up, dead labor become ever more massive, the capital of the capitalists becomes ever more colossal, while the wages of living labor constantly decrease, and the mass of workers living solely on wages grows ever more numerous and poverty-stricken. How is this contradiction to be solved? How can there remain a profit for the capitalist if the worker gets back the full value of the labor he adds to his product? And yet this should be the case, since only equal values are exchanged. On the other hand, how can equal values be exchanged, how can the worker receive the full value of his product, if, as is admitted by many economists, this product is divided between him and the capitalist? Economics up to now has been helpless in the face of this contradiction and writes or stutters embarrassed meaningless phrases. Even the previous socialist critics of economics were unable to do more than emphasize the contradiction; no one has solved it, until now at last Marx has traced the process by which this profit arises right to its birthplace and has thereby made everything clear.

In tracing the development of capital, Marx starts from the simple, notoriously obvious fact that the capitalists turn their capital to account by exchange: they buy commodities for their money and afterwards sell them for more money than they cost them. For example, a capitalist buys cotton for 1,000 talers and then sells it for 1,100, thus "earning" 100 talers. This excess of 100 talers over the original capital Marx calls *surplus-value*. Where does this surplus-value come from? According to the economists' assumption, only equal values are exchanged, and in the sphere of abstract theory this is correct. Hence, the purchase of cotton and its subsequent sale can just as little yield surplus-value as the exchange of a silver taler for thirty silver groschen and the re-exchange of the small coins for a silver taler, a process by which one becomes neither richer nor poorer. But surplus-value can just as little arise from sellers selling commodities above their value, or buyers buying them below their value, because each one is in turn buyer and seller and this would, therefore, again balance. No more can it arise from buyers and sellers reciprocally overreaching each other, for this would create no new or surplus-value, but would only distribute the existing capital differently between the capitalists. In spite of the fact that the capitalist buys the commodities at their value and sells them at their value, he gets more value out than he put in. How does this happen?

Under present social conditions the capitalist finds on the commodity market a *commodity* which has the peculiar property that *its use is a source of new value, is a creation of new value.* This commodity is *labor-power.*

What is the value of labor-power? The value of every commodity is measured by the labor required for its production. Labor-power exists in the shape of the living worker who needs a definite amount of means of subsistence for himself and for his family, which ensures the continuance of labor-power even after his death. Hence the labor-time necessary for producing these means of subsistence represents the value of labor-power. The capitalist pays him weekly and thereby purchases the use of one week's labor of the worker. So far, Messrs., the economists will pretty well agree with us as to the value of labor-power.

The capitalist now sets his worker to work. In a certain time the worker will have delivered as much labor as was represented by his weekly wage. Supposing that the weekly wage of a worker represents three labor days, then, if the worker begins on Monday he has by Wednesday evening *replaced* for the capitalist *the full value of the wage paid*. But does he then stop working? By no means. The capitalist has bought his *week's* labor and the worker must go on working during the last three days of the week too. This *surplus-labor* of the worker, over and above the time necessary to replace his wage, is the *source of surplus-value*, of profit, of the continually growing accumulation of capital.

Do not say it is an arbitrary assumption that the worker earns in three days the wages he has received and works the remaining three days for the capitalist. Whether he takes exactly three days to replace his wages, or two or four, is, of course, quite immaterial here and depends upon circumstances; the main point is that the capitalist, besides the labor he pays for, also extracts labor that he *does not pay for*; and this is no arbitrary assumption, for if the capitalist extracted from the worker over a long period only as much labor as he paid him for in wages, he would shut down his workshops, since indeed his whole profit would come to nought.

Here we have the solution of all those contradictions. The origin of surplus-value (of which the capitalist's profit forms an important part) is now quite clear and natural. The value of the labor-power is paid for, but this value is far less than that which the capitalist can extract from the labor-power, and it is precisely the difference, the *unpaid labor*, that constitutes the share of the capitalist, or more accurately, of the capitalist class. For even the profit that the cotton dealer made on his cotton in the above example must consist of unpaid labor, if cotton prices have not risen. The trader must have sold it to a cotton manufacturer, who is able to extract from his product a profit for himself besides the original 100 talers, and therefore shares with him the unpaid labor he has pocketed. In general, it is this unpaid labor which maintains all the non-working members of society. The state and municipal taxes, as far as they affect the capitalist class, the rent of the landowners, etc., are paid from it. On it rests the whole existing social system.

It would be absurd to assume that unpaid labor arose only under present conditions, where production is carried on by capitalists on the one hand and wage-workers on the other. On the contrary, the oppressed class at all times has had to perform unpaid labor. During the whole long period when slavery was the prevailing form of the organization of labor, the slaves had to perform much more labor than was returned to them in the form of means of subsistence. The same was the case under the rule of serfdom and right up to the abolition of peasant *corvée* labor; here in fact the difference stands out palpably between the time during which the peasant works for his own maintenance and the surplus-labor for the feudal lord, precisely because the latter is carried out separately from the former. The form has now been changed, but the substance remains and as long as "a part of society possesses the monopoly of the means of production, the laborer, free or not free, must add to the working-time necessary for his own maintenance an extra working-time in order to produce the means of subsistence for the owners of the means of production."

II

In the previous article we saw that every worker employed by the capitalist performs a twofold labor: during one part of his working-time he replaces the wages advanced to him by the capitalist, and this part of his labor Marx terms *necessary labor*. But afterwards he has to go on working and during that time he produces *surplus-value* for the capitalist, a significant portion of which constitutes profit. That part of the labor is called *surplus-labor*.

Let us assume that the worker works three days of the week to replace his wages and three days to produce surplus-value for the capitalist. Putting it otherwise, it means that with a twelve-hour working-day he works six hours daily for his wages and six hours for the production of surplus-value. One can get only six days out of the week, seven at most, even by including Sunday, but one can extract six, eight, ten, twelve, fifteen or even more hours of labor out of every working-day. The worker sells the capitalist a working-day for his day's wages. But, *what is a working-day? Eight hours or eighteen?*

It is in the capitalist's interest to make the working-day as long as possible. The longer it is, the more surplus-value is produced. The worker correctly feels that every hour of labor which he performs over and above the replacement of his wage is unjustly taken from him; he experiences with his own body what it means to work excessive hours. The capitalist fights for his profit, the worker for his health, for a few hours of daily rest, to be able, as a human being, to have other occupations than working, sleeping and eating. It may be remarked in passing that it does not depend at all upon the good will of the individual capitalists whether they desire to embark on this struggle or not, since competition compels even the most philanthropic among them to join with his colleagues and to make a working-time as long as theirs the rule.

The struggle for the fixing of the working-day has lasted from the first appearance of free workers in history up to the present day. In various trades different traditional working-days prevail, but in reality they are seldom observed. Only where the law fixes the working-day and supervises its observance can one really say that there exists a normal working-day. And up to now this is the case almost exclusively in the factory districts of England. Here the ten-hour working-day (ten-and-a-half hours on five days, seven-and-a-half hours on Saturday) has been fixed for all women and for youths of thirteen to eighteen; and since the men cannot work without them, they also come under the ten-hour working-day. This law has been won by English factory workers through years of endurance, through the most persistent, stubborn struggle with the factory owners, through freedom of the press, the right of association and assembly, and also through adroit utilization of the divisions within the ruling class itself. It has become the palladium of the English workers; it has gradually been extended to all important branches of industry and last year to almost *all trades*, at least to all those in which women and children are employed. The present work contains most exhaustive material on the history of this legislative regulation of the working-day in England. The next "North-German Reichstag" will also have factory regulations, and therefore the regulation of factory labor, to discuss. We expect that none of the deputies elected by German workers will go to discuss this bill without previously making themselves thoroughly conversant with *Marx's* book. *Much can be achieved there.* The divisions within the ruling classes are more favorable to the workers than they ever were in England, because *universal suffrage compels the ruling classes to court the favor of the workers.* Four or five representatives of the proletariat are a *power* under these circumstances, if they know how to use their position, if above all they know what is at issue, which the bourgeois do not know. And Marx's book gives them in ready form all the material required for this.

We will pass over a number of other very fine investigations of more theoretical interest and come to the final chapter which deals with the accumulation of capital. Here it is first shown that the capitalist mode of production, *i.e.*, that which presupposes capitalists on the one hand and wage-workers on the other, not only continually reproduces the capital of the capitalist, but also continually reproduces the poverty of the workers at the same time; so that it is ensured that there always exist anew, on the one hand, capitalists who are the owners of all means of subsistence, raw materials and instruments of labor, and, on the other, the great mass of workers who are compelled to sell their labor-power to these capitalists for an amount of the means of subsistence which at best just suffices to maintain them capable of working and to bring up a new generation of able-bodied proletarians. But capital is not merely reproduced; it is continually increased and multiplied—and so is its power over the propertyless class of workers. And just as capital itself is reproduced on an ever-greater scale, so the modern capitalist mode of production reproduces the class of propertyless workers also on an ever-greater scale and in ever-greater numbers. ". . . Accumulation [of capital] reproduces the capital-relation on a progressive scale, more capitalists or larger capitalists at this pole, more wage-workers at that. . . . *Accumulation of capital is, therefore, increase of the proletariat.*" Since, however, owing to the progress of machinery, owing to improved agriculture, etc., fewer and fewer workers are necessary in order to produce the same quantity of products, since this perfecting, *i.e.*, this making the workers superfluous, grows more rapidly than capital itself, what becomes of this ever-increasing number of workers? They form an industrial reserve army, which, during times of bad or moderate business, is paid *below* the value of its labor and is irregularly employed, or comes under the care of public Poor Law institutions, but which is indispensable to the capitalist class at times when business is especially lively, as is palpably evident in England— and which *under all circumstances* serves to break the power of resistance of the regularly employed workers and to keep their wages down. "The greater the social wealth . . . the greater is the [relative surplus-population or][1] industrial reserve army. . . . But the greater this reserve army in proportion to the active [regularly employed] labor army, the greater is the mass of a consolidated [permanent] surplus-population [or strata of workers] whose misery is in inverse ratio to its torment of labor. The more extensive, finally, the Lazarus-layers of the working class, and the industrial reserve army, the greater is official pauperism. *This is the absolute general law of capitalist accumulation.*"

These, strictly scientifically proved—and the official economists take great care not to make even an attempt at refutation—are some of the chief laws of the modern, capitalist social system. But with this is everything said? By no means. Just as sharply as Marx stresses the bad sides of capitalist production, does he also clearly prove that this social form was necessary to develop the productive forces of society to a level which will make possible an equal development, worthy of human beings, for *all* members of society. All earlier forms of society were too poor for this. Capitalist production for the first time creates the wealth and the productive forces necessary for this, but at the same time it also creates in the mass of oppressed workers the social class which is more and more compelled to claim the utilization of this wealth and these productive forces for the whole of society—instead of as today for a monopolist class.

Note

1. Insertions in brackets by Engels.—*Ed.*

READING #3
Marx
"Inaugural Address of the International Workingmen's Association"

Working Men,

It is a great fact that the misery of the working masses has not diminished from 1848 to 1864, and yet this period is unrivaled for the development of its industry and the growth of its commerce. In 1850, a moderate organ of the British middle class, of more than average information, predicted that if the exports and imports of England were to rise 50 per cent, English pauperism would sink to zero. Alas! on April 7, 1864, the Chancellor of the Exchequer* delighted his parliamentary audience by the statement that the total import and export trade of England had grown in 1863 "to £443,955,000! that astonishing sum about three times the trade of the comparatively recent epoch of 1843!" With all that, he was eloquent upon "poverty." "Think," he exclaimed, "of those who are on the border of that region," upon "wages . . . not increased"; upon "human life . . . in nine cases out of ten but a struggle of existence!" He did not speak of the people of Ireland, gradually replaced by machinery in the north, and by sheep-walks in the south, though even the sheep in that unhappy country are decreasing, it is true, not at so rapid a rate as the men. He did not repeat what then had been just betrayed by the highest representatives of the upper ten thousand in a sudden fit of terror. When the garrotte panic had reached a certain height, the House of Lords caused an inquiry to be made into, and a report to be published upon, transportation and penal servitude. Out came the murder in the bulky Blue Book of 1863, and proved it was, by official facts and figures, that the worst of the convicted criminals, the penal serfs of England and Scotland, toiled much less and fared far better than the agricultural laborers of England and Scotland. But this was not all. When, consequent upon the Civil War in America, the operatives of Lancashire and Cheshire were thrown upon the streets, the same House of Lords sent to the manufacturing districts a physician commissioned to investigate into the smallest possible amount of carbon and nitrogen, to be administered in the cheapest and plainest form, which on an average might just suffice to "avert starvation diseases." Dr. Smith, the medical deputy, ascertained that 28,000 grains of carbon, and 1,330 grains of nitrogen were the weekly allowance that would keep an average adult. . . just over the level of starvation diseases, and he found furthermore that quantity pretty nearly to agree with the scanty nourishment to which the pressure of extreme distress had actually reduced the cotton operatives.** But

---

* William Gladstone.—*Ed.*

** We need hardly remind the reader that, apart from the elements of water and certain inorganic substances, carbon and nitrogen form the raw materials of human food. However, to nourish the human system, those simple chemical constituents

now mark! The same learned Doctor was later on again deputed by the medical officer of the Privy Council to inquire into the nourishment of the poorer laboring classes. The results of his researches are embodied in the "Sixth Report on Public Health," published by order of Parliament in the course of the present year. What did the Doctor discover? That the silk weavers, the needle women, the kid glovers, the stocking weavers, and so forth, received, on an average, not even the distress pittance of the cotton operatives, not even the amount of carbon and nitrogen "just sufficient to avert starvation diseases."

> "Moreover," we quote from the report, "as regards the examined families of the agricultural population, it appeared that more than a fifth were with less than the estimated sufficiency of carbonaceous food, that more than one-third were with less than the estimated sufficiency of nitrogenous food, and that in three counties (Berkshire, Oxfordshire and Somersetshire) insufficiency of nitrogenous food was the average local diet." "It must be remembered," adds to official report, "that privation of food is very reluctantly borne, and that, as a rule, great poorness of diet will only come when other privations have preceded it. . . . Even cleanliness will have been found costly or difficult, and if there still be self-respectful endeavours to maintain it, every such endeavour will represent additional pangs of hunger." "These are painful reflections, especially when it is remembered that the poverty to which they advert is not the deserved poverty of idleness; in all cases it is the poverty of working populations. Indeed, the work which obtains the scanty pittance of food is for the most part excessively prolonged."

The report brings out the strange, and rather unexpected fact, "That of the divisions of the United Kingdom," England, Wales, Scotland, and Ireland, "the agricultural populations of England," the richest division, "is considerably the worst fed"; but that even the agricultural laborers of Berkshire, Oxfordshire, and Somersetshire, fare better than great numbers of skilled indoor operatives of the East of London.

Such are the official statements published by order of Parliament in 1864, during the millennium of free trade, at a time when the Chancellor of the Exchequer told the House of Commons that

---

must be supplied in the form of vegetable or animal substances. Potatoes, for instance, contain mainly carbon, while wheaten bread contains carbonaceous and nitrogenous substances in a due proportion. [*Note by Marx.*]

"the average condition of the British laborer has improved in a degree we know to be extraordinary and unexampled in the history of any country or any age."

Upon these official congratulations jars the dry remark of the official Public Health Report:

"The public health of a country means the health of its masses, and the masses will scarcely be healthy unless, to their very base, they be at least moderately prosperous."

Dazzled by the "Progress of the Nation" statistics dancing before his eyes, the Chancellor of the Exchequer exclaims in wild ecstasy:

"From 1842 to 1852 the taxable income of the country increased by 6 per cent; in the eight years from 1853 to 1861, it has increased from the basis taken in 1853 20 per cent! the fact is so astonishing as to be almost incredible! . . . This intoxicating augmentation of wealth and power," adds Mr. Gladstone, "is entirely confined to classes of property!"

If you want to know under what conditions of broken health, tainted morals and mental ruin, that "intoxicating augmentation of wealth and power entirely confined to classes of property" was, and is being produced by the classes of labor, look to the picture hung up in the last "Public Health Report" of the workshops of tailors, printers and dressmakers! Compare the "Report of the Children's Employment Commission" of 1863, where it is stated, for instance, that:

"The potters as a class, both men and women, represent a much degenerated population, both physically and mentally," that "the unhealthy child is an unhealthy parent in his turn, that a progressive deterioration of the race must go on," and that "the degenerescence of the population of Staffordshire would be even greater were it not for the constant recruiting from the adjacent country, and the intermarriages with more healthy races."

Glance at Mr. Tremenheere's Blue Book on the "Grievances complained of by the Journeymen Bakers"! And who has not shuddered at the paradoxical statement made by the inspectors of factories, and illustrated by the Registrar General, that the Lancashire operatives, while put upon the distress pittance of food, were actually improving in health, because of their temporary exclusion by the cotton famine from the cotton factory, and that the mortality of the children was decreasing, because their mothers were now at last allowed to give them, instead of Godfrey's cordial, their own breasts.

Again reverse the medal! The Income and Property Tax Returns laid before the House of Commons on July 20, 1864, teach us that the persons with yearly incomes, valued by the tax-gatherer at £50,000 and upwards, had, from April 5, 1862, to April 5, 1863, been joined by a dozen and one, their number having increased in that single year from 67 to 80. The same returns disclose the fact that about 3,000 persons divide amongst themselves a yearly income at about £25,000,000 sterling, rather more than the total revenue doled out annually to the whole mass of the agricultural laborers of England and Wales. Open the census of 1861, and you will find that the number of the male landed proprietors of England and Wales had decreased from 16,934 in 1851, to 15,066 in 1861, so that the concentration of land had grown in 10 years 11 per cent. If the concentration of the soil of the country in a few hands proceeds at the same rate, the land question will become singularly simplified, as it had become in the Roman empire, when Nero grinned at the discovery that half the Province of Africa was owned by six gentlemen.

We have dwelt so long upon these "facts so astonishing to be almost incredible," because England heads the Europe of commerce and industry. It will be remembered that some months ago one of the refugee sons of Louis Philippe publicly congratulated the English agricultural laborer on the superiority of his lot over that of his less florid comrade on the other side of the Channel. Indeed, with local colors changed, and on a scale somewhat contracted, the English facts reproduce themselves in all the industrious and progressive countries of the Continent. In all of them there has taken place, since 1848, an unheard-of development of industry, and an undreamed-of expansion of imports and exports. In all of them "the augmentation of wealth and power entirely confined to classes of property" was truly "intoxicating." In all of them, as in England, a minority of the working classes got their real wages somewhat advanced; while in most cases the monetary rise of wages denoted no more a real access of comforts than the inmate of the metropolitan poor-house or orphan asylum, for instance, was in the least benefited by his first necessaries costing £9 15s. 8d. in 1861 against £7 7s. 4d. in 1852. Everywhere the great mass of the working classes were sinking down to a lower depth, at the same rate, at least, that those above them were rising in the social scale. In all countries of Europe it has now become a truth demonstrable to every unprejudiced mind, and only denied by those, whose interest it is to hedge other people in a fool's paradise, that no improvement of machinery, no appliance of science to production, no contrivances of communication, no new colonies, no emigration, no opening of markets, no free trade, nor all these things put together, will do away with the miseries of the industrious masses; but that, on the present false base, every fresh development of the productive powers of labor must tend to deepen social contrasts and point social antagonisms. Death of starvation rose almost to the rank of an institution, during this intoxicating epoch of economical progress, in the metropolis of the British Empire. That epoch is marked in the annals of the world by the quickened return, the widening compass, and the deadlier effect of the social pest called a commercial and industrial crisis.

After the failure of the Revolutions of 1848, all party organizations and party journals of the working classes were, on the Continent, crushed by the iron hand of force, the most advanced sons of labor fled in despair to the Transatlantic Republic, and the short-lived dreams of emancipation vanished before an epoch of industrial fever, moral marasme, and political reaction. The defeat of the Continental working classes, partly owed to the diplomacy of the English Government, acting then as now in fraternal solidarity with the Cabinet of St. Petersburg, soon spread its contagious effects to this side of the Channel. While the rout of their Continental brethren unmanned the English working classes, and broke their faith in their own cause, it restored to the landlord and the money-lord their somewhat shaken confidence. They insolently withdrew concessions already advertised. The discoveries of new goldlands led to an immense exodus, leaving an irreparable void in the ranks of the British proletariat. Others of its formerly active members were caught by the temporary bribe of greater work and wages, and turned into "political blacks." All the efforts made at keeping up, or remodeling, the Chartist Movement, failed signally; the press organs of the working class died one by one of the apathy of the masses, and, in point of fact, never before seemed the English working class so thoroughly reconciled to a state of political nullity. If, then, there had been no solidarity of action between the British and the Continental working classes, there was, at all events, a solidarity of defeat.

And yet the period passed since the Revolutions of 1848 has not been without its compensating features. We shall here only point to two great facts.

After a thirty years' struggle, fought with most admirable perseverance, the English working classes, improving a momentaneous split between the landlords and money-lords, succeeded in carrying the Ten Hours' Bill. The immense physical, moral and intellectual benefits hence accruing to the factory operatives, half-yearly chronicled in the reports of the inspectors of factories, are now acknowledged on all sides. Most of the Continental governments had to accept the English Factory Act in more or less modified forms, and the English Parliament itself is every year compelled to enlarge its sphere of action. But besides its practical import, there was something else to exalt the marvelous success of this working men's measure. Through their most notorious organs of science, such as Dr. Ure, Professor Senior, and other sages of that stamp, the middle class had predicted, and to their heart's content proved, that any legal restriction of the hours of labor must sound the death knell of British industry, which, vampyre like, could but live by sucking blood, and children's blood, too. In olden times, child murder was a mysterious rite of the religion of Moloch, but it was practiced on some very solemn occasions only, once a year perhaps, and then Moloch had no exclusive bias for the children of the poor. This struggle about the legal restriction of the hours of labor raged the more fiercely since, apart from frightened avarice, it told indeed upon the great contest between the blind rule of the supply and demand laws which form the political economy of the middle class, and social production controlled by social foresight, which forms the political economy of the working class. Hence the Ten Hours' Bill was not only a great practical success; it was the victory of a principle; it was the first time that in broad daylight the political economy of the middle class succumbed to the political economy of the working class.

But there was in store a still greater victory of the political economy of labor over the political economy of property. We speak of the cooperative movement, especially the co-operative factories raised by the unassisted efforts of a few bold "hands." The value of these great social experiments cannot be over-rated. By deed, instead of by argument, they have shown that production on a large scale, and in accord with the behests of modern science, may be carried on without the existence of a class of masters employing a class of hands; that to bear fruit, the means of labor need not be monopolized as a means of dominion over, and of extortion against, the laboring man himself; and that, like slave labor, like serf labor, hired labor is but a transitory and inferior form, destined to disappear before associated labor plying its toil with a willing hand, a ready mind, and a joyous heart. In England, the seeds of the co-operative system were sown by Robert Owen; the working men's experiments, tried on the Continent, were, in fact, the practical upshot of the theories, not invented, but loudly proclaimed, in 1848.

At the same time, the experience of the period from 1848 to 1864 has proved beyond doubt that, however excellent in principle, and however useful in practice, co-operative labor, if kept within the narrow circle of the casual efforts of private workmen, will never be able to arrest the growth in geometrical progression of monopoly, to free the masses, nor even to perceptibly lighten the burden of their miseries. It is perhaps for this very reason that plausible noblemen, philanthropic middle-class spouters, and even keen political economists, have all at once turned nauseously complimentary to the very cooperative labor system they had vainly tried to nip in the bud by deriding it as the Utopia of the dreamer, or stigmatizing it as the sacrilege of the Socialist. To save the industrious masses, co-operative labor ought to be developed to national dimensions, and consequently, to be fostered by national means. Yet, the lords of land and the lords of capital will always use their political privileges for the defense and perpetuation of their economical monopolies. So far from promoting, they will continue to lay every possible impediment in the way of the emancipation of labor. Remember the sneer with which, last session, Lord Palmerston put down the advocates of the Irish Tenants' Right Bill. The House of Commons, cried he, is a house of landed proprietors.

To conquer political power has therefore become the great duty of the working classes. They seem to have comprehended this, for in England, Germany, Italy, and France there have taken place simultaneous revivals, and simultaneous efforts are being made of the political reorganization of the working men's party.

One element of success they possess—numbers; but numbers weigh only in the balance, if united by combination and led by knowledge. Past experience has shown how disregard of that bond of brotherhood which ought to exist between the workmen of different countries, and incite them to stand firmly by each other in all their struggle for emancipation, will be chastised by the common discomfiture of their incoherent efforts. This thought prompted the working men of different countries assembled on September 28, 1864, in public meeting at St. Martin's Hall, to found the International Association.

Another conviction swayed that meeting.

If the emancipation of the working classes requires their fraternal concurrence, how are they to fulfill that great mission with a foreign policy in pursuit of criminal designs, playing upon national prejudices, and squandering in piratical wars the people's blood and treasure? It was not the wisdom of the ruling classes, but the heroic resistance to their criminal folly by the working classes of England that saved the West of Europe from plunging headlong into an infamous crusade for the perpetuation and propagation of slavery on the other side of the Atlantic. The shameless approval, mock sympathy, or idiotic indifference, with which the upper classes of Europe have witnessed the mountain fortress of the Caucasus falling a prey to, and heroic Poland being assassinated by, Russia; the immense and unresisted encroachments of that barbarous power, whose head is at St. Petersburg, and whose hands are in every cabinet of Europe, have taught the working classes the duty to master themselves the mysteries of international politics; to watch the diplomatic acts of their respective Governments; to counteract them, if necessary, by all means in their power; when unable to prevent, to combine in simultaneous denunciations, and to vindicate the simple laws of morals and justice, which ought to govern the relations of private individuals, as the rules paramount of the intercourse of nations.

The fight for such a foreign policy forms part of the general struggle for the emancipation of the working classes.

Proletarians of all countries, Unite!

READING #4

Marx

"The Hague Congress of the IWA"

In the eighteenth century, he said, kings and potentates used to meet at The Hague to discuss the interests of their Houses.

That was where we wanted to hold the assizes of labor, despite the fears that people sought to inspire us with. It is in the midst of the most reactionary population that we wanted to assert the existence of our great Association, and its expansion and its hopes for the future.

It was said, upon hearing of our decision, that we had sent emissaries to clear the ground. We do not deny that we have emissaries everywhere; but most of them are unknown to us. Our emissaries at The Hague were those workers whose toil is so back-breaking, just as in Amsterdam they are also workers—from among those who work sixteen hours a day. *Those* are our emissaries, nor have we any others. And in all countries where we appear, we find them willing to give us a sympathetic welcome, for they realize very soon that it is improvement of their lot that we seek.

The Hague Congress did three principal things:

It proclaimed the necessity for the working classes to fight, in the political as well as the social sphere, against the old society, a society which is collapsing; and we are happy to see that the resolution of the London Conference is from now on included in our Rules. A group had formed in our midst advocating the workers' abstention from politics.

We have thought it important to point out how very dangerous and baneful to our cause we considered these principles to be.

The worker will some day have to win political supremacy in order to organize labor along new lines; he will have to defeat the old policy supporting old institutions, under penalty—as in the case of the ancient Christians, who neglected and scorned it—of never seeing their kingdom on earth.

But we have by no means affirmed that this goal would be achieved by identical means.

We know of the allowances we must make for the institutions, customs and traditions of the various countries; and we do not deny that there are countries such as America, England, and I would add Holland if I knew your institutions better, where the working people may achieve their goal by peaceful means. If that is true, we must also recognize that in most of the continental countries it is force that will have to be the lever of our revolutions; it is force that we shall some day have to resort to in order to establish a reign of labor.

The Hague Congress has vested the General Council with new and greater powers. Indeed, at a time when kings are gathered together in Berlin, where new and harsher measures of repression are to be adopted against us as a result of that meeting of powerful representatives of the feudal system and past times, and when persecution is being set on foot, the Hague Congress has deemed it wise and necessary to increase the powers of its General Council and to centralize, for the struggle that is about to begin, an action which isolation would render powerless. Besides, whom but our enemies could the authority of the General Council make suspicious? Has it, then, a bureaucracy and an armed police force to impose its will? Is not its authority purely moral, and does it not submit all its decisions to the federations which are entrusted with carrying them out? Under these conditions, kings without army, police and magistracy would be but feeble obstacles to the march of the revolution, were they ever reduced to maintaining their power through moral influence and authority.

Lastly, the Hague Congress has transferred the seat of the General Council to New York. Many people, even among our friends, seem to be surprised by that decision. Are they forgetting, then, that America is becoming a world chiefly of working people, that half a million persons—working people—emigrate to that continent every year, and that the International must take strong root in soil dominated by the working man? And then, the decision of the Congress authorizes the General Council to co-opt such members as it may find necessary and useful for the good of the common cause. Let us hope that it will be wise enough to choose people who will be equal to their task and will be able to bear firmly the banner of our Association in Europe.

Citizens, let us think of the fundamental principle of the International, solidarity! It is by establishing this vivifying principle on a strong basis, among all the working people of all countries, that we shall achieve the great goal we have set ourselves. The revolution needs solidarity, and we have a great example of it in the Paris Commune, which fell because a great revolutionary movement corresponding to that supreme rising of the Paris proletariat did not arise in all centers, in Berlin, Madrid and elsewhere.

As far as I am concerned, I shall continue my effort, and shall work steadily to establish for the future this fruitful solidarity among all working people. I am not withdrawing from the International at all, and the rest of my life will be devoted, as have been my past efforts, to the triumph of the social ideas which some day—you may rest assured of it— will lead to the world-wide victory of the proletariat.

Luxemburg

Rosa Luxemburg (1871–1919) was born in Poland (then divided under German and Russian domination), into a fairly well-to-do and cultured family which enabled this exceptionally bright daughter to pursue an education in Warsaw and then Zurich. By the early 1890s she was active in the Polish revolutionary movement, soon moving to Germany in order to play a more substantial role in the massive and internationally influential German Social Democratic Party. Here she took the lead—with her polemic *Reform or Revolution* (READING #6)—in opposing a reformist dilution of Marxist theory and politics that was being spearheaded by the "revisionist" spokesman Eduard Bernstein.

At the same time, Luxemburg was concerned that the bureaucratic organizational apparatus of the German Social Democracy would—despite a formal adherence to Marxist "orthodoxy"—fail to reach out to working people in a manner that would facilitate the development of the revolutionary energy which she felt was latent within them. This highlights the importance of her insistence that Marxism must not be allowed to stagnate (READING #5). It also helps explain her negative reaction to Lenin's emphasis on organizational centralism in Russia, although—in the wake of the 1905 wave of strikes and workers' uprisings throughout eastern Europe—she and Lenin soon found themselves standing closer together. By contrast, the 1905 experience compelled Luxemburg to write her 1906 classic, *Mass Strike, Political Party and Trade Unions* (READING #7), which criticized the bureaucratic conservatism permeating so much of German Social Democracy, and which analyzes the actual dynamics of revolutionary situations which are animated by spontaneous upsurges of largely unorganized masses unexpectedly swept into motion.

Luxemburg's opposition to those who stood for "business as usual" in the trade unions and party (even the "pope" of Marxist orthodoxy, Karl Kautsky) placed her unambiguously in the revolutionary wing of German Social Democracy. Refusing to occupy a "safer" and marginalized position as a women's spokesperson in the socialist movement, she nonetheless had a vibrant sense of the interpenetration of women's liberation and working-class liberation (READING #9). But her focus was on issues such as the development of capitalism into a new imperialist phase which threatened to bring about a devastating world war. Her major economic work, *The Accumulation of Capital* (1913), was inevitably followed up by a more practical and tragic political critique of 1915, *The Junius Pamphlet: The Crisis of German Social Democracy* (READING #8). This was written from a prison cell because of her opposition to the German war effort—while a majority of the de-radicalized, bureaucratic Social Democratic Party rallied to "the fatherland."

Luxemburg joined with a relative handful of revolutionary Marxists in Germany to organize the oppositional Spartakusbund. When kindred spirits in Russia—led by Lenin's Bolsheviks—brought about a workers' revolution in 1917, she was elated. Not uncritical of some of Lenin's and Trotsky's policies in Russia, she nonetheless strongly identified with what they represented, and she helped form the German Communist Party at the end of 1918. The monarchy had just collapsed—to be replaced by the Weimar Republic and a moderate Social-Democratic government—in the wake of the devastation and defeat of World War I. Amid the chaos and revolutionary ferment, masses of workers were rallying to the orientation with which Luxemburg was identified. But her enemies (including the Social Democratic bureaucracy) were spreading vicious and provocative slanders about "Red Rosa," and right-wing paramilitary units were being organized to combat insurgent workers and kill revolutionary militants. An abortive uprising in early 1919 was used as a pretext to murder Luxemburg, Karl Liebknecht, and others.

For some who reject revolutionary and Marxist perspectives—one thinks of Bertram D. Wolfe and Sidney Hook, but there have been many others—Rosa Luxemburg is seen as a "good" Marxist. . . good in spite of her Marxism. But as she actually lived her life, her Marxism was interwoven with her admirable personal qualities and inseparable from her penetrating analyses. Such things connect her intimately to the others featured in this reader.

READING #5

"Stagnation and Progress of Marxism"

In his shallow but at times interesting causerie entitled *Die soziale Bewegung in Frankreich und Belgien* (The Socialist Movement in France and Belgium), Karl Gruen remarks, aptly enough, that Fourier's and Saint-Simon's theories had very different effects upon their respective adherents. Saint-Simon was the spiritual ancestor of a whole generation of brilliant investigators and writers in various fields of intellectual activity; but Fourier's followers were, with few exceptions, persons who blindly parroted their master's words, and were incapable of making any advance upon his teaching. Gruen's explanation of this difference is that Fourier presented the world with a finished system, elaborated in all its details; whereas Saint-Simon merely tossed his disciples a loose bundle of great thoughts. Although it seems to me that Gruen pays too little attention to the inner, the essential, difference between the theories of these two classical authorities in the domain of utopian socialism, I feel that on the whole his observation is sound. Beyond question, a system of ideas which is merely sketched in broad outline proves far more stimulating than a finished and symmetrical structure which leaves nothing to be added and offers no scope for the independent efforts of an active mind.

Does this account for the stagnation in Marxist doctrine which has been noticeable for a good many years? The actual fact is that—apart from one or two independent contributions which mark a certain theoretical advance—since the publication of the last volume of *Capital* and of the last of Engels's writings there have appeared nothing more than a few excellent popularizations and expositions of Marxist theory. The substance of that theory remains just where the two founders of scientific socialism left it.

Is this because the Marxist system has imposed too rigid a framework upon the independent activities of the mind? It is undeniable that Marx has had a somewhat restrictive influence upon the free development of theory in the case of many of his pupils. Both Marx and Engels found it necessary to disclaim responsibility for the utterances of many who chose to call themselves Marxists! The scrupulous endeavor to keep "within the bounds of Marxism" may at times have been just as disastrous to the integrity of the thought process as has been the other extreme—the complete repudiation of the Marxist outlook, and the determination to manifest "independence of thought" at all hazards.

Still, it is only where economic matters are concerned that we are entitled to speak of a more or less completely elaborated body of doctrines bequeathed us by Marx. The most valuable of all his teachings, the materialist-dialectical conception of history, presents itself to us as nothing more than a method of investigation, as a few inspired leading thoughts, which offer us glimpses into an entirely new world, which open to us endless perspectives of independent activity, which wing our spirits for bold flights into unexplored regions.

Nevertheless, even in this domain, with few exceptions the Marxist heritage lies fallow. The splendid new weapon rusts unused; and the theory of historical materialism remains as unelaborated and sketchy as it was when first formulated by its creators.

It cannot be said, then, that the rigidity and completeness of the Marxist edifice are the explanation of the failure of Marx's successors to go on with the building.

We are often told that our movement lacks the persons of talent who might be capable of further elaborating Marx's theories. Such a lack is, indeed, of long standing; but the lack itself demands an explanation, and cannot be put forward to answer the primary question. We must remember that each epoch forms its own human material; that if in any period there is a genuine need for theoretical exponents, the period will create the forces requisite for the satisfaction of that need.

But is there a genuine need, an effective demand, for a further development of Marxist theory?

In an article upon the controversy between the Marxist and the Jevonsian schools in England, Bernard Shaw, the talented exponent of

Fabian semisocialism, derides Hyndman for having said that the first volume of *Capital* had given him a complete understanding of Marx, and that there were no gaps in Marxist theory—although Friedrich Engels, in the preface to the second volume of *Capital*, subsequently declared that the first volume with its theory of value, had left unsolved a fundamental economic problem, whose solution would not be furnished until the third volume was published. Shaw certainly succeeded here in making Hyndman's position seem a trifle ridiculous, though Hyndman might well derive consolation from the fact that practically the whole socialist world was in the same boat!

The third volume of *Capital*, with its solution of the problem of the rate of profit (the basic problem of Marxist economics), did not appear till 1894. But in Germany, as in all other lands, agitation had been carried on with the aid of the unfinished material contained in the first volume; the Marxist doctrine had been popularized and had found acceptance upon the basis of this first volume alone; the success of the incomplete Marxist theory had been phenomenal; and no one had been aware that there was any gap in the teaching.

Furthermore, when the third volume finally saw the light, whilst to begin with it attracted some attention in the restricted circles of the experts, and aroused here a certain amount of comment—as far as the socialist movement as a whole was concerned, the new volume made practically no impression in the wide regions where the ideas expounded in the original book had become dominant. The theoretical conclusions of volume 3 have not hitherto evoked any attempt at popularization, nor have they secured wide diffusion. On the contrary, even among the social democrats we sometimes hear, nowadays, reechoes of the "disappointment" with the third volume of *Capital* which is so frequently voiced by bourgeois economists—and thus these social democrats merely show how fully they had accepted the "incomplete" exposition of the theory of value presented in the first volume.

How can we account for so remarkable a phenomenon?

Shaw, who (to quote his own expression) is fond of "sniggering" at others, may have good reason here, for making fun of the whole socialist movement, insofar as it is grounded upon Marx! But if he were to do this, he would be "sniggering" at a very serious manifestation of our social life. The strange fate of the second and third volumes of *Capital* is conclusive evidence as to the general destiny of theoretical research in our movement.

From the scientific standpoint, the third volume of *Capital* must, no doubt, be primarily regarded as the completion of Marx's critique of capitalism. Without this third volume, we cannot understand, either the actually dominant law of the rate of profit; or the splitting up of surplus value into profit, interest, and rent; or the working of the law of value within the field of competition. But, and this is the main point, all these problems, however important from the outlook of pure theory, are comparatively unimportant from the practical outlook of the class war. As far as the class war is concerned, the fundamental theoretical problem is the origin of surplus value, that is, the scientific explanation of exploitation; together with the elucidation of the tendency towards the socialization of the process of production, that is, the scientific explanation of the objective groundwork of the socialist revolution.

Both these problems are solved in the first volume of *Capital*, which deduces the "expropriation of the expropriators" as the inevitable and ultimate result of the production of surplus value and of the progressive concentration of capital. Therewith, as far as theory is concerned, the essential need of the labor movement is satisfied. The workers, being actively engaged in the class war, have no direct interest in the question how surplus value is distributed among the respective groups of exploiters; or in the question how, in the course of this distribution, competition brings about rearrangements of production.

That is why, for socialists in general, the third volume of *Capital* remains an unread book.

But, in our movement, what applies to Marx's economic doctrines applies to theoretical research in general. It is pure illusion to suppose that the working class, in its upward striving, can of its own accord become immeasurably creative in the theoretical domain. True that, as Engels said, the working class alone has today preserved an understanding of and interest in theory. The workers' craving for knowledge is one of the most noteworthy cultural manifestations of our day. Morally, too, the working-class struggle denotes the cultural renovation of society. But active participation of the workers in the march of science is subject to the fulfillment of very definite social conditions.

In every class society, intellectual culture (science and art) is created by the ruling class; and the aim of this culture is in part to ensure the direct satisfaction of the needs of the social process, and in part to satisfy the mental needs of the members of the governing class.

In the history of earlier class struggles, aspiring classes (like the Third Estate in recent days) could anticipate political dominion by establishing an intellectual dominance, inasmuch as, while they were still subjugated classes, they could set up a new science and a new art against obsolete culture of the decadent period.

The proletariat is in a very different position. As a nonpossessing class, it cannot in the course of its struggle upwards spontaneously create a mental culture of its own while it remains in the framework of bourgeois society. Within that society, and so long as its economic foundations persist, there can be no other culture than a bourgeois culture. Although certain "socialist" professors may acclaim the wearing of neckties, the use of visiting cards, and the riding of bicycles by proletarians as notable instances of participation in cultural progress, the working class as such remains outside contemporary culture. Notwithstanding the fact that the workers create with their own hands the whole social substratum of this culture, they are only admitted to its enjoyment insofar as such admission is requisite to the satisfactory performance of their functions in the economic and social process of capitalist society.

The working class will not be in a position to create a science and an art of its own until it has been fully emancipated from its present class position.

The utmost it can do today is to safeguard bourgeois culture from the vandalism of the bourgeois reaction, and create the social conditions requisite for a free cultural development. Even along these lines, the workers, within the extant form of society, can only advance insofar as they can create for themselves the intellectual weapons needed in their struggle for liberation.

But this reservation imposes upon the working class (that is to say, upon the workers' intellectual leaders) very narrow limits in the field of intellectual activity. The domain of their creative energy is confined to one specific department of science, namely social science. For, inasmuch as "thanks to the peculiar connection of the idea of the Fourth Estate with our historical epoch," enlightenment concerning the laws of social development has become essential to the workers in the class struggle, this connection has borne good fruit in social science, and the monument of the proletarian culture of our day is—Marxist doctrine.

But Marx's creation, which as a scientific achievement is a titanic whole, transcends the plain demands of the proletarian class struggle for whose purposes it was created. Both in his detailed and comprehensive analysis of capitalist economy, and in his method of historical research with its immeasurable field of application, Marx has offered much more than was directly essential for the practical conduct of the class war.

Only in proportion as our movement progresses, and demands the solution of new practical problems do we dip once more into the treasury of Marx's thought, in order to extract therefrom and to utilize new fragments of his doctrine. But since our movement, like all the campaigns of practical life, inclines to go on working in old ruts of thought, and to cling to principles after they have ceased to be valid, the theoretical utilization of the Marxist system proceeds very slowly.

If, then, today we detect a stagnation in our movement as far as these theoretical matters are concerned, this is not because the Marxist theory upon which we are nourished is incapable of development or has become out-of-date. On the contrary, it is because we have not yet learned how to make an adequate use of the most important mental weapons which we had taken out of the Marxist arsenal on account of our urgent need for them in the earlier stages of our struggle. It is not true that, as far as the practical struggle is concerned, Marx is out-of-date, that we have superseded Marx. On the contrary, Marx, in his scientific creation, has outstripped us as a party of practical fighters. It is not true that Marx no longer suffices for our needs. On the contrary, our needs are not yet adequate for the utilization of Marx's ideas.

Thus do the social conditions of proletarian existence in contemporary society, conditions first elucidated by Marxist theory, take vengeance by the fate they impose upon Marxist theory itself. Though that theory is an incomparable instrument of intellectual culture, it remains unused because, while it is inapplicable to bourgeois class culture, it greatly transcends the needs of the working class in the matter of weapons for the daily struggle. Not until the working class has been liberated from its present conditions of existence will the Marxist method of research be socialized in conjunction with other means of production, so that it can be fully utilized for the benefit of humanity at large, and so that it can be developed to the full measure of its functional capacity.

Reading #6
"Reform or Revolution?" (excerpts)

Author's Introduction
At first view the title of this work may be found surprising. Can the social democracy be against reforms? Can we counterpose the social revolution, the transformation of the existing order, our final goal, to social reforms? Certainly not. The daily struggle for reforms, for the amelioration of the condition of the workers within the framework of the existing social order, and for democratic institutions, offers to the social democracy the only means of engaging in the proletarian class war and working in the direction of the final goal—the conquest of political power and the suppression of wage labor. Between social reforms and revolution there exists for the social democracy an indissoluble tie. The struggle for reforms is its means; the social revolution, its aim.

It is in Eduard Bernstein's theory, presented in his articles on "Problems of Socialism," *Neue Zeit* of 1897–98, and in his book *Die Voraussetzungen des Sozialismus and die Aufgaben der Sozialdemokratie* [The Preconditions of Socialism and the Tasks of Social Democracy—in English published under the title *Evolutionary Socialism*—Ed.] that we find for the first time, the opposition of the two factors of the labor movement. His theory tends to counsel us to renounce the social transformation, the final goal of the social democracy and, inversely, to make of social reforms, the means of the class struggle, its aim. Bernstein himself has very clearly and characteristically formulated this viewpoint when he wrote: "The final goal, no matter what it is, is nothing; the movement is everything."

But since the final goal of socialism constitutes the only decisive factor distinguishing the social democratic movement from bourgeois democracy and from bourgeois radicalism, the only factor transforming the entire labor movement from a vain effort to repair the capitalist order into a class struggle against this order, for the suppression of this order—the question: "Reform or revolution?" as it is posed by Bernstein, equals for the social democracy the question: "To be or not to be?" In the controversy with Bernstein and his followers, everybody in the party ought to understand clearly it is not a question of this or that method of struggle, or the use of this or that set of tactics, but of the very existence of the social democratic movement.

Upon a casual consideration of Bernstein's theory, this may appear like an exaggeration. Does he not continually mention the social democracy and its aims? Does he not repeat again and again, in very explicit language, that he too strives toward the final goal of socialism, but in another way? Does he not stress particularly that he fully approves of the present practice of the social democracy?

That is all true, to be sure. It is also true that every new movement, when it first elaborates its theory and policy, begins by finding support in the preceding movement, though it may be in direct contradiction with the latter. It begins by suiting itself to the forms found at hand and by speaking the language spoken hereto. In time, the new grain breaks through the old husk. The new movement finds its own forms and its own language.

To expect an opposition against scientific socialism at its very beginning, to express itself clearly, fully, and to the last consequence on the subject of its real content; to expect it to deny openly and bluntly the theoretic basis of the social democracy—would amount to underrating the power of scientific socialism. Today he who wants to pass as a socialist, and at the same time would declare war on Marxian doctrine, the most stupendous product of the human mind in the century, must begin with involuntary esteem for Marx. He must begin by acknowledging himself to be his disciple, by seeking in Marx's own teachings the points of support for an attack on the latter, while he represents this attack as a further development of Marxian doctrine. On this account, we must, unconcerned by its outer forms, pick out the sheathed kernel of Bernstein's theory. This is a matter of urgent necessity for the broad layers of the industrial proletariat in our party.

No coarser insult, no baser aspersion, can be thrown against the workers than the remark: "Theoretic controversies are only for academicians." Some time ago Lassalle said: "Only when science and the workers, these opposite poles of society, become one, will they crush in their arms of steel all obstacles to culture." The entire strength of the modern labor movement rests on theoretic knowledge.

But doubly important is this knowledge for the workers in the present case, because it is precisely they and their influence in the movement that are in the balance here. It is their skin that is being brought to market. The opportunist theory in the party, the theory formulated by Bernstein, is nothing else than an unconscious attempt to assure predominance to the petty bourgeois elements that have entered our party, to change the policy and aims of our party in their direction. The question of reform and revolution, of the final goal and the movement, is basically, in another form, but the question of the petty bourgeois or proletarian character of the labor movement.

It is, therefore, in the interest of the proletarian mass of the party to become acquainted, actively and in detail, with the present theoretic controversy with opportunism. As long as theoretic knowledge remains the privilege of a handful of "academicians" in the party, the latter will face the danger of going astray. Only when the great mass of workers take the keen and dependable weapons of scientific socialism in their own hands will all the petty bourgeois inclinations, all the opportunist currents, come to naught. The movement will then find itself on sure and firm ground. "Quantity will do it."

Berlin, April 18, 1899

The Opportunist Method

If it is true that theories are only the images of the phenomena of the exterior world in the human consciousness, it must be added, concerning Eduard Bernstein's system, that theories are sometimes inverted images. Think of a theory of instituting socialism by means of social reforms in the face of the complete stagnation of the reform movement in Germany. Think of a theory of trade-union control over production in face of the defeat of the metal workers in England. Consider the theory of winning a majority in Parliament, after the revision of the constitution of Saxony and in view of the most recent attempts against universal suffrage. However, the pivotal point of Bernstein's system is not located in his conception of the practical tasks of the social democracy. It is found in his stand on the course of the objective development of capitalist society, which, in turn is closely bound to his conception of the practical tasks of the social democracy.

According to Bernstein, a general decline of capitalism seems to be increasingly improbable because, on the one hand, capitalism shows a greater capacity of adaptation, and, on the other hand, capitalist production becomes more and more varied.

The capacity of capitalism to adapt itself, says Bernstein, is manifested first in the disappearance of general crises, resulting from the development of the credit system, employers' organizations, wider means of communication and informational services. It shows itself secondly, in the tenacity of the middle classes, which hails from the growing differentiation of the branches of production and the elevation of vast layers of the proletariat to the level of the middle class. It is furthermore proved, argues Bernstein, by the amelioration of the economic and political situation of the proletariat as a result of its trade-union activity.

From this theoretic stand is derived the following general conclusion about the practical work of the social democracy. The latter must not direct its daily activity toward the conquest of political power, but toward the betterment of the condition of the working class within the existing order. It must not expect to institute socialism as a result of a political and social crisis, but should build socialism by means of the progressive extension of social control and the gradual application of the principle of cooperation.

Bernstein himself sees nothing new in his theories. On the contrary, he believes them to be in agreement with certain declarations of Marx and Engels. Nevertheless, it seems to us that it is difficult to deny that they are in formal contradiction with the conceptions of scientific socialism.

If Bernstein's revisionism merely consisted in affirming that the march of capitalist development is slower than was thought before, he would merely be presenting an argument for adjourning the conquest of power by the proletariat, on which everybody agreed up to now. Its only consequence would be a slowing up of the pace of the struggle.

But that is not the case. What Bernstein questions is not the rapidity of the development of capitalist society, but the march of the development itself and, consequently, the very possibility of a change to socialism.

Socialist theory up to now declared that the point of departure for a transformation to socialism would be a general and catastrophic crisis. We must distinguish in this outlook two things: the fundamental idea and its exterior form.

The fundamental idea consists of the affirmation that capitalism, as a result of its own inner contradictions, moves toward a point when it will be unbalanced, when it will simply become impossible. There were good reasons for conceiving that juncture in the form of a catastrophic general commercial crisis. But that is of secondary importance when the fundamental idea is considered.

The scientific basis of socialism rests, as is well known, on three principal results of capitalist development. First, on the growing anarchy of capitalist economy, leading inevitably to its ruin. Second, on the progressive socialization of the process of production, which creates the germs of the future social order. And third, on the increased organization and consciousness of the proletarian class, which constitutes the active factor in the coming revolution.

Bernstein pulls away the first of the three fundamental supports of scientific socialism. He says that capitalist development does not lead to a general economic collapse.

He does not merely reject a certain form of the collapse. He rejects the very possibility of collapse. He says textually: "One could claim that by collapse of the present society is meant something else than a general commercial crisis, worse than all others, that is, a complete collapse of the capitalist system brought about as a result of its own contradictions." And to this he replies: "With the growing development of society a complete and almost general collapse of the present system of production becomes more and more improbable, because capitalist development increases on the one hand the capacity of adaptation and, on the other—that is, at the same time, the differentiation of industry" (*Neue Zeit*, 1897–98, vol. 18, p. 555).

But then the question arises: Why and how, in that case, shall we attain the final goal? According to scientific socialism, the historic necessity of the socialist revolution manifests itself above all in the growing anarchy of capitalism, which drives the system into an impasse. But if one admits with Bernstein that capitalist development does not move in the direction of its own ruin, then socialism ceases to be objectively necessary. There remain the other two mainstays of the scientific explanation of socialism, which are also said to be consequences of capitalism itself: the socialization of the process of production and the growing consciousness of the proletariat. It is these two matters that Bernstein has in mind when he says: "The suppression of the theory of collapse does not in any way deprive socialist doctrine of its power of persuasion. For, examined closely, what are all the factors enumerated by us that make for the suppression of the modification of the former crises?

Nothing else, in fact, than the conditions, or even in part the germs of the socialization of production and exchange" (ibid., p. 554).

Very little reflection is needed to understand that here, too, we face a false conclusion. Where lies the importance of all the phenomena that are said by Bernstein to be the means of capitalist adaptation—cartels, the credit system, the development of means of communication, the amelioration of the situation of the working class, etc.? Obviously, in that they suppress or, at least, attenuate the internal contradictions of capitalist economy, and stop the development or the aggravation of these contradictions. Thus the suppression of crises can only mean the suppression of the antagonism between production and exchange on the capitalist base. The amelioration of the situation of the working class, or the penetration of certain fractions of the class into the middle layers, can only mean the attenuation of the antagonism between capital and labor. But if the mentioned factors suppress the capitalist contradictions and consequently save the system from ruin, if they enable capitalism to maintain itself—and that is why Bernstein calls them "means of adaptation"—how can cartels, the credit system, trade unions, etc., be at the same time "the conditions and even, in part, the germs" of socialism? Obviously only in the sense that they express most clearly the social character of production.

But by presenting it in its capitalist form, the same factors render superfluous, inversely, in the same measure, the transformation of this socialized production into socialist production. That is why they can be the germs or conditions of a socialist order only in a theoretic sense and not in a historic sense. They are phenomena which, in the light of our conception of socialism, we know to be related to socialism but which, in fact, not only do not lead to a socialist revolution but render it, on the contrary, superfluous.

There remains one force making for socialism—the class consciousness of the proletariat. But it, too, is in the given case not the simple intellectual reflection of the growing contradictions of capitalism and its approaching decline. It is now no more than an ideal whose force of persuasion rests only on the perfection attributed to it.

We have here, in brief, the explanation of the socialist program by means of "pure reason." We have here, to use simpler language, an idealist explanation of socialism. The objective necessity of socialism, the explanation of socialism as the result of the material development of society, falls to the ground.

Revisionist theory thus places itself in a dilemma. Either the socialist transformation is, as was admitted up to now, the consequence of the internal contradictions of capitalism, and with the growth of capitalism will develop its inner contradictions, resulting inevitably, at some point, in its collapse, (in that case the "means of adaptation" are ineffective and the theory of collapse is correct); or the "means of adaptation" will really stop the collapse of the capitalist system and thereby enable capitalism to maintain itself by suppressing its own contradictions. In that case socialism ceases to be a historic necessity. It then becomes anything you want to call it, but is no longer the result of the material development of society.

The dilemma leads to another. Either revisionism is correct in its position on the course of capitalist development, and therefore the socialist transformation of society is only a utopia, or socialism is not a utopia, and the theory of "means of adaptation" is false. There is the question in a nutshell. . . .

Conquest of Political Power

The fate of democracy is bound up, we have seen, with the fate of the labor movement. But does the development of democracy render superfluous or impossible a proletarian revolution, that is, the conquest of the political power by the workers?

Bernstein settles the question by weighing minutely the good and bad sides of social reform and social revolution. He does it almost in the same manner in which cinnamon or pepper is weighed out in a consumers' cooperative store. He sees the legislative course of historic development as the action of "intelligence," while the revolutionary course of historic development is for him the action of "feeling." Reformist activity, he recognizes as a slow method of historic progress, revolution as a rapid method of progress. In legislation he sees a methodic force; in revolution, a spontaneous force.

We have known for a long time that the petty bourgeois reformer finds "good" and "bad" sides in everything. He nibbles a bit at all grasses. But the real course of events is little affected by such combination. The carefully gathered little pile of the "good sides" of all things possible collapses at the first fillip of history. Historically, legislative reform and the revolutionary method function in accordance with influences that are much more profound than the consideration of the advantages or inconveniences of one method or another.

In the history of bourgeois society, legislative reform served to strengthen progressively the rising class till the latter was sufficiently strong to seize political power, to suppress the existing juridical system, and to construct itself a new one. Bernstein, thundering against the conquest of political power as a theory of Blanquist violence, has the misfortune of labelling as a Blanquist error that which has always been the pivot and the motive force of human history. From the first appearance of class societies having the class struggle as the essential content of their history, the conquest of political power has been the aim of all rising classes. Here is the starting point and end of every historic period. This can be seen in the long struggle of the Latin peasantry against the financiers and nobility of ancient Rome, in the struggle of the medieval nobility against the bishops and in the struggle of the artisans against the nobles, in the cities of the Middle Ages. In modern times, we see it in the struggle of the bourgeoisie against feudalism.

Legislative reform and revolution are not different methods of historic development that can be picked out at pleasure from the counter of history, just as one chooses hot or cold sausages. Legislative reform and revolution are different *factors* in the development of class society. They condition and complement each other, and are at the same time reciprocally exclusive, as are the north and south poles, the bourgeoisie and the proletariat.

Every legal constitution is the *product* of a revolution. In the history of classes, revolution is the act of political creation, while legislation is the political expression of the life of a society that has already come into being. Work for reform does not contain its own force, independent from revolution. During every historic period, work for reforms is carried on only in the direction given to it by the impetus of the last revolution, and continues as long as the impulsion of the last revolution continues to make itself felt. Or, to put it more concretely, in each historic period work for reforms is carried on only in the framework of the social form created by the last revolution. Here is the kernel of the problem.

It is contrary to history to represent work for reforms as a long-drawn-out revolution and revolution as a condensed series of reforms. A social transformation and a legislative reform do not differ according to their duration but according to their content. The secret of historic change through the utilization of political power resides precisely in the transformation of simple quantitative modification into a new quality, or to speak more concretely, in the passage of a historic period from one given form of society to another.

That is why people who pronounce themselves in favor of the method of legislative reform *in place of and in contradistinction to* the conquest of political power and social revolution, do not really choose a more tranquil, calmer and slower road to the *same* goal, but a *different* goal. Instead of taking a stand for the establishment of a new society they take a stand for surface modification of the old society. If we follow the political conceptions of revisionism, we arrive at the same conclusion that is reached when we follow the economic theories of revisionism. Our program becomes not the realization of *socialism*, but the reform of *capitalism*: not the suppression of the system of wage labor, but the diminution of exploitation, that is, the suppression of the abuses of capitalism instead of the suppression of capitalism itself.

Does the reciprocal role of legislative reform and revolution apply only to the class struggles of the past? Is it possible that now, as a result of the development of the bourgeois juridical system, the function of moving society from one historic phase to another belongs to legislative reform, and that the conquest of state power by the proletariat has really become "an empty phrase," as Bernstein puts it?

The very opposite is true. What distinguishes bourgeois society from other class societies—from ancient society and from the social order of the Middle Ages? Precisely the fact that class domination does not rest on "acquired rights" but on *real economic relations*—the fact that wage labor is not a juridical relation, but purely an economic relation. In our juridical system there is not a single legal formula for the class domination of today. The few remaining traces of such formulas of class domination are (as that concerning servants) survivals of feudal society.

How can wage slavery be suppressed the "legislative way," if wage slavery is not expressed in laws? Bernstein, who would do away with capitalism by means of legislative reform, finds himself in the same situation as Uspensky's Russian policeman who tells: "Quickly I seized the rascal by the collar! But what do I see? The confounded fellow has no collar!" And that is precisely Bernstein's difficulty.

"All previous societies were based on an antagonism between an oppressing class and an oppressed class" (*Communist Manifesto*). But in the preceding phases of modern society, this antagonism was expressed in distinctly determined juridical relations and could, especially because of that, accord, to a certain extent, a place to new relations within the framework of the old. "In the midst of serfdom, the serf raised himself to the rank of a member of the town community" (*Communist Manifesto*). How was that made possible? It was made possible by the progressive suppression of all feudal privileges in the environs of the city: the corvee, the right to special dress, the inheritance tax, the lord's claim to the best cattle, the personal levy, marriage under duress, the right to succession, etc., which all together constituted serfdom.

In the same way, the small bourgeoisie of the Middle Ages succeeded in raising itself, while it was still under the yoke of feudal absolutism, to the rank of bourgeoisie (*Communist Manifesto*). By what means? By means of the formal partial suppression or complete loosening of the corporative bonds, by the progressive transformation of the fiscal administration and of the army.

Consequently, when we consider the question from the abstract viewpoint, not from the historic viewpoint, we can *imagine* (in view of the former class relations) a legal passage, according to the reformist method, from feudal society to bourgeois society. But what do we see in reality? In reality, we see that legal reforms not only did not obviate the seizure of political power by the bourgeoisie, but have, on the contrary, prepared for it and led to it. A formal social-political transformation was indispensable for the abolition of slavery as well as for the complete suppression of feudalism.

But the situation is entirely different now. No law obliges the proletariat to submit itself to the yoke of capitalism. Poverty, the lack of means of production, obliges the proletariat to submit itself to the yoke of capitalism. And no law in the world can give to the proletariat the means of production while it remains in the framework of bourgeois society, for not laws but economic development have torn the means of production from the producers' possession.

And neither is the exploitation inside the system of wage labor based on laws. The level of wages is not fixed by legislation, but by economic factors. The phenomenon of capitalist exploitation does not rest on a legal disposition, but on the purely economic fact that labor power plays in this exploitation the role of merchandise possessing, among other characteristics, the agreeable quality of producing value—*more* than the value it consumes in the form of the laborer's means of subsistence. In short, the fundamental relations of the domination of the capitalist class cannot be transformed by means of legislative reforms, on the basis of capitalist society, because these relations have not been introduced by bourgeois laws, nor have they received the form of such laws. Apparently Bernstein is not aware of this, for he speaks of "socialist reforms." On the other hand, he seems to express implicit recognition of this when he writes, on page 10 of his book, that "the economic motive acts freely today, while formerly it was masked by all kinds of relations of domination, by all sorts of ideology."

It is one of the peculiarities of the capitalist order that within it all the elements of the future society first assume, in their development, a form not approaching socialism but, on the contrary, a form moving more and more away from socialism. Production takes on a progressively increasing social character. But under what form is the social character of capitalist production expressed? It is expressed in the form of the large enterprise, in the form of the shareholding concern, the cartel, within which the capitalist antagonisms, capitalist exploitation, the oppression of labor-power, are augmented to the extreme.

In the army, capitalist development leads to the extension of obligatory military service, to the reduction of the time of service and, consequently, to a material approach to a popular militia. But all of this takes place under the form of modern militarism, in which the domination of the people by the militarist state and the class character of the state manifest themselves most clearly.

In the field of political relations, the development of democracy brings—in the measure that it finds a favorable soil—the participation of all popular strata in political life and, consequently, some sort of "people's state." But this participation takes the form of bourgeois parliamentarism, in which class antagonism and class domination are not done away with, but are, on the contrary, displayed in the open. Exactly because capitalist development moves through these contradictions, it is necessary to extract the kernel of socialist society from its capitalist shell. Exactly for this reason must the proletariat seize political power and suppress completely the capitalist system.

Of course, Bernstein draws other conclusions. If the development of democracy leads to the aggravation and not to the lessening of capitalist antagonisms, "the social democracy," he answers us, "in order not to render its task more difficult, must by all means try to stop social reforms and the extension of democratic institutions." Indeed, that would be the right thing to do if the social democracy found to its taste, in the petty bourgeois manner, the futile task of picking for itself all the good sides of history and rejecting the bad sides of history. However, in that case, it should at the same time "try to stop" capitalism in general, for there is no doubt that the latter is the rascal placing all these obstacles in the way of socialism. But capitalism furnishes besides the *obstacles* also the only *possibilities* of realizing the socialist program. The same can be said about democracy.

If democracy has become superfluous or annoying to the bourgeoisie, it is on the contrary and indispensable to the working class. It is necessary to the working class because it creates the political forms (autonomous administration, electoral rights, etc.) which will serve the proletariat as fulcrums in its task of transforming bourgeois society. Democracy is indispensable to the working class, because only through the exercise of its democratic rights, in the struggle for democracy, can the proletariat become aware of its class interests and its historic task.

In a word, democracy is indispensable not because it renders superfluous the conquest of political power by the proletariat, but because it renders this conquest of power both *necessary* and *possible*. When Engels, in his preface to the *Class Struggles in France*, revised the tactics of the modern labor movement and urged the legal struggle as opposed to the barricades, he did not have in mind—this comes out of every line of the preface—the question of a definite conquest of political power, but the contemporary daily struggle. He did not have in mind the attitude that the proletariat must take toward the capitalist state at the time of its seizure of power, but the attitude of the proletariat while in the bounds of the capitalist state. Engels was giving directions to the proletariat *oppressed*, and not to the proletariat victorious.

On the other hand, Marx's well-known sentence on the agrarian question in England (Bernstein leans on it heavily) in which he says: "We shall probably succeed easier by buying the estates of the landlords," does not refer to the stand of the proletariat *before, but after its victory*. For there evidently can be a question of buying the property of the old dominant class only when the workers are in power. The possibility envisaged by Marx is that of the *pacific exercise of the dictatorship of the proletariat* and not the replacement of the dictatorship with capitalist social reforms. There was no doubt for Marx and Engels about the necessity of having the proletariat conquer political power. It is left to Bernstein to consider the poultry-yard of bourgeois parliamentarism as the organ by means of which we are to realize the most formidable social transformation of history, *the passage from capitalist society to socialism.*

Bernstein introduces his theory by warning the proletariat against the danger of acquiring power too early. That is, according to Bernstein, the proletariat ought to leave the bourgeois society in its present condition and itself suffer a frightful defeat. If the proletariat came to power, it could draw from Bernstein's theory the following "practical" conclusion: to go to sleep. His theory condemns the proletariat, at the most decisive moments of the struggle, to inactivity, to a passive betrayal of its own cause.

Our program would be a miserable scrap of paper if it could not serve us in *all* eventualities, at *all* moments of the struggle, and if it did not serve us by its *application* and not by its non-application. If our program contains the formula of the historic development of society from capitalism to socialism, it must also formulate, in all its characteristic fundamentals, all the transitory phases of this development, and it should, consequently, be able to indicate to the proletariat what ought to be its corresponding action at every moment on the road toward socialism. There can be no time for the proletariat when it will be obliged to abandon its program or be abandoned by it.

Practically, this is manifested in the fact that there can be no time when the proletariat, placed in power by the force of events, is not in the condition, or is not morally obliged, to take certain measures for the realization of its program, that is, take transitory measures in the direction of socialism. Behind the belief that the socialist program can collapse completely at any point of the dictatorship of the proletariat lurks the other belief that *socialist program is, generally and at all times, unrealizable.*

And what if the transitory measures are premature? The question hides a great number of mistaken ideas concerning the real course of a social transformation.

In the first place, the seizure of political power by the proletariat, that is to say by a large popular class, is not produced artificially. It presupposes (with the exception of such cases as the Paris Commune, when power was not obtained by the proletariat after a conscious struggle for its goal, but fell into its hands, like a good thing abandoned by everybody else) a definite degree of maturity of economic and political relations. Here we have the essential difference between coups d'etat along Blanqui's conception, which are accomplished by an "active minority," and burst out like pistol shot, always inopportunely, and the conquest of political power by a great conscious popular mass, which can only be the product of the decomposition of bourgeois society and therefore bears in itself the economic and political legitimation of its opportune appearance.

If, therefore, considered from the angle of political effect, the conquest of political power by the working class cannot materialize itself "too early," then from the angle of conservation of power, the premature revolution, the thought of which keeps Bernstein awake, menaces us like a sword of Damocles. Against that neither prayers nor supplication, neither scares nor any amount of anguish, are of any avail. And this for two very simple reasons.

In the first place, it is impossible to imagine that a transformation as formidable as the passage from capitalist society to socialist society can be realized in one happy act. To consider that as possible is again to lend color to conceptions that are clearly Blanquist. The socialist transformation supposes a long and stubborn struggle, in the course of which, it is quite probable, the proletariat will be repulsed more than once, so that the first time, from the viewpoint of the final outcome of the struggle, it will necessarily come to power "too early."

In the second place, it will be impossible to avoid the "premature" conquest of state power by the proletariat precisely because these "premature" attacks of the proletariat constitute a factor, and indeed a very important factor, creating the political conditions of the final victory. In the course of the political crisis accompanying its seizure of power, in the course of the long and stubborn struggles, the proletariat will acquire the degree of political maturity permitting it to obtain in time a definitive victory of the revolution. Thus these "premature" attacks of the proletariat against the state power are in themselves important historic factors helping to provoke and determine the *point* of the definite victory.

Considered from this viewpoint, the idea of a "premature" conquest of political power by the laboring class appears to be a political absurdity derived from a mechanical conception of the development of society, and positing for the victory of the class struggle a point fixed *outside* and *independent of* the class struggle.

Since the proletariat is not in the position to seize political power in any other way than "prematurely," since the proletariat is absolutely obliged to seize power once or several times "too early" before it can maintain itself in power for good, the objection to the "premature" conquest of power is at bottom nothing more than a *general opposition to the aspiration of the proletariat to possess itself of state power.* Just as all roads lead to Rome, so too, do we logically arrive at the conclusion that the revisionist proposal to slight the final aim of the socialist movement is really a recommendation to renounce the socialist movement itself. . . .

Opportunism in Theory and Practice

Bernstein's book is of great importance to the German and the international labor movement. It is the first attempt to give a theoretic base to the opportunist currents common in the social democracy.

These currents may be said to have existed for a long time in our movement, if we take into consideration such sporadic manifestations of opportunism as the question of subsidization of steamers. But it is only since about 1890, with the suppression of the antisocialist laws, that we have had a trend of opportunism of a clearly defined character. Vollmar's "state socialism," the vote on the Bavarian budget, the "agrarian socialism" of South Germany, Heine's policy of compensation, Schippel's stand on tariffs and militarism are the high points in the development of our opportunist practice.

What appears to characterize this practice above all? A certain hostility to "theory." This is quite natural, for our "theory," that is, the principles of scientific socialism, impose clearly marked limitations to practical activity—insofar as it concerns the aims of this activity, the means used in attaining these aims, and the method employed in this activity. It is quite natural for people who run after immediate "practical" results to want to free themselves from such limitations and to render their practice independent of our "theory."

However, this outlook is refuted by every attempt to apply it in reality. State socialism, agrarian socialism, the policy of compensation, the question of the army all constituted defeats to our opportunism. It is clear that, if this current is to maintain itself, it must try to destroy the principle of our theory and elaborate a theory of its own. Bernstein's book is precisely an effort in that direction. That is why at Stuttgart all the opportunist elements in our party immediately grouped themselves about Bernstein's banner. If the opportunist currents in the practical activity of our party are an entirely natural phenomenon which can be explained in light of the special conditions of our activity and its development, Bernstein's theory is no less natural an attempt to group these currents into a general theoretic expression, an attempt to elaborate its own theoretic conditions and to break with scientific socialism. That is why the published expression of Bernstein's ideas should be recognized as a theoretic test for opportunism and as its first scientific legitimation.

What was the result of this test? We have seen the result. Opportunism is not in a position to elaborate a positive theory capable of withstanding criticism. All it can do is to attack various isolated theses of Marxist theory and, just because Marxist doctrine constitutes one solidly constructed edifice, hope by this means to shake the entire system, from the top to its foundation.

This shows that opportunist practice is essentially irreconcilable with Marxism. But it also proves that opportunism is incompatible with socialism (the socialist movement) in general, that its internal tendency is to push the labor movement into bourgeois paths, that opportunism tends to paralyze completely the proletarian class struggle. The latter, considered historically, has evidently nothing to do with Marxist doctrine. For, before Marx, and independently from him, there have been labor movements and various socialist doctrines, each of which, in its way, was the theoretic expression, corresponding to the conditions of the time, of the struggle of the working class for emancipation. The theory that consists in basing socialism on the moral notion of justice, on a struggle against the mode of distribution, instead of basing it on a struggle against the mode of production, the conception of class antagonism as an antagonism between the poor and the rich, the effort to graft the "cooperative principle" on capitalist economy—all the nice notions found in Bernstein's doctrine—already existed before him. And these theories were, *in their time*, in spite of their insufficiency, effective theories of the proletarian class struggle. They were the children's seven-league boots [thanks] to which the proletariat learned to walk upon the scene of history.

But after the development of the class struggle and its reflex in its social conditions had led to the abandonment of these theories and to the elaboration of the principles of scientific socialism, there could be no socialism—at least in Germany—outside of Marxist socialism, and there could be no socialist class struggle outside of the social democracy. From then on, socialism and Marxism, the proletarian struggle for emancipation, and the social democracy were identical. That is why the return to pre-Marxist socialist theories no longer signifies today a return to the seven-league boots of the childhood of the proletariat, but a return to the puny worn-out slippers of the bourgeoisie.

Bernstein's theory was the *first*, and at the same time, the *last* attempt to give a theoretic base to opportunism. It is the last, because in Bernstein's system, opportunism has gone—negatively through its renunciation of scientific socialism, positively through its marshalling of every bit of theoretic confusion possible—as far as it can. In Bernstein's book, opportunism has crowned its theoretic development (just as it completed its practical development in the position taken by Schippel on the question of militarism) and has reached its ultimate conclusion.

Marxist doctrine cannot only refute opportunism theoretically. It alone can explain opportunism as a historic phenomenon in the development of the party. The forward march of the proletariat, on a world historic scale, to its final victory is not, indeed, "so simple a thing." The peculiar character of this movement resides precisely in the fact that here, for the first time in history, the popular masses themselves, *in opposition* to the ruling classes, are to impose their will, but they must effect this outside of the present society, beyond the existing society. This *will* the masses can only form in a constant struggle against the existing order. The union of the broad popular masses with an aim reaching beyond the existing social order, the union of the daily struggle with the great world transformation, this is the task of the social democratic movement, which must logically grope on its road of development between the following two rocks: abandoning the mass character of the party or abandoning its final aim, falling into bourgeois reformism or into sectarianism, anarchism or opportunism.

In its theoretic arsenal, Marxist doctrine furnished, more than half a century ago, arms that are effective against both of these two extremes.

But because our movement is a mass movement and because the dangers menacing it are not derived from the human brain but from social conditions, Marxist doctrine could not assure us, in advance and once for always, against the anarchist and opportunist tendencies. The latter can be overcome only as we pass from the domain of theory to the domain of practice, but only with the help of the arms furnished us by Marx.

"Bourgeois revolutions," wrote Marx a half century ago, "like those of the eighteenth century, rush onward rapidly from success to success, their stage effects outbid one another, men and things seem to be set in flaming brilliants, ecstasy is the prevailing spirit; but they are short-lived, they reach their climax speedily, and then society relapses into a long fit of nervous reaction before it learns how to appropriate the fruits of its period of feverish excitement. Proletarian revolutions, on the contrary such as those of the nineteenth century, criticize themselves constantly; constantly interrupt themselves in their own course; come back to what seems to have been accomplished, in order to start anew; scorn with cruel thoroughness the half measures, weaknesses and meannesses of their first attempts; seem to throw down their adversary only to enable him to draw fresh strength from the earth and again to rise up against them in more gigantic stature; constantly recoil in fear before the undefined monster magnitude of their own objects—until finally that situation is created which renders all retreat impossible and conditions themselves cry out: 'Hic Rhodus, hic salta!' [Here is the rose. And here we must dance!]"

This has remained true even after the elaboration of the doctrine of scientific socialism. The proletarian movement has not as yet, all at once, become social democratic, even in Germany. But it is becoming more social democratic, surmounting continuously the extreme deviations of anarchism and opportunism, both of which are only determining phases of the development of the social democracy, considered as a process.

For these reasons, we must say that the surprising thing here is not the appearance of an opportunist current but rather its feebleness. As long as it showed itself in isolated cases of the practical activity of the party, one could suppose that it had a serious practical base. But now that it has shown its face in Bernstein's book, one can not help exclaim with astonishment: "What? Is that all you have to say?" Not the shadow of an original thought! Not a single idea that was not refuted, crushed, reduced into dust, by Marxism several decades ago!

It was enough for opportunism to speak out to prove it had nothing to say. In the history of our party that is the only importance of Bernstein's book.

Thus saying good-bye to the mode of thought of the revolutionary proletariat, to dialectics and to the materialist conception of history, Bernstein can thank them for the attenuating circumstances they provide for his conversion. For only dialectics and the materialist conception of history, magnanimous as they are, could make Bernstein appear as an unconscious predestined instrument, by means of which the rising working class expresses its momentary weakness, but which, upon closer inspection, it throws aside contemptuously and with pride.

Reading #7

"Mass Strike, Political Party and Trade Union" (excerpts)

An artificially arranged demonstration of the urban proletariat, taking place once, a mere mass strike action arising out of discipline, and directed by the conductor's baton of a party executive, could therefore leave the broad masses of the people cold and indifferent. But a powerful and reckless fighting action of the industrial proletariat, born of a revolutionary situation, must surely react upon the deeper-lying layers, and ultimately draw all those into a stormy general economic struggle who, in normal times, stand aside from the daily trade-union fight. . . .

It therefore inevitably follows that the pure political mass strike, which is operated with for preference, is, in Germany, a mere lifeless theoretical plan. If the mass strikes result, in a natural way from a strong revolutionary ferment, in a determined political struggle of the urban workers, they will equally naturally, exactly as in Russia, change into a whole period of elementary, economic struggles. The fears of the trade-union leaders, therefore, that the struggle for economic interests in a period of stormy political strife, in a period of mass strikes, can simply be pushed aside and suppressed rest upon an utterly baseless, schoolboy conception of the course of events. A revolutionary period in Germany would so alter the character of the trade-union struggle and develop its potentialities to such an extent that the present guerrilla warfare of the trade unions would be child's play in comparison. And on the other hand, from this elementary economic tempest of mass strikes, the political struggle would derive always new impetus and fresh strength. The reciprocal action of economic and political struggle, which is the mainspring of present-day strikes in Russia, and at the same time the regulating mechanism, so to speak, of the revolutionary action of the proletariat, would result also in Germany, and quite as naturally, from the conditions themselves.

Cooperation of Organized and Unorganized Workers Necessary for Victory

In connection with this, the question of organization in relation to the problem of the mass strike in Germany assumes an essentially different aspect.

The attitude of many trade-union leaders to this question is generally summed up in the assertion: "We are not yet strong enough to risk such a hazardous trial of strength as a mass strike." Now this position is so far untenable that it is an insoluble problem to determine the time, in a peaceful fashion by counting heads, when the proletariat are "strong enough" for any struggle. Thirty years ago the German trade unions had 50,000 members. That was obviously a number with which a mass strike on the above scale was not to be thought of. Fifteen years later the trade unions were four times as strong, and counted 237,000 members. If, however, the present trade-union leaders had been asked at the time if the organization of the proletariat was then sufficiently ripe for a mass strike, they would assuredly have replied that it was still far from it and that the number of those organized in trade unions would first have to be counted by millions.

Today the number of trade unionists already runs into the second million, but the views of the leaders are still exactly the same, and may very well be the same to the end. The tacit assumption is that the entire working class of Germany, down to the last man and the last woman, must be included in the organization before it "is strong enough" to risk a mass action, which then, according to the old formula, would probably be represented as "superfluous." This theory is nevertheless absolutely utopian, for the simple reason that it suffers from an internal contradiction, that it goes in a vicious circle. Before the workers can engage in any direct class struggle they must all be organized. The circumstances, the conditions, of capitalist development and of the bourgeois state make it impossible that, in the normal course of things, without stormy class struggles, certain sections—and these the greatest, the most important, the lowest and the most oppressed by capital, and by the state—can be organized at all. We see even in Britain, which has had a whole century of indefatigable trade-union effort without any "disturbances"—except at the beginning in the period of the Chartist movement—without any "romantic revolutionary" errors or temptations, it has not been possible to do more than organize a minority of the better-paid sections of the proletariat.

On the other hand the trade unions, like all fighting organizations of the proletariat, cannot permanently maintain themselves in any other way than by struggle, and that not struggles of the same kind as the war between the frogs and the mice in the stagnant waters of the bourgeois parliamentary period, but struggle in the troubled revolutionary periods of the mass strike. The rigid, mechanical-bureaucratic conception cannot conceive of the struggle save as the product of organization at a certain stage of its strength. On the contrary the living, dialectical explanation makes the organization arise as a product of the struggle. We have already seen a grandiose example of this phenomenon in Russia, where a proletariat almost wholly unorganized created a comprehensive network of organizational appendages in a year and a half of stormy revolutionary struggle.

Another example of this kind is furnished by the history of the German unions. In the year 1878 the number of trade-union members amounted to 50,000. According to the theory of the present-day trade-union leaders this organization, as stated above, was not nearly "strong enough" to enter upon a violent political struggle. The German trade unions however, weak as they were at the time, did take up the struggle—namely the struggle against the antisocialist law—and showed that they were "strong enough" not only to emerge victorious from the struggle, but to increase their strength fivefold: in 1891, after the repeal of the antisocialist laws, their membership was 277,659. It is true that the methods by which the trade unions conquered in the struggle against the antisocialist laws do not correspond to the ideal of a peaceful, bee-like, uninterrupted process: they first went into the fight absolutely in ruins, to rise again on the next wave and to be born anew. But this is precisely the specific method of growth corresponding to the proletarian class organizations: to be tested in the struggle and to go forth from the struggle with increased strength.

On a closer examination of German conditions and of the condition of the different sections of the working class, it is clear that the coming period of stormy political mass struggles will not bring the dreaded, threatening downfall of the German trade unions, but on the contrary, will open up hitherto unsuspected prospects of the extension of their sphere of power—an extension that will proceed rapidly by leaps and bounds. But the question has still another aspect. The plan of undertaking mass strikes as a serious political class action with organized workers only is absolutely hopeless. If the mass strike, or rather, mass strikes, and the mass struggle are to be successful they must become a real *people's movement*, that is, the widest sections of the proletariat must be drawn into the fight. Already in the parliamentary form the might of the proletarian class struggle rests not on the small organized group, but on the surrounding periphery of the revolutionary-minded proletariat. If the social democrats were to enter the electoral battle with their few hundred thousand organized members alone, they would condemn themselves to futility. And although it is the tendency of social democracy whereever possible to draw the whole great army of its voters into the party organization, its mass of voters after thirty years experience of social democracy is not increased through the growth of the party organization, but on the contrary, the new sections of the proletariat, won for the time being through the electoral struggle, are the fertile soil for the subsequent seed of organization. Here the organization does not supply the troops for the struggle, but the struggle, in an ever growing degree, supplies recruits for the organization.

In a much greater degree does this obviously apply to direct political mass action than to the parliamentary struggle. If the social democrats, as the organized nucleus of the working class, are the most important vanguard of the entire body of the workers and if the political clarity, the strength, and the unity of the labor movement flow from this organization, then it is not permissible to visualize the class movement of the proletariat as a movement of the organized minority. Every real, great class struggle must rest upon the support and cooperation of the widest masses, and a strategy of class struggle which does not reckon with this cooperation, which is based upon the idea of the finely stage-managed march out of the small, well-trained part of the proletariat is foredoomed to be a miserable fiasco.

Mass strikes and political mass struggles cannot, therefore, possibly be carried through in Germany by the organized workers alone, nor can they be appraised by regular "direction" from the central committee of a party. In this case, again—exactly as in Russia—they depend not so much upon "discipline" and "training" and upon the most careful possible regulation beforehand of the questions of support and cost, as upon a real revolutionary, determined class action, which will be able to win and draw into the struggle the widest circles of the unorganized workers, according to their mood and their conditions.

The overestimate and the false estimate of the role of organizations in the class struggle of the proletariat is generally reinforced by the underestimate of the unorganized proletarian mass and of their political maturity. In a revolutionary period, in the storm of great unsettling class struggles, the whole educational effect of the rapid capitalist development and of social democratic influences first shows itself upon the widest sections of the people, of which, in peaceful times the tables of the organized, and even election statistics, give only a faint idea.

We have seen that in Russia, in about two years a great general action of the proletariat can forthwith arise from the smallest partial conflict of the workers with the employers, from the most insignificant act of brutality of the government organs. Everyone, of course, sees and believes that, because in Russia "the revolution" is there. But what does that mean? It means that class feeling, the class instinct, is alive and very active in the Russian proletariat, so that immediately they regard every partial question of any small group of workers as a general question, as a class affair, and quick as lightning they react to its influence as a unity. While in Germany, France, Italy and Holland the most violent trade-union conflicts call forth hardly any general action of the working class—and when they do, only the organized part of the workers moves—in Russia the smallest dispute raises a storm. That means nothing else however, than that at present—paradoxical as it may sound—the class instinct of the youngest, least trained, badly educated and still worse organized Russian proletariat is immeasurably stronger than that of the organized, trained and enlightened working class of Germany or of any other west European country. And that is not to be reckoned a special virtue of the "young, unexhausted East" as compared with the "sluggish West," but is simply a result of direct revolutionary mass action.

In the case of the enlightened German worker the class consciousness implanted by the social democrats is *theoretical and latent*: in the period ruled by bourgeois parliamentarism it cannot, as a rule, actively participate in a direct mass action; it is the ideal sum of the four hundred parallel actions of the electoral sphere during the election struggle, of the many partial economic strikes and the like. In the revolution when the masses themselves appear upon the political battlefield this class consciousness becomes *practical and active*. A year of revolution has therefore given the Russian proletariat that "training" which thirty years of parliamentary and trade-union struggle cannot artificially give to the German proletariat. Of course, this living, active class feeling of the proletariat will considerably diminish in intensity, or rather change into a concealed and latent condition, after the close of the period of revolution and the erection of a bourgeois-parliamentary constitutional state.

And just as surely, on the other hand, will the living revolutionary class feeling, capable of action, affect the widest and deepest layers of the proletariat in Germany in a period of strong political engagement, and that the more rapidly and more deeply, more energetically the educational work of social democracy is carried on amongst them. This educational work and the provocative and revolutionizing effect of the whole present policy of Germany will express itself in the circumstances that all those groups which at present in their apparent political stupidity remain insensitive to all the organizing attempts of the social democrats and of the trade unions will suddenly follow the flag of social democracy in a serious revolutionary period. Six months of a revolutionary period will complete the work of the training of these as yet unorganized masses which ten years of public demonstrations and distribution of leaflets would be unable to do. And when conditions in Germany have reached the critical stage for such a period, the sections which are today unorganized and backward will, in the struggle, prove themselves the most radical, the most impetuous element, and not one that will have to be dragged along. If it should come to mass strikes in Germany, it will almost certainly not be the best organized workers—and most certainly not the printers—who will develop the greatest capacity for action, but the worst organized or totally unorganized—the miners, the textile workers, and perhaps even the land workers.

In this way we arrive at the same conclusions in Germany in relation to the peculiar tasks of *direction*, in relation to the role of social democracy in mass strikes, as in our analysis of events in Russia. If we now leave the pedantic scheme of demonstrative mass strikes artificially brought about by order of parties and trade unions, and turn to the living picture of a peoples' movement arising with elementary energy, from the culmination of class antagonisms and the political situation—a movement which passes, politically as well as economically, into mass struggles and mass strikes—it becomes obvious that the task of social democracy does not consist in the technical preparation and direction of mass strikes, but, first and foremost, in the *political leadership* of the whole movement.

The social democrats are the most enlightened, most class-conscious vanguard of the proletariat. They cannot and dare not wait, in a fatalist fashion, with folded arms for the advent of the "revolutionary situation," to wait for that which in every spontaneous peoples' movement, falls from the clouds. On the contrary, they must now, as always, hasten the development of things and endeavor to accelerate events. This they cannot do, however, by suddenly issuing the "slogan" for a mass strike at random at any odd moment, but first and foremost, by making clear to the widest layers of the proletariat the *inevitable advent* of this revolutionary period, the inner *social factors* making for it and the *political consequences* of it. If the widest proletarian layer should be won for a political mass action of the social democrats, and if, vice versa, the social democrats should seize and maintain the real leadership of a mass movement—should they become, in a *political sense*, the rulers of the whole movement, then they must, with the utmost clearness, consistency and resoluteness, inform the German proletariat of their tactics and aims in the period of coming struggle.

The Role of the Mass Strike in the Revolution

We have seen that the mass strike in Russia does not represent an artificial product of premeditated tactics on the part of the social democrats, but a natural historical phenomenon on the basis of the present revolution. . . .

The mass strike is the first natural, impulsive form of every great revolutionary struggle of the proletariat and the more highly developed the antagonism is between capital and labor, the more effective and decisive must mass strikes become. The chief form of previous bourgeois revolutions, the fight at the barricades, the open conflict with the armed power of the state, is in the revolution of today only the culminating point, only a moment on the process of the proletarian mass struggle. And therewith in the new form of the revolution there is reached that civilizing and mitigating of the class struggle which was prophesied by the opportunists of German social democracy—the Bernsteins, Davids, etc. It is true that these men saw the desired civilizing and mitigating of the class struggle in the light of petty bourgeois democratic illusions— they believed that the class struggle would shrink to an exclusively parliamentary contest and that street fighting would simply be done away with. History has found the solution in a deeper and finer fashion: in the advent of revolutionary mass strikes, which, of course, in no way replaces brutal street fights or renders them unnecessary, but which reduces them to a moment in the long period of political struggle, and which at the same time unites with the revolutionary period an enormous cultural work in the most exact sense of the words: the material and intellectual elevation of the whole working class through the "civilizing" of the barbaric forms of capitalist exploitation.

The mass strike is thus shown to be not a specifically Russian product, springing from absolutism but a universal form of the proletarian class struggle resulting from the present stage of capitalist development and class relations.

But if once the ball is set rolling then social democracy, whether it wills it or not, can never again bring it to a standstill. The opponents of the mass strike are in the habit of denying that the lessons and examples of the Russian Revolution can be a criterion for Germany because, in the first place, in Russia the great step must first be taken from an Oriental despotism to a modern bourgeois legal order. The formal distance between the old and the new political order is said to be a sufficient explanation of the vehemence and the violence of the revolution in Russia. In Germany we have long had the most necessary forms and guarantees of a constitutional state, from which it follows that such an elementary raging of social antagonisms is impossible here.

Those who speculate thus forget that in Germany when it once comes to the outbreak of open political struggles, even the historically determined goal will be quite different from that in Russia today. Precisely because the bourgeois legal order in Germany has existed for a long time, because therefore it has had time to completely exhaust itself and to draw to an end, because bourgeois democracy and liberalism have had time to die out—because of this there can no longer be any talk of a *bourgeois* revolution in Germany. And therefore in a period of open political popular struggles in Germany, the last historical necessary goal can only be the *dictatorship of the proletariat*. The distance, however, of this task from the present conditions of Germany is still greater than that of the bourgeois legal order from Oriental despotism, and therefore, the task cannot be completed at one stroke, but must similarly be accomplished during a long period of gigantic social struggles.

But is there not a gross contradiction in the picture we have drawn? On the one hand it means that in an eventual future period of political mass action the most backward layers of the German proletariat—the land workers, the railwaymen, and the postal slaves—will first of all win the right of combination, and that the worst excrescences of exploitation must first be removed, and on the other hand, the political task of this period is said to be the conquest of power by the proletariat! On one hand, economic, trade-union struggles for the most immediate interests, for the material elevation of the working class; on the other hand, the ultimate goal of social democracy! Certainly these are great contradictions, but they are not contradictions due to our reasoning, but contradictions due to capitalist development. It does not proceed in a beautiful straight line but in a lightninglike zigzag. Just as the various capitalist countries represent the most varied stages of development, so within each country the different layers of the same working class are represented. But history does not wait patiently till the backward countries, and the most advanced layers have joined together so that the whole mass can move symmetrically forward like a compact column. It brings the best prepared parts to explosion as soon as conditions there are ripe for it, and then in the storm of the revolutionary period, lost ground is recovered, unequal things are equalized, and the whole pace of social progress changed at one stroke to the double-quick.

Just as in the Russian Revolution all the grades of development and all the interests of the different layers of workers are united in the social democratic program of the revolution, and the innumerable partial struggles united in the great common class action of the proletariat, so will it also be in Germany when the conditions are ripe for it. And the task of social democracy will then be to regulate its tactics, not by the most backward phases of development but by the most advanced.

READING #8
"On Imperialism"
(excerpt from the *Junius Pamphlet*)

All demands for complete or gradual disarmament, for the abolition of secret diplomacy, for the dissolution of the great powers into smaller national entities, and all other similar propositions, are absolutely utopian so long as capitalist class-rule remains in power. For capitalism, in its present imperialist course, to dispense with present-day militarism, with secret diplomacy, with the centralization of many national states is so impossible that these postulates might, much more consistently, be united into the simple demand, "abolition of capitalist class society." The proletarian movement cannot reconquer the place it deserves by means of utopian advice and projects for weakening, taming or quelling imperialism within capitalism by means of partial reforms.

The real problem that the world war has placed before the socialist parties, upon whose solution the future of the working-class movement depends, *is the readiness of the proletarian masses to act in the fight against imperialism.* The international proletariat suffers, not from a dearth of postulates, programs, and slogans, but from a lack of deeds, of effective resistance, of the power to attack imperialism at the decisive moment, just in times of war. It has been unable to put its old slogan, war against war, into actual practice. Here is the Gordian knot of the proletarian movement and of its future.

Imperialism, with all its brutal policy of force, with the incessant chain of social catastrophe that it itself provokes, is, to be sure, a historic necessity for the ruling classes of the present world. Yet nothing could be more detrimental than that the proletariat should derive, from the present war, the slightest hope or illusion of the possibility of an idyllic and peaceful development of capitalism. There is but one conclusion that the proletariat can draw from the historic necessity of imperialism. To capitulate before imperialism will mean to live forever in its shadow, off the crumbs that fall from the tables of its victories.

Historic development moves in contradictions, and for every necessity puts its opposite into the world as well. The capitalist state of society is doubtless a historic necessity, but so also is the revolt of the working class against it. Capital is a historic necessity, but in the same measure is its gravedigger, the socialist proletariat. The world rule of imperialism is a historic necessity, but likewise its overthrow by the proletarian international. Side by side the two historic necessities exist in constant conflict with each other. And ours is the necessity of socialism. Our necessity receives its justification with the moment when the capitalist class ceases to be the bearer of historic progress, when it becomes a hindrance, a danger, to the future development of society. That capitalism has reached this stage the present world war has revealed.

Capitalist desire for imperialist expansion, as the expression of its highest maturity in the last period of its life, has the economic tendency to change the whole world into capitalistically producing nations, to sweep away all superannuated, precapitalistic methods of production and society, to subjugate all the riches of the earth and all means of production to capital, to turn the laboring masses of the peoples of all zones into wage slaves. In Africa and in Asia, from the most northern regions to the southernmost point of South America and in the South Seas, the remnants of old communistic social groups, of feudal society, of patriarchal systems, and of ancient handicraft production are destroyed and stamped out by capitalism. Whole peoples are destroyed, ancient civilizations are levelled to the ground, and in their place profiteering in its most modern forms is being established.

This brutal triumphant procession of capitalism through the world, accompanied by all the means of force, of robbery, and of infamy, has one bright phase: it has created the premises for its own final overthrow, it has established the capitalist world rule upon which, alone, the socialist world revolution can follow. This is the only cultural and progressive aspect of the great so-called works of culture that were brought to the primitive countries. To capitalist economists and politicians, railroads, matches, sewerage systems and warehouses are progress and culture. Of themselves such works, grafted upon primitive conditions, are neither culture nor progress, for they are too dearly paid for with the sudden economic and cultural ruin of the peoples who must drink down the bitter cup of misery and horror of two social orders, of traditional agricultural landlordism, of supermodern, superrefined capitalist exploitation, at one and the same time. Only as the material conditions for the destruction of capitalism and the abolition of class society can the effects of the capitalist triumphal march through the world bear the stamp of progress in a historical sense. In this sense imperialism, too, is working in our interest.

READING #9*

"Women's Suffrage and Class Struggle"

"Why are there no organizations for working women in Germany? Why do we hear so little about the working women's movement?" With these questions, Emma Ihrer, one of the founders of the proletarian women's movement of Germany, introduced her 1898 essay, "Working Women in the Class Struggle." Hardly fourteen years have passed since, but they have seen a great expansion of the proletarian women's movement. More than a hundred fifty thousand women are organized in unions and are among the most active troops in the economic struggle of the proletariat. Many thousands of politically organized women have rallied to the banner of Social Democracy: the Social Democratic women's paper [*Die Gleichheit*, edited by Clara Zetkin] has more than one hundred thousand subscribers; women's suffrage is one of the vital issues on the platform of Social Democracy.

Exactly these facts might lead you to underrate the importance of the fight for women's suffrage. You might think: even without equal political rights for women we have made enormous progress in educating and organizing women. Hence, women's suffrage is not urgently necessary. If you think so, you are deceived. The political and syndical awakening of the masses of the female proletariat during the last fifteen years has been magnificent. But it has been possible only because working women took a lively interest in the political and parliamentary struggles of their class in spite of being deprived of their rights. So far, proletarian women are sustained by male suffrage, which they indeed take part in, though only indirectly. Large masses of both men and women of the working class already consider the election campaigns a cause they share in common. In all Social Democratic electoral meetings, women make up a large segment, sometimes the majority. They are always interested and passionately involved. In all districts where there is a firm Social Democratic organization, women help with the campaign. And it is women who have done invaluable work distributing leaflets and getting subscribers to the Social Democratic press, this most important weapon in the campaign.

The capitalist state has not been able to keep women from taking on all these duties and efforts of political life. Step by step, the state has indeed been forced to grant and guarantee them this possibility by allowing them union and assembly rights. Only the last political right is denied women: the right to vote, to decide directly on the people's representatives in legislature and administration, to be an elected member of these bodies. But here, as in all other areas of society, the motto is: "Don't let things get started!" But things have been started. The present state gave in to the women of the proletariat when it admitted them to public assemblies, to political associations. And the state did not grant this voluntarily, but out of necessity, under the irresistible pressure of the rising working class. It was not least the passionate pushing ahead of the proletarian women themselves which forced the Prusso-German police state to give up the famous "women's section"[1] in gatherings of political associations and to open wide the doors of political organizations to women. This really set the ball rolling. The irresistible progress of the proletarian class struggle has swept working women right into the whirlpool of political life. Using their right of union and assembly, proletarian women have taken a most active part in parliamentary life and in election campaigns. It is only the inevitable consequence, only the logical result of the movement that today millions of proletarian women call defiantly and with self-confidence: *Let us have suffrage!*

Once upon a time, in the beautiful era of pre-1848 absolutism, the whole working class was said not to be "mature enough" to exercise political rights. This cannot be said about proletarian women today, because they have demonstrated their political maturity. Everybody knows that without them, without the enthusiastic help of proletarian women, the Social Democratic Party would not have won the glorious victory of January 12, [1912], would not have obtained four and a quarter million votes. At any rate, the working class has always had to prove its maturity for political freedom by a successful revolutionary uprising of the masses. Only when Divine Right on the throne and the best and noblest men of the nation actually felt the calloused fist of the proletariat on their eyes and its knee on their chests, only then did they feel confidence in the political "maturity" of the people, and felt it with the speed of lightning. Today, it is the proletarian woman's turn to make the capitalist state conscious of her maturity. This is done through a constant, powerful mass movement which has to use all the means of proletarian struggle and pressure.

Women's suffrage is the goal. But the mass movement to bring it about is not a job for women alone, but is a common class concern for women and men of the proletariat. Germany's present lack of rights for women is only one link in the chain of the reaction that shackles the people's lives. And it is closely connected with the other pillar of the reaction: the monarchy. In advanced capitalist, highly industrialized, twentieth-century Germany, in the age of electricity and airplanes, the absence of women's political rights is as much a reactionary remnant of the dead past as the reign by Divine Right on the throne. Both phenomena—the instrument of heaven as the leading political power, and woman, demure by the fireside, unconcerned with the storms of public life, with politics and class struggle—both phenomena have their roots in the rotten circumstances of the past, in the times of serfdom in the country and guilds in the towns. In those times, they were justifiable and necessary. But both monarchy and women's lack of rights have been uprooted by the development of modern capitalism, have become ridiculous caricatures. They continue to exist in our modern society, not just because people forgot to abolish them, not just because of the persistence and inertia of circumstances. No, they still exist because both—monarchy as well as women without rights—have become powerful tools of interests inimical to the people. The worst and most brutal advocates of the exploitation and enslavement of the proletariat are entrenched behind throne and altar as well as behind the political enslavement of women. Monarchy and women's lack of rights have become the most important tools of the ruling capitalist class.

In truth, our state is interested in keeping the vote from working women and from them alone. It rightly fears they will threaten the traditional institutions of class rule, for instance militarism (of which no thinking proletarian woman can help being a deadly enemy), monarchy, the systematic robbery of duties and taxes on groceries, etc. Women's suffrage is a horror and abomination for the present capitalist state because behind it stand millions of women who would strengthen the enemy within, i.e., revolutionary Social Democracy. If it were a matter of bourgeois ladies voting, the capitalist state could expect nothing but effective support for the reaction. Most of those bourgeois women who act like lionesses in the struggle against "male prerogatives" would trot like docile lambs in the camp of conservative and clerical reaction if they had suffrage. Indeed, they would certainly be a good deal more reactionary than the male part of their class. Aside from the few who have jobs or professions, the women of the bourgeoisie do not take part in social production. They are nothing but co-consumers of the surplus value their men extort from the proletariat. They are parasites of the parasites of the social body. And co-consumers are usually even more rabid and cruel in defending their "right" to a parasite's life than the direct agent of class rule and exploitation. The history of all great revolutionary struggles confirms this in a horrible way. Take the great French Revolution. After the fall of the Jacobins, when Robespierre was driven in chains to the place of execution the naked whores of the victory-drunk bourgeoisie danced in the streets, danced a shameless dance of joy around the fallen hero of the Revolution. And in 1871, in Paris, when the heroic workers' Commune was defeated by machine guns, the raving bourgeois females surpassed even their bestial men in their bloody revenge against the suppressed proletariat. The women of the property-owning classes will always fanatically defend the exploitation and enslavement of the working people by which they indirectly receive the means for their socially useless existence.

Economically and socially, the women of the exploiting classes are not an independent segment of the population. Their only social function is to be tools of the natural propagation of the ruling classes. By contrast, the women of the proletariat are economically independent. They are productive for society like the men. By this I do not mean their bringing up children or their housework which helps men support their families on scanty wages. This kind of work is not productive in the sense of the present capitalist economy no matter how enormous an achievement the sacrifices and energy spent, the thousand little efforts add up to. This is but the private affair of the worker, his happiness and blessing, and for this reason nonexistent for our present society. As long as capitalism and the wage system rule, only that kind of work is considered productive which produces surplus value, which creates capitalist profit. From this point of view, the music-hall dancer whose legs sweep profit into her employer's pocket is a productive worker, whereas all the toil of the proletarian women and mothers in the four walls of their homes is considered unproductive. This sounds brutal and insane, but corresponds exactly to the brutality and insanity of our present capitalist economy. And seeing this brutal reality clearly and sharply is the proletarian woman's first task.

For, exactly from this point of view, the proletarian women's claim to equal political rights is anchored in firm economic ground. Today, millions of proletarian women create capitalist profit like men—in factories, workshops, on farms, in home industry, offices, stores. They *are* therefore productive in the strictest scientific sense of our present society. Every day enlarges the hosts of women exploited by capitalism. Every new progress in industry or technology creates new places for women in the machinery of capitalist profiteering. And thus, every day and every step of industrial progress adds a new stone to the firm foundation of women's equal political rights. Female education and intelligence have become necessary for the economic mechanism itself. The narrow, secluded woman of the patriarchal "family circle" answers the needs of industry and commerce as little as those of politics. It is true, the capitalist state has neglected its duty even in this respect. So far, it is the unions and the Social Democratic organizations that have done most to awaken the minds and moral sense of women. Even decades ago, the Social Democrats were known as the most capable and intelligent German workers. Likewise, unions and Social Democracy have today lifted the women of the proletariat out of their stuffy, narrow existence, out of the miserable and petty mindlessness of household managing. The proletarian class struggle has widened their horizons, made their minds flexible, developed their thinking, shown them great goals for their efforts. Socialism has brought about the mental rebirth of the mass of proletarian women—and thereby has no doubt also made them capable productive workers for capital.

Considering all this, the proletarian woman's lack of political rights is a vile injustice, and the more so for being by now at least half a lie. After all, masses of women take an active part in political life. However, Social Democracy does not use the argument of "injustice." This is the basic difference between us and the earlier sentimental, utopian socialism. We do not depend on the justice of the ruling classes, but solely on the revolutionary power of the working masses and on the course of social development which prepares the ground for this power. Thus, injustice by itself is certainly not an argument with which to overthrow reactionary institutions. If, however, there is a feeling of injustice in large segments of society—says Friedrich Engels, the co-founder of scientific social-ism—it is always a sure sign that the economic bases of the society have shifted considerably, that the present conditions contradict the march of development. The present forceful movement of millions of proletarian women who consider their lack of political rights a crying wrong is such an infallible sign, a sign that the social bases of the reigning system are rotten and that its days are numbered.

A hundred years ago, the Frenchman Charles Fourier, one of the first great prophets of socialist ideals, wrote these memorable words: In any society, the degree of female emancipation is the natural measure of the general emancipation.[2] This is completely true for our present society. The current mass struggle for women's political rights is only an expres-sion and a part of the proletariat's general struggle for liberation. In this lies its strength and its future. Because of the female proletariat, general, equal, direct suffrage for women would immensely advance and inten-sify the proletarian class struggle. This is why bourgeois society abhors and fears women's suffrage. And this is why we want and will achieve it. Fighting for women's suffrage, we will also hasten the coming of the hour when the present society falls in ruins under the hammer strokes of the revolutionary proletariat.

Translated by Rosmarie Waldrop

Notes

*   Copyright © 1971 by Monthly Review Press. Reprinted by permission of Monthly Review Foundation.
1. The "women's section" had been instituted in 1902 by the Prussian Minister von Hammerstein. According to this disposition, a special section of the room was reserved for women at political meetings.
2. Marx and Engels sited these words of Fourier in several writings—the text most accessible to Luxemburg being Engels, *Herr Dühring's Revolution in Science (Anti-Dühring)* (New York: International Publishers, 1966), p. 284.

Lenin[*]

V. I. Lenin (1870–1924) was born Vladimir Ilyich Ulyanov in the Russian city of Simbrsk, into a moderately well-to-do family animated by cultural interests and liberal values. In the early 1890s young Ulyanov was already recognized as a brilliant Marxist thinker and activist committed to the overthrow of the tsarist autocracy. Among his writings were the massive study, *The Development of Capitalism in Russia* (1898), and such polemics against the populist (as opposed to working-class Marxist) revolutionaries as *What the "Friends of the People" Are*, as well as writings related to educational and organizing efforts among factory workers. Under repressive political conditions he utilized a number of aliases, Lenin being the best known.

By 1903 Lenin had organized the intransigently revolutionary wing of the Russian Social Democratic Labor Party known as the Bolsheviks (majorityites), as opposed to the Mensheviks (temporarily in the minority). The Bolsheviks called for a worker-peasant alliance and the blending of struggles for democratic rights and social reforms into a strategy that would overturn the regime. Essential for achieving such a goal, he had repeatedly emphasized, was the development of a highly disciplined revolutionary party (READING #10), the specifics of which he discussed in such polemical works as *What Is to Be Done?* (1902) and *One Step*

---

* "The Urgent Tasks of Our Movement," From V. I. Lenin, *Selected Works: In Three Volumes*, Vol. 1 (New York: International Publishers, 1967), pp. 91–96. "The Revolutionary Proletariat and the Right of Nations to Self-Determination," from V. I. Lenin, *The Right of Nations to Self-Determination: Selected Writings* (New York: International Publishers, 1951), pp. 66–69. "The State: A Lecture Delivered at the Sverdlov University, July 11, 1919," from V. I. Lenin, *Selected Works, In Three Volumes*, Vol. 3 (New York: International Publishers, 1967), pp. 243–258. Reprinted with permission.

Forward, Two Steps Back (1904). In the underground, from prison, and from exile he worked tirelessly to build such an organization—sometimes in thoroughgoing opposition to the more moderate Menshevik faction of the Russian Social Democratic Labor Party (their perspective of a worker-capitalist alliance to overthrow tsarism was the target of Lenin's 1905 polemic *Two Tactics in the Democratic Revolution*). In the wake of the 1905 revolutionary upsurge, he sought to work in common with the Mensheviks. By 1912, however, Lenin and the Bolsheviks had organized themselves into their own completely separate party. Over the next two years they became a powerful force in the growing workers' movement, although intensified government repression brought a temporary reversal of Bolshevik fortunes with the beginning of World War I.

During the war Lenin was among the most unyielding critics of imperialism—in 1916 he wrote the economic popularization *Imperialism: The Highest Stage of Capitalism*—and opposed support to any of the governments of the combatant nations. He urged the workers to "turn the imperialist war into a civil war," that is, to bring about the revolutionary overthrow of the capitalist regimes responsible for the mass slaughter and suffering of "the Great War." There was a dramatic deepening of his thinking on the relationship between democracy and revolution, as well well as on the right of oppressed nations to self-determination (READING #11), and in this period he began to retrieve the revolutionary perspectives on the state developed by Marx, but subsequently diluted by many Social-Democratic theorists. Lenin explained and documented these perspectives in his 1917 study, *The State and Revolution*, key points of which are summarized in his 1919 lecture "The State" (READING #12).

In 1917 the tsarist government was overthrown by masses of discontented working people, who organized themselves into *soviets* (democratic councils) while at first also supporting a Provisional Government consisting of (pro-capitalist) liberal and conservative politicians allied with some moderate socialist representatives. The Provisional Government stalled on land reform, other social changes, and continued Russian involvement in the unpopular war effort, and proved unable to overcome food shortages in the cities. The Bolsheviks called for "peace, bread, land" and "all power to the soviets," and Lenin interwove this in vibrant polemics with his analyses of imperialism, the state, workers' democracy, and revolution on the eve of his April return to Russia (READING #13). Despite fierce government repression in July, the Bolsheviks won decisive majorities in the working-class soviets by October and went on to lead a successful insurrection. Lenin became head of the Soviet government and also of the Communist International (the Third International), formed in 1919 for the purpose of helping revolutionary socialists of other countries aid each other and win similar victories.

Although Lenin's goals and perspectives had been permeated by a radically democratic orientation, his Bolshevik (renamed Communist) party regime implemented increasingly dictatorial policies in the face of a bitter civil war, military interventions involving fourteen different countries (including Britain, France, the United States, Germany and Japan), and a devastating blockade which contributed—along with mistakes in Communist economic policy—to the almost total wrecking of Soviet Russia's economy. While accused by hostile critics of being "the architect of totalitarianism" (and bearing some responsibility for the infamous Red Terror of the civil war period), Lenin spent his last years in desperate efforts to reverse the authoritarian economic measures of "war communism" and to push back conservative and bureaucratic tendencies that were undermining the Soviet regime and Communist movement as genuinely revolutionary forces.

To his critics he remains a fanatical and malevolent figure. In death he was turned into an icon to lend authority to the bureaucratic dictatorship which triumphed in the Soviet Union under Joseph Stalin (whose power Lenin attempted, too late, to eliminate). By his own lights, however, he was one of many dedicated to the liberation of the working class and all the oppressed—and Lenin's powerful intellect applied Marxist theory to the realities around him in a manner which helped, perhaps more than anyone else in the 20th century, to move those realities in a revolutionary direction.

READING #10: "The Urgent Tasks of Our Movement"—1900
READING #11: "The Revolutionary Proletariat and the Right of Nations to Self-Determination" (excerpt)—1915
READING #12: "The State"—1919
READING #13: "Letters from Afar" (excerpts)—1917

READING #10

"The Urgent Tasks of Our Movement"

Russian Social-Democracy has repeatedly declared the immediate political task of a Russian working-class party to be the overthrow of the autocracy, the achievement of political liberty. This was stated over fifteen years ago by the representatives of Russian Social-Democracy—the members of the Emancipation of Labour group. It was affirmed two and a half years ago by the representatives of the Russian Social-Democratic organizations that, in the spring of 1898, founded the Russian Social-Democratic Labour Party. Despite these repeated declarations, however, the question of the political tasks of Social-Democracy in Russia is prominent again today. Many representatives of our movement express doubt as to the correctness of the above-mentioned solution of the question. It is claimed that the economic struggle is of predominant importance; the political tasks of the proletariat are pushed into the background, narrowed down, and restricted, and it is even said that to speak of forming an independent working-class party in Russia is merely to repeat somebody else's words, that the workers should carry on only the economic struggle and leave politics to the intelligentsia in alliance with the liberals. The latest profession of the new faith (the notorious *Credo*) amounts to a declaration that the Russian proletariat has not yet come of age and to a complete rejection of the Social-Democratic program. *Rabochaya Mysl* (particularly in its *Separate Supplement*) takes practically the same attitude. Russian Social-Democracy is passing through a period of vacillation and doubt bordering on self-negation. On the one hand, the working-class movement is being sundered from socialism, the workers are being helped to carry on the economic struggle, but nothing, or next to nothing, is done to explain to them the socialist aims and the political tasks of the movement as a whole. On the other hand, socialism is being sundered from the working-class movement; Russian socialists are again beginning to talk more and more about the struggle against the government having to be carried on entirely by the intelligentsia because the workers confine themselves to the economic struggle.

In our opinion the ground has been prepared for this sad state of affairs by three circumstances. First, in their early activity, Russian Social-Democrats restricted themselves merely to work in propaganda circles.

When we took up agitation among the masses we were not always able to restrain ourselves from going to the other extreme. Secondly, in our early activity we often had to struggle for our right to existence against the Narodnaya Volya adherents, who understood by "politics" an activity isolated from the working-class movement and who reduced politics purely to conspiratorial struggle. In rejecting this sort of politics, the Social-Democrats went to the extreme of pushing politics entirely into the background. Thirdly, working in the isolation of small local workers' circles, the Social-Democrats did not devote sufficient attention to the necessity of organizing a revolutionary party which would combine all the activities of the local groups and make it possible to organize the revolutionary work on correct lines. The predominance of isolated work is naturally connected with the predominance of the economic struggle.

These circumstances resulted in concentration on one side of the movement only. The "economist" trend (that is, if we can speak of it as a "trend") has attempted to elevate this narrowness to the rank of a special theory and has tried to utilize for this purpose the fashionable Bernsteinism and the fashionable "criticism of Marxism," which peddles old bourgeois ideas under a new label. These attempts alone have given rise to the danger of a weakening of connection between the Russian working-class movement and Russian Social-Democracy, the vanguard in the struggle for political liberty. The most urgent task of our movement is to strengthen this connection.

Social-Democracy is the combination of the working-class movement and socialism. Its task is not to serve the working-class movement passively at each of its separate stages, but to represent the interests of the movement as a whole, to point out to this movement its ultimate aim and its political tasks, and to safeguard its political and ideological independence. Isolated from Social-Democracy, the working-class movement becomes petty and inevitably becomes bourgeois. In waging only the economic struggle, the working class loses its political independence; it becomes the tail of other parties and betrays the great principle: "The emancipation of the working classes must be the act of the working classes themselves." In every country there has been a period in which the working-class movement existed apart from socialism, each going its own way; and in every country this isolation has weakened both socialism and the working-class movement. Only the fusion of socialism with the working-class movement has in all countries created a durable basis for both. But in every country this combination of socialism and the working-class movement was evolved historically, in unique ways, in accordance with the prevailing conditions of time and place. In Russia, the necessity for combining socialism and the working-class movement was in theory long ago proclaimed, but it is only now being carried into practice. It is a very difficult process and there is, therefore, nothing surprising in the fact that it is accompanied by vacillations and doubts.

What lesson can be learned from the past?

The entire history of Russian socialism has led to the condition in which the most urgent task is the struggle against the autocratic government and the achievement of political liberty. Our socialist movement concentrated itself, so to speak, upon the struggle against the autocracy. On the other hand, history has shown that the isolation of socialist thought from the vanguard of the working classes is greater in Russia than in other countries, and that if this state of affairs continues, the revolutionary movement in Russia is doomed to impotence. From this condition emerges the task which the Russian Social-Democracy is called upon to fulfill—to imbue the masses of the proletariat with the ideas of socialism and political consciousness, and to organize a revolutionary party inseparably connected with the spontaneous working-class movement. Russian Social-Democracy has done much in this direction, but much more still remains to be done. With the growth of the movement, the field of activity for Social-Democrats becomes wider; the work becomes more varied, and an increasing number of activists in the movement will concentrate their efforts upon the fulfillment of various special tasks which the daily needs of propaganda and agitation bring to the fore. This phenomenon is quite natural and is inevitable, but it causes us to be particularly concerned with preventing these special activities and methods of struggle from becoming ends in themselves and with preventing preparatory work from being regarded as the main and sole activity.

Our principal and fundamental task is to facilitate the political development and the political organization of the working class. Those who push this task into the background, who refuse to subordinate to it all the special tasks and particular methods of struggle, are following a false path and causing serious harm to the movement. And it is being pushed into the background, firstly, by those who call upon revolutionaries to employ only the forces of isolated conspiratorial circles cut off from the working-class movement in the struggle against the government. It is being pushed into the background, secondly, by those who restrict the content and scope of political propaganda, agitation, and organization; who think it fit and proper to treat the workers to "politics" only at exceptional moments in their lives, only on festive occasions; who too solicitously substitute demands for partial concessions from the autocracy for the political struggle against the autocracy; and who do not go to sufficient lengths to ensure that these demands for partial concessions are raised to the status of a systematic, implacable struggle of a revolutionary, working-class party, against the autocracy.

"Organise!" *Rabochaya Mysl* keeps repeating to the workers in all keys, and all the adherents of the "economist" trend echo the cry. We, of course, wholly endorse this appeal, but we will not fail to add: organize, but not only in mutual benefit societies, strike funds, and workers' circles; organize also in a political party; organize for the determined struggle against the autocratic government and against the whole of capitalist society. Without such organization the proletariat will never rise to the class-conscious struggle; without such organization the working-class movement is doomed to impotency. With the aid of nothing but funds and study circles and mutual benefit societies the working class will never be able to fulfill its great historical mission—to emancipate itself and the whole of the Russian people from political and economic slavery. Not a single class in history has achieved power without producing its political leaders, its prominent representatives able to organize a movement and lead it. And the Russian working class has already shown that it can produce such men and women. The struggle which has developed so widely during the past five or six years has revealed the great potential revolutionary power of the working class; it has shown that the most ruthless government persecution does not diminish, but, on the contrary, increases the number of workers who strive towards socialism, towards political consciousness, and towards the political struggle. The Congress which our comrades held in 1898 correctly defined our tasks and did not merely repeat other people's words, did not merely express the enthusiasm of "intellectuals." . . . We must set to work resolutely to fulfill these tasks, placing the question of the Party's program, organization, and tactics on the order of the day. We have already set forth our views on the fundamental postulates of our program, and, of course, this is not the place to develop them in detail. We propose to devote a series of articles in forthcoming issues to questions of organization, which are among the most burning problems confronting us. In this respect we lag considerably behind the old workers in the Russian revolutionary movement. We must frankly admit this defect and exert all our efforts to devise methods of greater secrecy in our work, to propagate systematically the proper methods of work, the proper methods of deluding the gendarmes and of evading the snares of the police. We must train people who will devote the whole of their lives, not only their spare evenings, to the revolution; we must build up an organization large enough to permit the introduction of a strict division of labor in the various forms of our work. Finally, with regard to questions of tactics, we shall confine ourselves to the following: Social-Democracy does not tie its hands, it does not restrict its activities to some one preconceived plan or method of political struggle: it recognizes all methods of struggle, provided they correspond to the forces at the disposal of the Party and facilitate the achievement of the best results possible under the given conditions. If we have a strongly organized party, a single strike may turn into a political demonstration, into a political victory over the government. If we have a strongly organized party, a revolt in a single locality may grow into a victorious revolution. We must bear in mind that the struggles with the government for partial demands and the gain of certain concessions are merely light skirmishes with the enemy, encounters between outposts, whereas the decisive battle is still to come. Before us, in all its strength, towers the enemy fortress which is raining shot and shell upon us, mowing down our best fighters. We must capture this fortress, and we will capture it, if we unite all the forces of the awakening proletariat with all the forces of the Russian revolutionaries into one party which will attract all that is vital and honest in Russia. Only then will the great prophecy of the Russian worker-revolutionary, Pyotr Alexeyev, be fulfilled: "The muscular arm of the working millions will be lifted, and the yoke of despotism, guarded by the soldiers' bayonets, will be smashed to atoms!"

Reading #11

"The Revolutionary Proletariat and the Right of Nations to Self-Determination" (excerpt)

The Zimmerwald Manifesto, like the majority of the programs of the Social-Democratic parties or their resolutions on tactics, proclaims the right of nations to self-determination. Comrade Parabellum, in Nos. 252 and 523 of the *Berner Tagwacht* declares the "struggle for the non-existent right to self-determination" to be illusory; this struggle he contrasts with a "revolutionary mass struggle of the proletariat against capitalism," at the same time asserting that "we are against annexations" (this assertion is repeated five times in Comrade Parabellum's article), and against all "national acts of violence."

The arguments in favor of Comrade Parabellum's position reduce themselves to the assertion that all national problems of the present, like those of Alsace-Lorraine, Armenia, etc., are problems of imperialism; that capital has outgrown the framework of national states; that it is impossible to turn the wheel of history backward to the antiquated ideal of national states, etc.

Let us see whether Comrade Parabellum's arguments are correct.

First of all, it is Comrade Parabellum who looks backward and not forward when, at the beginning of his campaign against the acceptance by the working class "of the ideal of a national state," he directs his glance towards England, France, Italy, Germany, *i.e.*, countries where the national movement for liberation is a thing of the past, and not towards the Orient, Asia, Africa, the colonies, where this movement is a thing not of the past, but of the present and the future. Suffice it to mention India, China, Persia, Egypt.

Imperialism, further, means that capital has outgrown the framework of national states; it means the widening and sharpening of national oppression on a new historical basis. It follows from this, in contradiction to the conception of Comrade Parabellum, that we must *connect* the revolutionary struggle for socialism with a revolutionary program on the national question.

As to Comrade Parabellum, he, in the name of a socialist revolution scornfully rejects a consistently revolutionary program in the realm of democracy. This is incorrect. The proletariat cannot become victor save through democracy, *i.e.*, through introducing complete democracy and through combining with every step of its movement democratic demands formulated most vigorously, most decisively. It is senseless to *contrast* the socialist revolution and the revolutionary struggle against capitalism to *one* of the questions of democracy, in this case the national question. On the contrary, we must combine the revolutionary struggle against capitalism with a revolutionary program and revolutionary tactics relative to *all* democratic demands: a republic, a militia, officials elected by the people, equal rights for women, self-determination of nations, etc. While capitalism exists, all these demands are realizable only as an exception, and in an incomplete, distorted form. Basing ourselves on democracy as it already exists, exposing its incompleteness under capitalism, we advocate the overthrow of capitalism, expropriation of the bourgeoisie as a necessary basis both for the abolition of the poverty of the masses and for a complete and manifold realization of all democratic reforms. Some of those reforms will be started prior to the overthrow of the bourgeoisie, others in the process of the overthrow, still others after it has been accomplished. The socialist revolution is by no means a single battle; on the contrary, it is an epoch of a whole series of battles around *all* problems of economic and democratic reforms, which can be completed only by the expropriation of the bourgeoisie. It is for the sake of this final aim that we must formulate in a consistently revolutionary manner every one of our democratic demands. It is quite conceivable that the workers of a certain country may overthrow the bourgeoisie *before* even one fundamental democratic reform has been realized in full. It is entirely inconceivable, however, that the proletariat as an historical class will be able to defeat the bourgeoisie if it is not prepared for this task by being educated in the spirit of the most consistent and determined revolutionary democracy.

Imperialism is the progressing oppression of the nations of the world by a handful of great powers; it is an epoch of wars among them for the widening and strengthening of national oppression; it is the epoch when the masses of the people are deceived by the hypocritical social-patriots, *i.e.*, people who under the pretext of "freedom of nations," "right of nations to self-determination," and "defense of the fatherland" justify and defend the oppression of a majority of the world's nations by the great powers.

This is just why the central point in a program of Social-Democrats must be that distinction between oppressing and oppressed nations, since the distinction is the *essence* of imperialism, and is fraudulently evaded by the social-patriots, Kautsky included. This distinction is not important from the point of view of bourgeois pacifism, or the petty-bourgeois utopia of peaceful competition between independent nations under capitalism, but it is most important from the point of view of the revolutionary struggle against imperialism. From this distinction there follows *our* consistently democratic and revolutionary definition of the "right of nations to self-determination," which is in accord with the general task of the immediate struggle for socialism. It is in the name of this right, and fighting for its unequivocal recognition, that the Social-Democrats of the *oppressing* nations must demand the freedom of separation for the oppressed nations, for otherwise recognition of the equal rights of nations and international solidarity of the workers in reality remains an empty phrase, a hypocritical gesture. The Social-Democrats of the *oppressed* nations, however, must view as foremost the demand for the unity and the *fusion* of the workers of the oppressed nations with the workers of the oppressing nations, because otherwise those Social-Democrats involuntarily become the allies of one or the other national bourgeoisie, which *always* betrays the interest of the people and of democracy, and which in its turn is *always* ready for annexations and for oppressing other nations.

The approach to the national problem by the end of the sixties of the nineteenth century may serve as an instructive example. The petty-bourgeois democrats, devoid of every idea concerning the class struggle and the socialist revolution, pictured a utopia of peaceful competition between free and equal nations under capitalism. The Proudhonists "denied" entirely the national question and the right of self-determination of nations and precisely from the point of view of the immediate tasks of a social revolution. Marx scoffed at Proudhonism showing its affinity to chauvinism ("All Europe must sit quietly and obediently on its behind until the masters abolish 'poverty and ignorance' in France"; "by the denial of the national question, they seem to understand, without being aware of it, the swallowing up of the nations by the exemplary French nation"). Marx demanded the *separation of Ireland* from

England, "although after the separation there may come federation," and not from the standpoint of the petty-bourgeois utopia of a peaceful capitalism, not from considerations of "justice to Ireland," but from the standpoint of the interests of the revolutionary struggle of the prole-tariat of the *oppressing, i.e., the English, nation* against capitalism. The freedom of *that* nation was cramped and mutilated by the fact that it oppressed another nation. The internationalism of the *English* prole-tariat would have remained a hypocritical phrase were *it* not to demand the separation of Ireland. Marx never was in favor of small states, or of splitting up states, or of the federation principle. Still he considered the separation of an oppressed nation as a step towards federation, conse-quently not towards a splitting of nations but towards concentration, towards political and economic concentration, but concentration on the basis of democracy. From Comrade Parabellum's standpoint, Marx must have fought an "illusory" battle when he demanded the separa-tion of Ireland. In reality, however, only this demand was a consistent revolutionary program, only it corresponded to internationalism, only it represented concentration *not* along the lines of imperialism.

The imperialism of our days has brought about a situation where the oppression of nations by the great powers is a common phenomenon. It is precisely the standpoint of struggle against the social-patriots of the great-power nations that are now waging an imperialist war for the purpose of strengthening the oppression of nations—that are oppress-ing the majority of nations of the world and the majority of the earth's population—it is precisely this standpoint that must become the deci-sive, cardinal, basic point in the Social-Democratic national program.

READING #12

"The State"

Comrades, according to the plan you have adopted and which has been conveyed to me, the subject of today's talk is the state. I do not know how familiar you are already with this subject. If I am not mistaken your courses have only just begun and this is the first time you will be tackling this subject systematically. If that is so, then it may very well happen that in the first lecture of this difficult subject I may not succeed in making my exposition sufficiently clear and comprehensible to many of my listeners. And if this should prove to be the case, I would request you not to be perturbed by the fact, because the question of the state is a most complex and difficult one, perhaps one that more than any other has been confused by bourgeois scholars, writers and philosophers. It should not therefore be expected that a thorough understanding of this subject can be obtained from one brief talk, at a first sitting. After the first talk on this subject you should make a note of the passages which you have not understood or which are not clear to you, and return to them a second, a third and a fourth time, so that what you have not understood may be further supplemented and elucidated later, both by reading and by various lectures and talks. I hope that we may manage to meet once again and that we shall then be able to exchange opinions on all supplementary questions and see what has remained most unclear. I also hope that in addition to talks and lectures you will devote some time to reading at least a few of the most important works of Marx and Engels. I have no doubt that these most important works are to be found in the lists of books and in the handbooks which are available in your library for the students of the Soviet and Party school; and although, again, some of you may at first be dismayed by the difficulty of the exposition, I must again warn you that you should not let this worry you; what is unclear at a first reading will become clear at a second reading, or when you subsequently approach the question from a somewhat different angle. For I once more repeat that the question is so complex and has been so confused by bourgeois scholars and writers that anybody who desires to study it seriously and master it independently must attack it several times, return to it again and again and consider it from various angles in order to attain a clear, sound understanding of it. Because it is such a fundamental, such a basic question in all politics, and because not only in such stormy and revolutionary times as the present, but even in the most peaceful times, you will come across it every day in any newspaper in connection with any economic or political question it will be all the easier to return to it. Every day, in one context or another, you will be returning to the question: what is the state, what is its nature, what is its significance and what is the attitude of our Party, the party that is fighting for the overthrow of capitalism, the Communist Party—what is its attitude to the state? And the chief thing is that you should acquire, as a result of your reading, as a result of the talks and lectures you will hear on the state, the ability to approach this question independently, since you will be meeting with it on the most diverse occasions, in connection with the most trifling questions, in the most unexpected contexts and in discussions and disputes with opponents. Only when you learn to find your way about independently in this question may you consider yourself sufficiently confirmed in your convictions and able with sufficient success to defend them against anybody and at any time.

After these brief remarks, I shall proceed to deal with the question itself—what is the state, how did it arise and fundamentally what attitude to the state should be displayed by the party of the working class, which is fighting for the complete overthrow of capitalism—the Communist Party?

I have already said that you are not likely to find another question which has been so confused, deliberately and unwittingly, by representatives of bourgeois science, philosophy, jurisprudence, political economy and journalism, as the question of the state. To this day it is very often confused with religious questions; not only those professing religious doctrines (it is quite natural to expect it of them), but even people who consider themselves free from religious prejudice, very often confuse the specific question of the state with questions of religion and endeavor to build up a doctrine—very often a complex one, with an ideological, philosophical approach and argumentation—which claims that the state is something divine, something supernatural, that it is a certain force by virtue of which mankind has lived, that it is a force of divine origin which confers on people, or can confer on people, or which brings with it something that is not of man, but is given him from without. And it must be said that this doctrine is so closely bound up with the interests of the exploiting classes—the landowners and the capitalists—so serves their interests, has so deeply permeated all the customs, views and science of the gentlemen who represent the bourgeoisie, that you will meet with vestiges of it on every hand, even in the view of the state held by the Mensheviks and Socialist-Revolutionaries, although they are convinced that they can regard the state with sober eyes and reject indignantly the suggestion that they are under the sway of religious prejudices. This question has been so confused and complicated because it affects the interests of the ruling classes more than any other question (yielding place in this respect only to the foundations of economic science). The doctrine of the state serves to justify social privilege, the existence of exploitation, the existence of capitalism—and that is why it would be the greatest mistake to expect impartiality on this question, to approach it in the belief that people who claim to be scientific can give you a purely scientific view on the subject. In the question of the state, in the doctrine of the state, in the theory of the state, when you have become familiar with it and have gone into it deeply enough, you will always discern the struggle between different classes, a struggle which is reflected or expressed in a conflict of views on the state, in the estimate of the role and significance of the state.

To approach this question as scientifically as possible we must cast at least a fleeting glance back on the history of the state, its emergence and development. The most reliable thing in a question of social science, and one that is most necessary in order really to acquire the habit of approaching this question correctly and not allowing oneself to get lost in the mass of detail or in the immense variety of conflicting opinion— the most important thing if one is to approach this question scientifically is not to forget the underlying historical connection, to examine every question from the standpoint of how the given phenomenon arose in history and what were the principal stages in its development, and, from the standpoint of its development, to examine what it has become today.

I hope that in studying this question of the state you will acquaint yourselves with Engels's book *The Origin of the Family, Private Property and the State*. This is one of the fundamental works of modern socialism, every sentence of which can be accepted with confidence, in the assurance that it has not been said at random but is based on immense historical and political material. Undoubtedly, not all the parts of this work have been expounded in an equally popular and comprehensible way; some of them presume a reader who already possesses a certain knowledge of history and economics. But I again repeat that you should not be perturbed if on reading this work you do not understand it at once. Very few people do. But returning to it later, when your interest has been aroused, you will succeed in understanding the greater part, if not the whole of it. I refer to this book because it gives the correct approach to the question in the sense mentioned. It begins with a historical sketch of the origin of the state.

This question, like every other—for example, that of the origin of capitalism, the exploitation of man by man, socialism, how socialism arose, what conditions gave rise to it—can be approached soundly and confidently only if we cast a glance back on the history of its development as a whole. In connection with this problem it should first of all be noted that the state has not always existed. There was a time when there was no state. It appears wherever and whenever a division of society into classes appears, whenever exploiters and exploited appear.

Before the first form of exploitation of man by man arose, the first form of division into classes—slave-owners and slaves—there existed the patriarchal family, or, as it is sometimes called, the *clan* family. (Clan—tribe; at the time people of one kin lived together.) Fairly definite traces of these primitive times have survived in the life of many primitive peoples; and if you take any work whatsoever on primitive civilization, you will always come across more or less definite descriptions, indications and recollections of the fact that there was a time, more or less similar to primitive communism, when the division of society into slave-owners and slaves did not exist. And in those times there was no state, no special apparatus for the systematic application of force and the subjugation of people by force. It is such an apparatus that is called the state.

In primitive society, when people lived in small family groups and were still at the lowest stages of development, in a condition approximating to savagery—an epoch from which modern, civilized human society is separated by several thousand years—there were yet no signs of the existence of a state. We find the predominance of custom, authority, respect, the power enjoyed by the elders of the clan; we find this power sometimes accorded to women—the position of women then was not like the downtrodden and oppressed condition of women today—but nowhere do we find a special *category* of people set apart to rule others and who, for the sake and purpose of rule, systematically and permanently have at their disposal a certain apparatus of coercion, an apparatus of violence, such as is represented at the present time, as you all realize, by armed contingents of troops, prisons and other means of subjugating the will of others by force—all that which constitutes the essence of the state.

If we get away from what are known as religious teachings, from the subtleties, philosophical arguments and various opinions advanced by bourgeois scholars, if we get away from these and try to get at the real core of the matter, we shall find that the state really does amount to such an apparatus of rule which stands outside society as a whole. When there appears such a special group of men occupied solely with government, and who in order to rule need a special apparatus of coercion to subjugate the will of others by force—prisons, special contingents of men, armies, etc.—then there appears the state.

But there was a time when there was no state, when general ties, the community itself, discipline and the ordering of work were maintained by force of custom and tradition, by the authority or the respect enjoyed by the elders of the clan or by women—who in those times not only frequently enjoyed a status equal to that of men, but not infrequently enjoyed an even higher status—and when there was no special category of persons who were specialists in ruling. History shows that the state as a special apparatus for coercing people arose wherever and whenever there appeared a division of society into classes, that is, a division into groups of people some of which were permanently in a position to appropriate the labor of others, where some people exploited others.

And this division of society into classes must always be clearly borne in mind as a fundamental fact of history. The development of all human societies for thousands of years, in all countries without exception, reveals a general conformity to law, a regularity and consistency; so that at first we had a society without classes—the original patriarchal, primitive society, in which there were no aristocrats; then we had a society based on slavery—a slave-owning society. The whole of modern, civilized Europe has passed through this stage—slavery ruled supreme two thousand years ago. The vast majority of peoples of the other parts of the world also passed through this stage. Traces of slavery survive to this day among the less developed peoples; you will find the institution of slavery in Africa, for example, at the present time. The division into slave-owners and slaves was the first important class division. The former group not only owned all the means of production—the land and the implements, however poor and primitive they may have been in those times—but also owned people. This group was known as slave-owners, while those who labored and supplied labor for others were known as slaves.

This form was followed in history by another—feudalism. In the great majority of countries slavery in the course of its development evolved into serfdom. The fundamental division of society was now into feudal lords and peasant serfs. The form of relations between people changed.

The slave-owners had regarded the slaves as their property; the law had confirmed this view and regarded the slave as a chattel completely owned by the slave-owner. As far as the peasant serf was concerned, class oppression and dependence remained, but it was not considered that the feudal lord owned the peasants as chattels, but that he was only entitled to their labor, to the obligatory performance of certain services. In practice, as you know, serfdom, especially in Russia where it survived longest of all and assumed the crudest forms, in no way differed from slavery.

Further, with the development of trade, the appearance of the world market and the development of money circulation, a new class arose within feudal society—the capitalist class. From the commodity, the exchange of commodities and the rise of the power of money, there derived the power of capital. During the eighteenth century, or rather, from the end of the eighteenth century and during the nineteenth century, revolutions took place all over the world. Feudalism was abolished in all the countries of Western Europe. Russia was the last country in which this took place. In 1861 a radical change took place in Russia as well; as a consequence of this one form of society was replaced by another—feudalism was replaced by capitalism, under which division into classes remained, as well as various traces and remnants of serfdom, but fundamentally the division into classes assumed a different form.

The owners of capital, the owners of the land and the owners of the factories in all capitalist countries constituted and still constitute an insignificant minority of the population who have complete command of the labor of the whole people, and, consequently, command, oppress and exploit the whole mass of laborers, the majority of whom are proletarians, wage-workers, who procure their livelihood in the process of production only by the sale of their own worker's hands, their labor-power. With the transition to capitalism, the peasants, who had been disunited and downtrodden in feudal times, were converted partly (the majority) into proletarians, and partly (the minority) into wealthy peasants who themselves hired laborers and who constituted a rural bourgeoisie.

This fundamental fact—the transition of society from primitive forms of slavery to serfdom and finally to capitalism—you must always bear in mind, for only by remembering this fundamental fact, only by examining all political doctrines placed in this fundamental scheme, will you be able properly to appraise these doctrines and understand what they refer to; for each of these great periods in the history of mankind, slave-owning, feudal and capitalist, embraces scores and hundreds of centuries and presents such a mass of political forms, such a variety of political doctrines, opinions and revolutions, that this extreme diversity and immense variety (especially in connection with the political, philosophical and other doctrines of bourgeois scholars and politicians) can be understood only by firmly holding, as to a guiding thread, to this division of society into classes, this change in the forms of class rule, and from this standpoint examining all social questions—economic, political, spiritual, religious, etc.

If you examine the state from the standpoint of this fundamental division, you will find that before the division of society into classes, as I have already said, no state existed. But as the social division into classes arose and took firm root, as class society arose, the state also arose and took firm root. The history of mankind knows scores and hundreds of countries that have passed or are still passing through slavery, feudalism and capitalism. In each of these countries, despite the immense historical changes that have taken place, despite all the political vicissitudes and all the revolutions due to this development of mankind, to the transition from slavery through feudalism to capitalism and to the present world-wide struggle against capitalism, you will always discern the emergence of the state. It has always been a certain apparatus which stood outside society and consisted of a group of people engaged solely, or almost solely, or mainly, in ruling. People are divided into the ruled, and into specialists in ruling, those who rise above society and are called rulers, statesmen. This apparatus, this group of people who rule others, always possesses certain means of coercion, of physical force, irrespective of whether this violence over people is expressed in the primitive club, or in more perfected types of weapons in the epoch of slavery, or in the fire-arms which appeared in the Middle Ages, or, finally, in modern weapons, which in the twentieth century are technical marvels and are based entirely on the latest achievements of modern technology. The methods of violence changed, but whenever there was a state there existed in every society a group of persons who ruled, who commanded, who dominated and who in order to maintain their power possessed an apparatus of physical coercion, an apparatus of violence, with those weapons which corresponded to the technical level of the given epoch. And by examining these general phenomena, by asking ourselves why no state existed when there were no classes, when there were no exploiters and exploited, and why it appeared when classes appeared—only in this way shall we find a definite answer to the question of what is the nature and significance of the state.

The state is a machine for maintaining the rule of one class over another. When there were no classes in society, when, before the epoch of slavery, people labored in primitive conditions of greater equality, in conditions when the productivity of labor was still at its lowest, and when primitive man could barely procure the wherewithal for the crudest and most primitive existence, a special group of people whose function is to rule and to dominate the rest of society, had not and could not yet have emerged. Only when the first form of the division of society into classes appeared, only when slavery appeared, when a certain class of people, by concentrating on the crudest forms of agricultural labor, could produce a certain surplus, when this surplus was not absolutely essential for the most wretched existence of the slave and passed into the hands of the slave-owner, when in this way the existence of this class of slave-owners was secure—then in order that it might take firm root it was necessary for a state to appear.

And it did appear—the slave-owning state, an apparatus which gave the slave-owners power and enabled them to rule over the slaves. Both society and the state were then on a much smaller scale than they are now, they possessed incomparably poorer means of communication—the modern means of communication did not then exist. Mountains, rivers and seas were immeasurably greater obstacles than they are now, and the state took shape within far narrower geographical boundaries. A technically weak state apparatus served a state confined within relatively narrow boundaries and with a narrow range of action. Nevertheless, there did exist an apparatus which compelled the slaves to remain in slavery, which kept one part of society subjugated to and oppressed by another. It is impossible to compel the greater part of society to work systematically for the other part of society without a permanent apparatus of coercion. So long as there were no classes, there was no apparatus of this sort. When classes appeared, everywhere and always, as the division grew and took firmer hold, there also appeared a special institution—the state. The forms of state were extremely varied. As early as the period of slavery we find diverse forms of the state in the countries that were the most advanced, cultured and civilized according to the standards of the time—for example, in ancient Greece and Rome—which were based entirely on slavery. At that time there was already a difference between monarchy and republic, between aristocracy and democracy. A monarchy is the power of a single person, a republic is the absence of any none-lected authority; an aristocracy is the power of a relatively small minority, a democracy is the power of the people (democracy in Greek literally means the power of the people). All these differences arose in the epoch of slavery. Despite these differences, the state of the slave-owning epoch was a slave-owning state, irrespective of whether it was a monarchy or a republic, aristocratic or democratic.

In every course on the history of ancient times, in any lecture on this subject, you will hear about the struggle which was waged between the monarchical and republican states. But the fundamental fact is that the slaves were not regarded as human beings—not only were they not regarded as citizens, they were not even regarded as human beings. Roman law regarded them as chattels. The law of manslaughter, not to mention the other laws for the protection of the person, did not extend to slaves. It defended only the slave-owners, who were alone recognized as citizens with full rights. But whether a monarchy was instituted or a republic, it was a monarchy of the slave-owners or a republic of the slave-owners. All rights were enjoyed by the slave-owners, while the slave was a chattel in the eyes of the law; and not only could any sort of violence be perpetrated against a slave, but even the killing of a slave was not considered a crime. Slave-owning republics differed in their internal organization, there were aristocratic republics and democratic republics. In an aristocratic republic only a small number of privileged persons took part in the elections; in a democratic republic everybody took part—but everybody meant only the slave-owners, that is, everybody except the slaves. This fundamental fact must be borne in mind, because it throws more light than any other on the question of the state and clearly demonstrates the nature of the state.

The state is a machine for the oppression of one class by another, a machine for holding in obedience to one class other, subordinated classes. There are various forms of this machine. The slave-owning state could be a monarchy, an aristocratic republic or even a democratic republic. In fact the forms of government varied extremely, but their essence was always the same: the slaves enjoyed no rights and constituted an oppressed class; they were not regarded as human beings. We find the same thing in the feudal state.

The change in the form of exploitation transformed the slave-owning state into the feudal state. This was of immense importance. In slave-owning society the slave enjoyed no rights whatever and was not regarded as a human being; in feudal society the peasant was bound to the soil. The chief distinguishing feature of serfdom was that the peasants (and at that time the peasants constituted the majority; the urban population was still very small) were considered bound to the land—this is the very basis of "serfdom." The peasant might work a definite number of days for himself on the plot assigned to him by the landlord; on the other days the peasant serf worked for his lord. The essence of class society remained—society was based on class exploitation. Only the owners of the land could enjoy full rights; the peasants had no rights at all. In practice their condition differed very little from the condition of slaves in the slave-owning state. Nevertheless, a wider road was opened for their emancipation, for the emancipation of the peasants, since the peasant serf was not regarded as the direct property of the lord. He could work part of his time on his own plot, could, so to speak, belong to himself to some extent; and with the wider opportunities for the development of exchange and trade relations the feudal system steadily disintegrated and the scope of emancipation of the peasantry steadily widened. Feudal society was always more complex than slave society. There was a greater development of trade and industry, which even in those days led to capitalism. In the Middle Ages feudalism predominated. And here too the forms of state varied, here too we find both the monarchy and the republic, although the latter was much more weakly expressed. But always the feudal lord was regarded as the only ruler. The peasant serfs were deprived of absolutely all political rights.

Neither under slavery nor under the feudal system could a small minority of people dominate over the vast majority without coercion. History is full of the constant attempts of the oppressed classes to throw off oppression. The history of slavery contains records of wars of emancipation from slavery which lasted for decades. Incidentally, the name "Spartacist" now adopted by the German Communists—the only German party which is really fighting against the yoke of capitalism—was adopted by them because Spartacus was one of the most prominent heroes of one of the greatest revolts of slaves, which took place about two thousand years ago. For many years the seemingly omnipotent Roman Empire, which rested entirely on slavery, experienced the shocks and blows of a widespread uprising of slaves who armed and united to form a vast army under the leadership of Spartacus. In the end they were defeated, captured and put to torture by the slave-owners. Such civil wars mark the whole history of the existence of class society. I have just mentioned an example of the greatest of these civil wars in the epoch of slavery. The whole epoch of feudalism is likewise marked by constant uprising of the peasants. For example, in Germany in the Middle Ages the struggle between the two classes—the landlords and the serfs—assumed wide proportions and was transformed into a civil war of the peasants against the landowners. You are all familiar with similar examples of repeated uprisings of the peasants against the feudal landowners in Russia.

In order to maintain their rule and to preserve their power, the feudal lords had to have an apparatus by which they could unite under their subjugation a vast number of people and subordinate them to certain laws and regulations; and all these laws fundamentally amounted to one thing—the maintenance of the power of the lords over the peasant serfs. And this was the feudal state, which in Russia, for example, or in quite backward Asiatic countries (where feudalism prevails to this day) dif-fered in form—it was either a republic or a monarchy. When the state was a monarchy, the rule of one person was recognized; when it was a republic, the participation of the elected representatives of landowning society was in one degree or another recognized—this was in feudal society. Feudal society represented a division of classes under which the vast majority—the peasant serfs—were completely subjected to an insig-nificant minority—the owners of the land.

The development of trade, the development of commodity exchange, led to the emergence of a new class—the capitalists. Capital took shape as such at the close of the Middle Ages, when, after the discovery of America, world trade developed enormously, when the quantity of pre-cious metals increased, when silver and gold became the medium of exchange, when money circulation made it possible for individuals to possess tremendous wealth. Silver and gold were recognized as wealth all over the world. The economic power of the landowning class declined and the power of the new class—the representatives of capital—devel-oped. The reconstruction of society was such that all citizens seemed to be equal, the old division into slave-owners and slaves disappeared, all were regarded as equal before the law irrespective of what capital each owned; whether he owned land as private property, or was a poor man who owned nothing but his labor-power—all were equal before the law. The law protects everybody equally; it protects the property of those who have it from attack by the masses who, possessing no property, possessing nothing but their labor-power, grow steadily impoverished and ruined and become converted into proletarians. Such is capitalist society.

I cannot dwell on it in detail. You will return to this when you come to discuss the Program of the Party—you will then hear a description of capitalist society. This society advanced against serfdom, against the old feudal system, under the slogan of liberty. But it was liberty for those who owned property. And when feudalism was shattered, which occurred at the end of the eighteenth century and the beginning of the nineteenth century—in Russia it occurred later than in other countries, in 1861— the feudal state was then superseded by the capitalist state, which proclaims liberty for the whole people as its slogan, which declares that it expresses the will of the whole people and denies that it is a class state. And here there developed a struggle between the socialists, who are fighting for the liberty of the whole people, and the capitalist state— a struggle which has led to the creation of the Soviet Socialist Republic and which is going on throughout the world.

To understand the struggle that has been started against world capital, to understand the nature of the capitalist state, we must remember that when the capitalist state advanced against the feudal state it entered the fight under the slogan of liberty. The abolition of feudalism meant liberty for the representatives of the capitalist state and served their purpose, inasmuch as serfdom was breaking down and the peasants had acquired the opportunity of owning as their full property the land which they had purchased for compensation or in part by quit-rent—this did not concern the state: it protected property irrespective of its origin, because the state was founded on private property. The peasants became private owners in all the modern, civilized states. Even when the landowner surrendered part of his land to the peasant, the state protected private property, rewarding the landowner by compensation, by letting him take money for the land. The state as it was declared that it would fully preserve private property, and it accorded it every support and protection. The state recognized the property rights of every merchant, industrialist and manufacturer. And this society, based on private property, on the power of capital, on the complete subjection of the propertyless workers and laboring masses of the peasantry, proclaimed that its rule was based on liberty. Combating feudalism, it proclaimed freedom of property and was particularly proud of the fact that the state had ceased, supposedly, to be a class state.

Yet the state continued to be a machine which helped the capitalists to hold the poor peasants and the working class in subjection. But in outward appearance it was free. It proclaimed universal suffrage, and declared through its champions, preachers, scholars and philosophers, that it was not a class state. Even now, when the Soviet Socialist Republics have begun to fight the state, they accuse us of violating liberty, of building a state based on coercion, on the suppression of some by others, whereas they represent a popular, democratic state. And now, when the world socialist revolution has begun, and when the revolution has succeeded in some countries, when the fight against world capital has grown particularly acute, this question of the state has acquired the greatest importance and has become, one might say, the most burning one, the focus of all present-day political questions and political disputes.

Whichever party we take in Russia or in any of the more civilized countries, we find that nearly all political disputes, disagreements and opinions now center around the conception of the state. Is the state in a capitalist country, in a democratic republic—especially one like Switzerland or the U.S.A.—in the freest democratic republics, an expression of the popular will, the sum total of the general decision of the people, the expression of the national will, and so forth; or is the state a machine that enables the capitalists of those countries to maintain their power over the working class and the peasantry? That is the fundamental question around which all political disputes all over the world now center. What do they say about Bolshevism? The bourgeois press abuses the Bolsheviks. You will not find a single newspaper that does not repeat the hackneyed accusation that the Bolsheviks violate popular rule. If our Mensheviks and Socialist-Revolutionaries in their simplicity of heart (perhaps it is not simplicity, or perhaps it is the simplicity which the proverb says is worse than robbery) think that they discovered and invented the accusation that the Bolsheviks have violated liberty and popular rule, they are ludicrously mistaken. Today every one of the richest newspapers in the richest countries, which spend tens of millions on their distribution and disseminate bourgeois lies and imperialist policy in tens of millions of copies—every one of these newspapers repeats these basic arguments and accusations against Bolshevism, namely, that the U.S.A., Britain and Switzerland are advanced states based on popular rule, whereas the Bolshevik republic is a state of bandits in which liberty is unknown, and that the Bolsheviks have violated the idea of popular rule and have even gone so far as to disperse the Constituent Assembly. These terrible accusations against the Bolsheviks are repeated all over the world. These accusations lead us directly to the question— what is the state? In order to understand these accusations, in order to study them and have a fully intelligent attitude towards them, and not to examine them on hearsay but with a firm opinion of our own, we must have a clear idea of what the state is. We have before us capitalist states of every kind and all the theories in defense of them which were created before the war. In order to answer the question properly we must critically examine all these theories and views.

I have already advised you to turn for help to Engels's book *The Origin of the Family, Private Property and the State*. This book says that every state in which private ownership of the land and means of production exists, in which capital dominates, however democratic it may be, is a capitalist state, a machine used by the capitalists to keep the working class and the poor peasants in subjection; while universal suffrage, a Constituent Assembly, a parliament are merely a form, a sort of promissory note, which does not change the real state of affairs.

The forms of domination of the state may vary: capital manifests its power in one way where one form exists, and in another way where another form exists—but essentially the power is in the hands of capital, whether there are voting qualifications or some other rights or not, or whether the republic is a democratic one or not—in fact, the more democratic it is the cruder and more cynical is the rule of capitalism. One of the most democratic republics in the world is the United States of America, yet nowhere (and those who have been there since 1905 probably know it) is the power of capital, the power of a handful of multimillionaires over the whole of society, so crude and so openly corrupt as in America. Once capital exists, it dominates the whole of society, and no democratic republic, no franchise can change its nature.

The democratic republic and universal suffrage were an immense progressive advance as compared with feudalism: they have enabled the proletariat to achieve its present unity and solidarity, to form those firm and disciplined ranks which are waging a systematic struggle against capital. There was nothing even approximately resembling this among the peasant serfs, not to speak of the slaves. The slaves, as we know, revolted, rioted, started civil wars, but they could never create a class-conscious majority and parties to lead the struggle, they could not clearly realize what their aims were, and even in the most revolutionary moments of history they were always pawns in the hands of the ruling classes. The bourgeois republic, parliament, universal suffrage—all represent great progress from the standpoint of the world development of society. Mankind moved towards capitalism, and it was capitalism alone which, thanks to urban culture, enabled the oppressed proletarian class to become conscious of itself and to create the world working-class movement, the millions of workers organized all over the world in parties—the socialist parties which are consciously leading the struggle of the masses. Without parliamentarism, without an electoral system, this development of the working class would have been impossible. That is why all these things have acquired such great importance in the eyes of the broad masses of people. That is why a radical change seems to be so difficult. It is not only the conscious hypocrites, scientists and priests that uphold and defend the bourgeois lie that the state is free and that it is its mission to defend the interests of all; so also do a large number of people who sincerely adhere to the old prejudices and who cannot understand the transition from the old, capitalist society to socialism. Not only people who are directly dependent on the bourgeoisie, not only those who live under the yoke of capital or who have been bribed by capital (there are a large number of all sorts of scientists, artists, priests, etc., in the service of capital), but even people who are simply under the sway of the prejudice of bourgeois liberty, have taken up arms against Bolshevism all over the world because when the Soviet Republic was founded it rejected these bourgeois lies and openly declared: you say your state is free, whereas in reality, as long as there is private property, your state, even if it is a democratic republic, is nothing but a machine used by the capitalists to suppress the workers, and the freer the state, the more clearly is this expressed. Examples of this are Switzerland in Europe and the United States in America. Nowhere does capital rule so cynically and ruthlessly, and nowhere is it so clearly apparent, as in these countries, although they are democratic republics, no matter how prettily they are painted and notwithstanding all the talk about labor democracy and the equality of all citizens. The fact is that in Switzerland

and the United States capital dominates, and every attempt of the workers to achieve the slightest real improvement in their condition is immediately met by civil war. There are fewer soldiers, a smaller standing army, in these countries—Switzerland has a militia and every Swiss has a gun at home, while in America there was no standing army until quite recently—and so when there is a strike the bourgeoisie arms, hires soldiery and suppresses the strike; and nowhere is this suppression of the working-class movement accompanied by such ruthless severity as in Switzerland and the U.S.A., and nowhere does the influence of capital in parliament manifest itself as powerfully as in these countries. The power of capital is everything, the stock exchange is everything, while parliament and elections are marionettes, puppets. . . . But the eyes of the workers are being opened more and more, and the idea of Soviet government is spreading farther and farther a field, especially after the bloody carnage [of World War I] we have just experienced. The necessity for a relentless war on the capitalists is becoming clearer and clearer to the working class.

Whatever guise a republic may assume, however democratic it may be, if it is a bourgeois republic, if it retains private ownership of the land and factories, and if private capital keeps the whole of society in wage-slavery, that is, if the republic does not carry out what is proclaimed in the Program of our Party and in the Soviet Constitution, then this state is a machine for the suppression of some people by others. And we shall place this machine in the hands of the class that is to overthrow the power of capital. We shall reject all the old prejudices about the state meaning universal equality—for that is a fraud: as long as there is exploitation there cannot be equality. The landowner cannot be the equal of the worker, or the hungry man the equal of the full man. This machine called the state, before which people bowed in superstitious awe, believing the old tales that it means popular rule, tales which the proletariat declares to be a bourgeois lie—this machine the proletariat will smash. So far we have deprived the capitalists of this machine and have taken it over. We shall use this machine, or bludgeon, to destroy all exploitation. And when the possibility of exploitation no longer exists anywhere in the world, when there are no longer owners of land and owners of factories, and when there is no longer a situation in which some gorge while others starve, only when the possibility of this no longer exists shall we consign this machine to the scrap-heap. Then there will be no state and no exploitation. Such is the view of our Communist Party. I hope that we shall return to this subject in subsequent lectures, return to it again and again.

READING #13

"Letters from Afar" (excerpts)

THIRD LETTER: Concerning a Proletarian Militia

The conclusion I drew yesterday about [Menshevik politician] Chkheidze's vacillating tactics has been fully confirmed today, March 10 (23), by two documents. First—a telegraphic report from Stockholm in the *Frankfurter Zeitung* containing excerpts from the manifesto of the Central Committee of our Party, the Russian Social-Democratic Labour Party, in St. Petersburg. In this document there is not a word about either supporting the [pro-capitalist] Guchkov government or overthrowing it; the workers and soldiers are called upon to organize around the Soviet of Workers' Deputies, to elect representatives to it for the fight against tsarism and for a republic, for an eight-hour day, for the confiscation of the landed estates and grain stocks, and chiefly, for an end to the predatory war. Particularly important and particularly urgent in this connection is our Central Committee's absolutely correct idea that to obtain peace relations must be established with *the proletarians of all the belligerent countries*.

To expect peace from negotiations and relations between the bourgeois governments would be self-deception and deception of the people.

The second document is a Stockholm report, also by telegraph, to another German newspaper (*Vossische Zeitung*) about a conference between the Chkheidze group in the Duma, the workers' group (? Arbeiterfraction) and representatives of fifteen workers' unions on March 2 (15) and a manifesto published next day. Of the eleven points of this manifesto, the telegram reports only three: the first, the demand for a republic; the seventh, the demand for peace and immediate peace negotiations; and the third, the demand for "adequate participation in the government of representatives of the Russian working class".

If this point is correctly reported, I can understand why the bour-geoisie is praising Chkheidze. I can understand why the praise of the English Guchkovites in *The Times* which I quoted elsewhere has been supplemented by the praise of the French Guchkovites in *Le Temps*. This newspaper of the French millionaires and imperialists writes on March 22: "The leaders of the workers' parties, particularly M. Chkheidze, are exercising all their influence to moderate the wishes of the working classes."

Indeed, to demand workers'"participation" in the Guchkov-Milyukov government is a theoretical and political absurdity: to participate as a minority would mean serving as a pawn; to participate on an "equal foot-ing" is impossible, because the demand to continue the war cannot be reconciled with the demand to conclude an armistice and start peace negotiations; to "participate" as a majority requires the strength to *over-throw* the Guchkov-Milyukov government. In practice, the demand for "participation" is the worst sort of Louis Blancism, i.e., oblivion of the class struggle and the actual conditions under which it is being waged, infatuation with a most hollow-sounding phrase, spreading illusions among the workers, loss, in negotiations with Milyukov or Kerensky, of *precious* time which must be used to create a *real* class and revolutionary force, a proletarian militia that will *enjoy the confidence of all* the poor strata of the population, and they constitute the vast majority, and will *help them to organize*, help *them* to fight for bread, peace, freedom.

This mistake in the manifesto issued by Chkheidze and his group (I am not speaking of the O.C., Organizing Committee, *party*, because in the sources available to me there is not a word about the O.C.)—this mistake is all the more strange considering that at the March 2 (15) con-ference, Chkheidze's closest collaborator, Skobelev, said, according to the newspapers: "Russia is on the eve of a second, real [*wirklich*] revolution."

Now that is the truth, from which Skobelev and Chkheidze have forgotten to draw the practical conclusions. I cannot judge from here, from my accursed afar, how near this second revolution is. Being on the spot, Skobelev can see things better. Therefore, I am not raising for myself problems, for the solution of which I have not and cannot have the necessary concrete data. I am merely emphasizing the confirmation by Skobelev, an "outside witness," i.e., one who does not belong to our Party, of the *factual* conclusion I drew in my first letter, namely: that the February-March Revolution was merely the *first stage* of the revolution.

Russia is passing through a peculiar historical moment of *transition* to the next stage of the revolution, or, to use Skobelev's expression, to a "second revolution."

If we want to be Marxists and learn from the experience of revolution in the whole world, we must strive to understand in what, precisely, lies the *peculiarity* of this *transitional* moment, and what tactics follow from its objective specific features.

The peculiarity of the situation lies in that the Guchkov-Milyukov government gained the first victory with extraordinary ease due to the following three major circumstances: (1) assistance from Anglo-French finance capital and its agents; (2) assistance from part of the top ranks of the army; (3) the already existing organization of the entire Russian bourgeoisie in the shape of the rural and urban local government institutions, the State Duma, the war industries committees, and so forth.

The Guchkov government is held in a vise: bound by the interests of capital, it is compelled to strive to continue the predatory, robber war, to protect the monstrous profits of capital and the landlords, to restore the monarchy. Bound by its revolutionary origin and by the need for an abrupt change from tsarism to democracy, pressed by the bread-hungry and peace-hungry masses, the government is compelled to lie, to wriggle, to play for time, to "proclaim" and promise (promises are the only things that are very cheap even at a time of madly rocketing prices) as much as possible and do as little as possible, to make concessions with one hand and to withdraw them with the other.

Under certain circumstances, the new government can at best postpone its collapse somewhat by leaning on all the organizing ability of the entire Russian bourgeoisie and bourgeois intelligentsia. But even in that case it is *unable* to avoid collapse, because it is *impossible* to escape from the claws of the terrible monster of imperialist war and famine nurtured by world capitalism unless one renounces bourgeois relationships, passes to revolutionary measures, appeals to the supreme historic heroism of both the Russian and world proletariat.

Hence the conclusion: we cannot overthrow the new government at one stroke, or, if we can (in revolutionary times the limits of what is possible expand a thousandfold), we will not be able to maintain power *unless we counter* the magnificent organization of the entire Russian bourgeoisie and the entire bourgeois intelligentsia with an equally magnificent *organization of the proletariat*, which must lead the entire vast mass of urban and rural poor, the semi-proletariat and small proprietors.

Irrespective of whether the "second revolution" has already broken out in St. Petersburg (I have said that it would be absolutely absurd to think that it is possible from abroad to assess the actual tempo at which it is maturing), whether it has been postponed for some time, or whether it has already begun in individual areas (of which some signs are evident)—in *any* case, the slogan of the moment on the eve of the new revolution, during it, and on the morrow of it, must be *proletarian organization*.

Comrade workers! You performed miracles of proletarian heroism yesterday in overthrowing the tsarist monarchy. In the more or less near future (perhaps even now, as these lines are being written) you will again have to perform the same miracles of heroism to overthrow the rule of the landlords and capitalists, who are waging the imperialist war. You will not achieve *durable victory* in this next "real" revolution if you do not perform *miracles of proletarian organization*!

Organization is the slogan of the moment. But to confine oneself to that is to say nothing, for, on the one hand, organization is *always* needed; hence, mere reference to the necessity of "organizing the masses" explains absolutely nothing. On the other hand, he who confines himself solely to this becomes an abettor of the liberals, for the *very thing* the *liberals* want in order to strengthen their rule is that the questions *should not go beyond their ordinary* "legal" (from the standpoint of "normal" bourgeois society) organizations, i.e., that they should *only* join their party, their trade union, their co-operative society, etc., etc.

Guided by their class instinct, the workers have realized that in revolutionary times they need *not only* ordinary, but an entirely different organization. They have rightly taken the path indicated by the experience of our 1905 Revolution and of the 1871 Paris Commune; they have set up a *Soviet of Workers' Deputies*; they have begun to develop, expand and strengthen it by drawing in *soldiers'* deputies, and, undoubtedly, deputies from rural *wage*-workers, and then (in one form or another) from the entire peasant poor.

The prime and most important task, and one that brooks no delay, is to set up organizations of this kind in all parts of Russia without exception, for all trades and strata of the proletarian and semi-proletarian population without exception, i.e., for all the working and exploited people, to use a less economically exact but more popular term. Running ahead somewhat, I shall mention that for the entire mass of the peasantry our Party (its *special* role in the new type of proletarian organizations I hope to discuss in one of my next letters) should especially recommend Soviets of wage-workers and Soviets of small tillers who do not sell grain, to be formed *separately* from the well-to-do peasants. Without this, it will be impossible either to conduct a truly proletarian policy in general,* or correctly to approach the extremely important practical question which is a matter of life and death for millions of people: the proper distribution of *grain*, increasing its production, etc.

It might be asked: What should be the function of the Soviets of Workers' Deputies? They "must be regarded as organs of insurrection, of revolutionary rule," we wrote in No. 47 of the Geneva *Sotsial-Demokrat*, of October 13, 1915.

This theoretical proposition, deduced from the experience of the Commune of 1871 and of the Russian Revolution of 1905, must be explained and concretely developed on the basis of the practical experience of precisely the present stage of the present revolution in Russia.

We need revolutionary *government*, we need (for a certain transitional period) a *state*. This is what distinguishes us from the anarchists. The difference between the revolutionary Marxists and the anarchists is not only that the former stand for centralized, large-scale communist production, while the latter stand for disconnected small production. The difference between us precisely on the question of government, of the state, is that we are *for*, and the anarchists *against*, utilizing revolutionary forms of the state in a revolutionary way for the struggle for socialism.

We need a state. But *not the kind* of state the bourgeoisie has created everywhere, from constitutional monarchies to the most democratic republics. And in this we differ from the opportunists and Kautskyites of the old, and decaying, socialist parties, who have distorted, or have forgotten, the lessons of the Paris Commune and the analysis of these lessons made by Marx and Engels.

We need a state, but *not* the kind the bourgeoisie needs, with organs of government in the shape of a police force, an army and a bureaucracy

---

* In the rural districts a struggle will now develop for the small and, partly, middle peasants. The landlords, leaning on the well-to-do peasants, will try to lead them into subordination to the bourgeoisie. Leaning on the rural wage-workers and rural poor, we must lead them into the closest alliance with the urban proletariat.

(officialdom) separate from and opposed to the people. All bourgeois revolutions merely perfected *this* state machine, merely transferred *it* from the hands of one party to those of another.

The proletariat, on the other hand, if it wants to uphold the gains of the present revolution and proceed further, to win peace, bread and freedom, must "*smash*," to use Marx's expression, this "ready-made" state machine and substitute a new one for it by *merging* the police force, the army and the bureaucracy with *the entire armed people*. Following the path indicated by the experience of the Paris Commune of 1871 and the Russian Revolution of 1905, the proletariat must organize and arm *all* the poor, exploited sections of the population in order that they *themselves* should take the organs of state power directly into their own hands, in order that *they themselves should constitute* these organs of state power.

And the workers of Russia have already *taken* this path in the first stage of the first revolution, in February-March 1917. The whole task now is clearly to understand what this new path is, to proceed along it further, boldly, firmly and perseveringly.

The Anglo-French and Russian capitalists wanted "only" to remove, or only to "frighten," Nicholas II and to leave intact the old state machine, then police force, the army and the bureaucracy.

The workers went further and smashed it. And now, not only the Anglo-French, but also the German capitalists are *howling* with rage and horror as they see, for example, Russian soldiers shooting their officers, as in the case of Admiral Nepenin, that supporter of Guchkov and Milyukov.

I said that the workers have smashed the old state machine. It will be more correct to say: *have begun* to smash it.

Let us take a concrete example.

In St. Petersburg and in many other places the police force has been partly wiped out and partly dissolved. The Guchkov-Milyukov government *cannot* either restore the monarchy or, in general, maintain power *without restoring* the police force as a special organization of armed men under the command of the bourgeoisie, separate from and opposed to the people. That is as clear as daylight.

On the other hand, the new government must reckon with the revolutionary people, must feed them with half-concessions and promises, must play for time. That is why it resorts to half-measures: it establishes a "people's militia" with elected officials (this sounds awfully respectable, awfully democratic, revolutionary and beautiful!)—*but. . . but,* firstly, it places this militia under the control of the rural and urban local government bodies, i.e., under the command of landlords and capitalists who have been elected in conformity with laws passed by Nicholas the Bloody and Stolypin the Hangman!! Secondly, although calling it a "people's militia" in order to throw dust in the eyes of the "people," it does *not* call upon the *entire* people to join this militia, *and does not compel* the employers and capitalists to *pay* workers and office employees their ordinary wages *for the hours and days* they spend in the *public service,* i.e., in the militia.

That's their trick. That is how the landlord and capitalist government of the Guchkovs and Milyukovs manages to have a "people's militia" on paper, while in reality, it is restoring, gradually and on the quiet, the *bourgeois,* anti-people's militia. At first it is to consist of "eight thousand students and professors" (as foreign newspapers describe the present St. Petersburg militia)—an obvious plaything!—and will gradually be built up of the old and new *police force.*

Prevent restoration of the police force! Do not let the local government bodies slip out of your hands! Set up a militia that will really embrace the entire people, be really universal, and be led by the proletariat!—such is the task of the day, such is the slogan of the moment which equally conforms with the properly understood interests of furthering the class struggle, furthering the revolutionary movement, and the democratic instinct of every worker, of every peasant, of every exploited toiler who cannot help hating the policemen, the rural police patrols, the village constables, the command of landlords and capitalists over armed men with power over the people.

What kind of police force do *they* need, the Guchkovs and Milyukovs, the landlords and capitalists? The same kind as existed under the tsarist monarchy. After the briefest revolutionary periods *all* the bourgeois and bourgeois-democratic republics in the world set up or restored *precisely such* a police force, a special organization of armed men subordinate to the bourgeoisie in one way or another, separate from and opposed to the people.

What kind of militia do we need, the proletariat, all the toiling people? A genuine *people's* militia, i.e., one that, first, consists of the *entire* population, of all adult citizens of *both* sexes; and, second, one that combines the functions of a people's army with police functions, with the functions of the chief and fundamental organ of public order and public administration.

To make these propositions more comprehensible I will take a purely schematic example. Needless to say, it would be absurd to think of drawing up any kind of a "plan" for a proletarian militia: when the workers and the entire people set about it practically, on a truly mass scale, they will work it out and organize it a hundred times better than any theoretician. I am not offering a "plan," I only want to illustrate my idea.

St. Petersburg has a population of about two million. Of these, more than half are between the ages of 15 and 65. Take half—one million. Let us even subtract an entire fourth as physically unfit, etc., taking no part in public service at the present moment for justifiable reasons. There remain 750,000 who, serving in the militia, say one day in fifteen (and receiving their pay for this time from their employers), would form an army of 50,000.

That's the type of "state" we need!

That's the kind of militia that would be a "people's militia" in deed and not only in words.

That is how we must proceed in order to *prevent* the restoration either of a special police force, or of a special army separate from the people.

Such a militia, 95 hundredths of which would consist of workers and peasants, would express the *real* mind and will, the strength and power of the vast majority of the people. Such a militia would really arm, and provide military training for, the entire people, would be a safeguard, but *not* of the Guchkov or Milyukov type, against all attempts to restore reaction, against all the designs of tsarist agents. Such a militia would be the executive organ of the Soviets of Workers' and Soldiers' Deputies, it would enjoy the *boundless* respect and confidence of the people, for it itself would be an organization of the entire people. Such a militia would transform democracy from a beautiful signboard which covers up the enslavement and torment of the people by the capitalists, into a means of actually *training the masses* for participation in *all* affairs of state. Such a militia would draw the young people into political life and teach them not only by words, but also by action, by *work*. Such a militia would develop those functions which, speaking in scientific language, come within the purview of the "welfare police," sanitary inspection, and so forth, and would enlist for such work all adult women. If women are not drawn into public service, into the militia, into political life, if women are not torn out of their stupefying house and kitchen environment, it will be *impossible* to guarantee real freedom, it will be *impossible* to build even democracy, let alone socialism.

Such a militia would be a proletarian militia, for the industrial and urban workers would exert a guiding influence on the masses of the poor as naturally and inevitably as they came to hold the leading place in the people's revolutionary struggle both in 1905–07 and in 1917.

Such a militia would ensure absolute order and devotedly observed comradely discipline. At the same time, in the severe crisis that all the belligerent countries are experiencing, it would make it possible to combat this crisis in a really democratic way, properly and rapidly to distribute grain and other supplies, introduce "universal labor service," which the French now call "civilian mobilization" and the Germans "civilian service," and without which *it is impossible—it has proved to be impossible*—to heal the wounds that have been and are being inflicted by the predatory and horrible war.

Has the proletariat of Russia shed its blood only in order to receive fine promises of political democratic reforms and nothing more? Can it be that it will not demand, and secure, that *every* toiler should *forthwith* see and feel some improvement in his life? That every family should have bread? That every child should have a bottle of good milk and that not a single adult in a rich family should dare take extra milk until children are provided for? That the palaces and rich apartments abandoned by the tsar and the aristocracy should not remain vacant, but provide shelter for the homeless and the destitute? Who can carry out these measures except a people's militia, to which women must belong equally with men?

These measures do *not yet* constitute socialism. They concern the distribution of consumption, not the reorganization of production. They would not yet constitute the "dictatorship of the proletariat," only the "revolutionary-democratic dictatorship of the proletariat and the poor peasantry." It is not a matter of finding a theoretical classification. We would be committing a great mistake if we attempted to force the complex, urgent, rapidly developing practical tasks of the revolution into the Procrustean bed of narrowly conceived "theory" instead of regarding theory primarily and predominantly as a *guide to action*.

Do the masses of the Russian workers possess sufficient class-consciousness, fortitude and heroism to perform "miracles of proletarian organization" after they have performed miracles of daring, initiative and self-sacrifice in the direct revolutionary struggle? That we do not know, and it would be idle to indulge in guessing, for practice *alone* furnishes the answers to such questions.

What we do know definitely, and what we, as a party, must explain to the masses is, on the one hand, the immense power of the locomotive of history that is engendering an unprecedented crisis, starvation and incalculable hardship. That locomotive is the war, waged for predatory aims by the capitalists of *both* belligerent camps. This "locomotive" has brought a number of the richest, freest and most enlightened nations to the brink of doom. It is *forcing* the peoples to strain to the utmost all their energies, placing them in unbearable conditions, putting on the order of the day not the application of certain "theories" (an illusion against which Marx always warned socialists), but implementation of the most extreme practical measures; for *without* extreme measures, death—immediate and certain death from starvation—awaits millions of people.

That the revolutionary enthusiasm of the advanced class can do a *great deal* when the objective situation *demands* extreme measures from the entire people, needs no proof. *This* aspect is clearly seen and *felt* by everybody in Russia.

It is important to realize that in revolutionary times the objective situation changes with the same swiftness and abruptness as the current of life in general. And we must *be able to adapt* our tactics and immediate tasks to the *specific features* of every given situation. Before February 1917, the immediate task was to conduct bold revolutionary-internationalist propaganda, summon the masses to fight, rouse them. The February-March days required the heroism of devoted struggle to crush the immediate enemy—tsarism. Now we are in *transition* from that first stage of the revolution to the second, from "coming to grips" with tsarism to "coming to grips" with Guchkov-Milyukov landlord and capitalist imperialism. The immediate task is *organization*, not only in the stereotyped sense of working to form stereotyped organizations, but in the sense of drawing unprecedentedly broad masses of the oppressed classes into an organization that would take over the military, political and economic functions of the state.

The proletariat has approached, and will approach, this singular task in different ways. In some parts of Russia the February-March

Revolution puts nearly complete power in its hands. In others the proletariat may, perhaps, in a "usurpatory" manner, begin to form and develop
a proletarian militia. In still others, it will probably strive for immediate
elections of urban and rural local government bodies on the basis of
universal, etc., suffrage, in order to turn them into revolutionary centres,
etc., until the growth of proletarian organization, the coming together of
the soldiers with the workers, the movement among the peasantry and
the disillusionment of very many in the war-imperialist government of
Guchkov and Milyukov bring near the hour when this government will
be replaced by the "government" of the Soviet of Workers' Deputies.

Nor ought we to forget that close to St. Petersburg we have one of the
most advanced, factually republican, countries, namely, Finland, which,
from 1905 to 1917, shielded by the revolutionary battles of Russia, has in
a relatively peaceful way developed democracy and has won the *majority*
of the people for socialism. The Russian proletariat will guarantee the
Finnish Republic complete freedom, including freedom to secede (it is
doubtful now whether a single Social-Democrat will waver on this point
when the Cadet Rodichev is so meanly haggling in Helsingfors for bits
of privileges for the Great Russians)—and precisely in this way will win
the *complete* confidence and comradely assistance of the Finnish workers
for the all-Russian proletarian cause. In a difficult and big undertaking
mistakes are inevitable, nor will we avoid them. The Finnish workers are
better organizers, they will help us in this sphere, they will, *in their own
way*, push forward the establishment of the socialist republic.

Revolutionary victories in Russia proper—peaceful organizational
successes in Finland shielded by these victories—the Russian workers'
transition to revolutionary organizational tasks on a new scale—capture
of power by the proletariat and poorest strata of the population—encouragement and development of the socialist revolution in the West—this is
the road that will lead us to *peace* and *socialism*.

Fourth Letter: How to Achieve Peace

I have just (March 12/25) read in the *Neue Ziircher Zeitung* (No. 517 of
March 24) the following telegraphic dispatch from Berlin:

"It is reported from Sweden that Maxim Gorky has sent the government and the Executive Committee greetings couched in enthusiastic
terms. He greets the people's victory over the lords of reaction and calls
upon all Russia's sons to help erect the edifice of the new Russian state.

At the same time he urges the government to crown the cause of emancipation by concluding peace. It must not, he says, be peace at any price; Russia now has less reason than ever to strive for peace at any price. It must be a peace that will enable Russia to live in honor among the other nations of the earth. Mankind has shed much blood, the new government would render not only Russia, but all mankind, the greatest service if it succeeded in concluding an early peace."

That is how Maxim Gorky's letter is reported.

It is with deep chagrin that one reads this letter, impregnated through and through with stock philistine prejudices. The author of these lines has had many occasions, in meeting with Gorky in Capri, to warm and reproach him for his political mistakes. Gorky parried these reproaches with his inimitable charming smile and with the ingenuous remark: "I know I am a bad Marxist. And besides, we artists are all somewhat irresponsible." It is not easy to argue against that.

There can be no doubt that Gorky's is an enormous artistic talent which has been, and will be, of great benefit to the world proletarian movement.

But why should Gorky meddle in politics?

In my opinion, Gorky's letter expresses prejudices that are exceedingly widespread not only among the petty bourgeoisie, but also among a section of the workers under its influence. *All* the energies of our Party, all the efforts of the class-conscious workers, must be concentrated on a persistent, persevering, all-round struggle against these prejudices.

The tsarist government began and waged the present war as an *imperialist*, predatory war to rob and strangle weak nations. The government of the Guchkovs and Milyukovs, which is a landlord and capitalist government, is forced to continue, and wants to continue, *this very same kind* of war. To urge that government to conclude a democratic peace is like preaching virtue to brothel keepers.

Let me explain what is meant.

What is imperialism?

In my *Imperialism, the Highest Stage of Capitalism*, the manuscript of which was delivered to the Parus Publishers some time before the revolution, was accepted by them and announced in the magazine *Letopis*, I answered this question as follows:

"Imperialism is capitalism at that stage of development at which the dominance of monopolies and finance capital is established; in which the export of capital has acquired pronounced importance; in which the division of the world among the international trusts has begun; in which the division of all territories of the globe among the biggest capitalist powers has been completed" (Chapter VII of the above-mentioned book, the publication of which was announced in *Letopis*, when the censorship still existed, under the title: "Modern Capitalism," by V. Ilyin).

The whole thing hinges on the fact that capital has grown to huge dimensions. Associations of a small number of the biggest capitalists (cartels, syndicates, trusts) manipulate *billions* and divide the whole world among themselves. The world has been *completely* divided up. The war was brought on by the clash of the two most powerful groups of multimillionaires, Anglo-French and German, for the *redivision* of the world.

The Anglo-French group of capitalists wants first to rob Germany, deprive her of her colonies (nearly all of which have already been seized), and then to rob Turkey.

The German group of capitalists wants to seize Turkey for *itself* and to compensate itself for the loss of its colonies by seizing neighboring small states (Belgium, Serbia, Rumania).

This is the real truth; it is being concealed by all sorts of bourgeois lies about a "liberating," "national" war, a "war for right and justice," and similar jingle with which the capitalists always fool the common people.

Russia is waging this war with foreign money. Russian capital is a *partner* of Anglo-French capital. Russia is waging the war in order to rob Armenia, Turkey, Galicia.

Guchkov, Lvov and Milyukov, our present ministers, are not chance comers. They are the representatives and leaders of the entire landlord and capitalist class. They are *bound* by the interests of capital. The capitalists can no more renounce their interests than a man can lift himself by his bootstraps.

Secondly, Guchkov-Milyukov and Co. are *bound* by Anglo-French capital. They have waged, and are still waging, the war with foreign money. They have borrowed billions, promising to pay *hundreds of millions* in interest *every year*, and to squeeze this *tribute* out of the Russian workers and Russian peasants.

Thirdly, Guchkov-Milyukov and Co. are *bound* to England, France, Italy, Japan and other groups of robber capitalists by direct *treaties* concerning the predatory aims of this war. These treaties were concluded by *Tsar Nicholas II*. Guchkov-Milyukov and Co. took advantage of the workers' struggle against the tsarist monarch to seize power, and *they have confirmed the treaties* concluded by the tsar.

This was done by the whole of the Guchkov-Milyukov government in a manifesto which the St. Petersburg Telegraph Agency circulated on March 7 (20): "The government [of Guchkov and Milyukov] will faithfully abide by all the treaties that bind us with other powers," says the manifesto. Milyukov, the new Minister for Foreign Affairs, said the *same thing* in his telegram of March 5 (18), 1917 to all Russian representatives abroad.

These are all *secret* treaties, and Milyukov and Co. *refuse* to make them public for two reasons: (1) they fear the people, who are opposed to the predatory war; (2) they are bound by Anglo-French capital which insists that the treaties remain secret. But every newspaper reader who has followed events knows that these treaties envisage the robbery of China by Japan; of Persia, Armenia, Turkey (especially Constantinople) and Galicia by Russia; of Albania by Italy; of Turkey and the German colonies by France and England, etc.

This is how things stand.

Hence, to urge the Guchkov-Milyukov government to conclude a speedy, honest, democratic and good-neighborly peace is like the good village priest urging the landlords and the merchants to "walk in the way of God," to love their neighbors and to turn the other cheek. The landlords and merchants listen to these sermons, continue to oppress and rob the people and praise the priest for his ability to console and pacify the "muzhiks."

Exactly the same role is played—consciously or unconsciously—by all those who in the present imperialist war address pious peace appeals to the bourgeois governments. The bourgeois governments either refuse to listen to such appeals and even prohibit them, or they allow them to be made and assure all and sundry that they are only fighting to conclude the speediest and "justest" peace, and that all the blame lies with the enemy. Actually, talking peace *to bourgeois* governments turns out to be *deception of the people*.

The groups of capitalists who have drenched the world in blood for the sake of dividing territories, markets and concessions *cannot* conclude an "honorable" peace. They can conclude only a *shameful* peace, a peace based *on the division of the spoils, on the partition of Turkey and the colonies*.

Moreover, the Guchkov-Milyukov government is in general opposed to peace at the present moment, because the "*only*" "loot" it would get *now* would be Armenia and part of Galicia, whereas it *also* wants to get Constantinople *and* regain from the Germans Poland, which tsarism has always so inhumanly and shamelessly oppressed. Further, the Guchkov-Milyukov government is, in essence, only the agent of Anglo-French capital, which wants to retain the colonies it has wrested from Germany and, *on top of that*, compel Germany [to] hand back Belgium and part of France. Anglo-French capital helped the Guchkovs and Milyukovs remove Nicholas II in order that they might help it to "vanquish" Germany.

What, then, is to be done?

To achieve peace (and still more to achieve a really democratic, a really honorable peace), it is necessary that political power be in the hands *of the workers and poorest peasants*, not the landlords and capitalists. The latter represent an insignificant minority of the population, and the capitalists, as everybody knows, are making fantastic profits out of the war.

The workers and poorest peasants are the *vast* majority of the population. They are not making profit out of the war; on the contrary, they are being reduced to ruin and starvation. They are bound neither by capital nor by the treaties between the predatory groups of capitalists; they *can* and sincerely want to end the war.

If political power in Russia were in the hands of the *Soviets* of Workers', Soldiers' and Peasants' Deputies, these Soviets, and the *All-Russia Soviet* elected by them, could, and no doubt would, agree to carry out the peace program which our Party (the Russian Social-Democratic Labour Party) outlined as early as October 13, 1915, in No. 47 of its Central Organ, *Sotsial-Demokrat* (then published in Geneva because of the Draconic tsarist censorship).

This program would probably be the following:

1) The All-Russia Soviet of Workers', Soldiers' and Peasants' Deputies (or the St. Petersburg Soviet temporarily acting for it) would forthwith declare that it is *not* bound by *any* treaties concluded *either* by the tsarist monarchy *or* by the bourgeois governments.

2) It would forthwith publish *all* these treaties in order to hold up to public shame the predatory aims of the tsarist monarchy and of *all* the bourgeois governments without exception.

3) It would forthwith publicly call upon *all* the belligerent powers to conclude an *immediate armistice*.

4) It would immediately bring to the knowledge of all the people our, the workers' and peasants', *peace terms*: liberation of *all* colonies; liberation of *all* dependent, oppressed and unequal nations.

5) It would declare that it expects nothing good from the bourgeois governments and calls upon the workers of all countries to overthrow them and to transfer all political power to Soviets of Workers' Deputies.

6) It would declare that the *capitalist gentry themselves* can repay the billions of debts contracted by the bourgeois governments to wage this criminal, predatory war, and that the workers and peasants *refuse to recognize* these debts. To pay the interest on these loans would mean paying the capitalists *tribute* for many years for having graciously allowed the workers to kill one another in order that the capitalists might divide the spoils.

Workers and peasants!—the Soviet of Workers' Deputies would say—are you willing to pay these gentry, the capitalists, *hundreds of millions* of rubles *every year* for a war waged for the division of the African colonies, Turkey, etc.?

For *these* peace terms the Soviet of Workers' Deputies would, in my opinion, agree to *wage war* against *any* bourgeois government and against *all* the bourgeois governments of the world, because this would really be a just war, because *all* the workers and toilers in *all* countries would *work for its success*.

The German worker now sees that the bellicose monarchy in Russia is being replaced by a *bellicose* republic, a republic of capitalists who want to continue the imperialist war, and who have confirmed the predatory treaties of the tsarist monarchy.

Judge for yourselves, can the German worker trust *such* a republic?

Judge for yourselves, can the war continue, can the capitalist domination continue on earth, if the Russian people, always sustained by the living memories of the great Revolution of 1905, win complete freedom and transfer all political power to the Soviets of Workers' and Peasants' Deputies?

Trotsky

Leon Trotsky (1879–1940) was born Lev Davidovich Bronstein into a relatively prosperous farming family in the Ukraine, and at the age of ten was sent to live with a relative in Odessa in order to attend school. By the age of eighteen he was drawn into the socialist movement. Embracing Marxism and the struggle of the working class, he took on the pen-name Trotsky in the revolutionary underground.

At first close to Lenin's revolutionary orientation in the Russian Social Democratic Labor Party, Trotsky rejected the organizational intransigence of the Bolshevik faction—against which he polemicized in *Our Political Tasks*. A leading figure in the early Petersburg soviet during the 1905 revolutionary upheaval, Trotsky came to the conclusion that the kind of worker-peasant alliance advocated by Lenin was superior to the notion of a worker-capitalist alliance favored by the more moderate Menshevik faction. But he went further than most others in the revolutionary movement by arguing that such an alliance could bring the working class to power and put a transition to socialism on the agenda in backward Russia, if revolutions were also sparked in more industrially advanced countries. This outlook, reflected in his theoretical contribution *Results and Prospects* and his narrative account of the revolutionary struggle *1905*, became identified as the theory of permanent revolution.

While advocating unity among Russian socialists for many years, Trotsky found that those willing to participate in an all-inclusive unification could not maintain a coherent organization, and that the goal became utterly impossible when some of the Russian Social-Democrats supported their "own" government during World War I. He himself joined with many international socialists (including Lenin and Rosa Luxemburg) to organize open opposition to the imperialist war. By 1917, after the overthrow of the Tsar and the recreation of workers' soviets, Trotsky and some of his co-thinkers joined the Bolsheviks to help organize a working-class revolution to win "all power to the soviets."

Becoming a central leader of the Bolshevik (soon renamed Communist) Party and the new Soviet state, Trotsky was the organizer and commander of the Red Army, which beat back foreign invaders and triumphed over all enemies in the Russian Civil War. He was also a key figure in the newly organized Communist International and the author of its founding 1919 "Manifesto of the Communist International to the Workers of the World." Associated through works such as *Terrorism and Communism* (1920) with positions favoring dictatorial "expediency" in Soviet Russia, he soon joined with Lenin to oppose conservative, undemocratic, and bureaucratic developments that were wearing away the revolutionary fiber of the Communist regime, putting forward his views in the 1923 work *The New Course*. After Lenin's death he labored to build a Left Opposition to uphold and advance—in Russia and in the Communist International—the original Bolshevik-Leninist per-spectives, reiterated in numerous works, including a 1928 intervention into the Communist International later entitled the *Third International after Lenin*. These efforts were decisively defeated by the state and party apparatus led by Joseph Stalin, and Trotsky was expelled from the Soviet Union in 1929.

While in exile (in Turkey, France, Norway, Mexico), Trotsky wrote volumes of brilliant political works, including a restatement and elabo-ration of his distinctive theory, *The Permanent Revolution* (1930), and his three-volume classic *History of the Russian Revolution* (1932–33). Key ideas from both works are summarized in his 1932 lecture to left-wing Danish students "In Defense of the Russian Revolution" (READING #14). No less important were the critique of the bureaucratic dictatorship developed in *The Revolution Betrayed* (READING #15), followed up with perspectives for a political revolution to establish soviet democracy and working-class control of the economy (READINGS #16 and #17). More than this, Trotsky attempted to rally working-class militants and revo-lutionary-minded activists of the Communist and Socialist movements to an effective opposition against the rise of Hitlerism in Germany and the spread of fascism throughout Europe (READING #18), against the dilution and abandonment of revolutionary perspectives by Stalinism, against the imperialist stranglehold on Asia, Africa, and Latin America, and against the oncoming renewal of imperialist slaughter in a second world war. He insisted that an application of the revolutionary Marxist orientation was necessary to comprehend and to reverse the devastating developments of what turned out to be the interwar period. After 1933 he sought to advance this orientation by organizing revolutionary activists into the Fourth International, which was formally proclaimed in 1938 with the Transitional Program (READING #19). Condemned to death in absentia during the bloody purge trials of 1936–38 orchestrated in the USSR by Stalin, Trotsky was finally murdered by a Stalinist agent in 1940.

Ignored among innumerable revolutionary-minded people for many years—largely due to the slanders, pressures, and political influence of Stalinism—even today Trotsky suffers from a residue of hostility which sometimes takes the form of flippant dismissal. But revolutionary Marxism in the 20th century lacks coherence without the contributions of this heroic figure.

READING #14: "In Defense of the Russian Revolution"—1932
READING #15: *The Revolution Betrayed* (excerpt)—1936
READING #16: "The USSR and the Problems of the Transitional Epoch" (excerpt from Transitional Program)—1938
READING #17: "Letter to the Workers of the USSR"—1940
READING #18: "What Next? Vital Questions for the German Proletariat" (excerpt)—1932
READING #19: "The Transitional Program" (excerpts)—1938

READING #14

"In Defense of the Russian Revolution"

Permit me to begin by expressing my sincere regrets over my inability to speak before a Copenhagen audience in the Danish tongue. Let us not ask whether the listeners lose by it. As to the speaker, his ignorance of the Danish language deprives him of the possibility of familiarizing himself with Scandinavian life and Scandinavian literature immediately, at first hand and in the original. And that is a great loss.

The German language, to which I have had to take recourse, is rich and powerful. My German, however, is fairly limited. To discuss complicated questions with the necessary freedom, moreover, is possible only in one's own language. I must therefore beg the indulgence of the audience in advance.

The first time that I was in Copenhagen was at the International Socialist Congress, and I took away with me the kindest recollections of your city. But that was over a quarter of a century ago. Since then, the water in the Ore Sund and in the fjords has changed over and over again. And not the water alone. The war broke the backbone of the old European continent. The rivers and seas of Europe have washed down not a little blood. Mankind, and particularly European mankind, has gone through severe trials, has become more somber and more brutal. Every kind of conflict has become more bitter. The world has entered into the period of the great change. Its most extreme expressions are *war* and *revolution*.

Before I pass on to the theme of my lecture, the revolution, I consider it my duty to express my thanks to the organizers of this meeting, the Copenhagen organization of the Social Democratic student body. I do this as a political opponent. My lecture, it is true, pursues historico-scientific and not political aims. I want to emphasize this right from the beginning. But it is impossible to speak of a revolution, out of which the Soviet Republic arose, without taking up a political position. As a lecturer I stand under the same banner as I did when I participated in the events of the revolution.

Up to the war, the Bolshevik Party belonged to the International Social Democracy. On August 4, 1914, the vote of the German Social Democracy for the war credits put an end to this connection once and for all, and opened the period of uninterrupted and irreconcilable struggle of Bolshevism against Social Democracy. Does this mean that the organizers of this assembly made a mistake in inviting me as a lecturer? On this point the audience will be able to judge only after my lecture. To justify my acceptance of the kind invitation to present a report on the Russian Revolution, permit me to point to the fact that during the thirty-five years of my political life the question of the Russian Revolution has been the practical and theoretical axis of my interests and of my actions. The four years of my stay in Turkey were principally devoted to the historical elaboration of the problems of the Russian Revolution. Perhaps this fact gives me a certain right to hope that I will succeed, in part at least in helping not only friends and sympathizers, but also opponents, better to understand many features of the revolution which had escaped their attention before: At all events, the purpose of my lecture is: *to help to understand.* I do not intend to conduct propaganda for the revolution nor to call upon you to join the revolution. I intend to explain the revolution.

I do not know if in the Scandinavian Olympus there was a special goddess of rebellion. Scarcely! In any case, we shall not call upon her favor today. We shall place our lecture under the sign of Snotra, the old goddess of knowledge. Despite the passionate drama of the revolution as a living event, we shall endeavor to treat it as dispassionately as an anatomist. If the lecturer is drier because of it, the listeners will, let us hope, take it into the bargain.

Let us begin with some elementary sociological principles, which are doubtless familiar to you all, but as to which we must refresh our memory in approaching so complicated a phenomenon as the revolution.

Human society is an historically originated collaboration in the struggle for existence and the assurance of the maintenance of the generations. The character of a society is determined by the character of its economy. The character of its economy is determined by its means of productive labor.

For every great epoch in the development of the productive forces there is a definite corresponding social regime. Every social regime until now has secured enormous advantages to the ruling class.

Out of what has been said, it is clear that social regimes are not eternal. They arise historically, and then become fetters on further progress. "All that arises deserves to be destroyed."

But no ruling class has ever voluntarily and peacefully abdicated. In questions of life and death arguments based on reason have never replaced the argument of force. This may be sad, but it is so. It is not we that have made this world. We can do nothing but take it as it is.

Revolution means a change of the social order. It transfers the power from the hands of a class which has exhausted itself into those of another class which is on the rise. The insurrection is the sharpest and most critical moment in the struggle of two classes for power. The insurrection can lead to the real victory of the revolution and to the establishment of a new order only when it is based on a progressive class, which is able to rally around it the overwhelming majority of the people.

As distinguished from the processes of nature, a revolution is made by human beings and through human beings. But in the course of revolution, too, men act under the influence of social conditions which are not freely chosen by them, but are handed down from the past and imperatively point out the road which they must follow. For this reason, and only for this reason, a revolution follows certain laws.

But human consciousness does not merely passively reflect its objective conditions. It is accustomed to react to them actively. At certain times this reaction assumes a tense, passionate, mass character. The barriers of right and might are broken down. The active intervention of the masses in historical events is in fact the most indispensable element of a revolution.

But even the stormiest activity can remain in the stage of demonstration or rebellion, without rising to the height of revolution. The uprising of the masses must lead to the overthrow of the domination of one class and to the establishment of the domination of another. Only then have we a whole revolution. A mass uprising is no isolated undertaking, which can be conjured up any time one pleases. It represents an objectively conditioned element in the development of a revolution, as a revolution represents an objectively conditioned process in the development of society. But if the necessary conditions for the uprising exist, one must not simply wait passively, with open mouth. As Shakespeare says, "There is a tide in the affairs of men which, taken at the flood, leads on to fortune."

To sweep away the outlived social order, the progressive class must understand that its hour has struck, and set before itself the task of conquering power. Here opens the field of conscious revolutionary action, where foresight and calculation combine with will and courage. In other words: here opens the field of action of the party.

The revolutionary party unites within itself the flower of the progressive class. Without a party which is able to orient itself in its environment, evaluate the progress and rhythm of events, and early with the confidence of the masses, the victory of the proletarian revolution is impossible. These are the reciprocal relations of the objective and the subjective factors in insurrection and in revolution.

In disputations, particularly theological ones, it is customary, as you know, for the opponents to discredit scientific truth by driving it to an absurdity. This method is called in logic "reductio ad absurdum." We shall try to pursue the opposite method: that is, we shall start from an absurdity so as to approach the truth with all the greater safety. In any case, we cannot complain of lack of absurdities. Let us take one of the freshest and crassest.

The Italian writer, Malaparte, who is something in the nature of a fascist theoretician—there are such, too—not long ago launched a book on the technique of the coup d'etat. Naturally, the author devotes not an inconsiderable number of pages of his "investigation" to the October upheaval.

In contradistinction to the "strategy" of Lenin, which remained tied up with the social and political conditions of Russia in 1917, "the tactics of Trotsky," in Malaparte's words, "were, on the contrary, not tied up with the general conditions of the country." This is the main idea of the book! Malaparte compels Lenin and Trotsky, in the pages of his book, to carry on numerous dialogues in which both participants together show as much profundity as nature put at the disposal of Malaparte alone. In answer to Lenin's considerations on the social and political prerequisites of the upheaval, Malaparte has his alleged Trotsky say, literally, "Your strategy requires far too many favorable circumstances; the insurrection needs nothing, it suffices to itself." You hear: "The insurrection needs nothing!" There it is, my dear listeners, the absurdity which must help us to approach the truth. The author repeats persistently, that in the October Revolution, not the strategy of Lenin but the tactics of Trotsky won the victory. These tactics threaten, according to his words, even now the repose of the states of Europe. "The strategy of Lenin," I quote word for word, "is no immediate danger for the governments of Europe. But their present and, moreover, permanent danger is constituted by the tactics of Trotsky." Still more concretely, "Put Poincare in the place of Kerensky and the Bolshevik coup d'etat of October 1917 would succeed just as well." It is hard to believe that such a book has been translated into several languages and is taken seriously.

We seek in vain to discover what is the necessity altogether of the historically conditioned strategy of Lenin, if "Trotsky's tactics" can fulfill the same tasks in every situation. And why are successful revolutions so rare, if only a few technical recipes suffice for their success?

The dialogue between Lenin and Trotsky presented by the fascist author is in content, as well as form, an insipid invention from beginning to end. Of such inventions, there are not a few floating around the world. So, for example, in Madrid there has been printed a book, *La Vida del Lenin (The Life of Lenin)*, for which I am as little responsible as for the tactical recipes of Malaparte. The Madrid weekly, *Estampa*, published in advance whole chapters of this alleged book of Trotsky's on Lenin, which contain horrible desecrations of the memory of that man whom I valued and still value incomparably higher than anyone else among my contemporaries.

But let us leave the forgers to their fate. Old Wilhelm Liebknecht, the father of the unforgettable fighter and hero, Karl Liebknecht, liked to say, "A revolutionary politician must provide himself with a thick skin." Doctor Stockmann [protagonist in Ibsen's *Enemy of the People*] even more expressively recommended that anyone who proposed to act in a manner contrary to the opinion of society should refrain from putting on new trousers. We will take note of the two good pieces of advice, and go on to the order of the day.

What questions does the October Revolution raise in the mind of a thinking man?

1. Why and how did this revolution take place? More concretely, why did the proletarian revolution conquer in one of the most backward countries of Europe?
2. What have been the results of the October Revolution? and finally,
3. Has the October Revolution stood the test?

The first question, as to the causes, can now be answered more or less exhaustively. I have attempted to do this in great detail in my *History of the Russian Revolution*. Here I can formulate only the most important conclusions.

The fact that the proletariat reached power for the first time in such a backward country as the former czarist Russia seems mysterious only at first glance; in reality, it is fully in accord with historical law. It could have been predicted and it was predicted. Still more, on the basis of the prediction of this fact the revolutionary Marxists built up their strategy long before the decisive events.

The first and most general explanation is: Russia is a backward country, but only a part of world economy, only an element of the capitalist world system. In this sense Lenin exhausted the riddle of the Russian Revolution with the lapidary formula, "The chain broke at its weakest link."

A crude illustration: the Great War, the result of the contradictions of world imperialism, drew into its maelstrom countries of *different* stages of development, but made the *same claims* on all the participants. It is clear that the burdens of the war had to be particularly intolerable for the most backward countries. Russia was the first to be compelled to leave the field. But to tear itself away from the war, the Russian people had to overthrow the ruling classes. In this way the chain of war broke at its weakest link.

Still, war is not a catastrophe coming from outside, like an earthquake, but as old Clausewitz said, the continuation of politics by other means. In the last war, the main tendencies of the imperialistic system of "peacetime" only expressed themselves more crudely. The higher the general forces of production, the tenser the competition on the world markets, the sharper the antagonisms, and the madder the race for armaments, in that measure the more difficult it became for the weaker participants. For precisely this reason the backward countries assumed the first places in the succession of collapses. The chain of world capitalism always tends to break at its weakest link.

If, as a result of exceptional or exceptionally unfavorable circumstances—let us say, a successful military intervention from the outside or irreparable mistakes on the part of the Soviet government itself—capitalism should arise again on the immeasurably wide Soviet territory, together with it would inevitably arise also its historical inadequacy, and such capitalism would in turn soon become the victim of the same contradictions which caused its explosion in 1917. No tactical recipes could have called the October Revolution into being, if Russia had not carried it within its body. The revolutionary party in the last analysis can claim only the role of an obstetrician, who is compelled to resort to a Caesarean operation.

One might say in answer to this: "Your general considerations may adequately explain why old Russia had to suffer shipwreck, that country where backward capitalism and an impoverished peasantry were crowned by a parasitic nobility and a rotten monarchy. But in the simile of the chain and its weakest link there is still missing the key to the real riddle: How could the *socialist* revolution conquer in a *backward country?* History knows of more than a few illustrations of the decay of countries and civilizations accompanied by the collapse of the old classes for which no progressive successors had been found. The breakdown of old Russia should, at first sight, rather have changed the country into a capitalist colony than into a socialist state."

This objection is very interesting. It leads us directly to the kernel of the whole problem. And yet, this objection is erroneous; I might say, it lacks internal symmetry. On the one hand, it starts from an exaggerated conception of the backwardness of Russia; on the other, from a false theoretical conception of the phenomenon of historical backwardness in general.

Living beings, including man, of course, go through similar stages of development in accordance with their ages. In a normal five-year-old child, we find a certain correspondence between the weight, and the size of the parts of the body and the internal organs. But when we deal with human consciousness, the situation is different. In contrast with anatomy and physiology, psychology, both individual and collective, is distinguished by an exceptional ability of absorption, flexibility, and elasticity; therein consists the aristocratic advantage of man over his nearest zoological relatives, the apes. The absorptive and flexible psyche, as a necessary condition for historical progress, confers on the so-called social "organisms," as distinguished from the real, that is, biological organisms, an exceptional variability of internal structure. In the development of nations and states, particularly capitalist ones, there is neither similarity nor regularity. Different stages of civilization, even polar opposites, approach and intermingle with one another in the life of one and the same country.

Let us not forget, my esteemed listeners, that historical backwardness is a *relative* concept. There being both backward and progressive countries, there is also a reciprocal influencing of one by the other: there is the pressure of the progressive countries on the backward ones; there is the necessity for the backward countries to catch up with the progressive ones, to borrow their technology and science, etc. In this way arises the *combined type of development*: features of backwardness are combined with the last word in world technology and in world thinking. Finally, the historically backward countries, in order to escape from their backwardness, are often compelled to rush ahead of the others.

The flexibility of the collective consciousness makes it possible under certain conditions to achieve the result, in the social arena, which in individual psychology is called "overcoming the consciousness of inferiority." In this sense we can say that the October Revolution was an heroic means whereby the people of Russia were able to overcome their own economic and cultural inferiority.

But let us pass over from these historico-philosophic, perhaps somewhat too abstract, generalizations and put the same question in concrete form, that is, within the cross section of living economic facts. The backwardness of Russia expressed itself most clearly at the beginning of the twentieth century in the fact that industry occupied a small place in that country in comparison with agriculture, the city in comparison with the village, the proletariat in comparison with the peasantry. Taken as a whole, this mean a low productivity of the national labor. Suffice it to say that on the eve of the war, when czarist Russia had reached the peak of its well-being, the national income was eight to ten times lower than in the United States. This is expressed in figures, the "amplitude" of its backwardness, if the word "amplitude" can be used at all in connection with backwardness.

At the same time, however, the law of combined development expresses itself in the economic field at every step, in simple as well as in complex phenomena. Almost without highways, Russia was compelled to build railroads. Without having gone through the stage of European artisanry and manufacture, Russia passed on directly to mechanized production. To jump over intermediate stages is the fate of backward countries.

While peasant agriculture often remained at the level of the seventeenth century, Russia's industry, if not in scope, at least in type, stood at the level of the progressive countries and rushed ahead of them in some respects. It suffices to say that the giant enterprises, with over a thousand employees each, employed, in the United States, less than 18 percent of the total number of industrial workers, in Russia over 41 percent. This fact is hard to reconcile with the conventional conception of the economic backwardness of Russia. It does not, on the other hand, refute this backwardness, but complements it dialectically.

The same contradictory character was shown by the class structure of the country. The finance capital of Europe industrialized Russian economy at an accelerated tempo. Thereby the industrial bourgeoisie assumed a large-scale capitalistic and antipopular character. The foreign stockholders, moreover, lived outside of the country. The workers, on the other hand, were naturally Russians. Against a numerically weak Russian bourgeoisie, which had no national roots, stood therefore a relatively strong proletariat, with strong roots in the depths of the people.

The revolutionary character of the proletariat was furthered by the fact that Russia in particular, as a backward country, under the compulsion of catching up with its opponents, had not been able to work out its own conservatism, either social or political. The most conservative country of Europe, in fact of the entire world, is considered, and correctly, to be the oldest capitalist country—England. The European country freest of conservatism would in all probability be Russia.

But the young, fresh, determined proletariat of Russia still constituted only a tiny minority of the nation. The reserves of its revolutionary power lay outside of the proletariat itself—in the peasantry, living in half-serfdom, and in the oppressed nationalities.

The subsoil of the revolution was the agrarian question. The old feudal-monarchic system became doubly intolerable under the conditions of the new capitalist exploitation. The peasant communal areas amounted to some 140 million dessiatines [1 dessiatine = 2.7 acres]. But thirty thousand large landowners, whose average holdings were over two thousand dessiatines, owned altogether 70 million dessiatines, that is, as much as some 10 million peasant families or 50 millions of peasant population. *These statistics of land tenure constituted a ready-made program of agrarian revolt.*

The nobleman, Bokorkin, wrote in 1917 to the dignitary, Rodzianko, the chairman of the last municipal Duma, "I am a landowner and I cannot get it into my head that I must lose my land, and for an unbelievable purpose to boot, for the experiment of the socialist doctrine." But it is precisely the task of revolutions to accomplish that which the ruling classes cannot get into their heads.

In autumn 1917 almost the whole country was the scene of peasant revolts. On the 624 departments of old Russia, 482, that is, 77 percent, were affected by the movement! The reflection of the burning villages lit up the arena of the insurrections in the cities.

But the war of the peasants against the landowners—you will reply to me—is one of the classic elements of the bourgeois, by no means of the proletarian revolution!

Perfectly right, I reply—so it was in the past. But the inability of capitalist society to survive in an historically backward country was expressed precisely in the fact that the peasant insurrections did not drive the bourgeois classes of Russia forward, but on the contrary drove them back for good into the camp of the reaction. If the peasantry did not want to be completely ruined, there was nothing else left for it but to join the industrial proletariat. This revolutionary joining of the two oppressed classes was foreseen with genius by Lenin and prepared by him long ahead of time.

Had the bourgeoisie courageously solved the agrarian question, the proletariat of Russia would not, obviously, have been able to take the power in 1917. But the greedy and cowardly Russian bourgeoisie, too late on the scene, prematurely a victim of senility, did not dare to lift its hand against feudal property. But thereby it delivered the power to the proletariat and together with it the right to dispose of the destinies of bourgeois society.

In order for the Soviet state to come into existence, therefore, it was necessary for two factors of different historical nature to collaborate: the peasant war, that is, a movement which is characteristic of the dawn of bourgeois development, and the proletarian insurrection, that is, a movement which announces the decline of the bourgeois movement. Precisely therein consists the *combined* character of the Russian Revolution.

Once the peasant bear stands up on his hind feet, he becomes terrible in his wrath. But he is unable to give conscious expression to his indignation. He needs a leader. For the first time in the history of the world, the insurrectionary peasantry found a faithful leader in the person of the proletariat.

Four million industrial and transportation workers led a hundred million peasants. That was the natural and inevitable reciprocal relation between proletariat and peasantry in the revolution.

The second revolutionary reserve of the proletariat was constituted by the oppressed nationalities, who moreover were also predominantly made up of peasants. Closely tied up with the historical backwardness of the country is the extensive character of the development of the state, which spread out like a grease spot from the center at Moscow to the circumference. In the East, it subjugated the still more backward peoples, basing itself upon them, in order to stifle the more developed nationalities of the West. To the seventy million Great Russians, who constituted the main mass of the population, were added gradually some ninety millions of "other races."

In this way arose the empire, in whose composition the ruling nationality made up only 43 percent of the population, while the remaining 57 percent consisted of nationalities of varying degrees of civilization and legal deprivation. The national pressure was incomparably cruder in Russia than in the neighboring states, and not only those beyond the western boundary but beyond the eastern one, too. This conferred on the national problem a gigantic explosive force.

The Russian liberal bourgeoisie, in the national as well as in the agrarian question, would not go beyond certain ameliorations of the regime of oppression and violence. The "democratic" governments of Miliukov and Kerensky, which reflected the interests of the Great Russian bourgeoisie and bureaucracy, actually hastened to impress upon the discontented nationalities, in the course of the eight months of their existence, "You will obtain only what you tear away by force."

The inevitability of the development of the centrifugal national movement had been early taken into consideration by Lenin. The Bolshevik Party struggled obstinately for years for the right of self-determination for nations, that is, for the right of full secession. Only through this courageous position on the national question could the Russian proletariat gradually win the confidence of the oppressed peoples. The national independence movement, as well as the agrarian movement, necessarily turned against the official democracy, strengthened the proletariat, and poured into the stream of the October upheaval.

In these ways the riddle of the proletarian upheaval in an historically backward country loses its veil of mystery.

Marxist revolutionaries predicted, long before the events, the march of the revolution and the historical role of the young Russian proletariat. I may be permitted to repeat here passages from a work of my own in 1905:

"In an economically backward country the proletariat can arrive at power earlier than in a capitalistically advanced one. . . .

"The Russian revolution creates the conditions under which the power can (and in the event of a successful revolution must) be transferred to the proletariat, even before the policy of bourgeois liberalism receives the opportunity of unfolding its talent for government to its full extent."

"The fate of the most elementary revolutionary interests of the peasantry . . . is bound up with the fate of the whole revolution, that is, with the fate of the proletariat. The proletariat, once arrived at power, will appear before the peasantry as the liberating class."

"The proletariat enters into the government as the revolutionary representative of the nation, as the acknowledged leader of the people in the struggle with absolutism and the barbarism of serfdom."

"The proletarian regime will have to stand from the very beginning for the solution of the agrarian question, with which the question of the destiny of tremendous masses of the population of Russia is bound up." [From *Results and Prospects.*]

I have taken the liberty of quoting these passages as evidence that the theory of the October Revolution which I am presenting today is no casual improvisation, and was not constructed ex post facto under the pressure of events. No, in the form of a political prognosis it preceded the October upheaval by a long time. You will agree that a theory is in general valuable only insofar as it helps to foresee the course of development and influences it purposively. Therein, in general terms, is the invaluable importance of Marxism as a weapon of social and historical orientation. I am sorry that the narrow limits of the lecture do not permit me to enlarge the above quotation materially. I will therefore content myself with a brief resume of the whole work which dates from 1905.

In accordance with its immediate tasks, the Russian revolution is a bourgeois revolution. But the Russian bourgeoisie is antirevolutionary. The victory of the revolution is therefore possible only as a victory of the proletariat. But the victorious proletariat will not stop at the program of bourgeois democracy; it will go on to the program of socialism. The Russian revolution will become the first stage of the socialist world revolution.

This was the theory of the *permanent revolution* formulated by me in 1905 and since then exposed to the severest criticism under the name of "Trotskyism."

To be more exact, it is only a part of this theory. The other part, which is particularly timely now, states:

The present productive forces have long outgrown their national limits. A socialist society is not feasible within national boundaries. Significant as the economic successes of an isolated workers' state may be, the program of "socialism in one country" is a petty-bourgeois utopia. Only a European and then a world federation of socialist republics can be the real arena for a harmonious socialist society.

Today, after the test of events, I see less reason than ever to dissociate myself from this theory.

After all that has been said above, is it still worthwhile to recall the fascist writer, Malaparte, who ascribes to me tactics which are independent of strategy and amount to a series of technical recipes for insurrection, applicable in all latitudes and longitudes? It is a good thing that the name of the luckless theoretician of the coup d'etat makes it easy to distinguish him from the victorious practitioner of the coup d'etat; no one therefore runs the risk of confusing Malaparte with Bonaparte.

Without the armed insurrection of November 7, 1917, the Soviet state would not be in existence. But the insurrection itself did not drop from heaven. A series of historical prerequisites was necessary for the October Revolution.

1. The rotting away of the old ruling classes—the nobility, the monarchy, the bureaucracy.
2. The political weakness of the bourgeoisie, which had no roots in the masses of the people.
3. The revolutionary character of the peasant question.
4. The revolutionary character of the problem of the oppressed nations.
5. The significant social weight of the proletariat.
   To these organic preconditions we must add certain conjunctural conditions of the highest importance:
6. The revolution of 1905 was the great school, or in Lenin's words, the "dress rehearsal" of the revolution of 1917. The soviets, as the irreplaceable organizational form of the proletarian united front in the revolution, were created for the first time in the year 1905.
7. The imperialist war sharpened all the contradictions, tore the backward masses out of their immobility and thereby prepared the grandiose scale of the catastrophe.

But all these conditions, which fully sufficed for the *outbreak of the revolution*, were insufficient to assure the *victory of the proletariat* in the revolution. For this victory one condition more was needed:

8. The Bolshevik Party.

When I enumerate this condition as the last in the series, I do it only because it follows the necessities of the logical order, and not because I assign the party the last place in the order of importance.

No, I am far from such a thought. The liberal bourgeoisie—yes, it can seize the power and has seized it more than once as the result of struggles in which it took no part; it possesses organs of seizure which are admirably adapted to the purpose. But the working masses are in a different position; they have long been accustomed to give, and not to take. They work, are patient as long as they can be, hope, lose their patience, rise up and struggle, die, bring victory to the others, are betrayed, fall into despondency, again bow their necks, again work. This is the history of the masses of the people under all regimes. In order to take the power firmly and surely into its hands the proletariat needs a party, which far surpasses the other parties in the clarity of its thought and in its revolutionary determination.

The party of the Bolsheviks, which has been described more than once and with complete justification as the most revolutionary party in the history of mankind, was the living condensation of the modern history of Russia, of all that was dynamic in it. The overthrow of czarism had long since become the necessary condition for the development of economy and culture. But for the solution of this task, the forces were insufficient. The bourgeoisie feared the revolution. The intelligentsia tried to bring the peasant to his feet. The muzhik, incapable of generalizing his own miseries and his aims, left this appeal unanswered. The intelligentsia armed itself with dynamite. A whole generation was burned up in this struggle.

On March 1, 1887, Alexander Ulyanov carried out the last of the great terrorist plots. The attempted assassination of Alexander III failed. Ulyanov and the other participants were executed. The attempt to substitute a chemical preparation for the revolutionary class suffered shipwreck. Even the most heroic intelligentsia is nothing without the masses. Under the immediate impression of these facts and conclusions grew up Ulyanov's younger brother Vladimir, the later Lenin, the greatest figure of Russian history. Even in his early youth he placed himself on the foundations of Marxism, and turned his face toward the proletariat. Without losing sight of the village for a moment, he sought the way to the peasantry through the workers. Having inherited from his revolutionary predecessors their determination, their capacity for self-sacrifice, and their willingness to go to the limit, Lenin at an early age became the teacher of the new generation of the intelligentsia and of the advanced workers. In strikes and street fights, in prisons and in exile, the workers received the necessary tempering. They needed the searchlight of Marxism to light up their historical road in the darkness of absolutism.

In the year 1883 there arose among the emigres the first Marxist group. In the year 1898, at a secret meeting, the foundation of the Russian Social Democratic Workers' Party was proclaimed (we all called ourselves Social Democrats in those days). In the year 1903 occurred the split between Bolsheviks and Mensheviks. In the year 1912 the Bolshevik faction finally became an independent party.

It learned to recognize the class mechanics of society in struggle, in the grandiose events of twelve years (1905–1917). It educated cadres equally capable of initiative and subordination. The discipline of its revolutionary action was based on the unity of its doctrine, on the tradition of common struggles, and on confidence in its tested leadership.

Thus stood the party in the year 1917. Despised by the official "public opinion" and the paper thunder of the intelligentsia press, it adapted itself to the movement of the masses. Firmly it kept in hand the control of factories and regiments. More and more the peasant masses turned toward it. If we understand by "nation" not the privileged heads but the majority of the people, that is, the workers and peasants, then Bolshevism became in the course of the year 1917 a truly national Russian party.

In September 1917, Lenin, who was compelled to keep in hiding, gave the signal, "The crisis is ripe, the hour of the insurrection has approached." He was right. The ruling classes had landed in a blind alley before the problems of the war, the land, and national liberation. The bourgeoisie finally lost its head. The democratic parties, the Mensheviks and Social Revolutionaries, wasted the remains of the confidence of the masses in them by their support of the imperialist war, by their policy of ineffectual compromise and concession to the bourgeois and feudal property owners. The awakened army no longer wanted to fight for the alien aims of imperialism. Disregarding democratic advice, the peasantry smoked the landowners out of their estates. The oppressed nationalities at the periphery rose up against the bureaucracy of Petrograd. In the most important workers' and soldiers' soviets the Bolsheviks were dominant. The workers and soldiers demanded action. The ulcer was ripe. It needed a cut of the lancet.

Only under these social and political conditions was the insurrection possible. And thus it also became inevitable. But there is no playing around with the insurrection. Woe to the surgeon who is careless in the use of the lancet! Insurrection is an art. It has its laws and its rules.

The party carried through the October insurrection with cold calculation and with flaming determination. Thanks to this, it conquered almost without victims. Through the victorious soviets the Bolsheviks placed themselves at the head of a country which occupies one-sixth of the surface of the globe.

The majority of my present listeners, it is to be presumed, did not occupy themselves at all with politics in the year 1917. So much the better. Before the young generation lies much that is interesting, if not always easy. But the representatives of the older generation in this hall will surely well remember how the seizure of power by the Bolsheviks was received: as a curiosity, as a misunderstanding, as a scandal; most often as a nightmare which was bound to disappear with the first rays of dawn. The Bolsheviks would last twenty-four hours, a week, a month, a year. The period had to be constantly lengthened. The rulers of the whole world armed themselves against the first workers' state: civil war was stirred up, interventions again and again, blockade. So passed year after year. Meantime history has recorded fifteen years of existence of the Soviet power.

"Yes," some opponent will say, "the adventure of October has shown itself to be much more substantial than many of us thought. Perhaps it was not even quite an 'adventure.' Nevertheless, the question retains its full force: What was achieved at this high cost? Were then those dazzling tasks fulfilled which the Bolsheviks proclaimed on the eve of the revolution?"

Before we answer the hypothetical opponent, let us note that the question in and of itself is not new. On the contrary, it followed right at the heels of the October Revolution, since the day of its birth.

The French journalist, Claude Anet, who was in Petrograd during the revolution, wrote as early as October 27, 1917:

"The maximalists (which was what the French called the Bolsheviks at that time) have seized the power and the great day has come. At last, I say to myself, I shall behold the realization of the socialist Eden which has been promised us for so many years. . . . Admirable adventure! A privileged position!" And so on and so forth. What sincere hatred behind the ironical salutation! The very morning after the capture of the Winter Palace, the reactionary journalist hurried to register his claim for a ticket of admission to Eden. Fifteen years have passed since the revolution. With all the greater absence of ceremony our enemies reveal their malicious joy over the fact that the land of the Soviets, even today, bears but little resemblance to a realm of general well-being. Why then the revolution and why the sacrifices?

Worthly listeners—permit me to think that the contradictions, difficulties, mistakes, and want of the Soviet regime are no less familiar to me than to anyone else. I personally have never concealed them, whether in speech or in writing. I have believed and I still believe that revolutionary politics, as distinguished from conservative, cannot be built up on concealment. "To speak out that which is" must be the highest principle of the workers' state.

But in criticism, as well as in creative activity, perspective is necessary. Subjectivism is a poor adviser, particularly in great questions. Periods of time must be commensurate with the tasks, and not with individual caprices. Fifteen years! How much that is in the life of one man! Within that period not a few of our generation were borne to their graves and those who remain have added innumerable gray hairs. But these same fifteen years—what an insignificant period in the life of a people! Only a minute on the clock of history.

Capitalism required centuries to maintain itself in the struggle against the Middle Ages, to raise the level of science and technology, to build railroads, to stretch electric wires. And then? Then humanity was thrust by capitalism into the hell of wars and crises! But socialism is allowed by its enemies, that is, by the adherents of capitalism, only a decade and a half to install paradise on earth with all modern improvements. No, such obligations were never assumed by us. Such periods of time were never set forth.

The processes of great changes must be measured by scales which are commensurate with them. I do not know if the socialist society will resemble the biblical paradise. I doubt it. But in the Soviet Union there is no socialism as yet. The situation that prevails there is one of transition, full of contradictions, burdened with the heavy inheritance of the past, and in addition under the hostile pressure of the capitalistic states. The October Revolution has proclaimed the principle of the new society. The Soviet Republic has shown only the first stage of its realization. Edison's first lamp was very bad. We must know how to distinguish the future from among the mistakes and faults of the first socialist construction.

But the unhappiness that rains on living men! Do the results of the revolution justify the sacrifice which it has caused? A fruitless question, rhetorical through and through; as if the processes of history admitted of an accounting balance sheet! We might just as well ask, in view of the difficulties and miseries of human existence, "Does it pay to be born altogether?" To which Heine wrote, "And the fool expects an answer." Such melancholy reflections have not hindered mankind from being born and from giving birth. Suicides, even in these days of unexampled world crisis, fortunately constitute an unimportant percentage. But peoples never resort to suicide. When their burdens are intolerable, they seek a way out through revolution.

Besides, who becomes indignant over the victims of the socialist upheaval? Most often those who have paved the way for the victims of the imperialist war, and have glorified or, at least, easily accommodated themselves to it. It is now our turn to ask, "Has the war justified itself? What has it given us? What has it taught?"

The reactionary historian, Hippolyte Taine, in his eleven-volume pamphlet against the Great French Revolution describes, not without malicious joy, the sufferings of the French people in the years of the dictatorship of the Jacobins and afterward. The worst off were the lower classes of the cities, the plebeians, who as "sansculottes" had given up the best of their souls for the revolution. Now they or their wives stood in line through cold nights to return empty-handed to the extinguished family hearth. In the tenth year of the revolution Paris was poorer than before it began. Carefully selected, artificially pieced-out facts serve Taine as justification for his annihilating verdict against the revolution. Look, the plebeians wanted to be dictators and have precipitated themselves into misery!

It is hard to conceive of a more uninspired piece of moralizing. First of all, if the revolution precipitated the country into misery, the blame lay principally on the ruling classes who drove the people to revolution.

Second, the Great French Revolution did not exhaust itself in hungry lines before bakeries. The whole of modern France, in many respects the whole of modern civilization, arose out of the bath of the French Revolution!

In the course of the Civil War in the United States in the sixties of the last century, five hundred thousand men were killed. Can these sacrifices be justified?

From the standpoint of the American slaveholder and the ruling classes of Great Britain who marched with them—no! From the standpoint of the Negro or of the British working-man—absolutely! And from the standpoint of the development of humanity as a whole—there can be no doubt whatever. Out of the Civil War of the sixties came the present United States with its unbounded practical initiative, its rationalized technology, its economic energy. On these achievements of America, humanity will build the new society.

The October Revolution penetrated deeper than any of its predecessors into the holy of holies of society—into its property relations. So much the longer time is necessary to reveal the creative consequences of the revolution in all the spheres of life. But the general direction of the upheaval is already clear: the Soviet Republic has no reason whatever to hang its head before its capitalist accusers and speak the language of apology.

To evaluate the new regime from the standpoint of human development, one must first answer the question, "How does social progress express itself and how can it be measured?"

The deepest, the most objective, and the most indisputable criterion says—progress can be measured by the growth of the productivity of social labor. The evaluation of the October Revolution from this point of view is already given by experience. The principle of socialistic organization has for the first time in history shown its ability to record unheard-of results in production in a short space of time.

The curve of the industrial development of Russia, expressed in crude index numbers, is as follows, taking 1913, the last year before the war, as 100. The year 1920, the highest point of the civil war, is also the lowest point in industry—only 25, that is to say, a quarter of the prewar production. In 1925 it rose to 75, that is, three-quarters of the prewar production; in 1929 about 200, in 1932, 300, that is to say, three times as much as on the eve of the war.

The picture becomes even more striking in the light of the international index. From 1925 to 1932 the industrial production of Germany has declined one and a half times, in America twice; in the Soviet Union it has increased fourfold. These figures speak for themselves.

I have no intention of denying or concealing the seamy side of Soviet economy. The results of the industrial index are extraordinarily influenced by the unfavorable development of agriculture, that is to say, of that field which has essentially not yet risen to socialist methods, but at the same time has been led on the road to collectivization with insufficient preparation, bureaucratically rather than technically and economically. This is a great question, which however goes beyond the limits of my lecture.

The index numbers cited require another important reservation. The indisputable and, in their way, splendid results of Soviet industrialization demand a further economic checking-up from the standpoint of the mutual adaptation of the various elements of economy, their dynamic equilibrium, and consequently their productive capacity. Here great difficulties and even setbacks are inevitable. Socialism does not arise in its perfected form from the Five-Year Plan, like Minerva from the head of Jupiter, or Venus from the foam of the sea. Before it are decades of persistent work, of mistakes, corrections, and reorganization. Moreover, let us not forget that socialist construction in accordance with its very nature can only reach perfection on the international arena. But even the most unfavorable economic balance sheet of the results obtained so far could reveal only the incorrectness of the preliminary calculations, the errors of the plan, and the mistakes of the leadership, but could in no way refute the empirically firmly established fact—the possibility, with the aid of socialist methods, of raising the productivity of collective labor to an unheard-of height. This conquest, of world historical importance, cannot be taken away from us by anybody or anything.

After what has been said, it is scarcely worthwhile to spend time on the complaints, that the October Revolution has brought Russia to the downfall of its civilization. That is the voice of the disquieted ruling houses and the salons. The feudal-bourgeois "civilization" overthrown by the proletarian upheaval was only barbarism with decorations a la Talmi. While it remained inaccessible to the Russian people, it brought little that was new to the treasury of mankind.

But even with respect to this civilization, which is so bemoaned by the White emigres, we must put the question more precisely—in what sense is it ruined? Only in one sense; the monopoly of a small minority in the treasures of civilization has been destroyed. But everything of cultural value in the old Russian civilization has remained untouched. The Huns of Bolshevism have shattered neither the conquests of the mind nor the creations of art. On the contrary, they carefully collected the monuments of human creativeness and arranged them in model order. The culture of the monarchy, the nobility, and the bourgeoisie has now become the culture of the museums.

The people visit these museums eagerly. But they do not live in them. They learn. They build. The fact alone that the October Revolution taught the Russian people, the dozens of peoples of czarist Russia, to read and write, stands immeasurably higher than the whole former hothouse Russian civilization.

The October Revolution has laid the foundations for a new civilization, which is designed, not for a select few, but for all. This is felt by the masses of the whole world. Hence their sympathy for the Soviet Union, which is as passionate as once was their hatred for czarist Russia.

Worthy listeners—you know that human language is an irreplaceable tool, not only for giving names to events but also for evaluating them. By filtering out that which is accidental, episodic, artificial, it absorbs that which is essential, characteristic, of full weight. Notice with what nicety the languages of civilized nations have distinguished two epochs in the development of Russia. The culture of the nobility brought into world currency such barbarisms as *czar, Cossack, pogrom, nagaika*, [whip]. You know these words and what they mean. The October Revolution introduced into the language of the world such words as *Bolshevik, Soviet, kolkhoz* [collective farm], *Gosplan* [State Planning Commission], *Piatiletka* [Five-Year Plan]. Here practical linguistics holds its historical supreme court!

The profoundest significance, but the hardest to submit to immediate measurement, of that great revolution consists in the fact that it forms and tempers the character of the people. The conception of the Russian people as slow, passive, melancholy, mystical, is widely spread and not accidental. It has its roots in the past. But in Western countries up to the present time those far-reaching changes have not been sufficiently considered which have been introduced into the character of the people by the revolution. Could it have been otherwise?

Every man with experience of life can recall the picture of some youth that he has known, receptive, lyrical, all too susceptible, who later, all at once, under the influence of a powerful moral impetus, became hardened and unrecognizable. In the development of a whole nation, such moral transformations are wrought by the revolution.

The February insurrection against the autocracy, the struggle against the nobility, against the imperialist war, for peace, for land, for national equality, the October insurrection, the overthrow of the bourgeoisie, and of those parties which sought agreements with the bourgeoisie, three years of civil war on a front of five thousand miles, the years of blockade, hunger, misery, and epidemics, the years of tense economic reconstruction, of new difficulties and renunciations—these make a hard but a good school. A heavy hammer smashes glass, but forges steel. The hammer of the revolution forged the steel of the people's character.

"Who will believe," wrote a czarist general, Zalessky, with indignation, shortly after the upheaval, "that a porter or a watchman suddenly becomes a chief justice; a hospital attendant, the director of a hospital; a barber, an officeholder; a corporal, a commander-in-chief; a day worker, a mayor; a locksmith, the director of a factory?"

"Who will believe it?" They had to believe it. They could do nothing else but believe it, when the corporals defeated generals, when the mayor—the former day worker—broke the resistance of the old bureaucracy, the wagon-greaser put the transportation system in order, the locksmith as director put the industrial equipment into working condition. "Who will believe it?" Let them only try and not believe it.

For an explanation of the extraordinary persistence which the masses of the people of the Soviet Union are showing throughout the years of the revolution, many foreign observers rely, in accord with ancient habit, on the "passivity" of the Russian character. Gross anachronism! The revolutionary masses endure their privations patiently but not passively. With their own hands they are creating a better future and they want to create it, at any cost. Let the class enemy only attempt to impose his will from the outside on these patient masses! No, he would do better not to try it!

Let us now in closing attempt to ascertain the place of the October Revolution, not only in the history of Russia but in the history of the world. During the year 1917, in a period of eight months, two historical curves intersect. The February upheaval—that belated echo of the great struggles which had been carried out in past centuries on the territories of Holland, England, France, almost all of Continental Europe—takes its place in the series of bourgeois revolutions. The October Revolution proclaims and opens the domination of the proletariat. It was world capitalism that suffered its first great defeat on the territory of Russia. The chain broke at its weakest link. But it was the chain that broke, and not only the link.

Capitalism has outlived itself as a world system. It has ceased to fulfill its essential mission, the increase of human power and human wealth. Humanity cannot stand still at the level which it has reached. Only a powerful increase in productive forces and a sound, planned, that is, socialist organization of production and distribution can assure humanity—all humanity—of a decent standard of life and at the same time give it the precious feeling of freedom with respect to its own economy. Freedom in two senses—first of all, man will no longer be compelled to devote the greater part of his life to physical labor. Second, he will no longer be dependent on the laws of the market, that is, on the blind and dark forces which have grown up behind his back. He will build up his economy freely, that is, according to a plan, with compass in hand. This time it is a question of subjecting the anatomy of society to the X ray through and through, of disclosing all its secrets and subjecting all its functions to the reason and the will of collective humanity. In this sense, socialism must become a new step in the historical advance of mankind. To our ancestor, who first armed himself with a stone axe, the whole of *nature* represented a conspiracy of secret and hostile forces. Since then, the natural sciences, hand in hand with practical technology, have illuminated nature down to its most secret depths. By means of electrical energy, the physicist passes judgment on the nucleus of the atom. The hour is not far when science will easily solve the task of the alchemists, and turn manure into gold and gold into manure. Where the demons and furies of nature once raged, now rules ever more courageously the industrial will of man.

But while he wrestled victoriously with nature, man built up his relations to other men blindly, almost like the bee or the ant. Belatedly and most undecidedly he approached the problems of human society. He began with religion, and passed on to politics. The Reformation represented the first victory of bourgeois individualism and rationalism in a domain which had been ruled by dead tradition. From the church, critical thought went on to the state. Born in the struggle with absolutism and the medieval estates, the doctrine of the sovereignty of the people and of the rights of man and the citizen grew stronger. Thus arose the system of parliamentarism. Critical thought penetrated into the domain of government administration. The political rationalism of democracy was the highest achievement of the revolutionary bourgeoisie.

But between nature and the state stands economic life. Technology liberated man from the tyranny of the old elements—earth, water fire, and air—only to subject him to its own tyranny. Man ceased to be a slave to nature, to become a slave to the machine, and, still worse, a slave to supply and demand. The present world crisis testifies in especially tragic fashion how man, who dives to the bottom of the ocean, who rises up to the stratosphere, who converses on invisible waves with the antipodes, how this proud and daring ruler of nature remains a slave to the blind forces of his own economy. The historical task of our epoch consists in replacing the uncontrolled play of the market by reasonable planning, in disciplining the forces of production, compelling them to work together in harmony and obediently serve the needs of mankind. Only on this new social basis will man be able to stretch his weary limbs and—every man and every woman, not only a selected few—become a full citizen in the realm of thought.

But this is not yet the end of the road. No, it is only the beginning. Man calls himself the crown of creation. He has a certain right to that claim. But who has asserted that present-day man is the last and highest representative of the species homo sapiens? No, physically as well as spiritually he is very far from perfection, prematurely born biologically, feeble in thought, and without any new organic equilibrium.

It is true that humanity has more than once brought forth giants of thought and action, who tower over their contemporaries like summits in a chain of mountains. The human race has a right to be proud of its Aristotle, Shakespeare, Darwin, Beethoven, Goethe, Marx, Edison, and Lenin. But why are they so rare? Above all because, almost without exception, they came out of the upper and middle classes. Apart from rare exceptions, the sparks of genius in the suppressed depths of the people are choked before they can burst into flame. But also because the processes of creating, developing, and educating a human being have been and remain essentially a matter of chance, not illuminated by theory and practice, not subjected to consciousness and will.

Anthropology, biology, physiology, and psychology have accumulated mountains of material to raise up before mankind in their full scope the tasks of perfecting and developing body and spirit. Psychoanalysis, with the inspired hand of Sigmund Freud, has lifted the cover of the well which is poetically called the "soul." And what has been revealed? Our conscious thought is only a small part of the work of the dark psychic forces. Learned divers descend to the bottom of the ocean and there take photographs of mysterious fishes. Human thought, descending to the bottom of its own psychic sources, must shed light on the most mysterious driving forces of the soul and subject them to reason and to will.

Once he has done with the anarchic forces of his own society, man will set to work on himself, in the pestle and the retort of the chemist. For the first time mankind will regard itself as raw material, or at best as a physical and psychic semi-finished product. Socialism will mean a leap from the realm of necessity into the realm of freedom in this sense too, that the man of today, with all his contradictions and lack of harmony, will open the road for a new and happier race.

READING #15
The Revolution Betrayed (excerpt)

The present régime in the Soviet Union provokes protest at every step, a protest the more burning in that it is repressed. The bureaucracy is not only a machine of compulsion but also a constant source of provocation. The very existence of a greedy, lying, and cynical caste of rulers inevitably creates a hidden indignation. The improvement of the material situation of the workers does not reconcile them with the authorities; on the contrary, by increasing their self-respect and freeing their thought for general problems of politics, it prepares the way for an open conflict with the bureaucracy.

The unremovable "leaders" love to issue statements about the necessity of "studying," of "acquiring technique," "cultural self-education," and other admirable things. But the ruling layer itself is ignorant and little cultured; it studies nothing seriously, is disloyal and rude in social contacts. Its pretension to patronize all spheres of social life, to take command not only of cooperative shops but of musical compositions is the more intolerable for that. The Soviet population cannot rise to a higher level of culture without freeing itself from this humiliating subjection to a caste of usurpers.

Will the bureaucrat devour the workers' state, or will the working class clean up the bureaucrat? Thus stands the question upon whose decision hangs the fate of the Soviet Union. The vast majority of the Soviet workers are even now hostile to the bureaucracy. The peasant masses hate them with their healthy plebeian hatred. If in contrast to the peasants, the workers have almost never come out on the road of open struggle, thus condemning the protesting villages to confusion and impotence, this is not only because of the repressions. The workers fear lest, in throwing out the bureaucracy, they will open the way for a capitalist restoration. The mutual relations between state and class are much more complicated than they are represented by the vulgar "democrats." Without a planned economy the Soviet Union would be thrown back for decades. In that sense the bureaucracy continues to fulfill a necessary function. But it fulfills it in such a way as to prepare an explosion of the whole system which may completely sweep out the results of the revolution. The workers are realists. Without deceiving themselves with regard to the ruling caste—at least with regard to its lower tiers which stand near to them—they see in it the watchman for the time being of a certain part of their own conquests. They will inevitably drive out the dishonest, impudent, and unreliable watchman as soon as they see another possibility. For this it is necessary that in the West or the East another revolutionary dawn arise.

The cessation of visible political struggle is portrayed by the friends and agents of the Kremlin as a "stabilization" of the régime. In reality it signalizes only a temporary stabilization of the bureaucracy. With popular discontent driven deep, the younger generation feels with special pain the yoke of this "enlightened absolutism" in which there is so much more absolutism than enlightenment. The increasingly ominous vigilance of the bureaucracy against any ray of living thought, and the unbearable tensity of the hymns of praise addressed to a blessed providence in the person of the "leader," testify alike to a growing separation between the state and society. They testify to a steady intensifying of inner contradictions, a pressure against the walls of the state which seeks a way out and must inevitably find one.

In a true appraisal of the situation, the not infrequent terrorist acts against representatives of power have a very high significance. The most notorious of these was the murder of [Sergei] Kirov, a clever and unscrupulous Leningrad dictator, a typical representative of his corporation. In themselves, terrorist acts are least of all capable of overthrowing a Bonapartist oligarchy. Although the individual bureaucrat dreads the revolver, the bureaucracy of whole is able to exploit an act of terror for the justification of its own violences, and incidentally to implicate in the murder its own political enemies (the affair of Zinoviev, Kamenev, and the others).* Individual terror is a weapon of impatient or despairing individuals, belonging most frequently to the younger generation of the bureaucracy itself. But, as was the case in Tsarist times, political murders are unmistakable symptoms of a stormy atmosphere and foretell the beginning of an open political crisis.

In introducing the new constitution, the bureaucracy shows that it feels this danger and is taking preventive measures. However, it has happened more than once that a bureaucratic dictatorship, seeking salvation in "liberal" reforms, has only weakened itself. While exposing Bonapartism, the new constitution creates at the same time a semilegal cover for the struggle against it. The rivalry of bureaucratic cliques at the elections may become the beginning of a broader political struggle. The whip against "badly working organs of power" may be turned into a whip against Bonapartism. All indications agree that the further course of development must inevitably lead to a clash

---

* In January, 1935, Zinoviev, Kamenev, Smirnov and others were indicted and tried for being "politically and morally" responsible for assassinating Sergei M. Kirov, a Politburo member. They escaped death and were sentenced to various terms of imprisonment only to be retried in August, 1936, and executed on the ground that they had actually helped plot Kirov's murder. between the culturally developed forces of the people and the bureaucratic oligarchy. There is no peaceful outcome for this crisis. No devil ever yet voluntarily cut off his own claws. The Soviet bureaucracy will not give up its positions without a fight. The development leads obviously to the road of revolution.

With energetic pressure from the popular mass, and the disintegration of the government apparatus inevitable in such circumstances, the resistance of those in power may prove much weaker than now appears. But as to this, only hypotheses are possible. In any case, the bureaucracy can be removed only by a revolutionary force. And, as always, there will be fewer victims the more bold and decisive is the attack. To prepare this and stand at the head of the masses in a favorable historic situation—that is the task of the Soviet section of the Fourth International. Today it is still weak and driven underground. But the illegal existence of a party is not nonexistence. It is only a difficult form of existence. Repressions can prove fully effective against a class that is disappearing from the scene—this was fully proven by the revolutionary dictatorship of 1917 to 1923—but violences against a revolutionary vanguard cannot save a caste which, if the Soviet Union is destined in general to further development, has outlived itself.

The revolution which the bureaucracy is preparing against itself will not be social, like the October Revolution of 1917. It is not a question this time of changing the economic foundations of society, of replacing certain forms of property with other forms. History has known elsewhere not only social revolutions which substituted the bourgeois for the feudal régime, but also political revolutions which, without destroying the economic foundations of society, swept out an old ruling upper crust (1830 and 1848 in France, February, 1917, in Russia, etc.). The overthrow of the Bonapartist caste will, of course, have deep social consequences, but in itself it will be confined within the limits of political revolution.

This is the first time in history that a state resulting from a workers' revolution has existed. The stages through which it must go are nowhere written down. It is true that the theoreticians and creators of the Soviet Union hoped that the completely transparent and flexible soviet system would permit the state peacefully to transform itself, dissolve, and die away, in correspondence with the stages of the economic and cultural evolution of society. Here again, however, life proved more complicated than theory anticipated. The proletariat of a backward country was fated to accomplish the first socialist revolution. For this historic privilege, it must, according to all evidences, pay with a second supplementary revolution—against bureaucratic absolutism. The program of the new revolution depends to a great extent upon the moment when it breaks out, upon the level which the country has then attained, and to a great degree upon the international situation. . . .

It is not a question of substituting one ruling clique for another, but of changing the very methods of administering the economy and guiding the culture of the country. Bureaucratic autocracy must give place to soviet democracy. A restoration of the right of criticism and a genuine freedom of elections are necessary conditions for the further development of the country. This assumes a revival of freedom of soviet parties, beginning with the party of Bolsheviks, and a resurrection of the trade unions. The bringing of democracy into industry means a radical revision of plans in the interests of the toilers. Free discussion of economic problems will decrease the overhead expense of bureaucratic mistakes and zigzags. Expensive playthings—palaces of the soviets, new theatres, show-off subways—will be crowded out in favor of workers' dwellings. "Bourgeois norms of distribution" will be confined within the limits of strict necessity, and, in step with the growth of social wealth, will give way to Socialist equality. Ranks will be immediately abolished. The tinsel of decorations will go into the melting pot. The youth will receive the opportunity to breathe freely, criticize, make mistakes, and grow up. Science and art will be freed of their chains. And, finally, foreign policy will return to the traditions of revolutionary internationalism. . . .

READING #16

"The USSR and the Problems of the Transitional Epoch"

The Soviet Union emerged from the October Revolution as a workers' state. State ownership of the means of production, a necessary prerequisite to socialist development, opened up the possibility of rapid growth of the productive forces. But the apparatus of the workers' state underwent a complete degeneration at the same time: it was transformed from a weapon of the working class into a weapon of bureaucratic violence against the working class and more and more a weapon for the sabotage of the country's economy. The bureaucratization of a backward and isolated workers' state and the transformation of the bureaucracy into an all-powerful privileged caste constitute the most convincing refutation—not only theoretically but this time practically—of the theory of socialism in one country.

The USSR thus embodies terrific contradictions. But it still remains a *degenerated workers' state*. Such is the social diagnosis. The political prognosis has an alternative character: either the bureaucracy, becoming ever more the organ of the world bourgeoisie in the workers' state, will overthrow the new forms of property and plunge the country back to capitalism; or the working class will crush the bureaucracy and open the way to socialism....

A fresh upsurge of the revolution in the USSR will undoubtedly begin under the banner of the struggle against *social inequality* and *political oppression*. Down with the privileges of the bureaucracy! Down with Stakhanovism!* Down with the Soviet aristocracy and its ranks and orders! Greater equality of wages for all forms of labor!

The struggle for the freedom of the trade unions and the factory committees, for the right of assembly and freedom of the press, will unfold in the struggle for the regeneration and development of *Soviet democracy*.

The bureaucracy replaced the soviets as class organs with the fiction of universal electoral rights—in the style of Hitler-Goebbels. It is necessary to return to the soviets not only their free democratic form but also their class content. As once the bourgeoisie and kulaks were not permitted to enter the soviets, so now *it is necessary to drive the bureaucracy and the new aristocracy out of the soviets*. In the soviets there is room only for representatives of the workers, rank-and-file collective farmers, peasants, and Red Army men.

Democratization of the soviets is impossible without *legalization of soviet parties*. The workers and peasants themselves by their own free vote will indicate what parties they recognize as soviet parties.

A revision of *planned economy* from top to bottom in the interests of producers and consumers! Factory committees should be returned

---

* A Soviet system of work organization, introduced under Stalin in 1935, that stressed overfulfillment of production quotas and facilitated speedup. Name derived from Aleksey Stakhanov, a coal miner whose team increased daily output sevenfold. Stakhanovite workers were paid higher wages and received special privileges.

the right to control production. A democratically organized consumers' cooperative should control the quality and price of products.

Reorganization of the collective farms in accordance with the will and in the interests of the workers there engaged!

The reactionary *international policy* of the bureaucracy should be replaced by the policy of proletarian internationalism. The complete diplomatic correspondence of the Kremlin to be published. *Down with secret diplomacy!*

All political trials, staged by the Thermidorian bureaucracy, to be reviewed in the light of complete publicity and controversial openness and integrity. Only the victorious revolutionary uprising of the oppressed masses can revive the Soviet régime and guarantee its further development toward socialism.

There is but one party capable of leading the Soviet masses to insurrection—the party of the Fourth International!

Down with the bureaucratic gang of Cain-Stalin!

Long live Soviet democracy!

Long live the international socialist revolution!

READING #17

"Letter to the Workers of the USSR"

Greetings to the Soviet workers, collective farmers, soldiers of the Red Army, and sailors of the Red Navy! Greetings from distant Mexico where I found refuge after the Stalinist clique had exiled me to Turkey and after the bourgeoisie had hounded me from country to country!

Dear Comrades! The mendacious Stalinist press has been maliciously deceiving you for a long time on all questions, including those which relate to myself and my political co-thinkers. You possess no workers' press; you read only the press of the bureaucracy, which lies systematically so as to keep you in the dark and thus render secure the rule of a privileged parasitic caste.

Those who dare raise their voices against the universally hated bureaucracy are called "Trotskyists," agents of a foreign power; branded as spies—yesterday it was spies of Germany, today it is spies of England

and France—and then sent to face the firing squad. Tens of thousands of revolutionary fighters have fallen before the muzzles of GPU Mausers in the USSR and in countries abroad, especially in Spain. All of them were depicted as agents of Fascism. Do not believe this abominable slander! Their crime consisted of defending workers and peasants against the brutality and rapacity of the bureaucracy. The entire old guard of Bolshevism, all the collaborators and assistants of Lenin, all the fighters of the October Revolution, all the heroes of the civil war, have been murdered by Stalin. In the annals of history Stalin's name will forever be recorded with the infamous brand of Cain!

The October Revolution was accomplished for the sake of the toilers and not for the sake of new parasites. But because of the lag of the world revolution, and the fatigue, and, to a large measure, the backwardness of the Russian workers and especially the Russian peasants, there raised itself over the Soviet Republic and against its peoples a new oppressive and parasitic caste whose leader is Stalin. The former Bolshevik party was turned into an instrument of the caste. The world organization which the Communist International once was is today a pliant tool of the Moscow oligarchy. Soviets of Workers and Peasants have long perished. They have been replaced by degenerate Commissars, Secretaries, and GPU agents.

But, fortunately, among the surviving conquests of the October Revolution are the nationalized industry and the collectivized Soviet economy. Upon this foundation Workers' Soviets can build a new and happier society. This foundation cannot be surrendered by us to the world bourgeoisie under any conditions. It is the duty of revolutionists to defend tooth and nail every position gained by the working class, whether it involves democratic rights, wage scales, or so colossal a conquest of mankind as the nationalization of the means of production and planned economy. Those who are incapable of defending conquests already gained can never fight for new ones. Against the imperialist foe we will defend the USSR with all our might. However, the conquests of the October Revolution will serve the people only if they prove themselves capable of dealing with the Stalinist bureaucracy, as in their day they dealt with the Tsarist bureaucracy and the bourgeoisie.

If Soviet economic life had been conducted in the interests of the people; if the bureaucracy had not devoured and vainly wasted the major portion of the national income; if the bureaucracy had not trampled underfoot the vital interests of the population, then the USSR would have been a great magnetic pole of attraction for the toilers of the world and the inviolability of the Soviet Union would have been assured. But the infamous oppressive régime of Stalin has deprived the USSR of its attractive power. During the war with Finland, not only the majority of the Finnish peasants but also the majority of the Finnish workers, proved to be on the side of their bourgeoisie. This is hardly surprising since they know of the unprecedented oppression to which the Stalinist bureaucracy subjects the workers of nearby Leningrad and the whole of the USSR. The Stalinist bureaucracy, so bloodthirsty and ruthless at home and so cowardly before the imperialist enemies, has thus become the main source of war danger to the Soviet Union.

The old Bolshevik party and the Third International have disintegrated and decomposed. The honest and advanced revolutionists have organized abroad the Fourth International, which has sections already established in most of the countries of the world. I am a member of this new International. In participating in this work I remain under the very same banner that I served together with you or your fathers and your older brothers in 1917 and throughout the years of the civil war—the very same banner under which together with Lenin we built the Soviet state and the Red Army.

The goal of the Fourth International is to extend the October Revolution to the whole world and at the same time to regenerate the USSR by purging it of the parasitic bureaucracy. This can be achieved only in one way: by the workers, peasants, Red Army soldiers, and Red Navy sailors, rising against the new caste of oppressors and parasites. To prepare this uprising, a new party is needed—a bold and honest revolutionary organization of the advanced workers. The Fourth International sets as its task the building of such a party in the USSR.

Advanced workers! Be the first to rally to the banner of Marx and Lenin which is now the banner of the Fourth International! Learn how to create, in the conditions of Stalinist illegality, tightly fused, reliable revolutionary circles! Establish contacts between these circles! Learn how to establish contacts—through loyal and reliable people, especially the sailors—with your revolutionary co-thinkers in bourgeois lands! It is difficult, but it can be done.

The present war will spread more and more, piling ruins on ruins, breeding more sorrow, despair, and protest, driving the whole world toward new revolutionary explosions. The world revolution shall reinvigorate the Soviet working masses with new courage and resoluteness and shall undermine the bureaucratic props of Stalin's caste. It is necessary to prepare for this hour by stubborn systematic revolutionary work. The fate of our country, the future of our people, the destiny of our children and grandchildren are at stake.

> Down with Cain Stalin and his Camarilla!
> Down with the Rapacious Bureaucracy!
> Long Live the Soviet Union, the Fortress of the Toilers!
> Long Live the World Socialist Revolution!

Fraternally,
LEON TROTSKY
May, 1940

WARNING! Stalin's press will of course declare that this letter is transmitted to the USSR by "agents of imperialism." Be forewarned that this, too, is a lie. This letter will reach the USSR through reliable revolutionists who are prepared to risk their lives for the cause of socialism. Make copies of this letter and give it the widest possible circulation—L. T.

READING #18

"What Next? Vital Questions for the German Proletariat" (excerpts)

In the course of many decades, the workers have built up within the bourgeois democracy, by utilizing it, by fighting against it, their own strongholds and bases of *proletarian democracy*: the trade unions, the political parties, the educational and sport clubs, the cooperatives, etc. The proletariat cannot attain power within the formal limits of bourgeois democracy, but can do so only by taking the road of revolution: this has been proved both by theory and experience. And these bulwarks of workers' democracy within the bourgeois state are absolutely essential for taking the revolutionary road. The work of the Second International consisted in creating just such bulwarks during the epoch when it was till fulfilling its progressive historic labor.

Fascism has for its basic and only task the razing to their foundations of all institutions of proletarian democracy. Has this any "class meaning" for the proletariat, or hasn't it? The lofty theoreticians had better ponder over this. . . .

The wiseacres who boast that they do not recognize any difference "between Bruening and Hitler," are saying in reality: it makes no difference whether our organizations exist, or whether they are already destroyed. Beneath this pseudoradical phraseology there hides the most sordid passivity; we can't escape defeat anyway! Read over carefully the quotation from the French Stalinist periodical. They reduce the question to whether it is better to starve under Hitler or Bruening. To them it is a question of under whom to starve. To us, on the contrary, it is not a question of under which conditions it is better to die. We raise the question of how to fight and win. And we conclude thus: the major offensive must be begun before the bureaucratic dictatorship is replaced by the fascist regime, that is, before the workers' organizations are crushed. The general offensive should be prepared for by deploying, extending, and sharpening the sectional clashes. But for this one must have a correct perspective and, first of all, one should not proclaim victorious the enemy who is still a long way from victory.

Herein is the crux of the problem; herein is the strategical key to the background; herein is the operating base from which the battle must be waged. Every thinking worker, the more so every Communist, must give himself an accounting and plumb to the bottom the empty and rotten talk of the Stalinist bureaucracy about Bruening and Hitler being one and the same thing. You are muddling! we say in answer. You muddle disgracefully because you are afraid of the difficulties that lie ahead, because you are terrified by the great problems that lie ahead; you throw in the sponge before the fighting is begun, you proclaim that we have already suffered defeat. You are lying! The working class is split; it is weakened by the reformists and disoriented by the vacillations of its own vanguard, but it is not annihilated yet, its forces are not yet exhausted. No. The proletariat of Germany is powerful. The most optimistic estimates will be infinitely surpassed once its revolutionary energy clears the way for it to the arena of action.

Bruening's regime is the preparatory regime. Preparatory to what? Either to the victory of fascism, or to the victory of the proletariat. This regime is preparatory because both camps are only preparing for the decisive battle. If you identify Bruening with Hitler, you identify the conditions before the battle with the conditions after defeat; it means that you admit defeat beforehand; it means that you appeal for surrender without a battle.

The overwhelming majority of the workers, particularly the Communists, does not want this. The Stalinist bureaucracy, of course, does not want it either. But one must take into account not one's good intentions, with which Hitler will pave the road to his Hell, but the objective meaning of one's policies, of their direction, and their tendencies. . . .

But the proletariat moves toward revolutionary consciousness not by passing grades in school but by passing through the class struggle, which abhors interruptions. To fight, the proletariat must have unity in its ranks. This holds true for partial economic conflicts, within the walls of a single factory, as well as for such "national" political battles as the one to repel fascism. Consequently the tactic of the united front is not something accidental and artificial—a cunning maneuver—not at all; it originates, entirely and wholly, in the objective conditions governing the development of the proletariat. The words in the *Communist Manifesto* which state that the Communists are not to be opposed to the proletariat, that they have no interests separate and apart from those of the proletariat as a whole, carry with them the meaning that the struggle of the party to win over the majority of the class must in no instance come into opposition with the need of the workers to keep unity within their fighting ranks. . . .

Italian fascism was the immediate outgrowth of the betrayal by the reformists of the uprising of the Italian proletariat. From the time the war ended, there was an upward trend in the revolutionary movement in Italy, and in September 1920, it resulted in the seizure of factories and industries by the workers. The dictatorship of the proletariat was an actual fact; all that was lacking was to organize it, and to draw from it all the necessary conclusions. The Social Democracy took fright, and sprang back. After its bold and heroic exertions, the proletariat was left facing the void. The disruption of the revolutionary movement became the most important factor in the growth of fascism. In September, the revolutionary advance came to a standstill; and November already witnessed the first major demonstration of the fascists (the seizure of Bologna).

True, the proletariat, even after the September catastrophe, was capable of waging defensive battles. But the Social Democracy was concerned with only one thing: to withdraw the workers from under fire at the cost of one concession after the other. The Social Democracy hoped that the docile conduct of the workers would restore the "public opinion" of the bourgeoisie against the fascists. Moreover, the reformists even banked strongly upon the help of [King] Victor Emmanuel. To the last hour, they restrained the workers with might and main from giving battle to Mussolini's bands. It availed them nothing. The Crown, along with the upper crust of the bourgeoisie, swung over the side of fascism. Convinced at the last moment that fascism was not to be checked by obedience, the Social Democrats issued a call to the workers for a general strike. But their proclamation suffered a fiasco. The reformists had dampened the powder so long, in their fear lest it should explode, that when they finally and with a trembling hand applied a burning fuse to it, the powder did not catch.

In its politics as regards Hitler, the German Social Democracy has not been able to add a single word: all it does is repeat more ponderously whatever the Italian reformists in their own time performed with greater flights of temperament. The latter explained fascism as a postwar psychosis; the German Social Democracy sees in it a "Versailles" or crisis psychosis. In both instances, the reformists shut their eyes to the organic character of fascism as a mass movement growing out of the collapse of capitalism.

Fearful of the revolutionary mobilization of the workers, the Italian reformists banked all their hopes on "the state." Their slogan was, "Victor Emmanuel! Help! Intervene!" The German Social Democracy lacks such a democratic bulwark as a monarch loyal to the constitution. So they must be content with a president. "Hindenburg! Help! Intervene!" [Hindenburg was the conservative President.]

While waging battle against Mussolini, that is, while retreating before him, [Social Democratic leader Filippo] Turati let loose his dazzling motto, "One must have the manhood to be a coward." The German reformists are less frisky with their slogans. They demand, "Courage under unpopularity (*Mut zur Unpopularitaet*)." Which amounts to the same thing. One must not be afraid of the unpopularity which has been aroused by one's own cowardly temporizing with the enemy.

Identical causes produce identical effects. Were the march of events dependent upon the Social Democratic Party leadership, Hitler's career would be assured.

One must admit, however, that the German Communist Party has also learned little from the Italian experience.

The Italian Communist Party came into being almost simultaneously with fascism. But the same conditions of revolutionary ebb tide which carried the fascists to power served to deter the development of the Communist Party. It did not take account of the full sweep of the fascist danger; it lulled itself with revolutionary illusions; it was irreconcilably antagonistic to the policy of the united front; in short, it ailed from all the infantile diseases. Small wonder! It was only two years old. In its eyes fascism appeared to be only "capitalist reaction." The *particular* traits of fascism which spring from the mobilization of the petty bourgeoisie against the proletariat, the Communist Party was unable to discern. Italian comrades inform me that with the sole exception of Gramsci, the Communist Party wouldn't even allow the possibility of the fascists' seizing power. Once the proletarian revolution had suffered defeat, and capitalism had kept its ground, and the counterrevolution had triumphed, how could there be any further kind of counterrevolutionary upheaval? The bourgeoisie cannot rise up against itself! Such was the gist of the political orientation of the Italian Communist Party. Moreover, one must not let out of sight the fact that Italian fascism was then a new phenomenon, and only in the process of formation; it wouldn't have been an easy task even for a more experienced party to distinguish its specific traits.

The leadership of the German Communist Party reproduces today almost literally the position from which the Italian Communists took their point of departure: fascism is nothing else but capitalist reaction; from the point of view of the proletariat, the differences between divers types of capitalist reaction are meaningless. This vulgar radicalism is the less excusable because the German party is much older than the Italian was at a corresponding period; and in addition, Marxism has been enriched now by the tragic experience in Italy. To insist that fascism is already here, or to deny the very possibility of its coming to power—amounts politically to one and the same thing. By ignoring the specific nature of fascism, the will to fight against it becomes inevitably paralyzed. . . .

The last major defeat of the German party, which can be placed on the same historical board with the September days in Italy, dates back to 1923. During the more than eight years that have elapsed since, many wounds have been healed, and a new generation has risen to its feet. The German party represents an incomparably greater force than did the Italian Communists in 1922. The relative weight of the proletariat; the considerable time elapsed since its last defeat; the considerable strength of the Communist Party—these are the three advantages, which bear a great significance for the general summation of the background and of the perspectives. . . .

Should the Communist Party be compelled to apply the policy of the united front, this will almost certainly make it possible to beat off the fascist attack. In its own turn, a serious victory over fascism will clear the road for the dictatorship of the proletariat.

READING #19

"The Transitional Program" (excerpts)

[EDITOR'S NOTE: The Transitional Program was adopted at the founding congress of the Fourth International in 1938. It remains one of the central texts of the world Trotskyist movement. Its methodology continues to be vitally relevant, although in many ways it is a conjunctural document—dealing with tactics to use during the Great Depression in the advanced capitalist countries, in the anticolonial struggle, in fascist countries, and in the Soviet Union under Stalin's dictatorship.

Most importantly, it sketches a methodological approach toward the development of socialist strategy; within the context of actual struggles by working people, there should be developed "a system of transitional demands, stemming from today's conditions and today's consciousness of wide layers of the working class" and yet in fundamental conflict with the power of the capitalists, therefore "unalterably leading to one final conclusion: the conquest of power by the proletariat." This approach is alien to the dogmatic-sectarian approach which infects many on the revolutionary left (and which even affects some interpretations of the Transitional Program), instead combining a firm practical adherence to revolutionary goals with a serious involvement in actual mass movements and struggles for reforms, plus an extremely flexible approach to tactics.

The following excerpts give a sense of that approach, and of the way that the Fourth International presented itself when it was formally established. It has been widely and frequently published since 1938, although one of the most useful editions is Leon Trotsky, *The Transitional Program for Socialist Revolution*, Third Edition (New York: Pathfinder Press, 1977), which contains the entire document, plus valuable supplementary materials—including relevant transcripts of discussions between Trotsky and leaders of the SWP and useful essays by George Novack and Joseph Hansen.]

The Objective Prerequisites for a Socialist Revolution

The world political situation as a whole is chiefly characterized by a historical crisis of the leadership of the proletariat. The economic prerequisite for the proletarian revolution has already in general achieved the highest point of fruition that can be reached under capitalism. Mankind's productive forces stagnate. Already new inventions and improvements fail to raise the level of material wealth. Conjunctural crises under the conditions of the social crisis of the whole capitalist system afflict ever heavier deprivations and sufferings upon the masses. Growing unemployment, in its turn, deepens the financial crisis of the state and undermines the unstable monetary systems. Democratic regimes, as well as fascist, stagger on from one bankruptcy to another.

The bourgeoisie itself sees no way out. In countries where it has already been forced to stake its last upon the card of fascism, it now toboggans with closed eyes toward an economic and military catastrophe. In the historically privileged countries, i.e., in those where the bourgeoisie can still for a certain period permit itself the luxury of democracy at the expense of national accumulations (Great Britain, France, the United States, etc.), all of capital's traditional parties are in a state of perplexity bordering on a paralysis of will. The "New Deal," despite its first period pretentious resoluteness, represents but a special form of political perplexity, possible only in a country where the bourgeoisie succeeded in accumulating incalculable wealth. The present crisis, far from having run its full course, has already succeeded in showing that "New Deal" politics, like Popular Front politics in France, opens no new exit from the economic blind alley.[1]

International relations present no better picture. Under the increasing tension of capitalist disintegration, imperialist antagonisms reach an impasse at the height of which separate clashes and bloody local disturbances (Ethiopia, Spain, the Far East, Central Europe) must inevitably coalesce into a conflagration of world dimensions. The bourgeoisie, of course, is aware of the mortal danger to its domination represented by a new war. But that class is now immeasurably less capable of averting war than on the eve of 1914.

All talk to the effect that historical conditions have not yet "ripened" for socialism is the product of ignorance or conscious deception. The objective prerequisites for the proletarian revolution have not only "ripened"; they have begun to get somewhat rotten. Without a socialist revolution, in the next historical period at that, a catastrophe threatens the whole culture of mankind. The turn is now to the proletariat, i.e., chiefly to its revolutionary vanguard. The historical crisis of mankind is reduced to the crisis of the revolutionary leadership.

The Proletariat and Its Leaderships

The economy, the state, the politics of the bourgeoisie and its international relations are completely blighted by a social crisis, characteristic of a prerevolutionary state of society. The chief obstacle in the path of transforming the prerevolutionary into a revolutionary state is the opportunist character of proletarian leadership: its petty-bourgeois cowardice before the big bourgeoisie and its perfidious connection with it even in its death agony.

In all countries the proletariat is wracked by a deep disquiet. The multi-millioned masses again and again enter the road of revolution. But each time they are blocked by their own conservative bureaucratic machines.

The Spanish proletariat has made a series of heroic attempts since April 1931 to take power in its hands and guide the fate of society. However, its own parties (Social Democrats, Stalinists, Anarchists, POUMists)—each in its own way—acted as a brake and thus prepared Franco's triumphs.[2]

In France, the great wave of sit-down strikes, particularly during June 1936, revealed the wholehearted readiness of the proletariat to overthrow the capitalist system. However, the leading organizations (Socialists, Stalinists, Syndicalists) under the label of the Popular Front succeeded in canalizing and damming, at least temporarily, the revolutionary stream.[3]

The unprecedented wave of sit-down strikes and the amazingly rapid growth of industrial unionism in the United States (the CIO) is the most indisputable expression of the instinctive striving of the American workers to raise themselves to the level of the tasks imposed on them by history. But here, too, the leading political organizations, including the newly created CIO, do everything possible to keep in check and paralyze the revolutionary pressure of the masses.

"People's Fronts" on the one hand—fascism on the other; these are the last political resources of imperialism in the struggle against the proletarian revolution. From the historical point of view, however, both these resources are stopgaps. The decay of capitalism continues under the sign of the Phrygian cap of France as under the sign of the swastika in Germany.[4] Nothing short of the overthrow of the bourgeoisie can open a road out.

The orientation of the masses is determined first by the objective conditions of decaying capitalism, and second, by the treacherous politics of the old workers' organizations. Of these factors, the first of course is the decisive one: the laws of history are stronger than the bureaucratic apparatus. No matter how the methods of the social betrayers differ—from the "social" legislation of Blum to the judicial frame-ups of Stalin—they will never succeed in breaking the revolutionary will of the proletariat. As time goes on, their desperate efforts to hold back the wheel of history will demonstrate more clearly to the masses that the crisis of the proletarian leadership, having become the crisis in mankind's culture, can be resolved only by the Fourth International.

The Minimum Program and the Transitional Program

The strategic task of the next period—a prerevolutionary period of agitation, propaganda, and organization—consists in overcoming the contradiction between the maturity of the objective revolutionary conditions and the immaturity of the proletariat and its vanguard (the confusion and disappointment of the older generation, the inexperience of the younger generation). It is necessary to help the masses in the process of daily struggle to find a bridge between present demands and the socialist program of the revolution. This bridge should include a system of *transitional demands*, stemming from today's conditions and from today's consciousness of wide layers of the working class and unalterably leading to one final conclusion: the conquest of power by the proletariat.

Classical Social Democracy, functioning in an epoch of progressive capitalism, divided its program into two parts independent of each other: the *minimum program*, which limited itself to reforms within the framework of bourgeois society, and the *maximum program*, which promised substitution of socialism for capitalism in the indefinite future. Between the minimum and maximum program no bridge existed. And indeed Social Democracy has no need for such a bridge, since the word *socialism* is used only for holiday speechifying.[5] The Comintern has set out to follow the path of Social Democracy in an epoch of decaying capitalism: when, in general, there can be no discussion of systematic social reforms and the raising of the masses' living standards; when the bourgeoisie always takes away with the right hand twice what it grants with the left (taxes, tariffs, inflation, "deflation," high prices, unemployment, police supervision of strikes); when every serious demand of the proletariat and even every serious demand of the petty bourgeoisie inevitably reaches beyond the limits of capitalist property relations and of the bourgeois state.

The strategical task of the Fourth International lies not in reforming capitalism but in its overthrow. Its political aim is the conquest of power by the proletariat for the purpose of expropriating the bourgeoisie. However, the achievement of this strategic task is unthinkable without the most considerable attention to all, even small and partial questions of tactics. All sections of the proletariat, all its layers, occupations, and groups should be drawn into the revolutionary movement. The present epoch is distinguished not for the fact that it frees the revolutionary party from day-to-day work but because it permits this work to be carried on indissolubly with the actual tasks of the revolution.

The Fourth International does not discard the program of the old "minimal" demands to the degree to which these have preserved at least part of their vital forcefulness. Indefatigably, it defends the democratic rights and social conquests of the workers. But it carries on this day-to-day work within the framework of the correct actual, that is, revolutionary perspective. Insofar as the old, partial, "minimal" demands of the masses clash with the destructive and degrading tendencies of decadent capitalism—and this occurs at each step—the Fourth International advances a system of *transitional demands*, the essence of which is contained in the fact that ever more openly and decisively they will be directed against the very bases of the bourgeois regime. The old "minimal program" is superseded by the *transitional program*, the task of which lies in systematic mobilization of the masses for the proletarian revolution.

[EDITORS' NOTE: At this point, there is a discussion of possible transitional demands—a sliding scale of wages to keep pace with inflation, and a sliding scale of hours to eliminate unemployment by reducing the workday to provide jobs for all—which would seem reasonable to most people but which come into conflict with the continued existence of capitalism. This is followed by a discussion of building a class-struggle left wing in the trade unions, and also the development of democratic shop-floor and factory committees. The program calls for the elimination of "business secrets" used to cheat the workers ("open the books!") and calls for the development of structures to establish workers' control of the workplace. The expropriation of capitalist enterprises and industries, and the nationalization of banks and the credit system, under the control of the working-class majority, are also posed.

The Transitional Program then discusses the tactical escalation of factory seizures (through sit-down strikes) and picket lines, defense guards to protect picket lines and other workers' actions, the development of workers' militias, and the general arming of the working class—all within the context of mass struggles carried on through the radicalizing organized labor movement, which would be subject to attack by repressive governments, by thugs employed by employers, by fascist gangs, etc. A discussion of the need for a workers and farmers alliance, and a discussion of the struggle against imperialism and war, are followed by an examination of the formula of a "workers' and farmers' government," defined as a popularization of the concept of working-class political rule (or "dictatorship of the proletariat"), which should be based on the democratic councils in workplaces and communities that the Russians called soviets.

A substantial section on the struggle against colonialism and imperialism, and the fight for the interests of the workers and peasants, within the economically "backward" countries is followed by substantial sections focusing on struggles in fascist countries and in the USSR. There are critical discussions of left-wing currents that are seen as succumbing to "opportunism and unprincipled revisionism" on the one hand and to "sectarianism" on the other. This is followed by a section entitled:

"Open the road to the woman worker! Open the road to the youth!" The Transitional Program then concludes with the following section:]

Under the Banner of the Fourth International!

Skeptics ask: But has the moment for the creation of the Fourth International yet arrived? It is impossible, they say, to create an International "artificially"; it can arise only out of great events, etc., etc. All of these objections merely show that skeptics are no good for the building of a new International. They are good for scarcely anything at all.

The Fourth International has already arisen out of great events: the greatest defeats of the proletariat in history. The cause for these defeats is to be found in the degeneration and perfidy of the old leadership. The class struggle does not tolerate an interruption. The Third International, following the Second, is dead for purposes of revolution. Long live the Fourth International![6]

But has the time yet arrived to proclaim its creation? . . . the skeptics are not quieted down. The Fourth International, we answer, has no need of being "proclaimed." It exists and it fights. Is it weak? Yes, its ranks are not numerous because it is still young. They are as yet chiefly cadres. But these cadres are pledges for the future. Outside of these cadres there does not exist a single revolutionary current on this planet really meriting the name. If our International be still weak in numbers, it is strong in doctrine, program, tradition, in the incomparable tempering of its cadres. Who does not perceive this today, let him in the meantime stand aside. Tomorrow it will become more evident.

The Fourth International, already today, is deservedly hated by the Stalinists, Social Democrats, bourgeois liberals, and fascists. There is not and there cannot be a place for it in any of the People's Fronts. It uncompromisingly gives battle to all political groupings tied to the apron-strings of the bourgeoisie. Its task—the abolition of capitalism's domination. Its aim—socialism. Its method—proletarian revolution.

Without inner democracy—no revolutionary education. Without discipline—no revolutionary action. The inner structure of the Fourth International is based on the principles of *democratic centralism*: full freedom in discussion, complete unity in action.

The present crisis in human culture is the crisis in the proletarian leadership. The advanced workers, united in the Fourth International, show their class the way out of the crisis. They offer a program based on international experience in the struggle of the proletariat and of all the oppressed of the world for liberation. They offer a spotless banner.

Workers—men and women—of all countries, place yourselves under the banner of the Fourth International. It is the banner of your approaching victory.

Notes

1. The "New Deal" was the plan of the Democratic Party and the U.S. government under President Franklin D. Roosevelt from 1933 until 1939 (when there was a step-up in U.S. preparations for World War II), designed to preserve capitalism by conceding sweeping social reforms during the Great Depression in the face of ferment and radicalization within the working class and other sectors of the population. See Howard Zinn's critical-minded anthology, *New Deal Thought* (Indianapolis: Bobbs-Merrill Co., 1966), and Irving Bernstein's glowing yet informative *A Caring Society: The New Deal, the Worker, and the Great Depression* (Boston: Houghton Mifflin Co., 1985); for a Trotskyist critique, see Art Preis, *Labor's Giant Step* (New York: Pathfinder Press, 1972), pp. 9–18, 44–49, 66–70, 72–81, 113–124.

    The "Popular Front" (also known as the People's Front) was a strategy developed in the mid-1930s by the Communist International. At the Comintern's Seventh World Congress (1935), Georgi Dimitroff argued: "Now the toiling masses in a number of capitalist countries are faced with the necessity of making a *definite* choice, and of making it today, not between proletarian dictatorship and bourgeois democracy, but between bourgeois democracy and fascism." (See Dimitroff, *The United Front, The Struggle Against Fascism and War*, New York: International Publishers, 1938, p. 110.) There was a special concern that the rise of the virulently militaristic, anti-Communist, and anti-Soviet dictatorship of Adolf Hitler in Germany—due in part to Communist sectarianism in refusing to work with other left-wing forces to prevent the Nazi rise to power—posed a direct threat to the so-called "homeland of socialism," the USSR, as well as to the existence of the workers' movement throughout Europe.

    Therefore, Dimitroff and others insisted, Communists and Social-Democrats should immediately form a working-class united front, then form a cross-class Popular Front with petty-bourgeois and liberal capitalist forces, for the purpose of creating electoral coalitions to elect Popular Front governments. Such governments should preserve capitalism and bourgeois democracy, but also implement substantial social reforms, and—most important—form a foreign policy alliance with the Soviet Union against Nazi Germany. On the development of this orientation, see E. H. Carr, *Twilight of the Comintern, 1930–1935* (New York: Pantheon Books, 1982).

According to U.S. Communist leader Earl Browder, "Roosevelt's programmatic utterances of 1937, when combined with the legislative program of the C.I.O. (his main labor support), provides a People's Front program of an advanced type." (See Browder, *The People's Front*, New York: International Publishers, 1938, p. 13.)

2. In Spain there were several major currents on the left—the largest component made up of the Iberian Anarchist Federation (FAI) and anarcho-syndicalist labor federation (the CNT), next being the Socialist Party of Spain and its labor federation (the UGT). The Stalinist-led Communist Party was initially fairly small, and also participated in the UGT. Split-offs from the CP (including what had once been a sizable Trotskyist-influenced current) formed the Unified Marxist Workers Party (POUM).

   In 1935 the Socialists and Communists formed an electoral and governmental Popular Front with bourgeois liberal forces, narrowly winning national elections. When a combined conservative-fascist-military uprising in 1936, led by General Francisco Franco, sought to overturn the democratically elected government, a civil war erupted. The Popular Front government of the Spanish Republic followed relatively conservative policies so as not to alienate liberal procapitalist forces inside and outside of Spain. Nonetheless, the more radical anarchists and POUM made far-reaching concessions to the policies and power of the Popular Front government, which in turn (particularly due to Stalinist influence) savagely repressed them. The moderate social policies of the government during the Spanish Civil War, however, undermined the effort to mobilize the Spanish masses against the reactionary generals, landowners, and conservative businessmen who led the right-wing insurgents. Franco's forces finally won in 1939. See Pierre Broué and Emile Temime, *Revolution and the Civil War in Spain* (Cambridge: MIT Press, 1970), and Ronald Fraser, *Blood of Spain, An Oral History of the Spanish Civil War* (New York: Pantheon Books, 1979). Also see Leon Trotsky, *The Spanish Republic (1931–39)*, edited by Naomi Allen and George Breitman (New York: Pathfinder Press, 1973).

3. In France a right-wing coup attempt in 1934 galvanized the working class, which was organized into a Social Democratic formation, the French Section of the Second International (SFIO), the French Communist Party (PCF), and a divided trade union movement—the antipolitical (syndicalist) CGT, led by onetime anarcho-syndicalist Léon Jouhaux, and the pro-Communist CGT-U. A powerful working-class united front, under Socialist-Communist leadership, came into being, and it seemed that the workers might take power. Instead the ferment was channeled into a 1936 electoral coalition which resulted in a Popular Front government—composed of the SFIO under Léon Blum, the PCF under Maurice Thorez, and a small liberal-capitalist Radical Party under Edouard Daladier. The government, led by Blum, carried out some social reforms but made numerous compromises with liberal-capitalist elements, dampened popular enthusiasm, and then fell in 1938, giving way to a Radical Party government led by Daladier (which overturned many of the

1936 reforms). See Jacques Danos and Marcel Gibelin, *June '36, Class Struggle and the Popular Front in France* (London: Bookmarks, 1986). Also see: *Leon Trotsky on France*, edited by David Salner (New York: Monad Press, 1979), and Leon Trotsky, *The Crisis of the French Section (1935–36)*, edited by Naomi Allen and George Breitman (New York: Pathfinder Press, 1977).

4. The Phrygian cap refers to the liberty cap of the French Republic; the swastika, of course, to the mystical Nordic symbol utilized by the extreme fascistic Nazi (or "National-Socialist") movement led by Adolf Hitler. A classic Trotskyist-influenced analysis of German and Italian fascism is Daniel Guérin's *Fascism and Big Business* (New York: Monad Books/Pathfinder Press, 1973); although R. Palme Dutt's *Fascism and Social Revolution* (New York: International Publishers, 1934) presents a documented analysis, marred by the influence of Stalinism, it nonetheless offers much of interest. Also see Franz Neumann's classic, *Behemoth: The Structure and Practice of National Socialism, 1933–1944* (New York: Harper & Row, 1966), and Michael N. Dobkowski and Isidor Wallimann, eds., *Radical Perspectives on the Rise of Fascism in Germany, 1919–1945* (New York: Monthly Review Press, 1989). An invaluable memoir by a participant in the German workers' movement in the period leading up to, spanning, and following Nazi rule is Oskar Hippe's *And Red is the Color of Our Flag* (London: Index Books, 1991), which also provides information on German Trotskyism and thoughtful analyses of German realities from World War I to the 1970s. Also see Leon Trotsky, *The Struggle Against Fascism in Germany*, edited by George Breitman and Merry Maisel (New York: Pathfinder Press, 1971).

5. Two useful studies on this phenomenon are: Peter Gay, *The Dilemma of Democratic Socialism, Eduard Bernstein's Challenge to Marx* (New York: Columbia University Press, 1952), and Carl E. Schorske, *German Social Democracy, 1905–1917* (Harvard: Harvard University Press, 1955).

6. On the Second International, for a Social Democratic account, see: Julius Braunthal, *History of the International, 1914–1943*, 2 vols. (New York: Frederick A. Praeger, 1967), and *History of the International, World Socialism, 1943–1968* (Boulder: Westview Press, 1980); for a Stalinist account, see J. Lenz, *The Rise and Fall of the Second International* (New York: International Publishers, 1932); and for a brief academic account, see James Joll, *The Second International, 1889–1914* (New York: Harper & Row, 1975).

    On the Third International; for a Trotskyist-influenced account, see C. L. R. James, *World Revolution, 1917–1936: The Rise and Fall of the Communist International* (Atlantic Highlands: Humanities Press, 1993); for a Stalinist account, William Z. Foster, *History of the Three Internationals, The World Socialist and Communist Movements From 1848 to the Present* (New York: International Publishers, 1955); for a scholarly account by a former Communist, see Fernando Claudin, *The Communist Movement, From Comintern to Cominform*, 2 vols. (New York: Monthly Review Press 1975).

On the Fourth International, see: Pierre Frank, *The Fourth International: The Long March of the Trotskyists* (London: Ink Links, 1979); Tom Barrett, ed. *Fifty Years of the Fourth International* (New York: Fourth Internationalist Tendency, 1990); Robert J. Alexander, *International Trotskyism, 1929–1985: A Documented Analysis of the Movement* (Durham: Duke University Press, 1992).

Gramsci*

Antonio Gramsci (1891–1937) was born in Sardinia, an island off the western coast of the Italian mainland. His father was a lower-echelon government employee, and the family had upwardly mobile aspirations despite a downwardly mobile reality. Intellectually alert and thoughtful, Gramsci won a scholarship to the University of Turin in 1911. Within two years he had joined the Italian Socialist Party, within which he became an educator and journalist. In 1919 he helped found a new revolutionary socialist weekly, *L'Ordine Nuovo* (New Order), which sought to apply the lessons of the Russian Revolution to Italian realities. *L'Ordine Nuovo* became the voice of a mass factory council movement associated with the general strike and factory occupations of 1920, which—so it seemed to many—"threatened" to overturn capitalism and bring the workers to power. The moderate leaders of the trade unions and Socialist Party quickly effected a compromise which ended the occupations and secured (for a short time) the survival of a liberal capitalist regime. In the face of the workers' militancy, the landed aristocracy and factory owners concluded that a right-wing counter-force was needed, and poured money and resources into the rising fascist movement. In the face of the Social-Democratic sell-out, Gramsci and many others on the Left

---

* "Real Dialectics" (pp. 15–16), "What Is to Be Done?" (pp. 169–172), "Leader" (pp. 209–212), and "Once Again on the Organic Capacities of the Working Class" (pp. 417–421) in Antonio Gramsci, *Selections from Political Writings (1921–1926)*, ed. and trans. Quintin Hoare (New York: International Publishers, 1978). Excerpts from "The Modern Prince" (pp. 144–158 and 192–200) and "State and Civil Society" (pp. 229–236), from *Selections from the Prison Notebooks of Antonio Gramsci*, ed. and trans. Quintin Hoare and Geoffrey Nowell Smith (New York: International Publishers, 1971. Reprinted with permission.

concluded that a new, revolutionary workers' party was needed, resulting in the founding of the Italian Communist Party in 1921.

In the early 1920s, in addition to being an important leader of the Italian Communist Party, Gramsci worked for the Communist International in Moscow and Vienna. The rise and succession of victories by the fascist movement headed by ex-Socialist Benito Mussolini was—obviously—of primary concern to Gramsci and his comrades, but they could not agree on what the party's orientation should be. Gramsci began to develop a perspective independent of a moderate, semi-Social Democratic line advanced by Angelo Tasca and what he viewed as a sectarian and ultra-left line represented by Amadeo Bordiga. From 1924 (when he was elected to the Italian parliament) until 1926, when Gramsci was arrested by the fascist regime, his perspective predominated. We can see its popularization in columns for the Communist Party press emphasizing the practical meaning of dialectics in the class struggle in Italy; stressing the importance of developing within the working class a genuine understanding of Marxism as a critical-minded method for comprehending reality; describing the process—which should be replicated in Italy—through which the Bolsheviks developed as an adequate revolutionary party in Russia, culminating in working-class rule; and exploring specifics of Italy's recent history and class struggle, of special concern to revolutionary-minded workers (READINGS #20, #21, #22, #23).

After his 1926 arrest, Gramsci spent more than ten years in prison, where his health was finally broken, and was released only when his death seemed imminent. Throughout his imprisonment there were strict limitations on what he was able to read. The political impact of Stalinism on many of his comrades—inside and outside the prison walls—imposed additional limitations and confusion. Despite this, he was able to fill thirty-four thick notebooks with an impressive range of political, social, historical, and cultural writings. The fact that everything he wrote was reviewed by fascist censors forced him to use code names and obscure formulations. The problem of Stalinism introduces additional obscurities: sometimes Gramsci seems to be adapting and giving the benefit of many doubts to official Communist policy of the late 1920s and early '30s, and at other times he appears to be sharply critical—using harsh formulations that appear to be equally applicable to fascism and Stalinism.

Such prison writings as *The Modern Prince* (READING #24) appear to be profound elaborations (not repudiations) of revolutionary Marxist political thought. Some interpretations of Gramsci's thought argue that his discussions of gradually building up working-class "hegemony" and conducting a "war of attrition" against capitalism (as opposed a revolutionary "frontal assault") anticipate the reformist Popular Front policies of the late 1930s and after. But Gramsci himself appears to view what he wrote as reflections that are developed very much within the Leninist political framework that he embraced unambiguously in the early 1920s (READING #25).

In reading Gramsci's work—as in reading any of the revolutionaries in this volume—it is possible to identify distinct parts that can be counterposed to each other. If instead we see these varied aspects of his thought as being interlinked, and as part of a revolutionary continuity from 1848 to 1940 and beyond, we will discover creative tensions and a vibrancy that would not otherwise be there.

READING #20: "Real Dialectics"—1921
READING #21: "What Is to Be Done?"—1923
READING #22: "Leader"—1924
READING #23: "Once Again on the Organic Capacities of the Working Class"—1926
READING #24: Prison Notebooks: *The Modern Prince* (excerpts)—1930–34
READING #25: Prison Notebooks: "State and Civil Society" (excerpt)—1933–34

READING #20
"Real Dialectics"

Events are the real dialectics of history. They transcend all arguments, all personal judgments, all vague and irresponsible wishes. Events, with the inexorable logic of their development, give the worker and peasant masses, who are conscious of their destiny, these lessons. The class struggle at a certain moment reaches a stage in which the proletariat no longer finds in bourgeois legality, i.e. in the bourgeois State apparatus (armed forces, courts, administration), the elementary guarantee and defense of its elementary right to life, to freedom, to personal safety, to daily bread. It is then forced to create its own legality, to create its own apparatus of resistance and defense. At certain moments in the life of the people, this is an absolute historical necessity, transcending every desire, every wish, every whim, every personal impulse. Events present themselves as a universal fatality, with the overwhelming momentum of natural phenomena. Men, as individuals and *en masse*, find themselves placed brutally before the following dilemma: chances of death one hundred, chances of life ten, a choice must be made. And men always choose the chances of life, even if these are slight, even if they only offer a wretched and exhausted life. They fight for these slight chances, and their vitality is such and their passion so great that they break every obstacle and sweep away even the most awesome apparatus of power.

This is the situation which the real dialectics of history creates for men at certain moments—the decisive moments in the painful and bloody development of mankind. No human will can create situations of this kind; no little man, even if he puffs out his cheeks and distills from his brain the words which most touch hearts and stir the blood, can create situations of this kind. They are the blazing brazier in which flow together all the passions and all the hatreds which only the sight of violent death can arouse in the masses. Only this can be considered as a revolutionary situation in this historical period, which has as its immediate past experience the deeds of the Spartacists, Hungary, Ireland, Bavaria. In this situation, there is no middle term to choose; and if one fights, it is necessary to win.

Today, we do not find ourselves in such a situation. Today, we can still choose with a certain freedom. The freedom of choice imposes certain duties upon us, absolute duties which concern the life of the people and are inherent in the future of the masses who suffer and hope. Today, there exists only one form of revolutionary solidarity: to win. It therefore demands of us that we should not neglect any single element that might put us in a condition to win. Today, there exists a party that truly expresses the interests of the proletariat; that expresses the interests not only of the Italian proletariat, but of the workers' International as a whole. Today, the workers must have and can have faith. The Italian workers, maintaining an iron discipline, without a single exception, in response to the slogans of the Communist Party, will finally show that they have emerged from the state of revolutionary infantilism in which their movement has hitherto floundered. They will show that they are worthy and capable of victory.

READING #21

"What Is to Be Done?"

Dear Friends of the *Voce*,

I have read in *Voce*, no. 10 (15 September) the interesting discussion between comrade G. P. of Turin and comrade S. V. Is the discussion closed? Might one ask that the discussion remain open for many more issues, and invite all young workers of good will to take part in it, expressing their opinions on the subject sincerely and with intellectual honesty?

How the Problem Should Be Posed

I shall start off, and I shall certainly say that, at least in my view, comrade S. V. has not posed the problem properly and has fallen into certain errors that are extremely serious from his own point of view.

Why was the Italian working class defeated? Because it was not united? Because fascism succeeded in defeating the Socialist Party, the traditional party of the toiling population, not only physically but also ideologically? Because the Communist Party did not develop rapidly in the years 1921–2, and did not succeed in grouping around itself the majority of the proletariat and the peasant masses?

Comrade S. V. does not pose these questions. He replies to all the anguished concern expressed in comrade G. P.'s letter with the assertion that the existence of a true revolutionary party would have been enough, and that its future organization will be enough in the future, when the working class has recovered the possibility of movement. But is all that true, or at least in what sense and within what limits is it true?

Comrade S. V. suggests to comrade G. P. that he should not go on thinking in fixed schemas, but should think in other schemas—which he does not specify. But it is in fact essential to specify. So here is what seems immediately necessary to do. Here is what the "beginning" of the working class's task must be. It is necessary to carry out a pitiless self-criticism of our weakness, and to begin by asking ourselves why we lost, who we were, what we wanted, where we wished to go. But there is also something else which must be done first (one always finds that the beginning always has another . . . beginning!): it is necessary to fix the criteria, the principles, the ideological basis for our very criticism.

Does the Working Class Have Its Own Ideology?

Why have the Italian proletarian parties always been weak from a revolutionary point of view? Why have they failed, when they should have passed from words to action? They did not know the situation in which they had to operate, they did not know the terrain on which they should have given battle. Just think: in more than thirty years of life, the Socialist Party has not produced a single book which studies the socio-economic structure of Italy. There does not exist a single book which studies the Italian political parties, their class links, their significance. Why did reformism sink such deep roots in the Po valley? Why is the Catholic Popular Party more successful in northern and central than in southern Italy, where the population after all is more backward and should therefore more easily follow a confessional party? Why are the big landowners in Sicily separatists but not the peasants, whereas in Sardinia the peasants are separatists and not the big landowners? Why did the reformism of De Felice, Drago, Tasca di Cutó and their ilk develop in Sicily and not elsewhere? Why was there an armed struggle between fascists and nationalists in southern Italy which did not occur elsewhere?

We do not know Italy. Worse still: we lack the proper instruments for knowing Italy as it really is. It is therefore almost impossible for us to make predictions, to orient ourselves, to establish lines of action which have some likelihood of being accurate. There exists no history of the Italian working class. There exists no history of the peasant class. What was the importance of the 1898 events in Milan? What lesson did they furnish? What was the importance of the 1904 strike in Milan? How many workers know that then, for the first time, the necessity of the proletarian dictatorship was explicitly asserted? What significance has syndicalism had in Italy? Why has it been successful among agricultural workers and not among the industrial workers? What is the importance of the Republican party? Why are there republicans wherever there are anarchists? What is the importance and the meaning of the phenomenon of syndicalist elements going over to nationalism before the Libyan War, and the repetition of the phenomenon on a larger scale with fascism?

It is enough to pose these questions to perceive that we are completely ignorant, that we are without orientation. It seems that no one in Italy has ever thought, ever studied, ever done any research. It seems that the Italian working class has never had its own conception of the life, the history, the development of human society. And yet the working class does have its own conception: historical materialism. And yet the working class has had great teachers (Marx, Engels) who have shown how to examine facts and situations, and how to draw from one's examination guides to action.

This is our weakness, this is the main reason for the defeat of the Italian revolutionary parties: not to have had an ideology; not to have disseminated it among the masses; not to have strengthened the consciousness of their militants with certitudes of a moral and psychological character. What wonder that some workers have become fascists? What wonder if S. V. himself says at one point: "who knows, even we, if we were convinced, might become fascists"? (Such statements should not be made even as jokes, even as hypotheses for the sake of argument.) What wonder, if another article in the same issue of *Voce* says: "We are not anti-clerical"? Are we not anti-clerical? What does that mean? That we are not anti-clerical in a masonic sense, from the rationalist point of view of the bourgeois? It is necessary to say this, but it is also necessary to say that we, the working class, are indeed anti-clerical, inasmuch as we are materialists; that we have a conception of the world which transcends all religions and all philosophies born hitherto on the terrain of class-divided society. Unfortunately . . . we do not have that conception, and this is the reason for all these theoretical errors, which also have their reflection in practice and have so far led us to defeat and to fascist oppression.

The Beginning . . . of the Beginning!

What is to be done then? Where to begin? Well: in my view it is necessary to begin precisely from this. From a study of the doctrine which belongs to the working class, which is the philosophy of the working class, which is the sociology of the working class: from a study of historical materialism, from a study of Marxism. Here is an immediate task for the groups of friends of the *Voce*: to meet, buy books, organize lessons and discussions on this subject, form solid criteria for research and study, and criticize the past—in order to be stronger in the future and win.

The *Voce* should, in every possible way, help this attempt—by publishing courses of lessons and discussions, by giving rational bibliographical information, by replying to readers' questions, by stimulating their good will. The less that has been done up till now, the more it is necessary to do, and with the greatest possible rapidity. Destiny is pressing in upon us: the Italian petty bourgeoisie, which had placed its hopes and its faith in fascism, is daily seeing its house of cards collapse. Fascist ideology has lost its capacity to expand, and indeed is losing ground. The first dawn of the new proletarian day is appearing anew.

Signed Giovanni Masci, *Voce della Gioventù*,
1 November 1923.

READING #22
"Leader"

Every State is a dictatorship. Every State cannot avoid having a government, made up of a small number of men, who in their turn organize themselves around one who is endowed with greater ability and greater perspicacity. So long as a State is necessary, so long as it is historically necessary to govern men, whichever the ruling class may be, the problem will arise of having leaders, of having a "leader." The fact that socialists, even ones who call themselves Marxists and revolutionaries, say they want the dictatorship of the proletariat but not the dictatorship of leaders; say they do not want command to be individualized and personalized; in other words, say they want dictatorship, but not in the form in which it is historically possible—merely reveals a whole political stance, a whole "revolutionary" theoretical formation.

In the question of proletarian dictatorship, the key problem is not the physical personification of the function of command. The key problem consists in the nature of the relations which the leaders or leader have with the party of the working class, in the relations which exist between this party and the working class. Are these purely hierarchical, of a military type, or are they of a historical and organic nature? Are the leader and the party elements of the working class, are they a part of the working class, do they represent its deepest and most vital interests and aspirations, or are they an excrescence or simply a violent superimposition? How was this party formed, how did it develop, through what process did the selection of the men who lead it take place? Why did it become the party of the working class? Did this occur by chance?

The problem becomes that of the whole historical development of the working class, which is gradually formed in struggle against the bourgeoisie, winning a few victories and suffering many defeats: the historical development, moreover, not just of the working class of a single country, but of the entire working class of the world—with its superficial differentiations, which are nevertheless so important at any single moment in time, and with its basic unity and homogeneity. The problem also becomes that of the vitality of Marxism; of whether it is or is not the most certain and profound interpretation of nature and of history; of whether it can complement the politician's inspired intuition by an infallible method, an instrument of the greatest precision for exploring the future, foreseeing mass events, leading them and hence controlling them.

The international proletariat has had, and still has, the living example of a revolutionary party exercising working-class dictatorship. It has had, and unfortunately no longer has, the most typical and expressive living example of what a revolutionary leader is—comrade Lenin.

Comrade Lenin was the initiator of a new process of development of history. But he was this, because he was also the exponent and the last, most individualized moment of a whole process of development of past history, not just of Russia but of the whole world. Did he become the leader of the Bolshevik Party of chance? Did the Bolshevik Party become the leading party of the Russian proletariat, and hence of the Russian nation, by chance? The selection process lasted thirty years; it was extremely arduous; it often assumed what appeared to be the strangest and most absurd forms. It took place, in the international field, in contact with the most advanced capitalist civilizations of central and western Europe, in the struggle of the parties and factions which made up the Second International before the War. It continued within the minority of international socialism which remained at least partially immune from the social-patriotic contagion. It was renewed in Russia in the struggle to win the majority of the proletariat; in the struggle to understand and interpret the needs and aspirations of a numberless peasant class, scattered over an immense territory. It still continues, every day, because every day it is necessary to understand, to foresee, to take measures.

This selection process was a struggle of factions and small groups; it was also an individual struggle; it meant splits and fusions, arrest, exile, prison, assassination attempts; it meant resistance to discouragement and to pride; it meant suffering hunger while having millions in gold available; it meant preserving the spirit of a simple worker on the throne of the Tsars; it meant not despairing even when all seemed lost, but starting again, patiently and tenaciously; it meant keeping a cool head and a smile when others lost their heads. The Russian Communist Party, with its leader Lenin, bound itself up so tightly with the entire development of its Russian proletariat, with the whole development therefore of the entire Russian nation, that it is not possible even to imagine one without the other; the proletariat as a ruling class without the Communist Party being the governing party; hence without the Central Committee of the party being the inspirer of government policy; and hence without Lenin being the leader of the State.

The very attitude of the great majority of Russian bourgeois, who used to say "our ideal too would be a republic headed by Lenin without the Communist Party," had great historical significance. It was the proof that the proletariat no longer merely exercised physical domination, but dominated spiritually as well. At bottom, in a confused way, the Russian bourgeoisie too understood that Lenin could not have become and could not have remained leader of the State without the domination of the proletariat, without the Communist Party being the government party. Its class consciousness prevented it as yet from acknowledging, beyond its physical, immediate defeat, also its ideological and historical defeat. But already the doubt was there, expressed in that typical sentiment.

Another question arises. Is it possible, today, in the period of the world revolution, for there to exist "leaders" outside the working class; for there to exist non-Marxist leaders, who are not linked closely to the class which embodies the progressive development of all mankind? In Italy we have the fascist régime, we have Benito Mussolini as fascism's leader, we have an official ideology in which the "leader" is deified, declared to be infallible, prophesied as the organizer and inspirer of a reborn Holy Roman Empire. We see printed in the newspapers, every day, scores and hundreds of telegrams of homage from the vast local tribes to the "leader." We see the photographs: the hardened mask of a face which we have already seen at socialist meetings. We know that face: we know that rolling of the eyes in their sockets, eyes which in the past sought with their ferocious movements to bring shudders to the bourgeoisie, and today seek to do the same to the proletariat. We know that fist always clenched in a threat. We know the whole mechanism, the whole paraphernalia, and we understand that it may impress and tug at the heartstrings of bourgeois school-children. It is really impressive, even when seen close to, and has an awesome effect. But "leader"?

We saw the Red Week of June 1914. More than three million work-ers were on the streets, called out by Benito Mussolini, who for about a year since the Roccagorga massacre had been preparing them for the great day, with all the oratorical and journalistic means at the disposal of the then "leader" of the Socialist Party, of Benito Mussolini—from Scalarini's lampoon to his great trial at the Milan Assizes. Three mil-lion workers were on the streets: but the "leader," Benito Mussolini, was missing. He was missing as a "leader," not as an individual; for people say that as an individual he was courageous, and defied the cordons and the muskets of the *carabinieri* in Milan. He was missing as a "leader," because he was not one. Because, by his own admission, within the lead-ership of the Socialist Party he could not even manage to get the better of the wretched intrigues of Arturo Vella or Angelica Balabanoff.

He was then, as today, the quintessential model of the Italian petty bourgeois: a rabid, ferocious mixture of all the detritus left on the national soil by the centuries of domination by foreigners and priests. He could not be the leader of the proletariat; he became the dictator of the bour-geoisie, which loves ferocious faces when it becomes Bourbon again, and which hoped to see the same terror in the working class which it itself had felt before those rolling eyes and that clenched fist raised in menace.

The dictatorship of the proletariat is expansive, not repressive. A continuous movement takes place from the base upwards, a continuous replacement through all the capillaries of society, a continuous circula-tion of men. The leader whom we mourn today found a decomposing society, a human dust, without order or discipline. For in the course of five years of war, production—the source of all social life—had dried up. Everything was re-ordered and reconstructed, from the factory to the government, with the instruments and under the leadership and control of the proletariat, i.e. of a class new to government and to history.

Benito Mussolini has seized governmental power and is holding onto it by means of the most violent and arbitrary repression. He has not had to organize a class, but merely the personnel of an administration. He has dismantled a few of the State's mechanisms more to see how it is done and to learn the trade than from any primary necessity. His ideas are all contained in the physical mask, the eyes rolling in their sockets, the clenched fist ever raised in menace.

Rome has seen these dusty scenarios before. It saw Romulus, it saw Augustus Caesar, and at its twilight it saw Romulus Augustulus.

READING #23

"Once Again on the Organic Capacities of the Working Class"

Six years have passed since September 1920. In the intervening period, many things have changed among the working-class masses who in September 1920 occupied the factories in the metal-working industry. A notable part of the most active and combative workers, who in those years of heroic struggle represented the vanguard of the working class, are outside Italy. Marked with a triple cross on the black lists; after months and months of unemployment; after having tried every way (by changing trade, isolating themselves in small plants, etc., etc.) of remaining in their homeland to continue the revolutionary struggle, and to reconstruct each day the links which each day reaction was destroying; after unheard of sacrifices and sufferings—they were forced to emigrate. Six years are a long time. A new generation has already entered the factories: of workers who in 1920 were still adolescents or children, and who at most took part in political life by acting out in the streets the war between the Red Army and the Polish Army, and by refusing to be the Polish one even in a game. Yet the occupation of the factories has not been forgotten by the masses, and this is true not just of the working-class masses but also of the peasant masses. It was the general test of the Italian revolutionary class, which as a class showed that it was mature; that it was capable of initiative; that it possessed an incalculable wealth of creative and organizational energies. If the movement failed, the responsibility cannot be laid at the door of the working class as such, but at that of the Socialist Party, which failed in its duty; which was incapable and inept; which was at the tail of the working class not at its head.

The occupation of the factories is still on the agenda in the conversations and discussions which take place at the base, between vanguard elements and those who are more backward and passive, or between the former and class enemies. Recently, in a meeting of peasants and artisans in a village of Southern Italy (all sympathizers of our party), after a brief report on the present situation two kinds of questions were raised by those present.

1. What is happening in Russia? How are the local authorities organized in Russia? How do they succeed in getting the workers and peasants to agree, given that the former want to buy foodstuffs cheap and the latter want to sell them at a decent price? Are the officers of the Red Army and the functionaries of the Soviet State like officers and functionaries in our country? Are they a different class, or are they workers and peasants?

2. Explain to us why we workers (an artisan was speaking, a blacksmith) abandoned the factories which we had occupied in September 1920. The gentry still say to us: "Did you occupy the factories, yes or no? Why then did you abandon them? Certainly because without 'capital' one cannot do anything. You sent away the capitalists and so the 'capital' was not there, and you went bankrupt." Explain the whole question to us, so that we will be able to reply. We know that the gentry are wrong, but we do not know how to put our arguments and often have to shut our mouths.

The revolutionary impact of the occupation of the factories was enormous, both in Italy and abroad. Why? Because the working masses saw in it a confirmation of the Russian revolution, in a Western country more industrially advanced than Russia, with a working class that was better organized, technically more skilled, and industrially more homogenous and cohesive than was the Russian proletariat in October 1917. Are we capable of running production for ourselves, in accordance with our interests and a plan of our own?—wondered the workers. Are we capable of reorganizing production in such a way as to transfer society as a whole onto new tracks leading to the abolition of classes and economic equality? The test was positive, within the limits in which it took place and developed; within the limits in which the experiment could be carried through; in the sphere of the problems that were posed and resolved.

The experiment was limited, in general, to relations within the factory. Contacts between one factory and another were minimal from the industrial point of view; they occurred only for purposes of military defense, and even in this sense they were rather empirical and rudimentary.

The positive aspects of the occupation of the factories can be briefly resumed under the following headings.

1. Capacity for self-government of the mass of workers. In normal mass activity, the working class generally appears as a passive element waiting orders. During struggles, strikes, etc., the masses are required to

show the following qualities: solidarity, obedience to the mass organization, faith in their leaders, a spirit of resistance and sacrifice. But the masses are static, like an immense body with a tiny head.

The occupation of the factories required an unprecedented multiplicity of active, leading elements. Each factory had to put together its own government, which was invested at once with political and with industrial authority. Only a part of the technicians and white-collar employees remained at their posts; the majority deserted the plants. The workers had to choose from their own ranks technicians, clerks, managers, foremen, accountants, etc. etc. This task was performed brilliantly. The old management, when it took up its functions again, had no administrative difficulties to overcome. The normal functions of an enterprise had been kept up to date, in spite of the fact that the technical and administrative personnel was extremely limited and made up of "crude, ignorant" workers.

2. Capacity of the mass of workers to maintain or exceed the capitalist order's level of production. The following occurred. The work force was reduced—because a tiny proportion did desert their work; because a certain proportion was assigned to military defense; because a certain proportion was working to produce objects that were not precisely for current use, although they were very useful for the proletariat; and because workers had had to replace the majority of technicians and white-collar workers who had deserted—and in spite of all this, production kept up to the earlier level and often exceeded it. More cars were produced at FIAT than before the occupation, and the "workers'" cars displayed to the public daily by proletarian FIAT were not among the least of the reasons for the undeniable sympathy which the occupation enjoyed among the general population of the city of Turin, including among intellectuals and even tradesmen (who accepted the workers' goods as excellent currency).

3. Limitless capacity for initiative and creation of the working masses. An entire volume would be needed to cover this point fully. Initiative developed in every direction. In the industrial field, because of the need to resolve technical questions of industrial organization and production. In the military field, in order to turn every slight possibility into an instrument of defense. In the artistic field, through the capacity shown on Sundays to find ways of entertaining the masses by theatrical and other performances, in which *mise-en-scène*, production, everything was

devised by the workers. It was really necessary to see with one's own eyes old workers, who seemed broken down by decades upon decades of oppression and exploitation, stand upright even in a physical sense during the period of the occupation—see them develop fantastic activities; suggesting, helping, always active day and night. It was necessary to see these and other sights, in order to be convinced how limitless the latent powers of the masses are, and how they are revealed and develop swiftly as soon as the conviction takes root among the masses that they are arbiters and masters of their own destinies.

As a class, the Italian workers who occupied the factories revealed themselves to be up to their tasks and functions. All the problems which the needs of the movement posed for them to resolve were resolved brilliantly. They could not resolve the problems of re-stocking or communications, because the railways and merchant fleet were not occupied. They could not resolve the financial problems, because the institutes of credit and commercial firms were not occupied. They could not resolve the big national and international problems, because they did not conquer State power. These problems should have been confronted by the Socialist Party and by the unions, which instead capitulated shamefully, giving the immaturity of the masses as a pretext. In reality, it was the leaders who were immature and incapable, not the class. This was the reason why the Livorno split took place and a new party was created, the Communist Party.

READING #24
Prison Notebooks:
"The Modern Prince" (excerpts)

Elements of Politics

It really must be stressed that it is precisely the first elements, the most elementary things, which are the first to be forgotten. However, if they are repeated innumerable times, they become the pillars of politics and of any collective action whatsoever.

The first element is that there really do exist rulers and ruled, leaders and led. The entire science and art of politics are based on this primordial, and (given certain general conditions)[1] irreducible fact. The origins of this fact are a problem apart, which will have to be studied separately (at least one could and should study how to minimize the fact and eliminate it, by altering certain conditions which can be identified as operating in this sense), but the fact remains that there do exist rulers and ruled, leaders and led. Given this fact, it will have to be considered how one can lead most effectively (given certain ends); hence how the leaders may best be prepared (and it is more precisely in this that the first stage of the art and science of politics consists); and how, on the other hand, one can know the lines of least resistance, or the most rational lines along which to proceed if one wishes to secure the obedience of the led or ruled. In the formation of leaders, one premise is fundamental: is it the intention that there should always be rulers and ruled, or is the objective to create the conditions in which this division is no longer necessary? In other words, is the initial premise the perpetual division of the human race, or the belief that this division is only an historical fact, corresponding to certain conditions? Yet it must be clearly understood that the division between rulers and ruled—though in the last analysis it has its origin in a division between social groups—is in fact, things being as they are, also to be found within the group itself, even where it is a socially homogeneous one. In a certain sense it may be said that this division is created by the division of labor, is merely a technical fact, and those who see everything purely in terms of "technique," "technical" necessity, etc., speculate on this coexistence of different causes in order to avoid the fundamental problem.

Since the division between rulers and ruled exists even within the same group, certain principles have to be fixed upon and strictly observed. For it is in this area that the most serious "errors" take place, and that the most criminal weaknesses and the hardest to correct are revealed. For the belief is common that obedience must be automatic, once it is a question of the same group; and that not only must it come about without any demonstration of necessity or rationality being needed, but it must be unquestioning. (Some believe, and what is worse act in the belief, that obedience "will come" without being solicited, without the path which has to be followed being pointed out.) Thus it is difficult to cure leaders completely of "Cadornism"[2] or the conviction that a thing will be done because the leader considers it just and reasonable that it should be done: if it is not done, the blame is put on those who "ought to have . . . ," etc. Thus too it is hard to root out the criminal habit of permitting useless sacrifices through neglect. Yet common sense shows that the majority of collective (political) disasters occur because no attempt has been made to avoid useless sacrifice, or because manifestly no account has been taken of the sacrifices of others and their lives have been gambled with. Everyone has heard officers from the front recount how the soldiers were quite ready to risk their lives when necessary, but how on the other hand they would rebel when they saw themselves overlooked. For example: a company would be capable of going for days without food because it could see that it was physically impossible for supplies to get through; but it would mutiny if a single meal was missed as a result of neglect or bureaucratism, etc.

This principle extends to all actions demanding sacrifices. Hence, after every disaster, it is necessary first of all to enquire into the responsibility of the leaders, in the most literal sense. (For example: a front is made up of various sectors, and each sector has its leaders; it is possible that the leaders of one sector are more responsible for a particular defeat than those of another; but it is purely a question of degree—never of anybody being exempt from responsibility.)

The principle once posed that there are leaders and led, rulers and ruled, it is true that parties have up till now been the most effective way of developing leaders and leadership. (Parties may present themselves under the most diverse names, even calling themselves the anti-party or the "negation of the parties"; in reality, even the so-called "individualists" are party men, only they would like to be "party chiefs" by the grace of God or the idiocy of those who follow them.)[3]

Development of the general concept contained in the expression "State spirit."[4] This expression has a quite precise, historically determinate meaning. But the problem is raised: does there exist something similar to what is called "State spirit" in every serious movement, that is to say in every movement which is not the arbitrary expression of more or less justified individualisms? Meanwhile "State spirit" presupposes "continuity," either with the past, or with tradition, or with the future; that is, it presupposes that every act is a moment in a complex process, which has already begun and which will continue. The responsibility for this process, of being actors in this process, of being in solidarity with forces which are materially "unknown" but which nevertheless feel themselves to be active and operational—and of which account is taken, as if they were physically "material" and present—is precisely in certain cases called "State spirit." It is obvious that such awareness of "duration" must be concrete and not abstract, that is to say in a certain sense must not go beyond certain limits. Let us say that the narrowest limits are a generation back and a generation to come. This represents no short period, since generations cannot be calculated simply as thirty years each—the last thirty and the next thirty respectively. They have to be calculated organically, which at least as far as the past is concerned is easy to understand: we feel ourselves linked to men who are now extremely old, and who represent for us the *past* which still lives among us, which we need to know and to settle our accounts with, which is one of the elements of the present and one of the premises of the future. We also feel ourselves linked to our children, to the generations which are being born and growing up, and for which we are responsible. (The *cult* of tradition, which has a tendentious value, is something different; it implies a choice and a determinate goal—that is to say, it is the basis for an ideology.) However, if it can be said that a "State spirit" in this sense is to be found in everybody, it is necessary from time to time to combat distortions of it or deviations from it.

"The act for the act's sake," struggle for the sake of struggle, etc., and especially mean, petty individualism, which is anyway merely an arbitrary satisfying of passing whims, etc. (In reality, the question is still that of Italian "apoliticism," which takes on these various picturesque and bizarre forms.) Individualism is merely brutish apoliticism; sectarianism is apoliticism, and if one looks into it carefully is a form of personal following [*clientela*], lacking the party spirit which is the fundamental component of "State spirit." The demonstration that party spirit is the basic component of "State spirit" is one of the most critically important assertions to uphold. Individualism on the other hand is a brutish element, "admired by foreigners," like the behavior of the inmates of a zoological garden. [1933]

The Political Party

It has already been said that the protagonist of the new Prince could not in the modern epoch be an individual hero, but only the political party. That is to say, at different times, and in the various internal relations of the various nations, that determinate party which has the aim of founding a new type of State (and which was rationally and historically created for that end).

It should be noted that in those régimes which call themselves totalitarian,[5] the traditional function of the institution of the Crown is in fact taken over by the particular party in question, which indeed is totalitarian precisely in that it fulfills this function. Although every party is the expression of a social group, and of one social group only, nevertheless in certain given conditions certain parties represent a single social group precisely in so far as they exercise a balancing and arbitrating function between the interests of their group and those of other groups, and succeed in securing the development of the group which they represent with the consent and assistance of the allied groups—if not out and out with that of groups which are definitely hostile. The constitutional formula of the king, or president of the republic, who "reigns but does not govern" is the juridical expression of this function of arbitration, the concern of the constitutional parties not to "unmask" the Crown or the president. The formulae stating that it is not the head of State who is responsible for the actions of the government, but his ministers, are the casuistry behind which lies the general principle of safeguarding certain conceptions—the unity of the State; the consent of the governed to State action—whatever the current personnel of the government, and whichever party may be in power.

With the totalitarian party, these formulae lose their meaning; hence the institutions which functioned within the context of such formulae become less important. But the function itself is incorporated in the party, which will exalt the abstract concept of the "State," and seek by various means to give the impression that it is working actively and effectively as an "impartial force." [1933–34: first version 1930–32.]

Is political action (in the strict sense) necessary, for one to be able to speak of a "political party"? It is observable that in the modern world, in many countries, the organic and fundamental parties have been compelled by the exigencies of the struggle or for other reasons to split into fractions—each one of which calls itself a "party" and even an independent party. Hence the intellectual General Staff of the organic party often does not belong to any of these fractions, but operates as if it were a directive force standing on its own, above the parties, and sometimes is even believed to be such by the public. This function can be studied with greater precision if one starts from the point of view that a newspaper too (or group of newspapers), a review (or group of reviews), is a "party" or "fraction of a party" or "a function of a particular party." Think of the role of *The Times* in England; or that which *Corriere della Sera*[6] used to have in Italy; or again of the role of the so-called "informational press"[7] with its claim to be "apolitical"; or even of that of the sporting and technical press. Moreover, the phenomenon reveals interesting aspects in countries where there is a single, totalitarian, governing party. For the functions of such a party are no longer directly political, but merely technical ones of propaganda and public order, and moral and cultural influence. The political function is indirect. For, even if no other legal parties exist, other parties in fact always do exist and other tendencies which cannot be legally coerced; and, against these, polemics are unleashed and struggles are fought as in a game of blind man's buff. In any case it is certain that in such parties cultural functions predominate, which means that political language becomes jargon. In other words, political questions are disguised as cultural ones, and as such become insoluble.

But there is one traditional party too with an essentially "indirect" character—which in other words presents itself explicitly as purely "educative" (*lucus*, etc.),[8] moral, cultural [*sic*]. This is the anarchist movement. Even so-called direct (terrorist) action is conceived of a "propaganda" by example. This only further confirms the judgment that the anarchist movement is not autonomous, but exists on the margin of other parties, "to educate them." One may speak of an "anarchism" inherent in every organic party. (What are the "intellectual or theoretical anarchists" except an aspect of this "marginalism" in relation to the great parties of the dominant social groups?) The "economists sect"[9] itself was an historical aspect of this phenomenon.

Thus there seem to be the two types of party which reject the idea of immediate political action as such. Firstly, there is that which is constituted by an élite of men of culture, who have the function of providing leadership of a cultural and general ideological nature for a great movement of interrelated parties (which in reality are fractions of one and the same organic party). And secondly, in the more recent period, there is a type of party constituted this time not by an élite but by masses—who as such have no other political function than a generic loyalty, of a military kind, to a visible or invisible political center. (Often the visible center is the mechanism of command of forces which are unwilling to show themselves in the open, but only operate indirectly, through proxies and a "proxy ideology.")[10] The mass following is simply for "manœuvre," and is kept happy by means of moralizing sermons, emotional stimuli, and messianic myths of an awaited golden age, in which all present contradictions and miseries will be automatically resolved and made well. [1933]

To write the history of a political party, it is necessary in reality to confront a whole series of problems of a much less simple kind than

Robert Michels, for example, believes—though he is considered an expert on the subject. In what will the history of a party consist? Will it be a simple narrative of the internal life of a political organization? How it comes into existence, the first groups which constitute it, the ideological controversies through which its program and its conception of the world and of life are formed? In such a case, one would merely have a history of certain intellectual groups, or even sometimes the political biography of a single personality. The study will therefore have to have a vaster and more comprehensive framework.

The history will have to be written of a particular mass of men who have followed the founders of the party, sustained them with their trust, loyalty and discipline, or criticized them "realistically" by dispersing or remaining passive before certain initiatives. But will this mass be made up solely of members of the party? Will it be sufficient to follow the congresses, the votes, etc., that is to say the whole nexus of activities and modes of existence through which the mass following of a party manifests its will? Clearly it will be necessary to take some account of the social group of which the party in question is the expression and the most advanced element. The history of a party, in other words, can only be the history of a particular social group. But this group is not isolated; it has friends, kindred groups, opponents, enemies. The history of any given party can only emerge from the complex portrayal of the totality of society and State (often with international ramifications too). Hence it may be said that to write the history of a party means nothing less than to write the general history of a country from a monographic viewpoint, in order to highlight a particular aspect of it. A party will have had greater or less significance and weight precisely to the extent to which its particular activity has been more or less decisive in determining a country's history.

We may thus see that from the way in which the history of a party is written there emerges the author's conception of what a party is and should be. The sectarian will become excited over petty internal matters, which will have an esoteric significance for him, and fill him with mystical enthusiasm. The historian, though giving everything its due importance in the overall picture, will emphasize above all the real effectiveness of the party, its determining force, positive and negative, in having prevented other events from taking place. [1933–4: first version 1932.]

The problem of knowing when a party was actually formed, i.e., undertook a precise and permanent task, gives rise to many arguments and often too, unfortunately, to a kind of conceit which is no less absurd and dangerous than the "conceit of nations"[11] of which Vico speaks. It is true that one may say that a party is never complete and fully-formed, in the sense that every development creates new tasks and functions, and in the sense that for certain parties the paradox is true that they are complete and fully-formed only when they no longer exist—i.e., when their existence has become historically redundant. Thus, since every party is only the nomenclature for a class, it is obvious that the party which proposes to put an end to class divisions will only achieve complete self-fulfillment when it ceases to exist because classes, and therefore their expressions, no longer exist. But here I wish to refer to a particular moment of this process of development, the moment succeeding that in which something may either exist or not exist—in the sense that the necessity for it to exist has not yet become "imperative," but depends to a great extent on the existence of individuals of exceptional will-power and of exceptional will.

When does a party become historically necessary? When the conditions for its "triumph," for its inevitable progress to State power, are at least in the process of formation, and allow their future evolution—all things going normally—to be foreseen. But when can one say, given such conditions, that a party cannot be destroyed by normal means? To give an answer, it is necessary to develop the following line of reasoning: for a party to exist, three fundamental elements (three groups of elements) have to converge:

1. A mass element, composed of ordinary, average men, whose participation takes the form of discipline and loyalty, rather than any creative spirit or organizational ability. Without these the party would not exist, it is true, but it is also true that neither could it exist with these alone. They are a force in so far as there is somebody to centralize, organize and discipline them. In the absence of this cohesive force, they would scatter into an impotent diaspora and vanish into nothing. Admittedly any of these elements might become a cohesive force, but I am speaking of them precisely at the moment when they are not this nor in any condition to become it—or if they are, it is only in a limited sphere, politically ineffectual and of no consequence.

2. The principal cohesive element, which centralizes nationally and renders effective and powerful a complex of forces which left to themselves would count for little or nothing. This element is endowed with great cohesive, centralizing and disciplinary powers; also—and indeed

this is perhaps the basis for the others—with the power of innovation (innovation, be it understood, in a certain direction, according to certain lines of force, certain perspectives, even certain premises). It is also true that neither could this element form the party alone; however, it could do so more than could the first element considered. One speaks of generals without an army, but in reality it is easier to form an army than to form generals. So much is this true that an already existing army is destroyed if it loses its generals, while the existence of a united group of generals who agree among themselves and have common aims soon creates an army even where none exists.

3. An intermediate element, which articulates the first element with the second and maintains contact between them, not only physically but also morally and intellectually. In reality, for every party there exist "fixed proportions" between these three elements, and the greatest effectiveness is achieved when these "fixed proportions" are realized.

In view of these considerations, it is possible to say when it is that a party cannot be destroyed by normal means. The second element must necessarily be in existence (if it is not, discussion is meaningless); its appearance is related to the existence of objective material conditions, even if still in a fragmented and unstable state. The moment when it becomes impossible to destroy a party by normal means is reached when the two other elements cannot help being formed—that is, the first element, which in its turn necessarily forms the third as its continuation and its means of expressing itself.

For that to happen, the iron conviction has to have been formed that a particular solution of the vital problems is necessary. Without this conviction the second element will not be formed. This element can the more easily be destroyed in that it is numerically weak, but it is essential that if it is destroyed it should leave as its heritage a ferment from which it may be recreated. And where could this ferment better be formed and subsist than in the first and third elements, which, obviously, are the nearest in character to the second? The activity of the second element towards creating this ferment is therefore fundamental. The criteria by which the second element should be judged are to be sought; 1. in what it actually does; 2. in what provision it makes for the eventuality of its own destruction. It is difficult to say which of these two facts is the more important. Since defeat in the struggle must always be envisaged, the preparation of one's own successors is as important as what one does for victory.

With regard to party conceit, this may be said to be worse than the national conceit of which Vico speaks. Why? Because a nation cannot help existing; and in the fact that it exists it is always possible—maybe with a little goodwill and an invocation of the text—to discover that its existence is pregnant with destiny and significance. A party on the other hand may not exist by virtue of its own strength. It should *never* be forgotten that, in the struggle between the nations, it is in the interest of each one of them that the other should be weakened by internal struggles— and the parties are precisely the elements of internal struggle. Hence it is always possible to pose the question of whether the parties exist by virtue of their own strength, as their own necessity, or whether rather they only exist to serve the interests of others (and indeed in polemics this point is never overlooked, in fact it is even a recurring theme, especially when the answer is not in doubt—so that it takes hold and creates doubts). Naturally, anybody who allowed himself to be torn apart by such doubts would be a fool. Politically the question has only an ephemeral relevance. In the history of the so-called principle of nationality, foreign interventions in favor of national parties which trouble the internal order of enemy States are innumerable; so much so that when one speaks, for example, of Cavour's "Eastern" policy,[12] one wonders if it was really a question of a "policy," a permanent line of action, or not rather a stratagem of the moment to weaken Austria before 1859 and 1866. Similarly, in the Mazzinian movements of the early eighteen-seventies (the Barsanti affair, for instance)[13] one can discern the intervention of Bismarck, who with his eyes on the war with France and the danger of a Franco-Italian alliance thought to weaken Italy through internal conflict. Similarly, in the events of June 1914 some see the intervention of the Austrian General Staff with a view to the coming war. As can be seen, the list of examples is a long one, and it is essential to have clear ideas on the subject. Given that whatever one does one is always playing somebody's game, the important thing is to seek in every way to play one's own game with success—in other words, to win decisively. At all events, party conceit is to be despised, and replaced by concrete facts. Anyone who reinforces conceit, or prefers it to concrete facts, is certainly not to be taken seriously. It is unnecessary to add that it is essential for parties to avoid even the "justified" appearance of playing somebody else's game, especially if the somebody is a foreign State. But nobody can prevent speculations from being made.

It is difficult to deny that all political parties (those of subordinate as well as ruling groups) also carry out a policing function—that is to say, the function of safeguarding a certain political and legal order. If this were conclusively demonstrated, the problem would have to be posed in other terms; it would have to bear, in other words, on the means and the procedures by which such a function is carried out. Is its purpose one of repression or of dissemination; in other words, does it have a reactionary or a progressive character? Does the given party carry out its policing function in order to conserve an outward, extrinsic order which is a fetter on the vital forces of history; or does it carry it out in the sense of tending to raise the people to a new level of civilization expressed programmatically in its political and legal order? In fact, a law finds a lawbreaker: 1. among the reactionary social elements whom it has dispossessed; 2. among the progressive elements whom it holds back; 3. among those elements which have not yet reached the level of civilization which it can be seen as representing. The policing function of a party can hence be either progressive or regressive. It is progressive when it tends to keep the dispossessed reactionary forces within the bounds of legality, and to raise the backward masses to the level of the new legality. It is regressive when it tends to hold back the vital forces of history and to maintain a legality which has been superseded, which is anti-historical, which has become extrinsic. Besides, the way in which the party functions provides discriminating criteria. When the party is progressive it functions "democratically" (democratic centralism); when the party is regressive it functions "bureaucratically" (bureaucratic centralism). The party in this second case is a simple, unthinking executor. It is then technically a policing organism, and its name of "political party" is simply a metaphor of a mythological character. [1933]

The problem arises of whether the great industrialists have a permanent political party of their own. It seems to me that the reply must be in the negative. The great industrialists utilize all the existing parties turn by turn, but they do not have their own party. This does not mean that they are in any way "agnostic" or "apolitical." Their interest is in a determinate balance of forces, which they obtain precisely by using their resources to reinforce one party or another in turn from the varied political checkerboard (with the exception, needless to say, only of the enemy party, whose reinforcement cannot be assisted even as a tactical move). It is certain, however, that if this is what happens in "normal" times, in extreme cases—which are those which count (like war in the life of a nation)—the party of the great industrialists is that of the landowners, who for their part do have their own permanent party. The exemplification of this note may be seen in England, where the Conservative Party has swallowed up the Liberal Party, although the latter had traditionally appeared to be the party of the industrialists.

The English situation, with its great Trade Unions, explains this fact. In England, admittedly, there does not exist formally a party on the grand scale which is the enemy of the industrialists.[14] But there do exist mass organizations of the working-class, and it has been noted how at certain decisive moments they transform their constitution from top to bottom, shattering the bureaucratic carapace (for example, in 1919 and 1926). On the other hand the landowners and the industrialists have permanent interests which bind them together (especially now that protectionism has become general, covering both agriculture and industry); and it is undeniable that the landowners are "politically" far better organized than the industrialists, attract more intellectuals than they do, are more "permanent" in the directives they give, etc. The fate of the traditional "industrial" parties, like the English "liberal-radicals,"[15] the (very different) French radicals, and even the late, lamented "Italian radicals,"[16] is of considerable interest. What did they represent? A nexus of classes, great and small, rather than a single, great class. This is the cause of their various histories and their various ends. Their combat troops were provided by the petite bourgeoisie, which found itself in ever-changing conditions within the nexus until its total transformation. Today it provides the troops of the "demagogic parties,"[17] and it is not hard to understand why this should be.

In general it may be said that, in this history of the parties, comparison between different countries is highly instructive and indeed decisive in the search for the origin of the causes of transformation. It is true, too, of the polemics between parties in the "traditionalist" countries—where "remainders" are found from the entire historical "catalogue."

Conceptions of the World and Practical Stances: Global[18] and Partial

A prime criterion for judging either conceptions of the world or, especially, practical stances is the following: can the conception of the world or the practical action in question be conceived of as "isolated," "independent," bearing entire responsibility for the collective life? Or is that impossible, and must it be conceived of as "integration" or perfecting of—or counterweight to—another conception of the world or practical attitude? Upon reflection, it can be seen that this criterion is decisive for an ideal judgment on both ideal and practical changes, and it can also be seen that it has no small practical implications.

One of the commonest totems is the belief about everything that exists, that it is "natural" that it should exist, that it could not do otherwise than exist, and that however badly one's attempts at reform may go they will not stop life going on, since the traditional forces will continue to operate and precisely will keep life going on. There is some truth, certainly, in this way of thinking; it would be disastrous if there were not. All the same, beyond certain limits, this way of thinking becomes dangerous (certain cases of *"politique de pire"*),[19] and in any case, as has already been said, the criterion subsists for a philosophical, political and historical judgment. It is certain that, if one looks into it closely, certain movements conceive of themselves as being only marginal; that is, they presuppose a major movement onto which they graft themselves in order to reform certain presumed or real evils. In other words, certain movements are purely reformist.

This principle has political importance, because the theoretical truth that every class has a single party is demonstrated, at the decisive turning-points, by the fact that various groupings, each of which had up till then presented itself as an "independent" party, come together to form a united bloc. The multiplicity which previously existed was purely "reformist" in character, that is to say it was concerned with partial questions. In a certain sense, it was a political division of labor (useful, within its limits). But each part presupposed the other, so much so that at the decisive moments—in other words precisely when fundamental questions were brought into play—the unity was formed, the bloc came into existence. Hence the conclusion that in building a party, it is necessary to give it a "monolithic" character rather than base it on secondary questions; therefore, painstaking care that there should be homogeneity between the leadership and the rank and file, between the leaders and their mass following. If, at the decisive moments, the leaders pass over to their "true party," the rank and file militants are left suspended, paralyzed and ineffective. One may say that no real movement becomes aware of its global character all at once, but only gradually through experience—in other words, when it learns from the facts that nothing which exists is natural (in the non-habitual sense of the word), but rather exists because of the existence of certain conditions, whose disappearance cannot remain without consequences. Thus the movement perfects itself, loses its arbitrary, "symbiotic" traits, becomes truly independent, in the sense that in order to produce certain results it creates the necessary preconditions, and indeed devotes all its forces to the creation of these preconditions. [1933]

Number and Quality in Representative Systems of Government

One of the most banal commonplaces which get repeated against the elective system of forming State organs is the following: that in it numbers decide everything,[20] and that the opinions of any idiot who knows how to write (or in some countries even of an illiterate) have exactly the same weight in determining the political course of the State as the opinions of somebody who devotes his best energies to the State and the nation, etc.* But the fact is that it is not true, in any sense, that numbers decide everything, nor that the opinions of all electors are of "exactly" equal weight. Numbers, in this case too, are simply an instrumental value, giving a measure and a relation and nothing more. And what then is measured? What is measured is precisely the effectiveness, and the expansive and persuasive capacity, of the opinions of a few individuals, the active minorities, the élites, the avant-gardes, etc.—i.e. their rationality, historicity or concrete functionality. Which means it is untrue that all individual opinions have "exactly" equal weight. Ideas and opinions are not spontaneously "born" in each individual brain: they have had a center of formation, of irradiation, of dissemination, of persuasion—a group of men, or a single individual even, which has developed them and presented them in the political form of current reality. The counting

---

* There were numerous formulations of this, some more felicitous than the one quoted—which is due to Mario de Silva, in *Crilica Fascista*, 15 August 1932. But the content is always the same.

of "votes" is the final ceremony of a long process, in which it is precisely those who devote their best energies to the State and the nation (when such they are) who carry the greatest weight. If this hypothetical group of worthy men, notwithstanding the boundless material power which they possess, do not have the consent of the majority, they must be judged either as inept, or as not representative of "national" interests—which cannot help being decisive in inflecting the national will in one direction rather than in another. "Unfortunately" everyone tends to confound his own "private interest"[21] with that of the nation, and hence to find it "dreadful," etc. that it should be the "law of numbers" which decides; it is better of course to become an élite by decree. Thus it is not a question of the people who "have the brains" feeling that they are being reduced to the level of the lowest illiterate, but rather one of people who think they are the ones with the brains wanting to take away from the "man in the street" even that tiniest fraction of power of decision over the course of national life which he possesses.

These banal assertions have been extended from a critique (of oligarchic rather than élitist origin)[22] of the parliamentary system of government (it is strange that it should not be criticized because the historical rationality of numerical consensus is systematically falsified by the influence of wealth) to a critique of all representative systems—even those which are not parliamentary and not fashioned according to the canons of formal democracy.[23] These assertions are even less accurate. In these other systems of government, the people's consent does not end at the moment of voting, quite the contrary. That consent is presumed to be permanently active; so much so that those who give it may be considered as "functionaries" of the State, and elections as a means of voluntary enrollment of State functionaries of a certain type—a means which in a certain sense may be related to the idea of *self-government* (though on a different level). Since elections are held on the basis not of vague, generic programs, but of programs of immediate, concrete work, anyone who gives his consent commits himself to do something more than the simple, juridical citizen towards their realization—i.e. to be a vanguard of active and responsible work. The "voluntary" element in the whole undertaking could not be stimulated in any other way as far as the broader masses are concerned; and when these are not made up of amorphous citizens, but of skilled productive elements, then one can understand the importance that the demonstration of the vote may have.* [1933–34]

The proposition that society does not pose itself problems for whose solution the material preconditions do not already exist. This proposition immediately raises the problem of the formation of a collective will. In order to analyze critically what the proposition means, it is necessary to study precisely how permanent collective wills are formed, and how such will set themselves concrete short-term and long-term ends—i.e. a line of collective action. It is a question of more or less long processes of development, and rarely of sudden, "synthetic" explosions. Synthetic "explosions" do occur, but if they are looked at closely it can be seen that they are more destructive than reconstructive; they remove mechanical and external obstacles in the way of an indigenous and spontaneous development. . . .

It would be possible to study concretely the formation of a collective historical movement, analyzing it in all its molecular phases—a thing which is rarely done, since it would weigh every treatment down. Instead, currents of opinion are normally taken as already constituted around a group or a dominant personality. This is the problem which in modern times is expressed in terms of the party, or coalition of related parties: how a party is first set up, how its organizational strength and social influence are developed, etc. It requires an extremely minute, molecular process of exhaustive analysis in every detail, the documentation for which is made up of an endless quantity of books, pamphlets, review and newspaper articles, conversations and oral debates repeated countless times, and which in their gigantic aggregation represent this long labor which gives birth to a collective will with a certain degree of homogeneity—with the degree necessary and sufficient to achieve an action which is coordinated and simultaneous in the time and the geographical space in which the historical event takes place.

Importance of utopias and of confused and rationalistic ideologies in the initial phase of the historical processes whereby collective wills are formed. Utopias, or abstract rationalism, have the same importance as old conceptions of the world which developed historically by the

---

* These observations could be developed more amply and organically, stressing other differences as well between the various types of elective systems, according to the changes in general social and political relations: the relation between elected and career functionaries, etc.

accumulation of successive experience. What matters is the criticism to which such an ideological complex is subjected by the first representatives of the new historical phase. This criticism makes possible a process of differentiation and change in the relative weight that the elements of the old ideologies used to possess. What was previously secondary and subordinate, or even incidental, is now taken to be primary—becomes the nucleus of a new ideological and theoretical complex. The old collective will dissolves into its contradictory elements since the subordinate ones develop socially, etc.

After the formation of the party system—an historical phase linked to the standardization of broad masses of the population (communications, newspapers, big cities, etc.)—the molecular processes take place more swiftly than in the past, etc. [1931–32]

Continuity and Tradition

An aspect of the question alluded to elsewhere of "Dilettantism and Discipline," from the point of view of the organizing center of a grouping is that of the "continuity" which tends to create a "tradition"—understood of course in an active and not a passive sense: as continuity in continuous development, but "organic development". This problem contains in a nutshell the entire "juridical problem," i.e. the problem of assimilating the entire grouping to its most advanced fraction; it is a problem of education of the masses, of their "adaptation" in accordance with the requirements of the goal to be achieved. This is precisely the function of law in the State and in society; through "law" the State renders the ruling group "homogeneous," and tends to create a social conformism which is useful to the ruling group's line of development. The general activity of law (which is wider than purely State and governmental activity and also includes the activity involved in directing civil society, in those zones which the technicians of law call legally neutral—i.e. in morality and in custom generally) serves to understand the ethical problem better, in a concrete sense. In practice, this problem is the correspondence "spontaneously and freely accepted" between the acts and the admissions of each individual, between the conduct of each individual and the ends which society sets itself as necessary—a correspondence which is coercive in the sphere of positive law technically understood, and is spontaneous and free (more strictly ethical) in those zones in which "coercion" is not a State affair but is effected by public opinion, moral climate, etc. The "juridical" continuity of the organized center must be not of a Byzantine/ Napoleonic type, i.e. according to a code conceived of as perpetual, but Roman/Anglo-Saxon—that is to say, a type whose essential characteristic consists in its method, which is realistic and always keeps close to concrete life in perpetual development. This organic continuity requires a good archive, well stocked and easy to use, in which all past activity can be reviewed and "criticized." The most important manifestations of this activity are not so much "organic decisions" as explicative and reasoned (educative) circulars.

There is a danger of becoming "bureaucratized," it is true; but every organic continuity presents this danger, which must be watched. The danger of discontinuity, of improvisation, is still greater. Organ: the "Bulletin," which has three principal sections: 1. directive articles; 2. decisions and circulars; 3. criticism of the past, i.e. continual reference back from the present to the past, to show the differentiations and the specifications, and to justify them critically. [1930–32]

Spontaneity and Conscious Leadership

The term "spontaneity" can be variously defined, for the phenomenon to which it refers is many-sided. Meanwhile it must be stressed that "pure" spontaneity does not exist in history: it would come to the same thing as "pure" mechanicity. In the "most spontaneous" movement it is simply the case that the elements of "conscious leadership" cannot be checked, have left no reliable document. It may be said that spontaneity is therefore characteristic of the "history of the subaltern classes," and indeed of their most marginal and peripheral elements; these have not achieved any consciousness of the class "for itself," and consequently it never occurs to them that their history might have some possible importance, that there might be some value in leaving documentary evidence of it.

Hence in such movements there exist multiple elements of "conscious leadership," but no one of them is predominant or transcends the level of a given social stratum's "popular science"—its "common sense" or traditional conception of the world. This is precisely what De Man, empirically, counterposes to Marxism; but he does not realize (apparently) that he is falling into the position of somebody who, after describing folklore, witchcraft, etc., and showing that these conceptions have sturdy historical roots and are tenaciously entwined in the psychology of specific popular strata, believed that he had "transcended" modern science—taking as "modern science" every little article in the popular scientific journals and periodicals. This is a real case of intellectual teratology, of which there are other examples: precisely, the admirers of folklore, who advocate its preservation; the "magicalists" connected with Maeterlinck, who believe it is necessary to take up anew the thread—snapped by violence—of alchemy and witchcraft, so that science may be put back onto a course more fertile in discoveries, etc. However, De Man does have one incidental merit: he demonstrates the need to study and develop the elements of popular psychology, historically and sociologically, actively (i.e. in order to transform them, by educating them, into a modern mentality) and descriptively as he does. But this need was at least implicit (perhaps even explicitly stated) in the doctrine of Ilitch [Lenin]—something of which De Man is entirely ignorant. The fact that every "spontaneous" movement contains rudimentary elements of conscious leadership, of discipline, is indirectly demonstrated by the fact that there exist tendencies and groups who extol spontaneity as a method. Here one must distinguish between the realm of pure "ideology" and that of practical action, between scholars who argue that spontaneity is the immanent and objective "method" of the historical process, and political adventurers who argue for it as a "political" method. With the former it is a question of a mistaken conception, whereas with the latter what is involved is an immediate and vulgar contradiction which betrays its manifest practical origin—i.e. the immediate desire to replace a given leadership by a different one. Even in the case of the scholars the error does have a practical origin, but it is not an immediate one as in the latter case. The apoliticism of the French syndicalists before the war contained both these elements: there was a theoretical error and a contradiction (there was the "Sorelian" element, and the elements of rivalry between the anarcho-syndicalist political tendency and that of the socialists). That apoliticism was still a consequence of the terrible events of 1871 in Paris: the continuation, with new methods and a brilliant theory, of the thirty years of passivity (1870–1900) of the French working class. The purely "economic" struggle was not to the distaste of the ruling class—on the contrary. The same may be said of the Catalan movement,[24] which if it "displeased" the Spanish ruling class did so only because it objectively reinforced Catalan republican separatism, producing a real republican industrial bloc against the latifundists, the petite bourgeoisie and the royal army. The Turin movement was accused simultaneously of being "spontaneist" and "voluntarist" or Bergsonian. This contradictory accusation, if one analyzes it, only testifies to the fact that the leadership given to the movement was both creative and correct. This leadership was not "abstract"; it neither consisted in mechanically repeating scientific or theoretical formulae, nor did it confuse politics, real action, with theoretical disquisition. It applied itself to real men, formed in specific historical relations, with specific feelings, outlooks, fragmentary conceptions of the world, etc., which were the result of "spontaneous" combinations of a given situation of material production with the "fortuitous" agglomeration within it of disparate social elements. This element of "spontaneity" was not neglected and even less despised. It was *educated*, directed, purged of extraneous contaminations; the aim was to bring it into line with modern theory[25]—but in a living and historically effective manner. The leaders themselves spoke of the "spontaneity" of the movement, and rightly so. This assertion was a stimulus, a tonic, an element of unification in depth; above all it denied that the movement was arbitrary, a cooked-up venture, and stressed its historical necessity. It gave the masses a "theoretical" consciousness of being creators of *historical* and institutional *values*, of being founders of a State. This unity between "spontaneity" and "conscious leadership" or "discipline" is precisely the real political action of the subaltern classes, in so far as this is mass politics and not merely an adventure by groups claiming to represent the masses.

At this point, a fundamental theoretical question is raised: can modern theory be in opposition to the "spontaneous" feelings of the masses? ("Spontaneous" in the sense that they are not the result of any systematic educational activity on the part of an already conscious leading group, but have been formed through everyday experience illuminated by "common sense", i.e. by the traditional popular conception of the world—what is unimaginatively called "instinct," although it too is in fact a primitive and elementary historical acquisition.) It cannot be in opposition to them. Between the two there is a "quantitative" difference of degree, not one of quality. A reciprocal "reduction" so to speak, a passage from one to the other and vice versa, must be possible. (Recall that Immanuel Kant believed it important for his philosophical theories to agree with common sense; the same position can be found in Croce. Recall too Marx's assertion in *The Holy Family* that the political formulae of the French Revolution can be reduced to the principles of classical German philosophy.) Neglecting, or worse still despising, so-called "spontaneous" movements, i.e. failing to give them a conscious leadership or to raise them to a higher plane by inserting them into politics, may often have extremely serious consequences. It is almost always the case that a "spontaneous" movement of the subaltern classes is accompanied by a reactionary movement of the right-wing of the dominant class, for concomitant reasons. An economic crisis, for instance, engenders on the one hand discontent among the subaltern classes and spontaneous mass movements, and on the other conspiracies among the reactionary groups, who take advantage of the objective weakening of the government in order to attempt *coups d'état*. Among the effective causes of the *coups* must be included the failure of the responsible groups to give any conscious leadership to the spontaneous revolts or to make them into a positive political factor. N.B. the example of the Sicilian Vespers,[26] and the arguments among historians about whether this was a spontaneous movement or one planned in advance. In my view the two elements were combined in the case of the Vespers. On the one hand, a spontaneous rising of the Sicilian people against their Provençal rulers which spread so rapidly that it gave the impression of simultaneity and hence of preconcertation; this rising was the result of an oppression which had become intolerable throughout the national territory. On the other hand, there was the conscious element, of varying importance and effectiveness, and the success of Giovanni da Procida's plot with the Aragonese. Other examples can be drawn from all past revolutions in which several subaltern classes were present, with a hierarchy determined by economic position and internal homogeneity. The "spontaneous" movements of the broader popular strata make possible the coming to power of the most progressive subaltern class as a result of the objective weakening of the State. This is still a "progressive" example; but, in the modern world, the regressive examples are more frequent.

There exists a scholastic and academic historico-political outlook which sees as real and worthwhile only such movements of revolt as are one hundred per cent conscious, i.e. movements that are governed by plans worked out in advance to the last detail or in line with abstract theory (which comes to the same thing). But reality produces a wealth of the most bizarre combinations. It is up to the theoretician to unravel these in order to discover fresh proof of his theory, to "translate" into theoretical language the elements of historical life. It is not reality which should be expected to conform to the abstract schema. This will never happen, and hence this conception is nothing but an expression of passivity. (Leonardo was able to discern number in all the manifestations of cosmic life, even where profane eyes only saw blind chance and chaos.) [1930]

Notes

1. I.e. under the conditions of class society. For Gramsci's "first element" here, see Hegel: *Philosophy of History*, Dover 1956, p. 44: "The primary consideration is, then, the distinction between the governing and the governed...."

2. Luigi Cadorna (1850–1928) was commander-in-chief of the Italian armed forces until the defeat at Caporetto in 1917, for which he was held responsible. The war was widely unpopular by 1917, and the Italian soldiers' disaffection was certainly an important factor in the defeat. Cadorna was taken by Gramsci as the symbol of the authoritarian leader who makes no attempt to win the "consent" of those he is leading.

3. The fascists often described their party as an "anti-party," and Mussolini liked to expatiate on his own "individualism."

4. Term used by Hegel, e.g. in his *Philosophy of History*: "This Spirit of a People is a *determinate* and particular Spirit, and is, as just stated, further modified by the degree of its historical development. This Spirit, then, constitutes the basis and substance of those other forms of a nation's consciousness, which have been noticed.... In virtue of the original identity of their essence, purport, and object, these various forms are inseparably united with the Spirit of the State. Only in connection with this particular religion can this particular political constitution exist; just as in such or such a State, such or such a Philosophy or order of Art." Hegel, *op cit.*, p. 53.

    The notion of a "State spirit" was adopted by fascism, see e.g. Mussolini, Speech to the Chamber of Deputies, 13 May 1929: "What would the State be if it did not have a spirit, a morality, which is what gives the strength to its laws, and through which it succeeds in securing the obedience of its citizens?" It is not entirely clear exactly what Gramsci has in mind here, when he refers to the "precise, historically determine meaning" of the expression.

5. It is important to realize that Gramsci does not use this word in the pejorative sense which it has acquired in bourgeois ideology today—it is a quite neutral term for him, meaning approximately "all-embracing and unifying". We have sometimes translated it by "global."

6. The *Corriere*, under the editorship of Albertini . . . had been built up as the principal ideological expression of the Milan industrialists, and the nearest thing to a national organ of the Italian bourgeoisie, prior to fascism. Under fascism, it was aligned with the régime, but has since reassumed its former role.

7.   Literally newspapers. On Int. p. 152, Gramsci writes: "A distinction is made between the so-called informational or 'non-party' paper (without an explicit party) and the official organ of a particular party; between the paper for the popular masses or 'popular' paper and that which is aimed at a necessarily restricted public."

8.   *Lucus a non lucendo*: a famous example of mediaeval false etymology, meaning "a wood (*lucus*) is so called because it gives no light (*lux*)." I.e. the anarchists claim to be educators, and Gramsci suggests ironically that this is perhaps because they are nothing of the sort.

9.   I.e. the Physiocrats in eighteenth-century France.

10.   This second type of party must refer to fascism. The first type of "party" is probably a reference to the role of Croce; see MS. p. 172: "The party as general ideology, superior to the various more immediate groupings. In reality the liberal party in Italy after 1876 was characterized by the way in which it presented itself to the country as a number of national and regional fractions and groups 'in open order'. All of the following were fractions of political liberalism: the liberal Catholicism of the Popular Party; nationalism (Croce was a contributor to *Politica*, the journal of A. Rocco and F. Coppola); the monarchist unions; the Republican Party; a great part of socialism; the democratic radicals; the conservatives; Sonnino and Salandra; Giolitti, Orlando, Nitti and Co. Croce was the theorist of what all these groups, grouplets, *camarillas* and *mafias* had in common; the head of a central propaganda office which benefited all these groups and which they all made use of; the national leader of the cultural movements which arose to renovate the old political forms."

11.   "On the conceit of nations, there is a golden saying of Diodorus Siculus. Every nation, according to him, whether Greek or barbarian, has had the same conceit that it before all other nations invented the comforts of human life and that its remembered history goes back to the very beginning of the world." *The New Science of Giambattista Vico*, Cornell, 1968, p. 61. When Gramsci speaks of "party conceit" he may also have in mind a phrase of Zinoviev's at the Fourth World Congress, directed in particular against the PCI. Zinoviev referred to the danger of "*Kom-tchvanstvo*" = communist boastfulness or conceit.

12.   I.e. the policy whereby Piedmont allied itself with England and France and sent troops to fight in the Crimean War against Russia (1855).

13.   On May 24, 1870 Pietro Barsanti, a Mazzinian corporal, attacked a barracks in Pavia with forty republican followers, shouting "Long live Rome! Long live the Republic! Down with the monarchy!" He was arrested and shot on August 27, 1870.

14.   I.e. there is no mass Communist Party. Gramsci, of course, did not consider the Labour Party as an enemy of the industrialists.

15.   I.e. the Liberal Party of the latter half of the nineteenth century, with its radical wing, and perhaps especially with reference to the period after 1870 when the Radicals under Chamberlain, Dilke and Bradlaugh were republican and influenced by socialist ideas.

16. The Italian Radical Party was a small offshoot of the *Partido d'Azione*, which campaigned for social legislation, notably on working conditions, in the 1880s. It thereafter declined, and became a minor component of Giolitti's political bloc.
17. I.e. the fascist parties.
18. "Global" has been used here to translate "*totalitari*."
19. I.e. the idea that "the worse things get, the better that will be."
20. See, for example, Mussolini "The war was 'revolutionary' in the sense that it liquidated—in rivers of blood—the century of democracy, the century of number, of majority, of quantity", in *Which way is the world going?*, 1922; or again, "Fascism is against democracy which levels the people down to the largest number, bringing it down to the level of the majority," in *The Doctrine of Fascism*, 1932.
21. The Italian word here is "*particulare*", a term used by Guicciardini, who suggested that the best refuge from the trials of public life was one's own "*particulare*" or private interest. De Sanctis criticised this "egoism."
22. I.e. of conservative origin (concerned to restrict political power to a traditional ruling stratum—Mosca's "political class"), rather than élitist in the strict sense of the word (élite = chosen)—i.e. meritocratic, Pareto, fascist ideology, etc.).
23. I.e., presumably, soviets.
24. I.e. the syndicalist struggle in Barcelona between 1916 and 1923.
25. I.e. Marxism.
26. On March 31, 1282, the population of Palermo rose against the government of Charles of Anjou. The uprising, which came to be known as the Sicilian Vespers, spread rapidly throughout the island, and the French were expelled in less than a month. The throne was subsequently given to Frederick of Aragon. The rising had been the result of a combination of popular discontent and the plans of pro-Aragonese elements among the nobility, e.g. Giovanni da Procida (1210 approx.—1282), who became chancellor of the Kingdom after the rising had succeeded.

READING #25

Prison Notebooks:
"State and Civil Society" (excerpt)

Political Struggle and Military War

In military war, when the strategic aim—destruction of the enemy's army and occupation of his territory—is achieved, peace comes. It should also be observed that for war to come to an end, it is enough that the strategic aim should simply be achieved potentially: it is enough in other words that there should be no doubt that an army is no longer able to fight, and that the victorious army "could" occupy the enemy's territory. Political struggle is enormously more complex: in a certain sense, it can be compared to colonial wars or to old wars of conquest—in which the victorious army occupies, or proposes to occupy, permanently all or a part of the conquered territory. Then the defeated army is disarmed and dispersed, but the struggle continues on the terrain of politics and of military "preparation."

Thus India's political struggle against the English (and to a certain extent that of Germany against France, or of Hungary against the Little Entente) knows three forms of war: war of movement, war of position, and underground warfare. Gandhi's passive resistance is a war of position, which at certain moments becomes a war of movement, and at others underground warfare. Boycotts are a form of war of position, strikes of war of movement, the secret preparation of weapons and combat troops belongs to underground warfare. A kind of commando tactics[1] is also to be found, but it can only be utilized with great circumspection. If the English believed that a great insurrectional movement was being prepared, destined to annihilate their present strategic superiority (which consists, in a certain sense, in their ability to maneuver through control of the internal lines of communication, and to concentrate their forces at the "sporadically" most dangerous spot) by mass suffocation—i.e. by compelling them to spread out their forces over a theater of war which had simultaneously become generalized—then it would suit them to *provoke* a premature outbreak of the Indian fighting forces, in order to identify them and decapitate the general movement. Similarly it would suit France if the German Nationalist Right were to be involved in an adventurist *coup d'état*; for this would oblige the suspected illegal military organization to show itself prematurely, and so permit an intervention which from the French point of view would be timely. It is thus evident that in these forms of mixed struggle—fundamentally of a military character, but mainly fought on the political plane (though in fact every political struggle always has a military substratum)—the use of commando squads requires an original tactical development, for which the experience of war can only provide a stimulus, and not a model.

The question of the Balkan comitadjis[2] requires separate treatment; they are related to particular conditions of the region's geophysical environment, to the particular formation of the rural classes, and also to the real effectiveness of the governments there. The same is true with the Irish bands,[3] whose form of warfare and of organization was related to the structure of Irish society. The *comitadjis*, the Irish, and the other forms of partisan warfare have to be separated from the question of commandos, although they appear to have points of contact. These forms of struggle are specific to weak, but restive, minorities confronted by well-organized majorities: modern commandos on the contrary presuppose a large reserve-force, immobilized for one reason or another but potentially effective, which gives them support and sustenance in the form of individual contributions.

The relationship which existed in 1917–18 between the commando units and the army as a whole can lead, and has led, political leaders to draw up erroneous plans of campaign. They forget: 1. that the commandos are simple tactical units, and do indeed presuppose an army which is not very effective—but not one which is completely inert. For even though discipline and fighting spirit have slackened to the point where a new tactical deployment has become advisable, they still do exist to a certain degree—a degree to which the new tactical formation precisely corresponds. Otherwise there could only be rout, and headlong flight; 2. that the phenomenon of commandos should not be considered as a sign of the general combativity of the mass of the troops, but, on the contrary, as a sign of their passivity and relative demoralization. But in saying all this, the general criterion should be kept in mind that comparisons between military art and politics, if made, should always be taken *cum grano salts* [with a pinch of salt]—in other words, as stimuli to thought, or as terms in a *reductio ad absurdum*. In actual fact, in the case of the political militia there is neither any implacable penal sanction for whoever makes a mistake or does not obey an order exactly, nor do courts-martial exist—quite apart from the fact that the line-up of political forces is not even remotely comparable to the line-up of military forces.

In political struggle, there also exist other forms of warfare—apart from the war of movement and siege warfare or the war of position. True, i.e. modem, commandos belong to the war of position, in its 1914–18 form. The war of movement and siege warfare of the preceding periods also had their commandos, in a certain sense. The light and heavy cavalry, crack rifle corps,[4] etc.—and indeed mobile forces in general—partly functioned as commandos. Similarly the art of organising patrols contained the germ of modern commandos. This germ was contained in siege warfare more than in the war of movement: more extensive use of patrols, and particularly the art of organizing sudden sorties and surprise attacks with picked men.

Another point to be kept in mind is that in political struggle one should not ape the methods of the ruling classes, or one will fall into easy ambushes. In the current struggles this phenomenon often occurs. A weakened State structure is like a flagging army; the commandos—i.e. the private armed organizations—enter the field, and they have two tasks: to make use of illegal means, while the State appears to remain within legality, and thus to reorganize the State itself. It is stupid to believe that when one is confronted by illegal private action one can counterpose to it another similar action—in other words, combat commando tactics by means of commando tactics. It means believing that the State remains perpetually inert, which is never the case—quite apart from all the other conditions which differ. The class factor leads to a fundamental difference: a class which has to work fixed hours every day cannot have permanent and specialized assault organizations—as can a class which has ample financial resources and all of whose members are not tied down by fixed work. At any hour of day or night, these by now professional organizations are able to strike decisive blows, and strike them unaware. Commando tactics cannot therefore have the same importance for some classes as for other. For certain classes a war of movement and maneuver is necessary—because it is the form of war which belongs to them; and this, in the case of political struggle, may include a valuable and perhaps indispensable use of commando tactics. But to fix one's mind on the military model is the mark of a fool: politics, here too, must have priority over its military aspect, and only politics creates the possibility for maneuver and movement.

From all that has been said it follows that in the phenomenon of military commandos, it is necessary to distinguish between the technical function of commandos as a special force linked to the modern war of position, and their politico-military function. As a special force commandos were used by all armies in the World War. But they have only had a politico-military function in those countries which are politically enfeebled and non-homogeneous, and which are therefore represented by a not very combative national army, and a bureaucratized General Staff, grown rusty in the service. [1929–30]

On the subject of parallels between on the one hand the concepts of war of maneuver and war of position in military science, and on the other the corresponding concepts in political science, Rosa [Luxemburg]'s little book, translated (from French) into Italian in 1919 by C. Alessandri, should be recalled.[5]

In this book, Rosa—a little hastily, and rather superficially too—theorized the historical experiences of 1905. She in fact disregarded the "voluntary" and organizational elements which were far more extensive and important in those events than—thanks to a certain "economistic" and spontaneist prejudice—she tended to believe. All the same, this little book (like others of the same author's essays) is one of the most significant documents theorizing the war of maneuver in relation to political science. The immediate economic element (crises, etc.) is seen as the field artillery which in war opens a breach in the enemy's defenses—a breach sufficient for one's own troops to rush in and obtain a definitive (strategic) victory, or at least an important victory in the context of the strategic line. Naturally the effects of immediate economic factors in historical science are held to be far more complex than the effects of heavy artillery in a war of maneuver, since they are conceived of as having a double effect: 1. they breach the enemy's defenses, after throwing him into disarray and causing him to lose faith in himself, his forces, and his future; 2. in a flash they organize one's own troops and create the necessary cadres—or at least in a flash they put the existing cadres (formed, until that moment, by the general historical process) in positions which enable them to encadre one's scattered forces; 3. in a flash they bring about the necessary ideological concentration on the common objective to be achieved. This view was a form of iron economic determinism, with the aggravating factor that it was conceived of as operating with lighting speed in time and in space. It was thus out and out historical mysticism, the awaiting of a sort of miraculous illumination.

General Krasnov asserted (in his novel)[6] that the Entente did not wish for the victory of Imperial Russia (for fear that the Eastern Question would be definitively resolved in favor of Tsarism), and therefore obliged the Russian General Staff to adopt trench warfare (absurd, in view of the enormous length of the Front from the Baltic to the Black Sea, with vast marshy and forest zones), whereas the only possible strategy was a war of maneuver. This assertion is merely silly. In actual fact, the Russian Army did attempt a war of maneuver and sudden incursion, especially in the Austrian sector (but also in East Prussia), and won successes which were as brilliant as they were ephemeral. The truth is that one cannot choose the form of war one wants, unless from the start one has a crushing superiority over the enemy. It is well known what losses were caused by the stubborn refusal of the General Staffs to recognize that a war of position was "imposed" by the overall relation of the forces in conflict. A war of position is not, in reality, constituted simply by the actual trenches, but by the whole organizational and industrial system of the territory which lies to the rear of the army in the field. It is imposed notably by the rapid fire-power of cannons, machine-guns and rifles, by the armed strength which can be concentrated at a particular spot, as well as by the abundance of supplies which make possible the swift replacement of material lost after an enemy breakthrough or a retreat. A further factor is the great mass of men under arms; they are of very unequal caliber, and are precisely only able to operate as a mass force. It can be seen how on the Eastern Front it was one thing to make an incursion in the Austrian Sector, and quite another in the German Sector; and how even in the Austrian Sector, reinforced by picked German troops and commanded by Germans, incursion tactics ended in disaster. The same thing occurred in the Polish campaign of 1920; the seemingly irresistible advance was halted before Warsaw by General Weygand, on the line commanded by French officers.[7] Even those military experts whose minds are now fixed on the war of position, just as they were previously on that of maneuver, naturally do not maintain that the latter should be considered as expunged from military science. They merely maintain that, in wars among the more industrially and socially advanced States, the war of maneuver must be considered as reduced to more of a tactical than a strategic function; that it must be considered as occupying the same position as siege warfare used to occupy previously in relation to it.

The same reduction must take place in the art and science of politics, at least in the case of the most advanced States, where "civil society" has become a very complex structure and one which is resistant to the catastrophic "incursions" of the immediate economic element (crises, depressions, etc.). The superstructures of civil society are like the trench-systems of modern warfare. In war it would sometimes happen that a fierce artillery attack seemed to have destroyed the enemy's entire defensive system, whereas in fact it had only destroyed the outer perimeter; and at the moment of their advance and attack the assailants would find themselves confronted by a line of defense which was still effective. The same thing happens in politics, during the great economic crises. A crisis cannot give the attacking forces the ability to organize with lightning speed in time and in space; still less can it endow them with fighting spirit. Similarly, the defenders are not demoralized, nor do they abandon their positions, even among the ruins, nor do they lose faith in their own strength or their own future. Of course, things do not remain exactly as they were; but it is certain that one will not find the element of speed, of accelerated time, of the definitive forward march expected by the strategists of political Cadornism.[8]

The last occurrence of the kind in the history of politics was the events of 1917 [i.e. the Russian Revolution]. They marked a decisive turning-point in the history of the art and science of politics. Hence it is a question of studying "in depth" which elements of civil society correspond to the defensive systems in a war of position. The use of the phrase "in depth" is intentional, because 1917 has been studied—but only either from superficial and banal viewpoints, as when certain social historians study the vagaries of women's fashions, or from a "rationalistic" viewpoint—in other words, with the conviction that certain phenomena are destroyed as soon as they are "realistically" explained, as if they were popular superstitions (which anyway are not destroyed either merely by being explained).

The question of the meager success achieved by new tendencies in the trade-union movement should be related to this series of problems.[9] One attempt to begin a revision of the current tactical methods was perhaps that outlined by L. Dav. Br. [Trotsky] at the fourth meeting, when he made a comparison between the Eastern and Western fronts.[10] The former had fallen at once, but unprecedented struggles had then ensued; in the case of the latter, the struggles would take place "beforehand." The question, therefore, was whether civil society resists before or after the attempt to seize power; where the latter takes place, etc. However, the question was outlined only in a brilliant, literary form, without directives of a practical character. [1933–34; first version 1930–32.]

Notes

1. *"Arditismo."* During the First World War, the *"arditi"* were volunteer commando squads in the Italian army. The term was adopted by d'Annunzio for his nationalist volunteer "legions," and was also used by the *"arditi del popolo,"* formed to combat the fascist squads in the summer of 1921. This latter organization emerged outside the left parties, but the mass of its local leaders and members were communist or socialist. The PSI (who signed a "conciliation pact" with the fascists at this time) condemned the organization; they advocated a policy of non-resistance. The PCI also condemned the organization, for sectarian reasons, preferring to concentrate on its own, purely communist, defence squads. Gramsci had written and published articles welcoming the organization before the official condemnation, and even afterwards did so obliquely, by criticizing the PSI's attitude. However, as his comments later in this note indicate, he did not feel that working-class *"arditi"* could in fact hope to stand up to the fascist squads, who enjoyed the connivance of the State. It was only *mass* as opposed to *volunteer* action which could provide a viable response.

2. In the late nineteenth century, Turkey still occupied large parts of the Balkans—what are now Albania, Northern Greece, Southern Yugoslavia and Southern Bulgaria—including the whole of the area traditionally known as Macedonia (now divided between Yugoslavia, Greece and to a lesser extent Bulgaria). In 1893 a revolutionary Macedonian committee was set up in Sophia by the Macedonian nationalists Delcev and Gruev, and this committee began to send armed bands (*comitadjis*) across the border into Turkish territory. Their aim—strongly opposed by the Young Turks—was at least some measure of Macedonian autonomy. All the surrounding countries—Bulgaria, Serbia and Greece—formed their own armed bands (*čete*) in the years that followed (as did the Vlachs), to protect their own interests in the area. These bands fought each other at the same time as they fought the Turks.

3. Presumably a reference to the Fenian bands, who rose against British rule unsuccessfully in 1867 and continued sporadic activity during the latter years of the century.

4. *"Bersaglieri"*—an élite corps of the Italian army, founded by Lamarmora in 1836.

5. Rosa Luxemburg: *The Mass Strike, The Political Party and the Trade Unions.*

6. P. N. Krasnov, *From Two-headed Eagle to Red Flag*, Berlin, 1921. Italian edition, Florence, 1928.

7. The Red Army under Tukhachevsky was halted at the gates of Warsaw in August 1920, in its counter-offensive following Pilsudski's invasion of the Soviet Union. The defeat was followed by controversy both concerning the viability of the entire attempt to "export revolution" without the support of the local population, and concerning the specific responsibilities for the defeat (Budyenny and Egorov, supported by Stalin, had not followed the orders of S.

Kamenev, the commander-in-chief, and had marched on Lvov instead of linking up with Tukhachevsky before Warsaw.)

8. See note 2 on p. 312.

9. This is presumably a reference to the failure of communists in Italy between 1921 and 1926 to win more than a minority position within the trade-union movement, despite the betrayals of the CGL's reformist leaders.

10. The "fourth meeting" is the Fourth World Congress of the Comintern, at which Gramsci was present. Trotsky gave the report on Soviet Russia's New Economic Policy (NEP), in the course of which he said: ". . . it will hardly be possible to catch the European bourgeoisie by surprise as we caught the Russian bourgeoisie. The European bourgeoisie is more intelligent, and more farsighted; it is not wasting time. Everything that can be set on foot against us is being mobilized by it right now. The revolutionary proletariat will thus encounter on its road to power not only the combat vanguards of the counter-revolution but also its heaviest reserves. Only by smashing, breaking up and demoralizing these enemy forces will the proletariat be able to seize state power. By way of compensation, after the proletarian overturn, the vanquished bourgeoisie will no longer dispose of powerful reserves from which it could draw forces for prolonging the civil war. In other words, after the conquest of power, the European proletariat will in all likelihood have far more elbow room for its creative work in economy and culture than we had in Russia on the day after the overturn. The more difficult and gruelling the struggle for state power, all the less possible will it be to challenge the proletariat's power after the victory." Trotsky, *The First Five Years of the Communist International*, Vol. II, (New York: Pathfinder Press, 1972), pp. 221–22.

Bibliographical Essay

Many titles not listed here are in the reference notes of the lengthy introductory essay of this volume. More complete bibliographies of writings by and about Marx, Engels, Luxemburg, Lenin, Trotsky, and Gramsci (referred to here, for convenience, as "The Six") can be found in a number of works listed below. In the 1996 edition of this book, I offered a much more extensive listing of books and still felt it necessary to apologize for the many existing gaps. What follows is even shorter, but also more up to date.

Three valuable resources are: (1) the remarkable Marxists Internet Archive: https://www.marxists.org, which includes a treasure trove of writings from "The Six," and many others, and much additional information; (2) Immanuel Ness and others (including myself), eds., *The International Encyclopedia of Revolution and Protest*, 8 vols. (Malden, MA: Wiley-Blackwell, 2009), which includes an impressive number of biographical, historical, and theoretical entries relevant to the present volume; and (3) Tom Bottomore, with Laurence Harris, V. G. Kiernan, and Ralph Miliband, eds., *A Dictionary of Marxist Thought*, second revised edition (Oxford, UK: Basil Blackwell, 1991).

The broad historical context within which "The Six" developed is presented in Eric Hobsbawm's four volumes: *The Age of Revolution: 1789–1848* (New York: Vintage Books, 1996), *The Age of Capital: 1848–1875* (New York: Vintage Books, 1996), *The Age of Empire, 1875–1914* (New York: Vintage Books, 1989), and *The Age of Extremes: The Short Twentieth Century, 1914–1991* (New York: Vintage Books, 1996), and also in Geoff Eley, *Forging Democracy: The History of the Left in Europe, 1850–2000* (New York: Oxford University Press, 2002). More global contextualizations are provided by Chris Harman, *A People's History of the World* (London: Verso Books, 2008), Neill Ferguson, *A Marxist History of the World: From Neanderthals to Neoliberals* (London: Pluto Press, 2013), Samir Amin, *Global History: A View from the South* (Capetown/Dakar/Nairobi/Oxford: Pambazuka Press, 2011), and also by Leo Huberman's delightful though now somewhat dated (originally published in 1936) *Man's Worldly Goods: The Story of the Wealth of Nations* (New York: Monthly Review Press, 2009).

Karl Marx and Frederick Engels

There exists a fifty-volume Marx and Engels *Collected Works*, published by International Publishers in the United States and by Lawrence and Wishart in Britain. A substantial single-volume selection, Robert C. Tucker, ed., *The Marx-Engels Reader*, second edition (New York: W. W. Norton, 1978) contains essential writings, including excerpts from longer works. An eight-volume edition of Marx's writings was produced by the editors of *New Left Review* in the 1970s and early 1980s. The three volumes of political writings are currently available from Verso Books: Karl Marx, *The Revolutions of 1848: Political Writings*, ed. David Fernbach (London: Verso Books: Verso, 2010); *Surveys from Exile: Political Writings, ed. David Fernbach* (London: Verso Books: Verso, 2010); *The First International and After: Political Writings*, ed. David Fernbach (London: Verso Books: Verso, 2010). The other five volumes are currently available from Penguin: Karl Marx, *Early Writings* (London: Penguin Books, 1992); Karl Marx, *The Grundrisse: Foundations of the Critique of Political Economy* (London: Penguin Books, 1993); Karl Marx, *Capital, Volume 1: A Critique of Political Economy* (London: Penguin Books, 1992); Karl Marx, *Capital, Volume 2: A Critique of Political Economy* (London: Penguin Books, 1993); Karl Marx, *Capital, Volume 3: A Critique of Political Economy* (London: Penguin Books, 1993). The best version of the key work by Marx and Engels is to be found in Phil Gasper, ed., *The Communist Manifesto: A Road Map to History's Most Important Document* (Chicago: Haymarket Books, 2005), which provides the text along with incredibly helpful explanatory notes and much useful supplementary material.

The classic biographies Franz Mehring, *Karl Marx* and Gustav Mayer, *Friedrich Engels* (the English version being an abridgement) are presently out of print, although substantial and popularly written works on each—Francis Wheen, *Karl Marx: A Life* (New York: W.W. Norton, 2001) and Tristram Hunt, *Marx's General: The Revolutionary*

Life of Friedrich Engels (New York: Henry Holt and Co., 2009)—are easily available, as is the standard scholarly work by David McLellan, *Karl Marx: A Biography* (New York: Palgrave Macmillan, 2006). In some ways superior is the dual biography by the Bolshevik scholar David Riazanov, *Karl Marx and Friedrich Engels: An Introduction to Their Lives and Work* (New York: Monthly Review Press, 1974), out of print but available online through the Marxists Internet Archive: https://www.marxists.org/archive/riazanov/works/1927-ma/index.htm. One of the richest contributions is the well-researched and beautifully written book by Mary Gabriel, *Love and Capital: Karl and Jenny Marx and the Birth of a Revolution* (New York: Little Brown and Co., 2011), which brings Marx alive by placing him firmly in the vibrant context of family, friends (most prominently Engels), and others.

A brilliant and deliciously clever exposition and defense can be found in Terry Eagleton, *Why Marx Was Right* (New Haven, CT: Yale University Press, 2012). For those wishing to go in depth, a valuable resource is provided by the (alas unfinished) work of Hal Draper, *Karl Marx's Theory of Revolution*, 5 volumes (New York: Monthly Review Press, 1977–2005). More succinct but excellent is Michael Löwy, *The Theory of Revolution in the Young Marx* (Chicago: Haymarket Books, 2005). A well-researched and lucid exploration of the profoundly democratic nature of Marx's thought can be found in Richard N. Hunt, *The Political Ideas of Marx and Engels, 1818–1895*, 2 volumes (Pittsburgh: University of Pittsburgh Press, 1974, 1984). This is also a topic of an outstanding study by August H. Nimtz, Jr., *Marx and Engels: Their Contribution to the Democratic Breakthrough* (Albany: State University of New York Press, 2000). The development of Marx's economic analysis of capitalism is the focus of Ernest Mandel, *The Formation of the Economic Thought of Karl Marx* (New York: Monthly Review Press, 1971). For a discussion of what Marx saw as the alternative to capitalism, see Peter Hudis, *Marx's Concept of the Alternative to Capitalism* (Chicago: Haymarket Books, 2013). The allegation of "Eurocentrism" in Marx is addressed in different ways by Samir Amin, *Eurocentrism* (New York: Monthly Review Press, 2010), Kevin Anderson, *Marx at the Margins: On Nationalism, Ethnicity and Non-Western Societies* (Chicago: University of Chicago Press: 2010), and August H. Nimtz, Jr., *Marx, Tocqueville and Race in America: The 'Absolute Democracy' or 'Defiled Republic'* (Lanham, MD: Lexington Books, 2003).

Rosa Luxemburg

Verso Books, with the support of the Rosa Luxemburg Foundation in Germany, has committed to the publication of an anticipated seventeen-volume *Complete Works of Rosa Luxemburg*, all newly translated into English, edited by Peter Hudis and a team of scholars. The first two volumes, consisting of all her economic writings, have appeared as of this writing—Peter Hudis, ed., *The Complete Economic Writings of Rosa Luxemburg, Volume I: Economic Writings 1 (*London: Verso Books, 2013) and Peter Hudis and Paul Le Blanc, eds., *The Complete Economic Writings of Rosa Luxemburg, Volume II: Economic Writings 2* (London: Verso Books, 2015). As part of this project, a preliminary volume has also appeared: Annilies Laschitza, George Adler, and Peter Hudis, eds., *The Letters of Rosa Luxemburg* (London: Verso Books, 2011).

Several key works by Luxemburg can be found in Helen C. Scott, ed., *The Essential Rosa Luxemburg:* Reform or Revolution *and* The Mass Strike (Chicago: Haymarket Books, 2007), and *Rosa Luxemburg:* Reform or Revolution *and Other Writings*, ed. by Paul Buhle (Mineola, NY: Dover Publications, 2006). Mary-Alice Waters, ed., *Rosa Luxemburg Speaks* (New York: Pathfinder Press, 1979) has the great virtue of providing a much larger number of complete texts. Relying partly on excerpts, but in ways more comprehensive, is Peter Hudis and Kevin Anderson, eds., *The Rosa Luxemburg Reader* (New York: Monthly Review Press, 2004). For a compact, representative survey of her writings, see Paul Le Blanc and Helen Scott, eds., *Socialism or Barbarism, Selected Writings of Rosa Luxemburg* (London: Pluto Press, 2013).

The outstanding biographies of Rosa Luxemburg are those by her younger comrade Paul Frölich, *Rosa Luxemburg* (Chicago: Haymarket Books, 2010) and by the late scholar J. P. Nettl, *Rosa Luxemburg*, 2 volumes (Oxford, UK: Oxford University Press, 1966). Others worthy of attention include Elzbieta Ettinger, *Rosa Luxemburg: A Life* (Boston: Beacon Press, 1988) and especially Kate Evans (with Paul Buhle), *Red Rosa: A Graphic Biography of Rosa Luxemburg* (London: Verso, 2015). A partial selection of explorations of Luxemburg's life and thought would include: Norman Geras, *The Legacy of Rosa Luxemburg* (London: Verso Books, 2015), Paul Le Blanc, ed., *Rosa Luxemburg, Writings and Reflections* (Amherst, NY: Humanity Books, 1999), Ricardo Bellofiore, ed., *Rosa Luxemburg and the Critique of Political Economy* (London: Routledge, 2009), Raya Dunayevskaya, *Rosa Luxemburg, Women's Liberation, and*

Marx's Philosophy of Revolution (Urbana: University of Illinois Press, 1991), Andrea Nye, *Philosophia: The Thought of Rosa Luxemburg, Simone Weil, and Hannah Arendt* (London: Routledge, 1994).

Vladimir Ilyich Lenin

Most but not all of Lenin's writings were gathered in Vladimir Ilyich Lenin, *Collected Works*, 45 volumes (Moscow: Progress Publishers, 1960–1970), though a reasonable one-volume compilation of key works is available in Robert C. Tucker, ed., *The Lenin Anthology* (New York: W. W. Norton, 1975), and a compact selection, with substantial background material, can be found in *V. I. Lenin, Revolution, Democracy, Socialism*, ed. Paul Le Blanc (London: Pluto Press, 2008).

Lenin's life is presented in a number of more or less hostile biographies, but among the more reliable accounts are: Nadezhda Krupskaya, *Reminiscences of Lenin* (New York: International Publishers, 1979), Ronald H. Clark, *Lenin: A Biography* (New York: Harper and Row, 1988), Tony Cliff, *Lenin*, 3 volumes (London: Bookmarks, 2012), Lars Lih, *Lenin* (London: Reaktion Books, 2010).

Expositions of Lenin's political thought include three influential studies of the 1970s and 1980s: Marcel Liebman, *Leninism Under Lenin* (London: Merlin Press, 1985), Neil Harding, *Lenin's Political Thought: Theory and Practice in the Democratic and Socialist Revolutions* (Chicago: Haymarket Books, 2011), and Paul Le Blanc, *Lenin and the Revolutionary Party* (Chicago: Haymarket Books, 2015). In the twenty-first century, there has been a new wave of important studies: Sebastian Budgen, Stathis Kouvelakis, and Slavoj Žižek, eds., *Lenin Reloaded: Towards a Politics of Truth* (Chapel Hill, NC: Duke University Press, 2007); Lars Lih, *Lenin Rediscovered: 'What Is to Be Done?' in Context* (Chicago: Haymarket Books, 2008); Alan Shandro, *Lenin and the Logic of Hegemony: Political Practice and Theory in the Class Struggle* (Chicago: Haymarket Books, 2014); Tamás Krausz, *Reconstructing Lenin: An Intellectual Biography* (New York: Monthly Review Press, 2015); August H. Nimtz Jr., *Lenin's Electoral Strategy*, 2 volumes (New York: Palgrave Macmillan, 2014); Antonio Negri, *Factory of Strategy: Thirty-Three Lessons on Lenin* (New York: Columbia University Press, 2014). Also see Paul Le Blanc, *Unfinished Leninism: The Rise and Return of a Revolutionary Doctrine* (Chicago: Haymarket Books, 2014).

Leon Trotsky

Among Trotsky's crucial works are his three-volume *History of the Russian Revolution* (Chicago: Haymarket Books, 2008) and *The Revolution Betrayed: What Is the Soviet Union and Where Is It Going?* (Mineola, NY: Dover, 2004), but also *Permanent Revolution and Results and Prospects* (London: Resistance Books, 2007), *1905* (New York: Vintage Books, 1972), and *The Struggle Against Fascism in Germany*, ed. by George Breitman and Merry Meisel (New York: Pathfinder Press, 1971). George Breitman oversaw the immense editorial task of producing the invaluable collection, *Writings of Leon Trotsky, 1929-1940*, 14 volumes (New York: Pathfinder Press, 1973–79). A compact anthology can be found in Leon Trotsky, *Writings in Exile*, eds., Kunal Chattopadhyay and Paul Le Blanc (London: Pluto Press, 2012).

Trotsky's rich life is explored in his own *My Life: An Attempt at Autobiography* (Mineola, NY: Dover Books, 2007), and also in Victor Serge and Natalia Sedova, *The Life and Death of Leon Trotsky* (Chicago: Haymarket Books, 2015). Isaac Deutscher's three-volume classic has been merged into the massive *The Prophet: The Life of Leon Trotsky* (London: Verso Books, 2015). Pierre Broué, *Trotsky* (Paris: Fayard, 1988) is an essential text still awaiting translation into English. Tony Cliff provides a significant and informative interpretation in *Trotsky*, 4 volumes (London: Bookmarks, 1989–1993). Among the numerous critical to hostile biographies of Trotsky, one of the more serious and worthwhile works is Bertrand M. Patenaude, *Trotsky: Downfall of a Revolutionary* (New York: HarperCollins, 2009). For a succinct account, critical yet sympathetic, and nicely illustrated, see Paul Le Blanc, *Trotsky* (London: Reaktion Books, 2015).

Well worth consulting are the two editions of Michael Löwy, *The Politics of Combined and Uneven Development: The Theory of Permanent Revolution*—the first published by Verso Books (London, 1981), and a shortened version by Haymarket Books (Chicago: 2010). A valuable collection can be found in Bill Dunn and Hugo Radice, eds., *100 Years of Permanent Revolution: Results and Prospects* (London: Pluto Press, 2010). Searching and informative explorations are provided by Duncan Hallas, *Trotsky's Marxism and Other Essays* (Chicago: Haymarket Books, 2003) and Ernest Mandel, *Trotsky as Alternative* (London: Verso Books, 1995). A massive and critical study by Baruch Knei-Paz, *The Social and Political Thought of Leon Trotsky* (Oxford, UK: Oxford University Press, 1978) is matched by the massive yet more sympathetic Kunal Chattopadhyay, *The Marxism of Leon Trotsky* (Kolkata: Progress Publishers, 2006). An incredibly rich new study by Thomas M. Twiss, *Trotsky and the Problem of Soviet Bureaucracy* (Chicago: Haymarket Books, 2015) is complemented by Marcel van der Linden, *Western Marxism and the Soviet Union: A Survey of Critical Theories and Debates Since 1917* (Chicago: Haymarket Books, 2007). Also see Dianne Feeley, Paul Le Blanc, and Thomas Twiss, *Leon Trotsky and the Organizational Principles of the Revolutionary Party* (Chicago: Haymarket Books, 2014).

Antonio Gramsci

For some time, the primary works of Gramsci available to English-language readers were Antonio Gramsci, *Selections from Prison Notebooks*, eds., Quintin Hoare and Geoffrey Nowell Smith (New York: International Publishers, 1971) and Antonio Gramsci, *Selections from Political Writings, 1910–1926*, 2 volumes, ed., Quintin Hoare (New York: International Publishers, 1977, 1978)—both of which continue to have great value. There has been a fertile expansion of new translations. To date, these include Antonio Gramsci, *Prison Notebooks*, 3 volumes, ed., Joseph A. Buttigieg (New York: Columbia University Press, 1992), plus *Antonio Gramsci, A Great and Terrible World: The Pre-Prison Letters, 1908–1926*, ed., Derek Boothman (Chicago: Haymarket Books, 2014), and Antonio Gramsci, *Letters from Prison*, 2 volumes, ed., Frank Rosengarten (New York: Columbia University Press, 1993). For a one-volume selection, see David Forgacs, ed., *The Antonio Gramsci Reader: Selected Writings 1916–1935* (New York: New York University Press, 2000).

Biographies include John M. Cammett, *Antonio Gramsci and the Origins of Italian Communism* (Stanford, CA: Stanford University Press, 1967), Giuseppe Fiori, *Antonio Gramsci: Life of a Revolutionary* (London: Verso, 1990), and Dante Germano, *Antonio Gramsci: Architect of a New Politics* (Baton Rouge: Louisiana State University Press, 1990).

Among the more important studies of his thought are: Anne Shostock Sassoon, *Gramsci's Politics* (Minneapolis: University of Minnesota Press, 1988); Peter D. Thomas, *The Gramscian Moment* (Chicago: Haymarket Books, 2010); Antonio A. Santucci, *Antonio Gramsci* (New York: Monthly Review Press, 2010); and Carlos Nelson Coutinho, *Gramsci's Political Thought* (Chicago: Haymarket Books, 2013).

Surveys of Marxism

A brilliant short work by Ernest Mandel, *The Place of Marxism in History* (Atlantic Highlands, NJ: Humanities Press, 1994), also available online through the Ernest Mandel Internet Archive at http://ernest-mandel.org/en/works/pdf/PlaceofMarxisminHistory.pdf, provides what is essentially a dialectical exposition of how Marxism developed from the time of Marx and Engels down to the late twentieth century. Perry Anderson, *Considerations on Western Marxism* (London: Verso Books, 1976), is a succinct and influential summary of ebbs and flows of Marxist thought (predominantly in Western Europe) in the twentieth century. Michael Löwy, *On Changing the World: Essays in Marxist Political Philosophy from Karl Marx to Walter Benjamin* (Chicago: Haymarket Books, 2014) and Sobhanlal Datta Gupta, *Marxism in Dark Times: Select Essays for the New Century* (London/New York/Delhi: Anthem Press, 2012) both lucidly explore major issues and fascinating hidden pathways in the development of Marxism. Also worthy of consideration is Soma Marik, *Reinterrogating the Classical Marxist Discourses of Revolutionary Democracy* (Kolata: Aakar Books, 2008).

Marx and Engels started off as philosophy students, and philosophical concerns naturally permeated their work and that of those following them—as indicated in many studies, including Herbert Marcuse, *Reason and Revolution: Hegel and the Rise of Social Theory* (Amherst, NY: Humanity Books, 1999), Alex Callinicos, *Marxism and Philosophy* (Oxford, UK: Oxford University Press, 1985), John Rees, *The Algebra of Revolution: The Dialectic and the Classical Marxist Tradition* (London: Routledge, 1998), and Helena Sheehan, *Marxism and the Philosophy of Science: A Critical History* (Atlantic Highlands, NJ: Humanities Press, 1985). Among the many useful works on the interplay of Marxism and the discipline of history are: Eric Hobsbawm, *On History* (London: Abacus, 1997), Matt Perry, *Marxism and History* (New York: Palgrave Macmillan, 2002), Paul Blackledge, *Reflections on the Marxist Theory of History* (Manchester, UK: Manchester University Press, 2006), Jairus Banaji, *Theory as History: Essays on Modes of Production and Exploitation* (Chicago: Haymarket Books, 2011), and Neil Davidson, *We Cannot Escape History: States and Revolutions* (Chicago: Haymarket Books, 2015). On Marxism and politics, see Ralph Miliband, *Marxism and Politics* (London: Merlin Press, 2003), and Jules Townsend, *The Politics of Marxism: The Critical Debates* (London: Leicester University Press,

1996). In the realm of economics, classic works are Paul M. Sweezy, *The Theory of Capitalist Development* (New York: Monthly Review Press, 1968), Ernest Mandel, *Marxist Economic Theory*, 2 volumes (New York: Monthly Review Press, 1970), and Roman Rosdolsky, *The Making of Marx's Capital*, 2 volumes (London: Pluto Press, 1992). Also see the wide-ranging critical survey to be found in M. E. Howard and J. E. King, *A History of Marxian Economics, 1883–1990*, 2 volumes (New York: Palgrave Macmillan, 1992), the helpful collection, John Eatwell, Murray Milgate, Peter Newman, eds., *The New Palgrave Marxian Economics* (New York; W. W. Norton, 1990), and Richard D. Wolff and Stephen A. Resnick, *Contending Economic Theories: Neoclassical, Keynesian, and Marxian* (Cambridge, MA: MIT Press, 2012).

Among the interesting works that, in different ways, discuss the contemporary relevance of Marxism are Paul D'Amato, *The Meaning of Marxism* (Chicago: Haymarket Books, 2014), Michael A. Lebowitz, *The Socialist Imperative: From Gotha to Now* (New York: Monthly Review Press, 2015), and Colin Barker, John Krinsky, Laurence Cox, and Alf Gunvlad Nilsen, eds., *Marxism and Social Movements* (Chicago: Haymarket Books, 2014). A massive exploration of diverse and new pathways in Marxism can be found in Jacques Bidet and Stathis Kouvelakis, eds., *Critical Companion to Contemporary Marxism* (Chicago: Haymarket Books, 2009). Two classic works that focus on women in the Marxist schema are Sheila Rowbotham, *Women, Resistance, and Revolution* (London: Verso Books, 2014) and Lise Vogel, *Marxism and the Oppression of Women: Toward a Unitary Theory* (Chicago: Haymarket Books, 2014), and essential collections of writings can be found in Nancy Holmstrom, ed., *The Socialist-Feminist Project: A Contemporary Reader in Theory and Politics* (New York: Monthly Review, 2002) as well as Rosemary Hennessy and Chrys Ingraham, eds., *Materialist Feminism: A Reader in Class, Difference, and Women's Lives* (New York and London: Routledge, 1997). John Bellamy Foster, *Marx's Ecology: Materialism and Nature* (New York: Monthly Review, 2000) and Paul Burkett, *Marx and Nature: A Red-Green Perspective* (Chicago: Haymarket Books, 2014) are two of a growing number of valuable Marxist writings dealing with environmental concerns, and the more activist-oriented book by Chris Williams, *Ecology and Socialism: Solutions to Capitalist Ecological Crisis* (Chicago: Haymarket Books, 2010), should also consulted.

388 BIBLIOGRAPHICAL ESSAY

Many of the fine works cited above give too limited a sense of the truly global reach of Marxism. David McLellan, ed., *Marxism: Essential Writings* (Oxford, UK: Oxford University Press, 1988) has the virtue of attempting to include a little of Asia, Latin American, and Africa (in the form of Mao Zedong, Che Guevara, and Amílcar Cabral), although McLellan would undoubtedly be the first to admit that this is hardly adequate. A bare minimum in offering an overview of non-European Marxist perspectives would be to offer selections of diverse writings on a continental scale—a broad introductory volume such as Michael Löwy, ed., *Marxism in Latin America from 1909 to the Present* (Amherst, NY: Humanity Books, 1992). For some time, the one English-language survey on Asia has been the now-dated Cold War product, Stuart R. Schram and Hélène Carrère d'Encausse, ed., *Marxism and Asia: An Introduction with Readings* (London: Penguin Books, 1969), and English-speaking scholars and activists could be well served by a newer contribution.

In fact, China and India cry out for anthologies of their own. For many, "Chinese Marxism" is fixated on Mao Zedong, and Mao's works are easily available through the Marxists Internet Archive, but there were many others in China who have operated within the Marxist tradition (arguably much closer to Marx than was Mao), and the need for an updated collection on Chinese Marxism is indicated in Robert Ware, "Reflections on Chinese Marxism," *Socialism and Democracy*, 27:1 (2013), pp. 136–160. The richness of Indian Marxism cries out for something similar—as indicated by a mere sampling of such names as these: Aijaz Ahmad, Jairus Banaji, Kunal Chattopadhyay, Vivek Chibber, Sobhanlal Datta Gupta, Amalendu Guha, Irfan Habib, D. D. Kosambi, Soma Marik, Prabhat Patnaik, Vijay Prashad, Arundathi Roy, M. N. Roy, Randhir Singh, Achin Vanaik.

Africa and the African diaspora are the foci of a number of works that also indicate the need for similar circulation of Marxist-influenced writings from these realms, for instance: *The C.L.R. James Reader*, ed. by Anna Grimshaw (Oxford: Basil Blackwell, 1992), and *The Revolutionary Marxism of C.L.R. James: Selected Writings of C.L.R. James, 1939–1949*, ed. Scott McLemee and Paul Le Blanc (Atlantic Highlands, NJ: Humanities Press, 1994); George Padmore's writings, many of which are available through the Marxists Internet Archive, https://www.marxists.org/archive/padmore; Walter Rodney, *How Europe Underdeveloped Africa* (Washington, DC: Howard University Press, 1974); Cedric J. Robinson,

Black Marxism: The Making of the Black Radical Tradition (Chapel Hill, NC: University of North Carolina Press, 2000); Manning Marable, *African and Caribbean Politics: From Kwame Nkrumah to Maurice Bishop* (London: Verso Books, 1987). This barely gives a sense of the diversity and richness of Marxist thought on the African continent, from Egypt to South Africa, all crying out for rich collections of writings to benefit those who would understand and change the world.

Index

De Silva, Mario, 360
Deutscher, Isaac, 10, 24n9, 24n13,
    27n23, 125, 143n10
dialectics, dialectical material-
    ism, xiii, 7, 196, 219, 221, 334,
    336–337
dictatorship of the proletariat. *See*
    workers state
Dilke, Charles, 369n15
Dimitrov [also spelled Dimitroff],
    George, 14, 25n14, 329n1
Diodorus Siculus, 369n11
Dobkowski, Michael, 331n4
Domhoff, G. William, 143n18
Drago, Aurelio, 338
Draper, Hal, 7, 23n1, 24n7, 77n20
DuBois, W. E. B., 97n28
Duggan, Penny, 97n28
Duranty, Walter, 111, 118n27
Dutt, R. Palme, 331n4

Easton, Loyd, 23n2
Ebert, Teresa, 27n22
Ecology, 9, 136–137
Edison, Thomas, 301, 307
Egorov, Alexander I., 377n7
Engels, Frederick, xii, xiv, 3–4, 7, 12,
    18, 21, 22, 23n2, 27n23, 34, 36,
    37, 48, 49n2, 49n4, 49n5, 49n6,
    49n7, 50n12, 53, 54–55, 57, 60,
    70, 75n1, 76n2, 76n4, 76n7,
    76n10, 76n14, 81, 82, 83, 86,
    96n2, 96n4, 96n5, 96n6, 96n8,
    96n11, 97n17, 101–104, 106,
    110, 111, 116n2, 116n6, 116n7,
    116n9, 117n10, 117n11, 123,
    141, 145n25, 195, 197, 198, 204,
    235, 249, 251, 262–263, 269,
    339; biography, 149–150; on
    Marx, 175–180
Enlightenment, 3, 149

Evans, Les, 52n27

factory committees, 124, 142n7, 313,
    327
Fagen, Richard R., 143n11
Fairbank, John K., 52n27
Fanon, Franz, 20
fascism, fascists, 14, 66, 72–74, 314,
    318, 322, 327, 328, 329n1,
    330n2, 330n3, 331n4, 333, 334,
    339, 340–341, 343–344, 353,
    358, 368n4, 368n6, 369n10;
    links to capitalism, 72, 73, 74,
    320, 321, 324, 344; methods,
    72–73, 313, 353, 358; social
    base, 72, 74, 321, 340; takes
    power at certain moments, 72,
    73, 74, 319–320, 321
Fernbach, David, 26n17, 96n5,
    116n2, 116n6
Feuerbach, Ludwig, 3, 149
Fine, Ben, 49n5
Finley, M. I., 143n18
Fiori, Giuseppe, 27n23
First International (International
    Workingmen's Association), 64,
    150
Fischer, Louis, 25n14, 78n24
Form, William, 145n26
Foster, John Bellamy, 27n22
Foster, William Z., 25n14, 331n6
Fourier, Charles, 3, 149, 175, 195,
    235
Fourth International, 16, 283, 311,
    314, 316–317, 322, 325, 326–
    327, 328, 331n6
Franco, Francisco, 330n2
Frank, Pierre, 26n16, 331n6
Frankfurt School, 15
Franklin, Bruce, 52n27, 117n23

Victor Emmanuel, 320
Vogt-Downey, Marilyn, 141n1
Volkoganov, Dmitri, 24n13
Vollmar, Georg Heinrich von, 215

Wald, Alan, 26n16
Wallerstein, Immanuel, 49n9
Wallimann, Isidore, 331n4
Wang Fan-hsi, 52n27
War of maneuver (movement). *See*
    insurrection; mass strikes, mass
    actions war of position. *See*
    reforms, reform struggles
Waters, Mary-Alice, 24n8, 49n3,
    117n18
Weber, Max, 49n1
Weeks, John, 40
Weiss, Murry, 132
welfare state, 14, 129, 131–132,
    133–138, 137
Williams, Raymond, 20, 97n28
Wills, Garry, 143n18
Wilson, Edgar, 143n18
Wilson, Edmund, 141n1
Wolf, Eric, 49n9
Wolfe, Bertram D., xii, xiii, xvn2, 6,
    24n5, 123–124, 125, 131, 132,
    133, 134, 135, 137–138, 142n4,
    142n6, 143n16, 194
women's oppression and women's
    rights, 8, 89, 139, 159, 169–170,
    193, 230–235, 246, 327
Wood, Ellen Meiksins, 27n22
workers' militia, 265–266, 327
workers' state [dictatorship of the
    proletariat], 7, 9–10, 47, 54, 55,
    67, 88, 90, 100–108, 113–115,
    120, 123–125, 171–172, 190,
    207, 213, 226, 262, 268–273,
    279–288, 295, 296, 299–301,
    319, 322, 327, 334, 339, 341,

342, 344, 348; bureaucratic
    degeneration, 67–69, 108–110,
    113–115, 120–121, 238–239,
    281–282, 309–317; transitional,
    104–105
working class [proletariat], 53–74,
    100–108, 111, 120, 123,
    126–128, 130–135, 137–143,
    139–140, 149–151, 158–164,
    175–180, 182–189, 193, 198–
    200, 201, 204–205, 230–235,
    241–245, 297–307, 309–310,
    314–317, 336–348; capitalism
    generates (proletarianization),
    30–31, 40, 53–79, 158–159, 161,
    175–176, 180, 255, 259–260,
    263; consciousness, 58–59,
    60–61, 69–72, 75, 81, 83, 87–90,
    93–94, 120, 130–131, 138–140,
    205, 206–207, 224, 225, 234–
    235, 263, 273; defined, 9, 53,
    130, 152; democracy, 7, 9, 48,
    69–72, 82–83, 89–90, 99, 100,
    103, 104–105, 106–108, 120,
    163, 171–172, 189, 234–235,
    238, 246, 268–273; hegemony
    (predominance, leadership),
    82–86, 88, 93–94, 334; inter-
    nationalism, 11, 12, 69, 95,
    100–104, 113, 149, 150–151,
    189, 190–191, 228–230, 312,
    313, 341–342; political inde-
    pendence, 82, 83, 162, 189, 190,
    241, 242; reserve army of labor
    (unemployed, underemployed),
    180; revolution, 7, 12–14, 21–23,
    47, 81–98, 100–103, 104, 120,
    138, 140, 163–165, 171–172,
    173, 189–191, 207–215,
    222–224, 226–227; stratification,
    60–61, 65–66, 88, 97–98, 120,

About the Author

Paul Le Blanc is a professor of history at La Roche College, has written on and participated in the US labor, radical, and civil rights movements, and is author of such books as *Marx, Lenin and the Revolutionary Experience*, *A Short History of the U.S. Working Class* and *Work and Struggle: Voices from U.S. Labor Radicalism*. In addition, he has coauthored, with economist Michael Yates, the highly acclaimed *A Freedom Budget for All Americans: Recapturing the Promise of the Civil Rights Movement in the Struggle for Economic Justice Today*.